HONEST TO JESUS

HONEST
^{TO} JESUS

*Jesus for a
New Millennium*

ROBERT W. FUNK

A Polebridge Press Book

HarperSanFrancisco
An Imprint of HarperCollins *Publishers*

A TREE CLAUSE BOOK

HarperSanFrancisco and the author, in association with The Basic Foundation, a not-for-profit organization whose primary mission is reforestation, will facilitate the planting of two trees for every one tree used in the manufacture of this book.

A Polebridge Press Book

FIRST EDITION

Library of Congress Cataloging-in-Publication Data
Funk, Robert Walter
Honest to Jesus : Jesus for a new millennium / Robert W. Funk.—1st ed.
"A Polebridge Press book."
Includes bibliographical references and index.
ISBN 0–06–062757–3 (cloth)
ISBN 0–06–062758–1 (pbk.)
1. Jesus Christ—Historicity. 2. Jesus Christ—Person and offices. I. Title.
BT303.2.F85   1996
232.9′08—dc20   96–9234

96 97 98 99 00 RRDH 10 9 8 7 6 5 4 3 2 1

Honest to Jesus is dedicated to

CHAR

who has robbed me of the desire to dissemble

Contents

Acknowledgments

Many of the insights informing this book have grown out of more than a decade of vigorous exchanges with the Fellows of the Jesus Seminar. Dom, Marc, Roy, Art, Ron, John, Karen, Kathleen, Sandy, Lane, Bob, Bill, Steve, Sara, Gerd, Walter, Mahlon, Barnes, Paul, and many others among the seventy-five active Fellows are entitled to as much credit as they want to claim. They will no doubt be given an ample helping of blame by my critics.

The members of the Thursday night Associates group at Westar have been patient partners in an extended conversation through many months, even years. Thank you Charlie, Earl, Enola, Ed, Fred, Gene, John, Harvey, Jim, Karen, Oak, Sarah, Sue, Tom, Tink, and dozens more, for the candor, the good will, the gut-wrenching sessions that lasted far into the night.

The process of turning years of learning, occasional glimpses beyond the rim of present sight, and a flood of passion into a disciplined manuscript is sheer agony—unadulterated hell. I would not have succeeded alone. I am indebted to Julian Hills for many miniature homilies scattered through heavily corrected paragraphs. Daryl Schmidt has proved once again to be the master of endless detail, for which I am grateful. Ed Beutner has replaced my failed prose with his scintillating metaphors on more than one occasion. John and Mary Dosier have caught stray slips in their final combing of the manuscript. Geneviève Duboscq, our in-house editor at Polebridge Press, and Charlene Matejovsky, the CEO of Polebridge Press, have been tireless in demanding clarity of my too often befuddled mind. My Harper editor, Mark Chimsky, has once more worked his magic in giving shape to my thoughts. If the wisdom of these friends is not evident in the end product, I have only myself to thank for not paying closer heed to their advice.

Robert W. Funk
Westar Institute
Santa Rosa, California

FIGURE 1

This woodcut of a young person peeking through the firmament of the heavens to catch a glimpse of how the universe works is believed to be the work of an early sixteenth-century artist. It was first published in *L'Astronomie* by Camille Flammarion (1842–1925).

HONEST TO JESUS

*Those who begin by loving Christianity
more than truth, proceed to love their sect
more than Christianity, and end by
loving themselves most of all.*

Samuel Taylor Coleridge

AUTHORS AND READERS

Books are an exchange between authors and readers. Readers need to know a few essential things about the authors they read, and authors had better know their readers. The ideal match of reader and author consists of the right questions joined to the relevant answers. I begin with that problem. Then I want to tell you about this author, about myself, so you will understand the set of interests and perspectives I bring to the topic of Jesus. Eventually I will reveal how I perceive you, the reader.

Paul Tillich, the great twentieth-century theologian, used to say that theologians spend a great deal of time answering questions that are not being asked. But then he regularly reframed the questions his students posed before he responded to them. The beginning of knowledge is knowing the right questions to ask. In this volume I will be answering questions as I have formulated them, but they had better be framed so that they are also the questions my readers are asking. If the two sets of questions do not match, my remarks will be wide of the mark.

Let me illustrate.

At a summer seminar on the historical Jesus, Janet Meeker, a lay participant, reported a question posed by her newly baptized grand-daughter: Did Jesus become a Christian at his baptism? Was he being confirmed by John the Baptist? While the young lady had anachronistically transferred her own experience to the remote past, a profound contemporary question actually lurked in her query. Let me rephrase her question in more sophisticated terms: Did Christianity begin with Jesus himself? Was he in fact the first "Christian"? Or did it begin at Easter with his resurrection? That is a trenchant and troubling question. We will return anon to the question of when Christianity began in the epilogue to this book.

On a radio talk show when we were discussing the historical Jesus, a caller asked me if there was such a place as hell. As teachers are wont to do, I restated her question: Do you mean, did Jesus believe there was such a place as hell?

She said, no, she was not concerned about what Jesus believed. She just wanted to know whether there is a hell. Yes or no.

I was taken aback. I am not often faced with such candor. Hell belongs, I replied, to the mythological world, the symbolic universe, that governed the perspective of most ordinary folk in the ancient Mediterranean world. That universe is no longer viable for most of us. Heaven cannot be a place located in the vault above a flat, pancakelike earth, and hell cannot be a fiery place found in the bowels of the earth. Modern observations of the physical universe have made many aspects of the ancient mythological world obsolete. Of course, we have not yet determined whether there are modern counterparts of heaven and hell and, if so, what they are.

The caller's question was one I had answered for myself many years earlier. I assumed—wrongly—that she was as interested as I primarily in historical questions. Those of us who have devoted a lifetime to the study of the New Testament and Christian origins tend to be preoccupied with questions about the past. Such questions will play a large role in this study. Historical questions often appear unrelated and irrelevant to contemporary concerns, but I also believe that the answers to historical questions have some bearing on other kinds of questions.

To be sure, I am not of the opinion that facts of themselves will provide us with the ultimate truth about Jesus, about ourselves, and about our world. But whatever we come to believe about those ultimate issues should be informed by the facts, insofar as we can discover them. I am not an empiricist, much less a positivist, contrary to some of my critics. But the pressure to discover all we can know about our own past, about the history of Jesus, and about the physical universe has a cathartic way of disciplining our imaginations.

When we put the origins of Christianity under heavy historical pressure, it is surprising what fault lines open up in the monolithic edifice of Christian mythology—that is, in the prevailing, unexamined narrative frame of the gospels and creeds. That is the real function of historical investigation—to subject the prevailing symbolic vehicles of encapsulation to close rigorous examination.

The truths of religion are more like the truths of poetry than the truths of the empirical sciences. That is one reason I prefer to think of Jesus as a poet rather than as the second person of the Trinity. Yet the truths of religion and the truths of science are divorced only at grave risk.

Similarly, we segregate the truths of history from the truths of religion only at our peril.

By analogy, I think it also to our detriment that we divorce our own real questions about life from our work as interpreters of the Bible, from our profession as historians, or just from our knowledge of how the world works. I propose to try to keep the truths of history and the sciences together with the truths of religion—not to confuse them, but to let them inform each other. For that reason, I will often turn from the past to the present in pursuing questions of interest to people today. So while I will focus on questions about Jesus, the gospels, and the distant past, nevertheless, these two faces of truth—the truth of religion and the truth of history—will be in constant contact with each other.

As a beginning, I want to tell you a little about myself, particularly about my convictions at this stage of my own history. And I want to indicate how I perceive those who will read this book. In doing so, I will be keeping the two kinds of truth in touch with each other from the outset.

CONFESSION OR COVER-UP?

Christians are given to confession, which is assumed to be good for the soul. I cannot confirm that confession actually nourishes the soul, but I am quite certain that the acknowledgment of warts and other blemishes is essential in the religion business: it is disarming. It will disarm me and, I hope, my critics. I can ill afford to be armed against myself—against the honesty to which I aspire—and I certainly do not need armed adversaries.

In practice, confession is often no more than a license to wallow in sentiment and self-pity. Confessions, like prayer, can be the most deceptive cover-ups of all our pious practices. It is actually quite easy to conceal from the left hand what the right hand is up to. Confessions are really intended to be the occasion to own up to the blinders that inhibit sight, to the earplugs that impede hearing—in short, to the proclivities that dictate how one is predisposed to face life. Unfortunately, those with dimmed sight and impaired hearing rarely have an inkling of their real limitations. In such cases, confession turns out to be a cover-up.

My confession, or cover-up, as the case may be, has tentacles that reach far back into the past. I must begin there if I am to come clean.

Youthful Discretions and Indiscretions

I began quite young with a string of beliefs and very little faith. Back then, in the exuberance of youth, I thought it extremely important to hold the correct opinions. I didn't really know what the correct opinions were, but friends and others around me seemed to know, so I embraced theirs when I could understand them and sometimes when I couldn't.

Among them was the good confession. In response to prompting, I said Jesus was my personal savior. Nobody explained to me what that entailed. It has taken me several decades to get even a hint of what it could mean.

Most of us cling to opinions received secondhand and worn like used clothing. I grew up in the Great Depression and know both the shame and the occasional joy of having to wear hand-me-down clothing. In fact, I found it almost impossible to break the habit: years later, living in a New York suburb and reasonably affluent, I frequented a Goodwill store located in a bedroom community just outside Manhattan and acquired an expensive but used tuxedo for which I had only occasional use. On that same trip I saw a chesterfield hanging nearby on the same rack. I had admired those elegant, close-fitting coats with the velvet collar and flap pockets—I had seen them in the movies—but had never worn one. Urged on by a friend, I could not resist the temptation to acquire my own, even secondhand. Soon thereafter we wore tuxedos and chesterfields into the city for an evening at the theater and learned one vital fact: if you slip on the ice and fall down in a chesterfield, you cannot get up without help.

It is the same with secondhand opinions that have the narrow, confining fit of a chesterfield: if you fall down in them—if they don't serve you well or if you find them stiff and inflexible—you can't get back up without assistance.

As a youngster I was looking for help. I am happy to report that I am the victim of a good education. I would undoubtedly have grown up opinionated, narrow-minded, and bigoted like many Americans, but I had the misfortune, or the good fortune, of having excellent teachers. Ruth Stamps, Lloyd Deckard, and Janet Macdonald, among many others, pried open a closed mind and introduced me to the larger world. In Reitz High School in Evansville, Indiana, I first learned the name Albert Einstein from some brave teacher whose name I have forgotten and who taught me that mass is the equivalent of energy. She had the audacity to surprise me with ideas the range of which I have been struggling all these years to comprehend. If the creationists had their way, I would not have learned anything of that revolutionary theory— the theory of general relativity—and would have been stuck with a literalist reading of Genesis 1 and 2, which I had already acquired from attending Sunday school.

In high school I majored in drama and debate. My teachers urged me to go to Indiana University, where I intended to study law. My grades had earned me a full scholarship. But the pastor of the church I had been attending thought I would make a good minister. Rice Kello was a gifted musician with a penetrating sense of humor. In Evansville he was very much in demand as a public speaker and a civic leader. He was unable to dissemble, either with me or with the members of his congregation. I liked his candor and admired his skills. He sent me to a Bible college located in the hills of eastern Tennessee. I promptly became a teenage evangelist, using my rhetorical skills to make my audiences laugh and cry almost at will.

But I was uneasy. Learning at the college was mostly by memorization and rehearsal. Truth was already encoded in the simplistic creed of the school. A doctrinal straitjacket did not suit me. At the end of the second year I transferred to Butler University in Indianapolis and enrolled in the classics department. I discovered that real learning is *agony*—a struggle, a contest with ourselves, with superficial, entrenched ideas, and with the lore we absorb from the surrounding cultural atmosphere. Learning the truth about the Christian tradition can be the most agonizing of all exercises. I had set out on a quest for knowledge that would continue for the rest of my life.

Professional Migrations

My odyssey began in the church. It has followed trails blazed by many before me and followed by others since. I started out to be a parish minister but soon learned that passion for truth was not compatible with that role. In self-defense I became a scholar. To stay near the church, I taught in theological seminaries for the next two decades. When I returned to Vanderbilt University toward the end of that period, I learned, to my regret, that the old theological issues had become limp and lifeless. In *Jesus as Precursor,* a book I wrote while teaching in the Divinity School, I concluded that theologians should abandon the cloistered precincts of the church and seminary where nothing real was on the agenda. I soon followed my own advice.

The longing for intellectual freedom drove me out of the seminary and into a secular university. I don't believe I was fully aware of it at the time, but the university had become my church and learning my real vocation. Yet my odyssey was not yet complete. The University of Montana taught me another hard lesson: universities are much like churches, replete with orthodoxies of various kinds, courts of inquisition, and severe penalties for those who do not embrace mediocrity and the teachers' union. Preoccupation with political trivia and insulation from the real world eventually pushed me to abandon that final sanctuary. I retired as soon as I could afford to and, with my wife as partner, founded my own publishing house, Polebridge Press, and organized the Westar Institute for private research. My exodus was complete. I had finally found my home in an industrial park in an urban California wilderness.

I weep to think that I spent thirty-five years in the classroom, in concert with thousands of other colleagues, to have had so little lasting impact on students, ministerial candidates, and the American mind. In our time, religious literacy has reached a new low in spite of our scholarship, in spite of the remarkable advances in research and publication our academic disciplines have made.

Where have all the students gone? Apparently out into the dark night of consumerism, professional sports, and mindless television. There is no institution to fan the spark, to feed that tiny appetite for knowledge we so painstakingly implanted in them. Our graduates are embarrassed to confess their interest in religion and at a loss to know where to turn for comradeship in the intellectual pursuit of religious knowledge. They can't find good books on the subject, in part because scholars haven't written them, in part because scholarly books don't sell well enough to be stocked by ordinary booksellers. In the void they either read pulp or turn to other pursuits.

I might have expected more from the churches. I did at one time. Then I discovered that by and large what my students learned in seminary did not get passed on to parish members; in fact, it seems to have little or no bearing on the practice of ministry at all. I was chagrined to learn that I was investing in an enterprise with no prospect of return. Ecclesiastical bureaucrats, by and large, resisted and resist real theological education. My grief at this discovery is beyond expression.

I finally came to see that my academic colleagues and I were trapped in a perpetual holding pattern dictated to us by a system of rewards and sanctions in the university. That system prevented us, or at least discouraged us, from entering the public domain with learning that mattered. In their book, *The Social Construction of Reality,* Peter Berger and Thomas Luckman define intellectuals as experts whose specialized knowledge is not wanted, is not even tolerated, by the general public. We scholars of the Bible and theology have defined ourselves as intellectuals and glory in the fact that what we produce is of no real interest or obvious use to anyone outside a narrow circle of specialists.

Insulated and isolated in the university, rebuffed by the church, and scorned by the public, we have retreated into our academic towers and pretend that what we know is beyond the ken of average mortals. Scholarship in religion, especially in the biblical field, is all but bankrupt.

The Westar Institute

Rather than view this situation with despair, I took it as a challenge. To my delight and comfort, I found other academic colleagues who shared my regrets and my hopes. Together we founded the Westar Institute and set out to respond to the challenges facing us. The Westar Institute was formed to bring the best in high scholarship—the best we can enlist—to bear on the religious issues that matter in our time, and to do so within earshot of literate readers. We have not asked ourselves to popularize or "write down" to our readers but to say the profoundest things we have to say in plain English. In this enterprise, we are mounting a frontal assault on a pervasive religious illiteracy that blinds and intimidates, even those, or perhaps especially those, in positions of authority in the church and in our society.

That is Westar in a nutshell.

The first thing we had to do was to identify the issues that matter—issues to which the best scholarship can make a material and significant contribution and issues that are of interest to everyone concerned with religion and religious practice.

The second task was to enlist scholars who were willing to address those issues in a serious way—serious enough to warrant the investment of research time, writing, and extended conversations. Participation in the programs of Westar involves a certain amount of risk—risk in relation to the academic system of rewards and sanctions I mentioned earlier. To some of our academic colleagues, to be successful in the public arena is to sacrifice the approval of professional elitists. At the same time, we scholars had to draw a significant number of listeners and readers into our work to form an essential listening post and to serve as our critics.

The next issue confronting us was to learn how to package the product of our research and deliberations in a form or forms that would make it attractive to the public and accessible to nonspecialists. For scholars this was perhaps the most formidable—and threatening—challenge of all.

The Jesus Seminar

The first project of the new institute was the Jesus Seminar. Jesus is a topic of wide public interest, and the ancient gospels are the subject of profound public ignorance. In addition, in recent years there has been an awakening in scholarly circles to new ways of viewing the Jesus tradition preserved in the gospels.

It appeared that no one had ever collected and evaluated all the words and deeds attributed to Jesus. That in itself was surprising. I wrote to thirty colleagues and asked them to join me in collecting and analyzing all the words and deeds ascribed to Jesus in all the ancient sources up to about 300 C.E. They in turn were to invite other colleagues to join the project. About two hundred of us formed the Jesus Seminar.

The concept of the seminar transgressed established academic protocol. The Jesus Seminar was to be a collaborative enterprise; for researchers accustomed to working in isolation booths in dusty libraries, collaboration is difficult. In addition, our work was to be cumulative; for academics who love to reinvent the wheel each time they gather, it was a genuine innovation to build at each meeting on the conclusions that had been reached at previous meetings. Furthermore, the parochial and denominational and confessional perspectives that once dominated biblical studies had receded sufficiently to make the seminar truly ecumenical. *Ecumenical* in this context means more than transcending confessional affiliations, though it includes that; it means a common method and a shared goal: the historical truth at all costs. Method and goal set the terms for participation: competence rather than theological commitment, rigor and candor rather than posturing. In addition, we determined to discover whether there was a broad scholarly consensus. That decision prompted us to emphasize the accumulated lore of the biblical guild and subject private deviations to serious review. Out of our attempts to talk and listen to each other, we learned to enlarge on the area of agreement by negotiation. That proved to be the little touch that made the Jesus Seminar different from other academic symposia.

We agreed at the outset, although reluctantly, to come to some decision, however tentative and belated, however provisional, this side of the millennium. So we adopted the simple expedient of voting to see whether a consensus existed among us and, if so, what its magnitude might be. We employed our now notorious colored beads for voting purposes.*

We further agreed—again reluctantly—to make a public report and to do so in clear and unequivocal terms, no matter what the results of our deliberations. At first it was difficult to formulate unambiguous statements. And it was hard not to attempt to control how our decisions were to be interpreted. Reporters and interviewers serving the media are themselves often innocent of nuances to which their ears are not attuned. Moreover, reporters prefer confrontations and the sensational and so tend to exaggerate differences. Our experiences with the media were at first uniformly negative. In spite of such experiences, we learned to speak our minds without excessive qualifications. And as we did so, our inclination to be honest, to come clean, increased. Posturing gave way to candor. This was, and is, an unusual and refreshing experience for academics.

We have now completed the first two parts of a three-part agenda. We first inventoried and then evaluated all the words ascribed to Jesus in *all* the gospels. Our public report was published as *The Five Gospels: The Search for the Authentic Words of Jesus* (Scribner, 1993). The second phase was to assemble and assess all the acts attributed to Jesus in those same texts. A report covering the acts of Jesus will appear in 1997. The seminar has now embarked on its third phase, which is to "read" or interpret the database of authentic words and deeds it has identified. As a part of that endeavor, Fellows of the seminar are compiling individual

---

*For the words of Jesus, the seminar adopted the following brief definitions of the four colors: Red—Jesus said it or something very close to it. Pink—Jesus probably said something like it, although his words have suffered in transmission. Gray—these are not his words, but the ideas are close to his own. Black—Jesus did not say it; the words represent the Christian community or a later point of view.

For the acts of Jesus, the colors indicate: Red—the report is historically reliable. Pink—the report is probably reliable. Gray—the report is possible but unreliable; it lacks supporting evidence. Black—the report is improbable; it is not congruent with verifiable evidence, and it may well be fictive.

profiles of Jesus. They are also asking how their profiles affect the way in which we now understand the origins of Christianity. In due course, the seminar will inquire what impact its findings have on ancient versions of Christian orthodoxy, on definitions of heresy, and on Christian life and practice in the modern world.

The Spiritual Trek

I have been on a spiritual trek that parallels my professional odyssey at most points. However, the course of my quest for knowledge has been steadier, less hesitant than my spiritual adventure. Spiritually I have gradually exchanged my youthful convictions for a certain amount of faith. By faith I do not mean "belief"; I mean "trust." The confusion, in popular usage, of faith as trust with faith as belief in a set of propositions has almost made the term in its proper sense unusable. In spite of progress, I still have trouble acting as though I trust that things will work out. I continue to be anxious about what I will eat and wear. I don't trust the people who are in charge, and I tend to let that distrust spill over into the cosmos. There are many days when I am inclined to reorganize things for God. Most of the time I have doubts that truth will be victorious, that the innocent won't suffer, that good will triumph over evil. In my office hangs an anonymous six-stage outline of what happens to most projects, which means to most of our grand designs:

1. Enthusiasm
2. Disillusionment
3. PANIC
4. Search for the guilty
5. Punishment of the innocent
6. Praise and reward for the nonparticipants.

That often seems to me to reflect the way things are likely to go. Yet there are rare instances when I recognize that what I think is important may not in fact be significant, that I may not understand what truth is all about, and that the values I cherish may not be worth much. It is tough to have faith when the evidence doesn't support your private convictions. But then, that is what faith is—toughness in the face of rampant confusion and contrary evidence. My faith in the order and Orderer of the universe is in short supply most of the time.

In recent years I have occasionally had the thought that there is some advantage to dying young. Thirty comes to mind as a good age to go. You can make up your mind initially, broadcast your convictions without apology, and not have to worry about revisions, regrets, and mistakes that you learn about only with experience, age, and maturity. It was not my lot to pass on at a tender age. I have lingered around well beyond the customary three score.

On the other hand, being a senior scholar—one who is over the hill—has certain advantages as well: age and experience permit one to gather enough data to imagine what the whole is all about, to posit a horizon, to envision a world, and to get beyond the fear of rejection and failure, possibilities denied to the young and inexperienced. That is a distinct advantage, if the vision is informed; a disadvantage if it comes only with the hardening of the arteries. My arteries have certainly hardened, but I have also been visited by a vision of sorts.

The life of a scholar can easily be moved into the fast lane. It requires a flurry of activity to keep up with the latest fashions in theory and practice, to keep abreast with what is politically correct, to learn to quote the right sources, and to interpret in the categories considered à la mode. I spent a great deal of my life keeping up with those currents. It is easy to be seduced by one or all of them. That is the right word: seduced. The better part of wisdom is not to be entranced by the fashionable, not to be taken in by the politically correct, not to fall victim to the politics of theory and quotation. To practice wisdom in that form is a delicate matter. As always, it is very difficult to tell the difference between real progress and a change in style. To stick to what is good and true and dodge the allure of current fads. I cannot claim that I have done so. My way of looking at things may be merely old-fashioned. But I have allowed myself the belated luxury of forming certain convictions, which I am now ready to confess.

1. I confess that my confession may be a cover-up. Reader beware.

2. I fear that the confession Christians make when they recite the Apostles' Creed is very likely a cover-up. (It is a cover-up of the real Jesus.)

Here I must digress for a moment.

The fellow who runs the granary down the street in the industrial park where my office is located frequently plays "fetch the ball" with his dog. Every so often he will pretend to throw the ball and then, while the dog is looking away, he will actually throw it. Because the dog has not noticed this deception, he sits patiently at his master's feet and waits. His master points in the direction of the ball. The dog, not understanding the meaning of that gesture, barks at the pointing finger.

The first and many subsequent followers of Jesus are like that dog: Jesus points to some horizon in his parables, some fabulous yonder, something he called God's estate, which he sees but to which the rest of us are blind. Like dogs, we bark at the pointing finger, oblivious to the breathtaking scene behind us. All we need do is turn around and look.

The Jesus movement very early on exchanged the vision for the visionary. Those first enthusiastic followers were enthralled by the world Jesus encapsulated in the parables and aphorisms, but, since they were unable to hold on to the vision embodied in those verbal vehicles, they turned from the story to the storyteller. They didn't know how else to celebrate the revelation. They turned the iconoclast into an icon.

3. I confess I am more interested in what Jesus thought about God's domain than in what Peter the fisherman and Paul the tentmaker thought about Jesus of Nazareth.

4. I am inclined to the view that Jesus caught a glimpse of what the world is really like when you look at it with God's eyes. He endeavored to pass that glimpse along in disturbing short stories we call parables and in subversive proverbs we call aphorisms. But he did not spell out what he meant.

5. I have a glimpse of the real Jesus stealing a peek at God's domain. My glimpse is informed by, but bypasses, the Jesus of the gospels—the Christ superimposed by the evangelists on their own glimpse of the real Jesus.

6. I am convinced that the New Testament conceals the real Jesus as frequently as it reveals him.

7. I believe that the world "out there," the world we take to be real, is a product for the most part of our descriptions of it and the stories we tell about it. We are inclined to think our scientific descriptions and our mythic tales are unassailable. Because we do not recognize them as fictions, they can be dangerously deceptive. Nevertheless, I concede that there is a world out there and that it is solidly real. I just don't know for sure which aspects are real and which are illusions supplied by our myths and descriptions.

8. I believe in original sin, but I take original sin to mean the innate infinite capacity of human beings to deceive themselves.

9. I have come to see that the self-deception inherent in "original sin" prompts human beings to believe that what they want is what they are really entitled to and what they will eventually get—things like unending life in another world and absolute justice in this. I doubt that it will work out that way.

10. I am inclined to the view that we are free to cross over to the kingdom of God, to God's estate, so long as we never arrive. Perpetual leave-taking and the hope of homecoming is our common human fate.

CLASSES OF READERS

There are six classes of potential readers for *Honest to Jesus*. I have endeavored to keep all these readers in mind as I write.

The first group consists of those who are bitter from an initial deception by parent, clergy, or the church. These are the dispossessed, the alienated members of "the church alumni association," as Bishop John Shelby Spong terms them. They once thought they were instructed in the truth, only to discover that their parents and the church had misled them.

They had asked for bread but were given a stone. The bitterness and pain of that initial deception lingers on. They are the walking wounded.

If they are not too embittered, they have become truth seekers, questers. They welcome new, reliable information, mentors who refuse to dissemble, and a hearty challenge. They are not afraid to embark on the great adventure under less than auspicious circumstances.

A second group, closely related to the first, is made up of those who have patiently remained within the community of faith. They are there in the pews Sunday after Sunday, studying and learning, but they are not compliant, mindless adherents of the received tradition. They are there in spite of their dissatisfaction. They are undernourished, even starved, unless they provide for their own sustenance. They wait quietly for a crumb for the mind, a morsel to sate the moral appetite. They are the loyal, the forbearing, the hopeful, perpetually looking for a star in the East. They hang on in spite of the fact that the church's sun is setting. If the first group can be characterized as the walking wounded, this second group may be described as the ambient hungry.

For the first two groups I have some affection because they are kindred spirits. I will subsequently refer to them as catacomb questers.

A third cadre is made up of those who are innocent of the Christian tradition altogether. They have often wondered what the Bible and religion were all about but did not have—or at least did not seize—the opportunity to find out. They are the victims of the separation of church and state, of the wariness of university faculties to allow Judaism and Christianity to be taught as bona fide subject matters, or of the hypocrisy of pastors and parents who either did not know the truth or refused to divulge it. I have come to know this group intimately after many years facing freshmen in the university classroom.

A fourth company—probably of limited number once the news about this book gets out—is comprised of those who are certain they know the truth and who read only to confirm their own prior convictions. In all probability, they will be suspicious that this book is the work of the devil, simply because they consider any view they cannot endorse without further thought to be born of Satan. They will anticipate that *Honest to Jesus* is one more attempt to deceive and mislead the public by a parade of scholarship. These readers are those who already know, or think they know, what the Bible means. They are mostly well-intentioned but unwitting victims of clerical or parental tyrannies, forms of child abuse that are even more damaging, in some cases, than physical abuse. Where their capacity to entertain alternative points of view has not been permanently impaired, there is hope that some chance remark or small insight will awaken them to new possibilities. They are the students who enrolled in a class to set the instructor straight but lingered on to enlarge their horizons. One should never abandon hope. However, the terminally intransigent are the dogs to whom one should not offer what is sacred, the swine before whom one should not cast pearls. Since we don't know in advance who they are, we just cast away indiscriminately.

A fifth body is comprised of clergy and lay leaders. A few of them have been waiting a long time for an honest statement. They were overjoyed at the appearance of *The Five Gospels,* which is a report of the search for the authentic words of Jesus. They read John Dominic Crossan and Thomas Sheehan, Elaine Pagels and Marcus Borg with delight. A few rare souls among clergy and laity have been in the territory of *Honest to Jesus* ahead of me. I have learned from them. One pastor, Culver Nelson, who was the instructor of his huge congregation for more than three decades, has been my mentor; his ideas run well ahead of those of most academics. I am also deeply indebted to laypersons who think a sermon should be more than three points and a poem. They have encouraged me when my zeal has flagged; they have alerted me to the real questions; they have pushed and probed and prodded until I agreed to come clean.

I am running into increasing numbers of both clergy and laypersons who are quitting or have quit the church. For them *Honest to Jesus* may have come too late. Yet they have not lost their interest in the Jesus question. They have channeled their energies into other venues, such as social work or carpentry or counseling. I have a special affinity for them because I belong to their number.

On the whole, though, the rank and file of clergy and lay leaders suffer from theological dry rot: institutional fungi have eaten away the heart of the faith, leaving behind a soft skeleton, prone to disintegrate into dust. Their attention spans have shortened. Their reading time has eroded. Their personal libraries have become dated. They are perhaps the least likely to be looking for a challenge, owing, undoubtedly, to a lack of interest and to the loss of the habit of circumspective reading and reflection.

A final group consists of other professional scholars, especially other biblical scholars. Also included in this august company are the journalists and reporters who cover the religion beat. Some of these literati will read, like any genuine intellectual, to discover another point of view, perhaps even to pick up new information. I am always pleasantly surprised by journalists and academic colleagues who read with understanding, often at a level that exceeds the original input.

But many in this category, while technically literate, read poorly, read with inattention, read only to confirm their own biases, read to find fault, or read to foster confrontation, which is the bread and butter of both journalistic and academic existence. To the extent that this subgroup does read, they do so not so much to learn as to smirk. They look out on the world from the pedestal of "superior knowledge." They will furnish the slings and arrows that wound the truth in the name of some private view and contribute further to the collapse of credibility where biblical scholars and scholarship are concerned. As trigger-happy gunslingers, they will shoot themselves in the foot without even clearing the holster.

I, too, aspire to be a reader. I write principally to find out what I think, or aspire to think, and so am my own first reader. I know that we cannot have and then retain the visions that we are unable to articulate and thereby share with other readers and listeners. As a first step, I want to share any glimpse with myself through the medium of the well-constructed sentence.

Literary critics speak frequently of the *implied author,* the author who pens my sentences but from whom I want to distinguish myself the moment I become my own reader. I am not infrequently amazed and often amused at what I write. The delete key on my computer is a close friend. As a consequence, I want to be among those "other" readers of this work, all of whom are seekers, many of whom are innocent of guile, some of whom have set out on the same odyssey or related quest as I. Together we are at risk before the mysteries of life. The quest for the historical Jesus is a small piece of that great adventure. Minor though it may be, it requires the same devotion to truth as all our other pursuits, the resolute willingness to confront the facts, and the unblinking determination to tell all.

In other words, it demands that we be honest to Jesus.

PART ONE

Return
to Nazareth

Chapter One

THE JESUS QUESTION

THE PERENNIAL JESUS

The longing to know who Jesus really was seems to persist in North America. People wonder about Jesus; they feel some spiritual kinship with him, although they are often unable to say precisely what that means. The Jesus question persists but it does not lead to the quest of the historical Jesus, the Jesus that lies behind the popular image. Why is that?

Americans do not view Jesus as a hero, according to reports now and then in the newspapers. "Heroes make history," writes Daniel Boorstin, Pulitzer prize-winning author; "they are known for their achievements." Celebrities, on the other hand, are known for being known; they make news, not history. A celebrity functions for many contemporary folk as a role model, as someone to be emulated and imitated because he or she makes news—and makes money.

Although Jesus is not considered a hero, he is thought by some to be a "role model." It is unclear what that could mean. After all, Jesus was not successful in any of the categories most people regard as marks of success; instead, he was executed as a common criminal. Since they know so little about him, people around the world must view Jesus as a celebrity rather than as a hero. Jesus is known for being known; everybody knows *about* Jesus: his name is mentioned on talk shows, he is frequently the subject of TV documentaries, athletes form prayer circles around him, and he commands the untiring adoration of evangelists and advocates of public prayer. All of this in the face of very little hard information about his real achievements.

In the popular imagination Jesus does not appear to have the definable stature of, let us say, Martin Luther King Jr., Mohandas K. Gandhi, Mother Teresa, John Wayne, or Elvis Presley, but he is there on the mental landscape, in faded form, a figure with an indistinct profile, not really to be distinguished from God in many minds but who has also been reduced from a genuinely transcendent being to something more accessible and personal—a friend available for a stroll in the garden in the cool of the evening.

In other segments of American society, Jesus leads a more influential but not necessarily more robust existence: he is an available endorser of favorite virtues and values, an occasional inciter of good deeds, and an inspiration for those who must suffer some terrible pain. In these roles he is the equivalent of the Good Housekeeping Seal of Approval for the charities we espouse and a perpetual presence at our hospital bedsides.

In yet other quarters, Jesus is the icon of the full gospel believers; he is a still life dictated by a fixed reading of the gospels and creeds. Nothing is at issue for this group because selected facts drawn from the New Testament gospels and the meaning of those facts are etched in stone, like the ten commandments—or in this case, in the concrete of the King James Version and its fundamentalist interpreters. Lest it sound as though there is only one fundamentalist view of Jesus, we do well to recall that there are about as many fundamentalist pictures of Jesus as there are fundamentalists. There is nothing quite so fractious as a good fight on the religious right. In spite of the fact that the Christian right recites a common litany of theological affirmations, its members multiply churches at a phenomenal rate because they are unable to accommodate each other beyond a few special, political causes.

The tendency to take Jesus captive for this reason or that, to confiscate his name as slogan for one crusade or another, belies a hankering to know the real Jesus, the Jesus no one knows, to get around and behind the Jesus that is paraded on television in ideological chains and heralded in cheap paperbacks as someone held hostage by objectives militantly prosecuted. There is an underlying but ultimately suppressed impulse to turn the Jesus question into a quest for Jesus. There are numerous impediments that block that impulse; we will explore those blockages subsequently.

The Jesus of the gospel records is an enigma to us because he belongs to an alien time and place. On the authority of those same records, he belonged to yet another time and place even for his contemporaries; by virtue of his vision he did not belong to their everyday world either. We should not be surprised to learn that the Jesus no one really knows is a subverter of causes. That he tramples with disdain on our saccharine sentiments. That he contradicts the labels we pin on him. That he rejects our honors and adoration. That Jesus, like the real Abraham Lincoln and the real Socrates, floats there in the collective imagination as an elusive but endlessly tantalizing figure who, if liberated, promises to help us discover who we really are and what life is all about.

THE JESUS OF THE GLIMPSE

I share an interest in who Jesus is and especially who he *was*. I am intrigued by the provocative but shadowy figure that one occasionally catches sight of in the ancient gospel texts. In his authentic parables and aphorisms, Jesus provides a glimpse into another reality, one that lies beyond present conceptual horizons. His words and deeds open onto that reality. His vision, in my view, is worth exploring. The Jesus of that alternative world encourages me to celebrate life, to suck the marrow out of existence, to explore, and probe, and experiment, to venture into uncharted seas, without fear of a tyrannical and vindictive God. He does not set limits on my curiosity, on my drive to challenge every axiom. That same Jesus prompts me to give myself to tasks that exceed, even contradict, my own self-interest. I am not infrequently startled at the tasks I find myself willing to undertake.

As I look around me, I am distressed by those who are enslaved by a Christ imposed on them by a narrow and rigid legacy. There are thousands, perhaps millions, of Americans who are the victims of a mythical Jesus conjured up by modern evangelists to whip their followers into a frenzy of guilt and remorse—and cash contributions. I agonize over their slavery in contrast to my freedom. I have a residual hankering to free my fellow human beings from that bondage, which can be as abusive as any form of slavery known to humankind. I believe that such a hankering is inspired by Jesus himself, who seems to be untouched by religious bigotry and tyranny and unacquainted with the straitjacket of literalism and dogmatism. Liberation from fear and ignorance is always a worthy cause, with or without the endorsement of Jesus. In the last analysis, however, it is because I occasionally glimpse an unknown Jesus lurking in and behind Christian legend and piety that I persist in my efforts to find my way through the mythical and legendary debris of the Christian tradition. And it is the lure of this glimpse that I detect in other questers and that I share with them.

JESUS SUBVERTS JESUS

The real reason for rediscovering the historical Jesus is to allow an ancient Jesus to confront the many faces of the modern Jesus. The Jesus we begin with is the Jesus we have enshrined in our images and creeds, our reconstructions and convictions, our hopes and our fears. The Jesus that lies at the end of the return to Nazareth is someone we do not yet know. Whatever he turns out to be, he will subvert the Jesus we think we know, the Jesus we venerate and cherish. We must be prepared for the potential emotional and intellectual turmoil that discovery will produce.

"It is a good thing," Albert Schweitzer wrote in *The Quest of the Historical Jesus* nearly a century ago, "that the true historical Jesus should overthrow the modern Jesus."[1] The modern Jesus he had in mind was the Jesus as reconstructed by critical scholars during the nineteenth century. But the modern Jesus also includes popular, naive, and fundamentalist notions of Jesus. It embraces the kind of Jesus proclaimed from the pulpits of many mainline churches on any average Sunday morning—if and when he is proclaimed at all. Scholarly reconstructions of Jesus are not immune from their own critical virus either; in fact, scholarly reconstructions of the historical Jesus are the special targets of professional scholars, who eke out their intellectual existence by preying on the work of others—prey in both senses of the term: to loot and to destroy.

To this list of things at which to take aim Schweitzer might have added others: It is also a good thing that the true historical Jesus should overthrow the Christ of Christian orthodoxy, the Christ of the creeds. The creedal Christ, no less than the best scholarly reconstructions of Jesus, is an idol that invites shattering. Both must "yield to the facts, which . . . are sometimes the most radical critics of all," as Schweitzer put it.[2] Finally, it has become clear that even the Christ of the gospels is a further impediment to any serious effort to rediscover Jesus of Nazareth. It is the gospel of *Jesus* and his acts that we seek to identify and isolate amid the rich variety of early Christian reminiscences and affirmations preserved by all the surviving gospels.

Those who are searching for the origins of Christianity are actually in quest of the "real" Christianity, the "golden age" of the tradition, according to Elaine Pagels. We long, she says, for "a simpler and purer" form of religion. But if we are astute, if we are bona fide seekers, we will discover, as she did in her brilliant book, *Adam, Eve, and the Serpent,* that "there is no single, 'real Christianity.'"[3] Instead of simplicity and purity, historical investigation uncovers the complexity and rich diversity of the origins of Christianity. The Jesus movement was, from the very beginning, in the minds of Jesus' first and most intimate companions, a welter of responses —impulses, convictions, emotions, memories, typifications, practices, false starts, new hopes, struggles for power, and related human reactions. It is possible to isolate many of these tiny blips on the screen of history if we pay sufficient attention to detail and do not let our preconceptions overrule what our texts tell us on their own terms.

In and among that plethora of responses, we will be able, if our historical antennae are well tuned, to catch sight of a particular person— a solitary face in a Galilean crowd—among the many other faces and voices that echo from that specific past. Of course, if we hope to be successful, we will have to find and isolate the historical figure in the ancient gospels, the only sources we have that provide us with access to him as a historical person. We can never hope to establish more than a few features, this or that aspect, a trace here and there, of Jesus of Nazareth. And we can achieve that much only by means of more than one angle of vision. Locating a solitary person in history requires a series of triangulation points. As a consequence, the historian searches for and attempts to isolate as many of these responses and reactions as the records preserve. By tracing out their converging lines, we may hope, in this detail or that, to catch sight of what each response and respondent had in view. But this venture will not result in a final, fixed, immutable destination. The picture of Jesus that emerges will be tentative, subject to further investigation and new information.

If we cannot arrive at a final profile, what then is our goal? If we cannot reach the original, the real Jesus, the true Christianity, what is the purpose of the quest? The answer is worth repeating: The aim of the quest of the historical Jesus is to set Jesus free, to liberate him from prevailing captivities. Truth is a moving target. It is always necessary to remind ourselves that the liberated Jesus will eventually be imprisoned again and reentombed. Then it will be time to start all over again.

JESUS AS THREAT

The quest of the historical Jesus can be a hazardous undertaking. If we search the sources diligently, with all our natural and contrived defenses down, if we make use of the best information we can gather, if we allow the evidence to invade our closely guarded castle of assurances, we will probably discover a Jesus that explodes our inherited and acquired notions, a Jesus we cannot readily mold to our preformed images or bend to our favorite moral causes. In that case, we will be embarrassed by our own discoveries. At the same time, by unearthing the real Jesus, we may be prompted to jettison much of the traditional baggage we acquired at our cultural birth and brought with us as carry-on luggage.

When Jesus manages to escape from our creedal and experiential dungeons, he asserts his preemptive right to the use of his name and may want to object to the title we have assigned him. He demands his prerogatives. As in reformations of the past, we may find, to our chagrin, that he objects as much to the church established on his behalf as he did to the religious practices of his day, to the priests and temple, the scholars and their affluent sponsors in Galilee and Jerusalem. His protest might well be aimed at popes and bishops, televangelists and evangelical declaimers, ministers and priests, biblical scholars and their cousins, along with messianic pretenders, in every age. He may well even resist what you and I want to do for him. That prospect may become the most formidable roadblock of all.

The strength and vitality of any tradition can be measured by the depth and integrity of its continuous self-criticism. Christianity is in danger of dozing off. We need to wake it up with a powerful new reformation, one that matches, or perhaps even exceeds, the quake produced by the great reformers of the fifteenth through the nineteenth centuries. Seismic activity has been too long dormant.

The prospect of a theological quake generated by a prison break on the part of the historical Jesus is intolerable to many. There is the suppressed fear that an emancipated Jesus might break down old barriers, cross unacknowledged frontiers, and open up new fissures in the body of Christ. For the most part, we prefer the comfortable creeds we brought with us from our earliest memories of church, Sunday school, and reassuring baritone pastors. We find the fuzzy, cuddly Jesus of our youth quite satisfactory.

It is quite possible that we do not want to readmit Jesus of Nazareth back into Christianity. We probably prefer things as they are. The letter writers whose loud protests on the editorial page champion a Jesus of the miraculous birth, many ostentatious miracles, an atoning blood sacrifice, and a bodily resurrection are merely announcing their preference for a Jesus who demands nothing of them—except to reiterate such high-sounding but largely empty assertions. Persons of this type can believe and believe and then call for more belief, in loud and resonant tones, and not suffer the slightest urge to modify their own behavior; the sole impetus they seem to share with others of similar persuasions is to condemn the rest of us who do not agree with their formulations.

There are some, to be sure, for whom the liberation of Jesus spells the liberation of the spirit. For them an encounter with Joseph's son is relief, release, and reclamation. The historical truth about Jesus is no more a threat to their faith than a dentist is a threat to teeth, as one pastor put it. For these the demands of Jesus may well be like a painful visit to the dentist. But in spite of the trauma, many Christians, in company with those who have already left the church, have welcomed the exploratory work of critical scholarship because new information has brought them release from the tyranny of dogma.

How the scholarly investigation of the gospels affects Christian convictions cannot be the immediate concern of this study or of the work of the Jesus Seminar. Our allegiance is to history—to the historical data we collect and to their interpretation—and not to particular religious interests, not to the Apostles' Creed or the Westminster Confession of Faith. Whether liberating or not, historical knowledge is the best check we have on the human capacity to deceive ourselves. We are all prone to believe what we want to believe. It is not an act of faith to take the Bible at face value; it is a betrayal, a violation of the trust scripture bestows on its custodians.

To find oneself suddenly free in a dizzying realm without a polestar can be truly exhilarating, unbelievably liberating, but it can also produce sheer terror. For those hardy enough to brave the unknown, it is the opportunity to discover what it is like to chart a new course, to sail to the edge of the world, to put down boundary stakes on a vast, undifferentiated prairie, to erect a shelter from the endless reaches of the cold, boundless heavens overhead. For the less hardy pioneers of the spirit, a genuine quest may result in unanticipated trauma. The loss of received notions of the Bible regularly produces an emotionally devastating experience. I do not wish to rob those vulnerable souls of their mythic shelters if they cannot weather that loss. For those who fear that result, the end of this paragraph is a good place to exit the adventure that lies before us.

If you have elected to continue this adventure, please be reminded that there is no truth so profound, no conviction so sacred, no fact so certain that it is immune to repeated critical review. There are no theologies or sciences without question marks trailing behind. And there is no institution that can guarantee the truth of anything. We are all pilgrims in a wondrous and strange land of latent possibilities and unknown potential.

In any genuine attempt to recover the historical Jesus, everything is at stake. The church, as it faces the beginning of its third millennium, is in crisis regarding what it believes about Jesus.[4] Believers are in crisis about their convictions, to judge by the emotional and strident responses to any aberration in popular orthodoxy. And the previous reconstructions of who Jesus was, what he said, and what he did are coming unraveled in the light of new information, new methodologies, and new perspectives. What scholars of the gospels discover about their sources and the Jesus who fills those pages will affect what is believed and believable. We should make no mistake: historical research does affect belief. The Protestant and Catholic theologians who attempted to put the convictions of faith beyond the reach of historical reconstruction and human reason have failed. The Jesus that is emerging from a reevaluation of the ancient records in the light of new discoveries will shake the temple to its foundations.

The quest of the historical Jesus is also about the religion to which he gave rise. The historical truth about this man may help us discover the truth about the faith he evoked. Or, conversely, the truth about the faith may open our eyes to the truth about the man. The distinction between the Jesus of history and the Jesus of the gospels and creeds threatens traditional orthodoxy and other "doxies" that constitute the formidable ramparts guarding our previous convictions. But the discrepancy may also prove to be salutary for a flabby community of faith, provided it is explored with rigor and honesty.

GROUND RULES FOR THE QUEST

The quest for truth should be framed by certain ground rules, particularly where religious truth is concerned. The discussion of religion is a difficult matter in polite society. It is even more difficult in impolite contexts in which truth-telling is the primary goal. Before we sketch the rules themselves, some preliminary observations will be helpful.

An argument about religious beliefs is rarely a profitable undertaking. It usually involves two parties attacking each other from entrenched and impregnable positions. In such disputes there are no victories, only casualties. Beyond the emotional encumbrances that dog theological debate at the popular level, arguments about religion are never simple. Solitary points are like the flower in the crannied wall: if we knew everything there was to know about that solitary Wordsworthian flower, we would know what God and humankind are. Ostensibly simple points are linked to most other important issues. As a consequence of these limitations, for hostility and acrimony we should substitute the desire to learn what we can from our written sources, from our ancestors, from each other. Learning requires a large dose of humility to offset our built-in arrogance, which is usually supported by deafness and massive ignorance.

New knowledge can prompt us to modify our beliefs. If we want to stick to our prior convictions, we should avoid new information like the plague and close our minds to everything but the opinions that square with our own. This is the way of censors and bookburners.

On the other hand, if we are to learn something about our religious heritage, we should agree on the ground rules for investigation and discussion. Ground rules will reduce frustration and help produce satisfactory results. Here are several ground rules that are operative among genuine learners:

Rule One

Human knowledge is finite. It is fallible, limited, subject to correction. If it were not, study and learning would be unnecessary. This rule applies, willy-nilly, to the Bible, to the pope, to ecclesiastical bureaucrats and contemporary preachers alike. And to scholars.

Even if the revelation contained in the Bible were infallible and inerrant, as some claim, how we understand it is not—unless, of course, particular interpreters have been granted the only correct interpretation by divine right and light. But if interpreters have the only correct interpretation, then they, too, must be equally inspired if their interpretations are to be infallible. And even if their interpretations are infallible, I must share their inspiration, and hence their infallibility, if I am perfectly to understand their interpretations. This progression suggests that we are confronted with an endless sequence in which everyone who pretends to understand must participate in the original inspiration to be part of the chain. It is best to admit that our knowledge is finite and open-ended and therefore subject to modification, and that we have acquired it by toil— by study and learning. The admission puts us all on a level playing field and makes a genuine exchange of ideas possible.

Rule Two

The frame of reference for our questions should be as large as the world and all that's in it; it should not be confined to the Bible and religion. We should place our questions in the broadest possible context. Narrowing the frame of reference limits the perspectives we can bring to bear on our deepest queries. For students of the Bible this means setting the Bible in the larger context of Western history—indeed, in the global perspective of all the world's religions.

For Americans, it is essential to frame our religious questions in relation to the development of the American tradition, both religious and secular. Further, the intellectual and scientific advances made since the Enlightenment (roughly, since the seventeenth century) should be allowed to inform the issues we pose. We have to take account of Galileo, Kepler, Descartes, Spinoza, and others who have given the modern world its perceived shape. And, of course, we cannot ponder the God question without some contemporary knowledge of the physical universe. The Hubbell telescope, for example, enables us to see some fourteen thousand million light-years into space and thus see stars that were forming close to the time the universe originated. And, finally, we cannot do without the best scholarship of the Jewish and Christian traditions performed by all qualified investigators. To ignore any of these frames of reference is to circumscribe the validity of our answers.

Rule Three

Our questions and their answers should be informed by all the information we can gather. And the facts depend on what we can observe.

If we kick a rock, we can be reasonably confident that we will hurt our toes. That is a fact of life. I do not advocate kicking rocks four times a day in the hope that the fact will be proved false on some future occasion. It is essential to be aware of some of the rocks that lie along the paths of our intellectual journey. There is not much point in kicking them.

Whether we like it or not, there are presently no fragments of any of the books of the New Testament older than about 125 C.E., and no copies of any substantial portions of any Christian writings that can be dated to a time before 200 C.E. And these are copies of copies made long after the originals. There are no copies of the Hebrew Bible older than the Qumran documents, now dated to the second century B.C.E. We cannot change these facts; only new discoveries can alter them. We cannot change the fact that all copies of the Bible were made by hand prior to the invention of the printing press in 1454 or thereabouts and consequently contain mistakes and inaccuracies. Such facts as these and many, many others should make a difference in our assessment of the reliability of the original-language texts of the Bible.

Rule Four

Those to whom we go for information and evaluation must be those who qualify as scholars and experts. Scholars are those (a) who have acquired the necessary linguistic and methodological skills; (b) who are thoroughly acquainted with the ancient texts and archaeological data, together with correlative comparative materials; (c) who undertake their own investigations and draw their own conclusions in relation to an established body of knowledge and critical theory; (d) who have put their own work in the public domain and thereby subjected it to critical peer review; (e) who put truth above personal preference or conviction.

We may not get exactly what we want from scholars, and we may not get everything we would like, and we may not like what we get, but high scholarship is the best we can do. In Chapter Three, I will express several reservations about the scholarly fraternity and the way it functions. Meanwhile, I can do no less than commend learning.

Rule Five

In spite of the sciences, impressive methodological advances, and the knowledge explosion, we still cannot be certain that we can tell the difference between illusion and reality.

Aspects of what we think we see and hear, of what we believe we know, are almost certainly illusory. The social world we inhabit as human beings was created for us by our historical and social contexts and by our own imaginations. We are products, to a greater or lesser extent, of our own creative activity. In a word, we are autocreators. One consequence of this arrangement is that we are constantly being deceived. If this assertion seems false, ask yourself whether you know anyone who has never been wrong about anything. We may safely assert that illusion and error are a part of the human condition.

This rule has its positive side. A lively imagination is a basic ingredient in the scholarly enterprise. There are undoubtedly realities all around us we have not yet recognized because our imaginations lack the requisite capacity. There are explanations we have not yet invented for phenomena already encountered in the world we do know. Imagination itself is sparked by metaphor, misstatement, subversion, and other forms of pliant creativity. The illusions we presently have may turn out to be real, and the realities we now think we know may turn out to be illusory. The wise are always open to surprise, ready for reconstruals.

Rule Six

Our investigations, our quest for truth, should be sprinkled with humor. We must not take ourselves too seriously. As serious as this business of the Bible and Jesus and religion is, we should remember that we are all buffoons of one sort or another, clowns strutting about on life's stage or waiting in the wings, as Paul suggests in his second letter to the Corinthians.

Rule Seven

No matter how many illusions we dispel, no matter how firm the conclusions we reach this time around, we will turn out to be wrong in some way, perhaps in many ways, down the road. Someone, somewhere, sometime will have to come along and correct our mistakes while adding their own. This brings us back to Rule One: Human knowledge is finite.

LOCATORS

Ground rules specify the boundaries, more or less, for the kind of search, or investigation, or conversation appropriate to a common intellectual enterprise. Beyond these ground rules are "locators," more subjective in nature, that "place" the odyssey to be embarked upon. I am not speaking of private opinions but of clues that show up in many conversations among informed and thoughtful people, of the concerns and issues that are identified by established writers in their books and essays, of the problems to which scholars and thinkers return again and again in the course of an age. These locators do not have the status of ground rules. Their purpose is to situate the conversation or debate in relation to a definite complex of issues. Locators are themselves part of the imaginative landscape of thinkers in a particular time and place. Locators indicate what the real frame of reference is for a specific line of investigation. What follows is a series of locators that indicate the landscape on which this book—my own approach to the issues raised by Jesus—is situated. These markers reflect the widespread conviction of many scholars and theologians. I have borrowed them from many sources and conversations, although my formulation of them may vary from the way others would have stated them.

Locator One

Traditional answers to theological questions no longer completely satisfy: we can no longer simply repeat the old creeds and pre-Enlightenment shibboleths and expect thinking people to regard them as illuminating and persuasive.

Locator Two

The mainline churches face a fundamental crisis of faith: in a pre-emptory way they have suppressed the questions people are asking, or would ask if empowered to do so, and so have left themselves and their parishioners vulnerable. Church bureaucrats too often admonish, "Don't rock the boat," or they urge us not to injure the good work the church is doing in other domains by posing embarrassing questions. Worst of all, they ask us not to disturb the faith of simple believers, as though the suppression of knowledge can somehow advance the faith. In so doing, they are postponing a rendezvous with the issues that are emptying the churches and crippling the intellectual integrity of the Christian tradition.

Locator Three

Fundamentalisms of various types are efforts to turn back the clock to the sixteenth century, to the infancy of the Enlightenment, to the clear and distinct idea, much as the Essenes attempted to reverse time in Jesus' day by moving out into the desert and establishing isolated, insulated, uncontaminated enclaves.

Locator Four

Insecurity and uncertainty have produced a plethora of political bullies: fundamentalists on the right and politically correct liberals on the left insist that we all adopt their points of view. I don't like bullies, big or little, human or divine, smart or dumb. I prefer to make up my own mind after careful review.

Locator Five

Criticism of current orthodoxies, right and left, is coming principally from scholars outside the church, scholars whose base of operations consists of independent colleges or secular universities or private research institutes. This owes in large measure to the fact that scholars are being driven out of the seminaries, just as they were earlier driven out of Bible colleges; and the mainline churches, for their part, are often forcing out perfectly loyal laymen and laywomen who are unable to hew to the party line. The Southern Baptists may be more efficient at the excommunication of their intelligentsia, but a few Roman Catholic bishops aspire to equal them. All of this is unfortunate but true.

Locator Six

Scholars of religion are themselves under heavy pressure to conform, even in institutions whose supposed allegiance is to academic freedom. Academic appointments and even visiting speakers are subject to veto by the politically correct, who insist on conformity to the current line. Straitjackets of opinion are as restrictive among liberals as they are among fundamentalists.

As biblical scholars make the transition from cloistered to secular contexts, some are finding the stress of that shift paralyzing. In a few cases scholars become cop-outs because they want to avoid conclusions or consequences that would have been unwelcome in their previous ecclesiastical context. Those left behind in the monastic shelters are whining because they understand the transformation of the questions, the methodologies, and the answers but are unable to abandon their intellectual pensions. They are constrained by church traditions but are expected by their academic colleagues to perform as if they were secular scholars. The strain in both cases is agonizing. The secular context is actually hostile to religion, even to religious questions addressed candidly; our former ecclesiastical homes are wary of us. We are trapped between the two.

The first six locators are mostly negative in character. The following locators will fix the positive horizon.

Locator Seven

Those of us who care about the truth, about each other, about the earth, even about God cannot—must not—give in to barbarism, to chaos, to naïveté, to intellectual bullies, even to traditional, comfortable answers. We must face ourselves and our ultimate future—death—unafraid and unsullied.

Locator Eight

The chief test of the authentic quest for truth in our time is not ideological but ethical. It is not what we believe that is crucial but what we do. In some circles, joining a church means accepting an ideology; it should mean caring for one's neighbor. When ideology dominates, the ethical light dims. It is no accident, for instance, that fundamentalist groups have the highest racial bigotry ratios among religious bodies in the United States. They are also the most vigorous supporters of a military solution to world problems. I want to know what the right-to-lifers have done for the starving children here and abroad before I listen to their theories about the beginning of life. But I also want to know what those who oppose the death penalty have done about violence in the streets and in government operations before I entertain their extended arguments about the sacredness of life. It is not clear to me either how those who have cultivated a culture of complaint can contribute in a meaningful way to the betterment of society.

Locator Nine

Finally, I am inclined to the view that life is a leave-taking and a home-coming, all at the same time. There is no place for humankind to lay its head and rest. We are pilgrims, one and all, for all time. We are vagrants on the playing field of life.

The quest of the historical Jesus is a quest in the spirit of Homer's Odysseus and Arthur's knights of the Round Table. It does not involve sailing ships, the one-eyed Cyclops, Sirens, broadswords, and grateful maidens. Yet it is no less a quest story, and it is no less beset by dangers and pitfalls of every kind. The search for the Jesus of history is a quest for the holy grail of truth.

Chapter Two

FROM NAZARETH TO NICEA

HOW THE ICONOCLAST BECAME THE ICON

THE FOUNDERS OF THE FAITH

Christianity as we know it did not originate with Jesus of Nazareth. Jesus was not the first Christian. Tradition has it that Peter, the leader of an inner circle of three followers of Jesus, was the first to identify Jesus as the expected messiah. Incipient Christianity was formed around the conviction that Jesus had been exalted to God's right hand at his death and would return as the heavenly son of Adam to sit in cosmic judgment at the end of the age. His first coming was to be followed by his second coming. From that relatively modest beginning, Jesus was gradually elevated to godhood in the second and third centuries. But Christianity took its definitive form—the form defined by the emperor and the church councils as "orthodox"—in the fourth century with the creation of the first creeds and canons.

These developments, from the death of Jesus about 30 C.E. to the Council of Nicea in 325 C.E., have led modern critical scholars to distinguish Jesus of Nazareth—often referred to as the historical Jesus—from the so-called Christ of faith—the Christ embodied in the first confessions of Peter and Paul and the creedal formulations of the fourth and later centuries. The quest of the historical Jesus is an effort to emancipate the Galilean sage from the tangle of Christian overlay that obscures, to some extent, who Jesus was and what he said, to distinguish the religion *of* Jesus from the religion *about* Jesus. That quest has been under way since the eighteenth century, when the first critical scholars asserted their independence from ecclesiastical control. It has continued unabated in the nineteenth and twentieth centuries. Yet the struggle for independence is not over; would-be inquisitors inside and outside the churches continue to fashion straitjackets of orthodoxy to restrain their critics.

The Christian tradition in all its forms and guises everywhere claims to be descended from a historical person, Jesus of Nazareth, who belonged to a specific time and place in world history. The link between Jesus and the Christ, or between Jesus and Christianity, is limited in the Apostles' Creed to the birth and death of Jesus, but a link however narrow and specific is nevertheless a link. The New Testament gospels, in contrast, posit a link that covers a much broader spectrum of historical events, running from Jesus' baptism by John to his final days in Jerusalem. It is impossible to imagine any form of Christianity without Jesus as its basic component.

The question for both Christians and Jews is what role to assign Jesus the Jew in the Jewish sect known as Christianity. Do Jesus' words and deeds play a formative role in the religion that bears his name? Does Jesus have anything to say about the religion formed around his life and death? Or did the first Christians merely borrow his name and his death as the pretext for a religion that has little or nothing to do with the sage from Nazareth?

It is not possible to answer these questions unless we discover who the real Jesus was. In seeking the real Jesus, all the creeds and confessions in the world will not supply us with a single historical datum: belief has not and cannot create a solitary fact. Faith may suggest an imaginative configuration of many isolated facts, but it cannot supply the foundations on which that construction is erected. For that purpose, substantial, well-attested, critically screened historical evidence is required.

ASSORTED FACTS AND FIGURES

What do we know about this shadowy figure who is depicted in snapshots in more than twenty gospels and gospel fragments that have survived from antiquity?

The short answer is that we don't know a great deal. But there are a few assorted facts to which most critical scholars subscribe. Jesus lived in a period bounded by 6 or 7 B.C.E. on the one side and by 36 C.E. on the other. Those limits are set by the death of Herod the Great in 4 B.C.E. and the end of Pilate's tenure in 36 C.E. Jesus' life was played out on the stage we know as Palestine, consisting in his day of Galilee to the north and Judea to the south. Dividing the two provinces was the territory of Samaria, through which Jesus may have occasionally passed on his way to and from Jerusalem. He may also have traveled in the region across the Jordan, on the east bank, since, like other Judean pilgrims, he may have chosen to avoid contact with hostile Samaritans by crossing and recrossing the Jordan on pilgrimages to the holy city.

We do not know much about the persons who played a role in Jesus' story. We are fairly certain he was attracted to the movement of John the Baptist at one point, perhaps prior to the inauguration of his own public career. John the Baptist was almost certainly a historical figure. We know the names of a few followers of Jesus, such as Simon Peter, and James and John, the sons of Zebedee affectionately known as the "thunder brothers," whose own stories are sketchy at best. Jesus is linked with the reign of King Herod the Great (38–4 B.C.E.), during whose incumbency Jesus was allegedly born. We also have the name of Herod Antipas the Tetrarch, who ruled Galilee during Jesus' adult life, and the name of Pontius Pilate, the Roman procurator (26–36 C.E.) under whom Jesus was crucified. Then, too, we know the names of a few women associates, such as Mary of Magdala, who belonged to his retinue and was later to play such a prominent role in legend. Beyond these few shadowy faces, we have very little hard information. Nevertheless, there is substantial evidence that a person by the name of Jesus once existed.

Some additional isolated facts can be gleaned from the surviving records. These are data that a disinterested, neutral observer could have attested. Jesus' home was semipagan Galilee, whose inhabitants, because they were often of mixed blood and open to foreign influence, were despised by the ethnically pure Judeans living to the south. His hometown was Nazareth, and he was probably born there as well, contrary to later legends that assign his birth to Bethlehem to satisfy an ancient prophecy. Since Jesus was a Jew, he belonged to the ethnic group we now more accurately call Judeans, the ancestors of present-day Jews. Jesus' father,[1] as well as Jesus himself, may have been a carpenter or a craftsman of some kind. His mother's name was Mary. Jesus had four brothers whose names were James, Joses, Judas, and Simon.[2] According to the Gospel of Mark, Jesus' mother and his brothers were originally skeptical of Jesus' program but later became part of the Christian movement.[3] Jesus may also have had sisters.[4] These details square with what we otherwise know of the period and place, and scholars see no reason why the Jesus movement would have invented them.

Jesus' native tongue was Aramaic, a Galilean dialect that Judeans apparently could identify, as suggested by Matthew's account of the confrontation with Peter in the courtyard during Jesus' trial.[5] We do not know whether Jesus could read and write; the story of Jesus in the synagogue reading from Isaiah[6] may well be a fiction invented by Luke, the author of the third gospel. The "orphan story" of the woman caught in an adulterous act pictures Jesus stooping down and "drawing" in the sand while those ready with stones are making up their minds who among them is sinless. This is called an orphan story because it does not have a fixed home in gospel manuscripts, appearing as it does in various locations; it probably did not belong originally to any of the gospels known to us but may be a fragment of an unknown gospel. It cannot be taken as evidence that Jesus could read and write. The critical reader must be constantly alert to fictional embellishments in the gospels. We do not know whether Jesus knew Hebrew, in his day only a literary language. There is now evidence that suggests he may have been bilingual; Greek was probably his second language, learned from the pagan environment that surrounded him in Galilee, especially in Sepphoris, a hellenistic city located only four miles from his home village. In any case, the written gospels were all composed in Greek, and judging by the poetic shape of much of the language, it seems certain that the Jesus tradition took its formative shape in Greek as well. If Jesus did not speak Greek, his original words have been lost to us forever.

Jesus was active during his public career in the towns and hamlets of Galilee, but no mention is made in the written gospels of comparable activity in hellenistic towns in the same region.

The Fellows of the Jesus Seminar and scholars generally regard it as highly probable that Jesus was baptized by John the Baptist. Scholars are also relatively certain that he quit John and launched his own career in Galilee. These events are not likely to have been invented by Christian apologists. Jesus was evidently an itinerant sage, wandering about from place to place, teaching and healing and living on handouts. He practiced exorcism. He and his followers, unlike John the Baptist, did not practice baptism in the beginning. We are not certain that Jesus deliberately formed a group of disciples, but it is clear that followers gathered around him. He was popular with the people. He was opposed, however, by some religious authorities, in both Galilee and Jerusalem, although much of the controversy in the gospels between adherents of the new sect and Judaism may reflect later conditions, subsequent to the destruction of Jerusalem and the temple (70 C.E.), when the budding church was competing with the synagogue.

We do not know how long his public career lasted, but the narrative gospels imply a relatively short period, from one to three years. As a final act, Jesus went to Jerusalem, either spoke or acted against the temple and the temple authorities, and was executed by the Romans.

Much of the story of his arrest, trial, and crucifixion was suggested by prophecies that early Christian storytellers arranged to have fulfilled as they told and retold the story. This part of the gospel story will be examined in detail in Chapter Twelve.

In addition to these meager facts, we also have a compendium of teachings consisting of parables, aphorisms, and dialogues, together with a few dubious anecdotes told about him by his first admirers. The authentic words of Jesus can be isolated, to a greater or lesser degree, from other words borrowed from the old scriptures or common lore and put on his lips and from words created by the evangelists under the poetic license exercised by storytellers the world over. The content of this body of authentic speech material tells us a great deal more about Jesus, but it does so indirectly. The central section of this book will examine the parables and aphorisms for a fresh glimpse into the outlook of the Galilean sage.

Meanwhile, the scattered facts we can muster do not of themselves produce a Jesus who is the object of the Christian faith. For the author, or rather authors, of the faith—those who first conceived and articulated that faith—we must turn to Peter and Paul.

FOUNDERS AND RIVALS: PETER AND PAUL

In his startling book, *The First Coming,* Thomas Sheehan asserts that the faith of the church can only be traced back to Peter, not to Jesus. Actually Sheehan has the Roman Catholic tradition in mind when he makes that statement. The commissioning of Peter as the foundation upon which the new church would be built, reported in the Gospel of Matthew, is almost certainly legendary.

Protestants, beginning with Martin Luther, would probably prefer to trace their beginnings back to Paul, who was converted only three or four years after the death of Jesus, perhaps as early as 33 or 34 C.E. Paul of Tarsus, a Jew living in the hellenistic world—in the Diaspora—was the pioneer missionary of the incipient Christian movement. This cultured, educated Jew, who did not know Jesus personally, identified Jesus as a savior figure of the hellenistic type, a dying/rising god, such as Osiris in the Isis cult, popular in Egypt. Isis, the royal queen of heaven and mother of all, was the wife of Osiris, who, according to the myth, was murdered by his twin brother Seth and his dismembered body thrown into the Nile. Isis searches for the body parts, reunites them, becomes pregnant by Osiris, and gives birth to Horus. This holy family played a significant role in a hellenistic cult that won adherents all over the empire. It was not the life and teachings of Jesus but the death of Jesus and his appearance to Paul in a vision on the Damascus road that became the focal points of Paul's gospel. Jesus' death as saving event and the subsequent vision that provided Paul with the "truth of the gospel"—this is how Paul puts it in his letter to the Galatians—were the two incidents that comprise the formal content of his gospel. (We will explore these matters subsequently.) Paul enjoys popularity among Protestants in large measure because he is the counterweight to, and critic of, Peter, whom the later Roman tradition designated the first pope.

The work of the two competing apostles, Peter and Paul, are storied in the Book of Acts—Peter in the first half, Paul in the second. Peter left nothing written for us to be able to judge his views (the letters that bear his name were ascribed to him by anonymous authors). As a consequence, we have to measure his contribution to the new movement by reports in the gospels and Acts and in the letters of Paul. Paul, on the other hand, produced an extensive correspondence, which provides us with much of the information we have about the advance of the new movement; they also tell us a great deal about Paul himself. His writings, which are occasional rather than systematic treatises, were the first to be regarded as sacred to the new movement. They were first collected and circulated toward the close of the first century c.e. (Anonymous authors also wrote letters in Paul's name.) The lives of Peter and Paul both ended in the sixties of the first century.

Peter and Paul were rivals from the beginning. In his first letter to the Corinthians, Paul tells of the report he has received about factions in the church at Corinth: Some members, he writes, claim Peter (whom Paul usually refers to as Cephas, his Aramaic name) as their leader, some claim Paul himself, others endorse Apollos, and some even belong to a Christ party. In his letter to the Galatians, Paul tells the story of his conflict with Peter over eating openly with gentiles, those who do not observe kosher (Peter did not approve), and over requiring gentiles like Titus, Paul's assistant, to be circumcised (Paul did not think it necessary). Paul interprets his stand on open-table fellowship and freedom from circumcision as the "truth of the gospel." He is adamant about his understanding.

At an earlier conference held in Jerusalem, attended by Peter, James (the brother of Jesus), and John, along with Paul, Paul thought they had settled these matters. It appears that they had not. When Peter later came to Antioch, he reneged on the agreement that gentiles should not be forced to live like Jews in order to become Christian. Paul confronted Peter personally on that occasion and reprimanded him. Peter appears to have resisted the notion that ethnic origin, religious practice, gender, or social status does not give one a favored status in God's eyes. We must assume that Peter was a slow learner, to put it in the kindest possible way.

Broadly speaking, in the rivalry with Paul, Peter represents the connection with the historical Jesus. After all, Peter had been a close companion and confidant of Jesus until his arrest. Paul, on the other hand, claimed only to know the risen Jesus, the Christ of vision and spirit possession. It is perhaps ironic that it was Paul, and not Peter, who understood the heart of Jesus' parables and aphorisms. The conflict between Peter and Paul may be the reason that Paul remained alienated from the original disciples and, as a consequence, from the written gospel tradition, which was just then taking its first form in a collection of Jesus' sayings that has come to be known as the Sayings Gospel Q, later incorporated into the Gospels of Matthew and Luke. It was at this same time that Paul was writing his letters to the Corinthians and Galatians.

FROM NAZARETH TO NICEA: PAUL AND CONSTANTINE

Christianity took shape and became successful in the Mediterranean basin primarily as the result of the work of two very different persons: Paul and the Emperor Constantine.

Paul was an excellent promoter. He spearheaded the new movement as it marched from Antioch in Syria across Asia Minor and Greece to Rome. Paul worked the synagogues of Diaspora Judaism as the entry to numerous communities and employed his not inconsiderable rhetorical skills to great effect. To top it off, he must have been a superb administrator and correspondent, if we may judge by the letters that form his literary legacy. He also laid the foundations for the early creeds. Paul underwent his conversion experience on the Damascus road not long after the death of Jesus. He arrived in Rome about 60 C.E. and died a couple of years later.

There were other pioneer missionaries in the early church, to be sure. We know the movement spread first to Galilee from Jerusalem, then to Damascus and Antioch in Syria, before Paul came on the scene. And Egypt must have been invaded at an early date by Christian emissaries. Yet we know very little about these other important endeavors. Paul appears as the giant among early leaders because of the correspondence he left behind and because of his theological prowess.

The culmination of the missionary work of Paul and others occurred later, when the Emperor Constantine issued the edict of toleration in 313 C.E., which acknowledged Christianity as a legitimate religion for the first time. Later, in 381 C.E., the Emperor Theodosius adopted Christianity as the official religion of the sagging Roman Empire. In 325 C.E., Constantine summoned the leaders of the church to Nicea, a suburb of Constantinople (modern Istanbul), to adjudicate controversies among warring factions in the ecclesiastical world. He presided at that council himself, although not yet a Christian. The first form of the Nicene Creed (it was later expanded), which contained the formulations of that council, was intended to unify the various parties. Constantine saw to it that the vote was unanimous by banishing the bishops who did not put their signatures to the creed. There was now an official statement of correct beliefs, an orthodoxy, to which everyone had to subscribe. Those who did not became "heretics"—dissenting parties. But we are anticipating the end of the story.

THE DECADE OF THE FIFTIES: LETTERS AND GOSPELS

Paul did not know the historical Jesus; his gospel consisted only of the death and resurrection of Jesus Christ, as he called him. (Many people today think there was a Joseph Christ and a Mary Christ to complete the holy family; *Christ* is actually a title, meaning the "anointed one" and is the Greek term that corresponds to the Hebrew title *messiah*.) This gospel he had learned from his predecessors at Antioch in Syria, but the development of it owes to Paul's own creative mind, as he makes clear in the first two chapters of Galatians.

Paul wrote his letters during the decade 50–60 C.E. The authentic letters include Romans, 1 and 2 Corinthians, Galatians, 1 Thessalonians, Philippians, and Philemon. Some scholars add 2 Thessalonians and Colossians; whether authentic or not, these letters do not add anything material to what we learn about Paul from the first seven enumerated here.

During the same decade that Paul was dictating his letters to a scribe, the earliest gospels were being turned from oral tradition into writing. Memories of what Jesus had said and done were circulated for two decades by word of mouth. As the anticipation faded that Jesus would soon return as the son of Adam (the cosmic figure described in Daniel 7), Jesus' followers began to think of creating written records. The earliest gospels known to us are collections of the sayings of Jesus. They, too, were first written down in the decade 50–60 C.E. One of these early gospels was the Sayings Gospel Q, which must be reconstructed from Matthew and Luke, since no copies of it have so far turned up. However, Matthew and Luke incorporated most of it into their gospels in one form or another, so it was not lost altogether. A second early gospel has survived in the Gospel of Thomas, which, like Q, is simply a collection of the sayings of Jesus. Neither Q nor Thomas contained a passion narrative —the story of Jesus' arrest, trial, and crucifixion. The first narrative gospel, the Gospel of Mark, was not created until a decade or more later, probably during the decade 70–80 C.E. Matthew and Luke employed an early copy of Mark as the narrative framework for their gospels, which were composed in the next two decades. To Mark, Matthew and Luke added material they derived from Q. The Gospel of John, also frequently called the Fourth Gospel, was the last to appear—at the end of the century. John overlaps the other three canonical gospels at several points, but it also contains much unique material. We will return to the specific content of the several gospels in Chapter Seven. The names attached to the various gospels do not help us identify their real authors; these names were assigned by scribes at a later date.

The sayings gospels Q and Thomas must have been competitors of the Pauline gospel during the formative decades of the Christian movement, since all three came into being at approximately the same time.

THE GOSPEL OF PAUL

The roots of the later creeds—the Apostles' Creed and the Nicene Creed—are to be found in the early, pre-Pauline confessions of faith like the one recorded in Corinthians:

> Please remember that I passed on to you as first and foremost the
>   account I was taught:
> Christ died for our sins in accordance with the scriptures,
> and was buried;

he was raised on the third day in accordance with the scriptures,
and appeared to Cephas and then to the twelve.

1 Corinthians 15:3–5

This simple formulation was suggested by fragments of certain "prophetic" texts—Isaiah 53 and Psalm 16—and by the myth of the dying/rising lord of some hellenistic mystery cults. It encapsulates the earliest known summary of what was to become the Christian "gospel." The technical name scholars use for this form of the "gospel" is *kerygma,* the Greek term for "proclamation" or "message." Since it is necessary to distinguish various forms of the Christian "gospel," the term *kerygma* will come in handy later.

This version of the gospel is limited to two events, or rather to a single event conceived as an uninterrupted downward and upward trajectory. Jesus as the Christ *descends* into the tomb and then *ascends* from the grave to heaven, where he sits at the right hand of the Father. The short form of the kerygma consists of this steep "V" movement.

Paul also knows a more expansive version of this same V-shaped trajectory. In the redeemer hymn recorded in Philippians, the savior descends from heaven to carry out his redemptive mission and then ascends back to heaven as triumphant savior following his death:

Adopt the frame of mind that belonged to Christ Jesus:
Although he was divine by nature
he did not regard being equal with God
as something to use for his own advantage,
but abandoned self-interest
and took on the nature of a servant
and assumed the appearance of a mortal.
And when he had taken on the role of a human being
he humbled himself
and became obedient to the point of death,
even to death on a cross.
For that reason God raised him higher than anyone
and granted him the title that exceeds every other,
so that at the name of Jesus
every knee should bend
above the earth, on earth, and under the earth,
and every tongue acknowledge
that the Ruler of All is Jesus Christ
to the majestic honor of God, the Father.

Philippians 2:5–11

This larger trajectory, which begins before the birth of the savior, is reflected also in the Gospel of John 1:1–18. In outline it became the basis of the Apostles' Creed.

How did this "gospel" develop?

The crucifixion of Jesus must have been a disappointment to his first followers. It certainly frightened them, to judge by their response. With his arrest and crucifixion they fled from Jerusalem, returned to Galilee, and resumed their humble lives as fishermen and peasants. To die as ignominiously as Jesus did was not the fate a true Davidic messiah ought to suffer, since David's successor was supposed to restore the kingdom of Israel. Ironically, it was the disappointing execution of Jesus that kept the new faith anchored in history, in the life and destiny of the peasant from Nazareth. The crucifixion was an ugly fact that the new movement could not deny and for which it was compelled to account. Without that link, the Christ might well have originated as a cult figure risen from the dead but with no earthly credentials.

The conviction that Jesus was no longer dead but was risen began as a series of visions, initiated, according to the records, by Peter. Paul claimed to have had a similar vision on the road to Damascus. We do not know the content of Peter's vision, but Paul gives us an explanatory account of his revelation in the opening chapters of his letter to the Galatians, and Luke provides a detailed description, twice repeated, in the Book of Acts. The conviction that this Jesus, who had once lived among them, was now risen from the dead and seated at the right hand of God became the cornerstone of the confession that he was the son of God, a heavenly savior figure who had come to earth incognito to perform his redemptive task. This conviction was an intermediate stage on the way to the later affirmation that Jesus was divine.

THE GOSPEL OF JESUS

The memory of what Jesus had said during his brief public appearance circulated for two decades or more by word of mouth. As a result, only sayings that were short, pithy, and memorable were likely to survive; Jesus' ordinary words, like "hello" and "good-bye," would not have been remembered as such, nor would lengthy discourses such as we find in the Gospel of John. Sayings that could readily be repeated and adapted to new situations would have entered the stream of oral tradition and later have been written down. Some sayings and parables continued to be transmitted orally, of course, long after the first gospels were written, and some of these were captured in writing in later gospels, like Matthew and Luke. All the authentic words of Jesus derive ultimately from this fund of oral tradition.

Jesus belonged to an oral culture. Learning and wisdom were transferred from teacher to student by word of mouth, rather than through written texts. At the popular level, authorship was not highly regarded; plagiarism was an unknown concept. In the judgment of many critical scholars, wise teachers such as Moses, King Solomon, King David, Socrates, and Jesus became repositories of anonymous and proverbial wisdom, much of it secular. Moses was credited with the five books of the law, very little of which can actually be traced back to him. David is supposed to have composed the psalms; he may have been a poet and musician, but he is not the author of the Book of Psalms. Solomon is credited with the Book of Proverbs, the Song of Solomon, the Wisdom of Solomon, the Psalms of Solomon, the Odes of Solomon, and the Testament of Solomon. He wrote none of them. Plato creates a Socrates in his dialogues who probably never existed precisely as Plato represents him, although Plato's Socrates is undoubtedly a mixture of historical reminiscence, philosophical theory, and a rich helping of Plato's imagination. Jesus, too, became the repository of words he did not originate and probably did not even say. In addition, Christian evangelists imagined things for him to say—things that gave voice to their own beliefs. For these reasons, the Jesus Seminar concluded on a case-by-case basis that less than 20 percent of the words attributed to Jesus in the gospels were actually spoken by him. The miracle is that any authentic aphorisms and parables of Jesus may actually have survived for us to ponder.

The two early sayings gospels, Q and Thomas, permit us to reconstruct, to a limited extent, what the religion *of* Jesus must have been—as distinguished from the religion *about* Jesus, conceived by his first followers and amplified by Paul. Put in other terms, these first gospels provide the basis for discriminating the gospel of Jesus from the kerygma (the "message") of the Jesus movement.

The gospel of Jesus came to expression in the parables and aphorisms preserved in Q, Thomas, and other gospels. The message of the parables and aphorisms is first and foremost the announcement of good news: sinners and outcasts are welcome in God's kingdom; indeed, God's domain belongs to them. The bad news is that those who think they are leading upright lives will be surprised to learn that they have missed the messianic banquet, the great supper, because they were too preoccupied with misleading and deceptive aspects of life. According to Jesus' parables and aphorisms, the social roles—marginal versus respectable—will be reversed: the first will be last and the last first, according to Jesus.

God's domain was for Jesus something already present. It was also something to be celebrated because it embraces everyone—Jew, gentile, slave, free, male, female. In God's domain, circumcision, keeping kosher, and sabbath observance are extraneous. The kingdom represents an unbrokered relationship to God: temple and priests are obsolete.

This Jesus had nothing to say about himself, other than that he had no permanent address, no bed to sleep in, no respect on his home turf. He did not ask his disciples to convert the world and establish a church. He did not believe the world was going to end immediately, unlike John the Baptist, who was an eschatological prophet who expected God to intervene directly in history in the near future. Jesus apparently did not even call on people to repent, and he did not practice baptism. He may have eaten a last meal with the inner circle of his followers, but he did not initiate what we know as the eucharist. In short, very little of what we associate with traditional Christianity originated with him.

THE MERGER OF THE JESUS OF HISTORY WITH THE CHRIST OF FAITH

The evangelists merged the Jesus of history with the Christ of faith in the narrative gospels, Mark, Matthew, Luke, and John. Using our alternative terms again, the gospel of Jesus was combined with the kerygma of the early Christian movement—the "gospel" of Paul and others—to create the Jesus of the narrative gospels.

The merger in Mark, the earliest of the group, is incomplete, yet it is clearly under way. Mark begins his story with the baptism of Jesus at the hands of John the Baptist and concludes it with the passion story and the empty tomb. Jesus is portrayed as an eschatological prophet, like John, who calls for repentance in the face of the impending doom.[7] But there are no birth and childhood stories and no resurrection appearances. Nevertheless, Jesus three times predicts that he will suffer and die in Jerusalem and after three days rise up.[8] Mark has Jesus say that "the son of Adam came to give his life as a ransom for many."[9]

Both Matthew and Luke adopt Mark as the narrative framework of their gospels. Fortunately, they also embed material from the Sayings Gospel Q in that frame; if they had not done so, we would have much less on which to base a reconstruction of the historical Jesus. And to Mark they have both added birth and childhood stories at the front of their gospels, including claims of a miraculous birth; at the end they have appended a variety of appearance stories not found in Mark. Matthew locates the appearances to the followers of Jesus in Galilee; Luke confines them to Jerusalem. Matthew is here following Mark. The epiphany story in the middle of Mark—where Jesus takes Peter, James, and John with him up the mountain and is there transfigured before them—may well have originally been an appearance story set in Galilee.

The competition between the gospel of Jesus and the gospel of Paul, represented by the sayings gospels on the one hand and by the Pauline letters on the other, has thus been resolved: the historical Jesus has been given a more encompassing role as the Christ of faith. In the narrative gospels, Jesus still tells parables and pronounces aphorisms as he does in Q, but he is made to talk like the expected messiah whose miraculous birth and even more amazing resurrection identify him as the redeemer from heaven.

In the Fourth Gospel the pretense of a flesh-and-blood figure is dropped: Jesus has been made coeternal with the Father and he doesn't mind telling us so in episode after episode. The history of Jesus the man has been smothered by the myth of the Christ. Nevertheless, the author of the Fourth Gospel has preserved some important insights into the historical person: Jesus speaks in puzzling, enigmatic figures and tropes, as he does in the other gospels, and performs signs of enigmatic rather than ironclad interpretation, such as changing the water into wine. These features probably mirror aspects of the performances of the historical Jesus.

THE CREED WITH AN EMPTY CENTER

The merger created by the narrative gospels did not endure. The Christ of faith eventually overpowered the Jesus of history. The Apostles' Creed, which may go back to the second century in some rudimentary version, has been preserved in a form it had in the eighth century. In translation from its Greek original, the second article runs like this:

> I believe in Jesus Christ, God's only Son, our Lord,
> who was conceived by the Holy Spirit,
> born of the Virgin Mary,
> . . . .
> suffered under Pontius Pilate,
> was crucified, died, and was buried;
> he descended to the dead.
> On the third day he rose again;
> he ascended into heaven,
> he is seated at the right hand of the Father,
> and he will come again to judge the living and the dead.

It scarcely requires notice that this creed calls on the believer to affirm nothing about the historical Jesus other than his virgin birth at the beginning of his life and his suffering, execution, and resurrection at the end. *It is a creed with an empty center.* (The dotted line represents the missing center.)

Further, Jesus plays a passive role in the events mentioned: things happen or are done to him, but nothing he does depends on his own initiative or resolution. In grammatical terms, Jesus is the recipient of the action; he is never the agent. As a savior, he is only a pawn in the divine plan. Finally, the ethical dimensions of the gospels of both Jesus and Paul have been lost in this creedal formulation: believers only have to believe; they are not required to modify their behavior in any other respect. Like Jesus, they, too, are passive.

THE PARADOX OF THE DEAD GOD

The religion about Jesus, as mentioned earlier, took as its point of departure the fact of Jesus' noble death, in tandem with the vision of him as risen lord. This composite Jesus became the object of a cult—a system of religious practices focused on him as a fresh new deity, whose real name is Christ, rather than Jesus. This Christ, except for his execution as Jesus of Nazareth, is mythic in character. A myth is a story of the activities of a god. The Apostles' Creed, except for the two lines that have to do with Jesus' suffering, death, and burial, details the activities of a god: he is conceived miraculously, he descends to the regions of the dead, rises from the grave, ascends to heaven, sits at the right hand of the Father, and will come again. Those are actions that can only be performed by a deity. The Christ of this Christian confession of faith has all but eliminated the Jesus of history.

The traditional combination of elements—death, resurrection—forms a curious paradox. It is the paradox of a god who died, of immortality succumbing to mortality. It juxtaposes the historical and the mythical. The tension between these contradictory elements has produced endless turmoil in the Christian tradition. Anxieties on the part of believers, especially in modern times, have tended to be high on the mythic side of the equation: I am frequently asked whether I believe Jesus is the son of God and therefore divine, as though to give a negative answer disqualifies me for further conversation. I have never been asked whether I believe Jesus is fully human by any of the modern-day not-so-grand inquisitors. Perhaps this is the reason there is so little interest in, and even disdain for, the quest of the historical Jesus on the part of those who embrace traditional orthodoxy.

The insistence on the divinity test and the absence of the humanity test suggest that many poorly informed inquisitors are guilty of the docetic heresy—the belief, condemned by early Christian theologians, that Jesus Christ only *seemed* to be human. According to the Chalcedonian definition of 451 c.e., another creedal formulation of the ancient church, to deny the full humanity of Jesus is as much a heresy as to doubt that he is divine.

> . . . We all with one accord teach men to acknowledge one and the same Son, our Lord Jesus Christ, at once complete in Godhead and complete in manhood, truly God and truly man, consisting also of a reasonable soul and body; of one substance with the Father as regards his Godhead, and at the same time of one substance with us as regards his manhood; like us in all respects, apart from sin . . .[10]

The paradox of the dead god represents the marriage of the imageless tradition of Israel with the iconic mentality of the Graeco-Roman world. For descendants of Abraham, no one has ever seen God, and God cannot be pictured. For the Greeks, to consort with the gods was an everyday matter, and it was commonplace to make images of every imaginable deity. For hellenized Christians, Jesus the iconoclast became Christ the icon. Because Christianity has a twin heritage—its ancestors are both Jews and Greeks—it has never quite made up its mind whether it is iconic or iconoclastic. Yet, except for brief outbursts inspired by reformers and heretics, it has veered predominantly in the iconic direction. The quest of the historical Jesus is a way of restoring interest in the iconoclastic dimension.

HOW FAR IS IT FROM NAZARETH TO NICEA?

It is about a thousand miles from Nazareth to Nicea as the crow flies. It is a world away if we are thinking not of geographical space but of the relation of Jesus as Jewish teacher and sage to the theological debates and political intrigue that took place at Nicea. The three hundred years that separate the death of Jesus from the council of Nicea were filled with intrigue, controversy, struggle, martyrdom, conflict, success, triumph. Much of what happened in those centuries is unknown to us. But the broad outlines of development can be reconstructed from surviving records, principally from the gospels, Acts, and the letters of Paul, along with the writings of the first leaders of the church, such as Ignatius of Antioch, Justin Martyr, Clement of Alexandria, and Irenaeus of Lyon, as well as from the interpreters of Christianity who were later branded heretics: Valentinus, Marcion of Pontus, Arius, and the British monk Pelagius.

In this chapter we have sketched in barest outline how the Jesus movement got from Nazareth to Nicea. It will next be our aim to retrace the steps critical scholars take in working their way back from modern forms of orthodoxy to the historical Jesus. The way back from Nicea— from later orthodoxies—to Nazareth is beset with roadblocks and pitfalls. We will examine some of them in Chapter Three. In Chapter Four, we will detail the factors that have set the renewed quest in motion and suggest why it is an advance over earlier quests. In Chapter Five, we will discuss the difficulties translators face in putting ancient languages into modern idiom. Chapter Six describes how the New Testament came into being. How scholars approach the gospels as sources for the history of Jesus is the subject of Chapter Seven.

Once back in Nazareth, we will develop a profile of the historical Jesus based on his authentic words and deeds (Chapters Eight through Eleven). The third division of this book (Chapters Twelve through Fifteen) will be devoted to the death of Jesus, the stories of his resurrection, and the myth of the divine child. The domestication of the Jesus tradition and the marketing of the messiah are the subject of Chapter Thirteen, which marks the end of the history of Jesus and the beginning of the mythical Christ.

Chapter Three

BARRIERS BLOCKING THE WAY

A wink is as good as a nod to a blind horse.

The return road to Nazareth is beset with numerous roadblocks and detours, obstacles and pitfalls. They are mostly of recent vintage, but some of them are hoary with age. It is necessary to be aware of these impediments and barriers and be prepared to do battle with the trolls and dragons that guard the way back, exacting heavy tolls from submissive travelers. And formidable monsters they are because we ourselves have created and nourished them, often in spite of ourselves.

This territory will seem familiar, to be sure. In traversing that terrain, however, it is possible to lose one's way almost immediately. Confusion results from the lack of clear signing at forks in the road. The demons that patrol the route and thwart discovery, that blind us to fresh perception, that cloud the open mind are especially resistant to dragon slayers because the fire-breathers we aspire to destroy turn out to be our alter egos! Among these barriers are the following:

Ignorance

Popular images of Jesus

The gospels as inerrant and infallible

Monolithic literalisms and the death of the imagination

Spirituality as self-indulgence

A self-serving church and clergy

The foibles of biblical scholarship

All of this treacherous territory must be mastered if we hope to recover the faint figure of the Galilean, now encrusted with centuries of adoration and piety but more recently tarnished with disdain and suspicion.

IGNORANCE

The strategy immediately available to many Americans for frustrating any attempt to recover the historical Jesus is to remain piously ignorant while rigidly opinionated. This contradictory combination is unassailable. Americans of all ethnic origins and every religious persuasion take the doctrine of the separation of church and state to imply their right to remain ignorant about religion. It is a right exercised with untiring vigor. For example, opinion polls reveal that a majority of Americans believe that the Bible is the word of God; more than half of those who adhere to this conviction cannot name the four canonical gospels. They apparently have not read them in English, much less in Greek. As a consequence, it is difficult to take seriously their strident defense of the Bible as divine communication. In spite of their ignorance, many have deceived themselves into thinking that their judgments are beyond criticism and correction.

The reason for this strange posture is that Americans consider religion entirely a private affair. For most, in matters religious one opinion is deemed to be as good as another. In the university lecture hall, the professor of theoretical physics or biochemistry is seldom contradicted by the heady student; the distinguished scholar of classics or the teacher of Chinese rarely faces students who think they know better; but instructors in religion are repeatedly confronted by untutored sophomores who demand equal time and disproportionate attention for their ill-conceived certitudes. They do so usually on the basis of something they have learned from crusaders on campus sponsored by fundamentalist promoters. Knowledge appears to make no contribution to the credentials of an authority; opinions firmly held, expressed loudly, and buttressed by ignorance are quite adequate.

POPULAR IMAGES OF JESUS

Popular piety in the United States rests on what may be called a primal "childhood package" of Christian convictions. This package, based on surveys and polls, consists of six assertions:

- There is a God in heaven.
- God loves me.
- Jesus is God's son.
- Jesus died for my sins.
- God speaks to us through the Bible.
- I must believe these teachings; if I don't believe them, I won't go to heaven when I die.

The childhood version is later replaced by what is regarded as a more sophisticated package of the type often advocated by televangelists. The adult edition consists of a five-pronged creed:

- Jesus is the son of God.
- Jesus was born of a virgin.
- Jesus died on the cross as a blood sacrifice to atone for the sins of the world.
- Jesus rose bodily from the tomb.
- Jesus will come again to sit in judgment.

Many Americans, with and without church affiliation, will affirm these doctrines. They have apparently become societal norms to be accepted without question and without understanding. While many factors and forces have produced this state of affairs, a poorly understood gospel of Paul and a creed with an empty center are the chief culprits.

On the basis of one or the other of those tenets, the marginally informed like to mount their own inquisitions. In public forums, on radio talk shows, in television interviews, there are always those who want to know what axes scholars of the Bible have to grind, as though the inquisitors themselves were innocent believers without bias. To find out about axes they want to know what one believes. If the scholar does not immediately subscribe to the basic litany of affirmations, he or she is presumed to have an agenda, undoubtedly hidden. So the inquisition is intended to smoke out the unbeliever, perhaps even the heretic.

In my fifty years of public appearances, I have only rarely been asked about my academic credentials. Inquisitors seem not to be interested in whether I can read Greek, the original language of the gospels, whether I have had firsthand experience in Palestinian archaeology, whether I have submitted my work to peer review in journals and books, whether I am quoted in the scholarly literature, or what my fields of specialization have been. The acquisition of skills and information seem to be irrelevant to the subject of religion in the eyes of Americans who belong to the anti-intellectual, know-nothing party. What counts is whether one can assent to orthodox propositions. Any hesitation on the scholar's part brings on sudden hearing loss in the inquisitor.

THE GOSPELS AS INERRANT AND INFALLIBLE

The simple expedient that thousands use to impede the way back to Nazareth is to declare the Bible, and hence the gospels, inerrant. The Roman Catholic counterpart is to declare the magisterium of the church to be infallible—or, if not infallible, unimpeachable. The two forms of absolute authority are actually two faces of the same coin. This exceedingly effective strategy instantly puts the gospels out of reach and thus beyond critical review. But it does more than that. It opens the gospels to naive harmonizing (discrepancies are piously ironed out) and to proof-texting (the scriptures are mined for words, phrases, and sentences that reinforce doctrinaire positions). Moreover, this strategy puts up "no trespassing" signs at three levels: At the first, personal level it insists that the understanding of the person or community of belief is beyond question because it rests on the canonical gospels. At the second level, this view claims that the gospels are completely reliable and historically accurate. At a third level, this position insists that the Jesus pictured by the canonical gospels, and exclusively by them, is the true, the real, Jesus. The progression from a private preserve of understanding to the canonical gospels and finally to the only true Jesus is taken to be self-evident. Jesus lies entombed at the bottom of this three-tiered defense.

The proponents of this point of view—Protestant and Catholic alike—are rarely completely content with the view that their creedal formulations are beyond question for believers. This is merely the outer line of defense. The inner wall of defense, the second level indicated in the previous paragraph, is the insistence that the reports of the canonical gospels are based on the evidence of eyewitnesses and confirmed by unequivocal archaeological and textual data and by common sense. The question the representatives of this view regularly pose in inquisitional tests is this: How can modern scholars know more about what happened than the eyewitnesses who penned the gospels? We will return to that question later when we show that the gospels were not written by eyewitnesses. Meanwhile, the need for that second defensive trench is occasioned by the fact that the inerrancy creed falls not only with the close and detailed analysis of the gospels but even on superficial observation. The defenders of the sacred text and the teaching magisterium are kept busy plugging the gaping holes in the doctrine with contrived harmonizing constructs allegedly assembled by impartial historians.

It is possible to understand the call to affirm that the New Testament gospels are all that is needed for faith, but it appears to be a contradiction in terms to ask us to accept the argument that they are historically reliable on the same basis. If the evidence supports the historical accuracy of the gospels, where is the need for faith? And if the historical reliability of the gospels is so obvious, why have so many scholars failed to appreciate the incontestable nature of the evidence?

Inerrancy, infallibility, and special pleading inspired by prior theological commitments are strategies that are shattered on the shoals of the most reliable data we can assemble and their accompanying critical analysis.

MONOLITHIC LITERALISMS AND THE DEATH OF THE IMAGINATION

Inerrancy and infallibility are the offspring of literalism. Literalism takes theological affirmations to be objectively descriptive. If it didn't happen literally, we are told by the literalists, it didn't happen. Thus when Paul announces that Jesus died for the sins of humankind, the literalist takes that to mean that Jesus either made some kind of atoning sacrifice to appease an angry God, or that Jesus takes on the guilt of human beings and suffers in their place because suffering is the price God exacts for disobedience. This redemptive act on the part of Jesus is understood to be something that happened in the past, once and for all, and so cannot be repeated.

The crucifixion of Jesus is an event of the past, to be sure. In its literal descriptive sense it cannot be repeated. However, the redemptive function of that event is something that can be repeated, or at least newly appropriated, if it is to make a difference to us. As an event of the past, Jesus' death is said to have taken place *for* us; as something to be appropriated on later occasions, it can be understood as something that happens *to* us. In the first sense, the death of Jesus is literally true; in the second sense, it may be said to be true nonliterally.

The redemptive function of Jesus' death is usually expressed in mythological language. It is termed mythological because it refers to an act that was performed by God, or by God's son, on behalf of humankind. Such an act can be neither verified (nor falsified) on the basis of empirical data, by facts established by historical investigation. His death as redemptive event was not an act visible to the disinterested observer. All such mythological acts lie outside the purview of the empirical sciences and hence of the historian.

When, on the other hand, literalists claim that certain biblical stories are descriptively true, they are making claims that are an affront to common sense. Such stories include accounts of Mary's conception while still a virgin, Jesus' exorcisms of demons, references to seven heavens in the vault above the earth and to Sheol or hell below the earth, and Jesus' resurrection as the resuscitation of a corpse. If this form of misunderstanding were not so deeply entrenched in the literalistic mind, it would make us snicker. In the wake of the Enlightenment, when scriptural and ecclesiastical authority were abandoned by scholars, natural explanations were sought for all such phenomena. That strategy was born of the desire to be rid of the mythical parading as the historical.

Now we presumably know better. But our better knowledge has not been disseminated much beyond the university classroom, so we go on confusing the two categories. We either reject the mythical as pure unadulterated fancy or conflate the mythical and the historical as though they were one. Both positions are in error because they have fallen under the spell of literalism.

Literalism has created what Northrop Frye has termed the "imaginative illiterate." This product of the ascendancy of the empirical sciences, who can understand things only literally, dominates both high and naive levels of culture. It doesn't seem to matter that the literalist understands the term *literal* in different senses on different occasions. At times, the literalist takes "literal" to mean the descriptive, true-to-fact assertion; at other times, he or she understands the "literal" to mean the conventional, what everybody takes for granted. When used to mean what everybody takes for granted, the "literal" sense may thus also include the nonliteral. For example, everyone knows that there are no real oats in "sowing wild oats," and there is neither iron nor curtain in "the iron curtain." Yet these popular expressions are understood to refer "literally" to youthful indiscretions and an impenetrable political boundary. Similarly, the literalist will claim that Jesus dying for sins quite "literally" means that he paid the price demanded by God with his sacrificial blood.

The physical sciences and preoccupation with the literal have nearly killed the imagination. That does not mean that I want to give up my refrigerator and modern medicine, both of which owe their efficacy to the sciences. But it does mean that refrigeration and surgery do not cover all the needs of the mind and spirit. There are some things that cooling and lancing will not cure. The ability to perceive the nonliteral dimensions of our world is the victim of our inclination to exchange a refreshed sense of the world for a mess of technical pottage.

SPIRITUALITY AS SELF-INDULGENCE

Another numbing strategy is to insist that the Bible is a sourcebook for private spiritual nurture. Because scripture is considered "spiritual," individuals are entitled to extract their own "spirituality" in private, without the assistance of historical or critical analysis or, for that matter, without reference to what the text meant originally. The doctrine that the state may not interfere with religious thought and practice and may not abridge freedom in that sector is taken as a guarantee that religion is a private and personal matter. Accordingly, everyone is permitted to be his or her own expert. Everyone is his or her own authority on the subject; no one has the right to tell an individual what the Bible or the gospels mean.

This conviction has considerable merit. I subscribe to it myself. However, for many it is no more than a shield for self-indulgence, a prescription for do-it-yourself brain surgery. If in private meditation we are satisfied with our own secret responses to a text that we may not, in fact, understand, then we have done no more than confirm our prejudices, invoking the text as an ally in self-deceit. In this interpretive scheme, who is to gainsay Charles Manson's assertion that the Book of Revelation presages in detail the arrival of the Beatles in America? To listen to what the gospels actually say for their own time and place, as opposed to what we would like them to say, means that individuals must acquire some knowledge of how and when that text was composed and what it meant to its original authors and readers. Bible study often means no more than mining this collection of books composed over more than a millennium for incidental sentences, phrases, images, and schemes that we can employ to indulge our own system of prejudices and preferences. All too often Bible study is a case of the blind congratulating the blind.

A SELF-SERVING CHURCH AND CLERGY

American society is woefully illiterate in matters religious. By almost any standard or poll, Christians and Jews fail to exhibit minimal knowledge of their own religious traditions, to say nothing of Islam and Buddhism. Yet those same Americans are outspoken in their endorsement of religion, conspicuous in their participation in the Easter parade and, more recently, flagrant in their fixation with public piety, to judge by the politicians who endorse public prayer and by the display in end zones by professional athletes. How are we to account for that discrepancy?

It is difficult to avoid the conclusion that the churches have failed to educate their constituencies, that pastors have failed to inform their parishioners, and that instructors in seminaries have somehow short-changed ordinands. In American society, with its preoccupation with the separation of church and state, nobody else seems to care.

The colleges and universities that dot the land owe their origins more often than not to the churches. Education was once a top priority of religious institutions of every stripe. In addition, the churches mounted their own vigorous, internal educational program through their Sunday schools and study groups. Pastors and priests were once the most highly educated professionals in the local community. Theological seminaries were the most advanced graduate institutions until faculties of medicine began to displace them late in the nineteenth century. Church members were expected to be knowledgeable in their own religious traditions, and they were expected to support an educated clergy. That has all changed. The churches no longer have a serious educational program. They no longer sponsor or support educational institutions to the extent they once did. Pastors are not as well trained. The churches have become self-serving and introspective because they are beleaguered and defensive. They no longer know what their mission is. They are content to endorse the United Way and drift.

As a consequence, the churches have ceased to be part of the solution to religious illiteracy; they have become a major contributor to the problem—which, if not reversed, will lead to their own demise.

Clergy have decided that what they learned in seminary is a secret to be kept. Under duress by crusading fundamentalisms, the mainline churches have retreated into their cloisters and dissembled. The pulpit has become the locus of the soft assurance rather than the source of hard information. Parish members wither and die on a vine that is neither pruned nor watered—unless they take matters into their own hands. The least common denominator and the collection plate have taken over Christian education. Worse yet, the spiritual and intellectual leaders of

Christian communities have allowed uninformed parishioners to determine the content of the gospel. In a television interview, a Lutheran pastor insisted that his parishioners would go down the street to a church that taught fundamentalism if he did not teach it. That does not strike me as a particularly prophetic response to the requirements of the gospel. I wonder what happened to his moral integrity.

There are striking exceptions to these generalizations, of course. When asked to speak at a large urban church, I asked the pastor what topics to avoid as a way of assuring him that I didn't want to cause him trouble. He told me to say anything I liked, since his parishioners had already heard it all. I took him at his word. I learned in the responses from his parishioners what a teaching pastor can achieve in thirty-seven years. "If you tell the truth," he reminded me, "you need not remember what you told them, and you need not worry about what others will tell them." I found that experience very refreshing but exceptional.

For those who prefer gargantuan detours, there is the claim, occasionally made, that the Bible is the property of the church. These property rights, it is argued, give the church the prerogative to determine what the Bible means. If one wants to reinterpret the Bible, one must first persuade the church to change its mind. Those who make this claim often use the singular *church* as though there were only one, and they seem to assume that they belong to that one imaginary church.

Journalists appear to have adopted this doctrine. They frequently presuppose that there is one authority, ecclesiastical in nature, that is the final, undisputed arbiter in theological disputes. Cardinal Joseph Ratzinger and Billy Graham are members of this exclusive club. Scholars are not included. In news stories, academics are reported briefly and then the problems they raise papered over with piety supplied by reassuring priests and pastors. The Fellows of the Jesus Seminar are usually referred to as "self-appointed," thereby suggesting that they are intruders, usurpers, without proper endorsement by those who know the "real" answers. To be an authority, one has to be "appointed" by other authorities of higher rank. It should be a great comfort to readers and listeners to know that journalists have a direct pipeline to the truth on the subject of religion and the Bible.

THE FOIBLES OF BIBLICAL SCHOLARSHIP

Biblical scholars went indoors about 1923 and have refused to come out. We are closet scholars. Since the controversy over Darwin and evolution (*Origin of Species* was published in 1869) erupted, we have been wary of public discourse. The Scopes trial taught us that it was dangerous to speak and write in plain language. (The trial was held in Tennessee in 1923 and involved a high school teacher who was convicted of teaching the doctrine of evolution against state law, a law that was not repealed until 1963 but is now being reconsidered.) As a result of this case and similar controversies, biblical scholars learned to speak to and write for each other in codes that cannot be broken by the uninitiated. Like other academicians struggling for a place in the sun, we have made a virtue out of the trivial, articulated in bloated and esoteric rhetoric, and published in journals in which the footnote is king, in order to skirt or obscure the real issues.

In our academic ghettos, we have learned to live in a limbo between the heaven of the knowledge we possess and the hell of the ignorance we have taken oaths to dispel. We have learned to manage the discrepancy in our students, in our larger constituencies (college alumni and the church), and in ourselves by cultivating ambiguity, by the suspended and therefore equivocating judgment, and by the feigned respect for opinions at all levels. We have also acquired the skill of the parry and thrust with the rapier of wit in order to wound the opponent without resolving the dispute. In short, we have become adept at the intellectual gamesmanship played out in the classroom, in seminars, and in the annual ritual gatherings of professionals. It is loads of fun, but it leaves intellectuals impotent and sterile.

This uncertainty about roles corresponds to another pair of poles. As scholars of the Bible and religion, we cannot make up our minds whether we belong to the community of faith or to the academy. Some serious critical scholars teach in seminaries or church-related colleges and universities. They are under constant pressure from scholars in the field to adhere to scientific methods while giving lip service to the creeds in the college chapel. The conflict between what we think we know under those circumstances and what we are willing to admit often becomes acute.

Biblical scholars who labor outside cloistered precincts are equally ambivalent; those of us who have taught or teach in secular universities lack a significant public base: we do not appear to be working for, or in service to, a particular constituency. We are not training students for specific roles in the larger world. A major in religion, like a major in English or history, does not prepare one for a specific vocation. Like other humanists, instructors in religion are likely to be divorced from issues that matter beyond a relatively small circle of similarly situated professionals.

These extremely difficult conditions have left their mark on the scholarship of the Bible. We are fragmented; we lack common goals; we have no formal agendas or even hidden agendas; we have no major problems to solve. So we play trivial pursuit, like many other scholars in the humanistic wing of the modern university—specialists in literature, philosophy, linguistics, history, the arts. We are hounded by the anxiety of influence for fear that we will not be able to establish our own identities; we turn on our academic ancestry and disavow our didactic parentage because we believe ourselves to be intellectual orphans in need of adoption. Naturally, this syndrome produces tendencies toward fratricide among colleagues. Scholars turn on each other in the struggle for power and place, which results in the substitution of political for ideational goals. It is no wonder the ethics of biblical scholarship is in collapse. Self-esteem is low, and self-identity is weak. There is an abiding nostalgia for the European tradition where scholarship is honored and honored and honored, beyond reason—where Herr Professor Dr. Dr. is the unsolicited mode of address in the grocery for persons with two doctoral degrees and a lifetime appointment. It is no wonder that at the first chance and with the help of the National Endowment for the Humanities, American scholars are off to Europe to have their academic achievements recognized and their egos refurbished.

The worst enemy of all for scholars of the Bible—indeed, for all scholars—is elitism. In the academic world, penalties are severe for the author who writes a book that sells well, or for sponsors of the lucid sentence, or for teachers who can teach but fail to publish. Promotion and tenure committees look askance at such successes: after all, if a work is well written and elicits a broad readership, if a sentence is understandable, if students actually learn, that scholarship cannot be very profound. The inevitable result is that academics deliberately write in convoluted jargon merely to please their elitist colleagues.

Elitism breeds hypocrisy. Scholarship without a real public—without a real agenda—must pretend to be significant, when, in fact, it may be entirely or mostly irrelevant. Unlike Descartes, modern-day academics no longer have private patrons who will pay them to lie abed until noon to ponder the fundamental verities. Scholars produce at the behest and in accordance with the agendas of government agencies or private foundations that fund research. Their product is unwanted—indeed, unusable —by the society at large. In a democracy, that is very nearly fatal for the humanities. But it may not matter that their results are unsalable, particularly if their products are not distributed beyond a small, elite circle.

Scholars are basically the recipients of patronage. They are, in fact, clients of broker deans and committees on promotion and tenure and behave much like enslaved intellectuals. They have mortgaged most of their freedom to think and act as they please or as their research dictates. Tenure for them means job security rather than independence. They pretend to exercise unfettered judgments about important matters, but do so mostly when that exercise doesn't count for much or when it is merely a fashion statement.

Under such circumstances, how is it possible for scholars to muster the integrity to be honest to Jesus? It does not come easily. But in spite of my misgivings about myself and my colleagues, I believe that scholars and teachers, learning and scholarship are the last best hope we have to stave off the dire consequences of a waxing ignorance in matters religious and a waning tolerance on the part of the public for divergent points of view. In the next chapter I intend to award scholars a messianic assignment.

Chapter Four

THE RENEWED QUEST

RETURN TO NAZARETH

THE SEARCH FOR A SINGLE FACE IN A GALILEAN CROWD

What are scholars looking for when they go in quest of the historical Jesus? What do they expect to find?

The broad answer is this: we expect to identify and describe a particular person who lived in a particular time and place and who said and did particular things. To identify and describe a particular person it is necessary to distinguish that person from other persons living in the same time and place. In this case, it is essential to isolate a single face in a Galilean crowd. Of course, we must also depict the behavior of the many faceless people who make up Galilean crowds in order to give a concrete, plausible setting to the Galilean Jesus. Jesus will be defined both by what he has in common with his contemporaries and by how he differs from them.

The particulars for which the historian searches must be derived from the surviving primary and secondary reports of what Jesus did and said. In addition to about twenty known gospels, the Book of Acts provides some information, along with the letters of Paul and other early Christian documents. To be sure, we can also learn a great deal about his time and place from reports of what other people did and said. That will be the second major source of information: comparative or contemporary evidence. Once again, the profile that eventually emerges will be the product of determining what Jesus had in common with his world and how he differed from the behavior of others. This dialectic of how he was like and how he was unlike his contemporaries is the essence of historical reconstruction.

We must now take an additional step.

The sources we must rely on for information will often give us biased or slanted information. Of course, those same sources may also include very good historical or factual data. The trick will be to know which is which.

We will have to make allowances for bias in the reports of the Jewish historian Josephus; in the works of Philo, the Alexandrian philosopher; in the Dead Sea Scrolls of the Qumran Essenes; in rabbinic works such as the Mishnah; and in the writing of Christian sects such as the group that buried the Nag Hammadi library. We will also have to factor in the powerful convictions of the canonical gospel writers as we evaluate the information they provide. We will want to compare and contrast the perspectives of each of the gospels, including those not included in the New Testament. *As historians we are obliged not to take anybody's word for anything; we must attempt to verify every scrap of information we decide to use in our reconstructions.* That involves an assessment of the proclivities of our sources along with an evaluation of the sources from which they got *their* information.

To recap: we are faced with a double distinction. We must compare and contrast Jesus with his contemporaries in order to distinguish Jesus from other Galileans. But we must also distinguish Jesus from the reports about him preserved in the gospels, since that Jesus is the product, in large part, of his early admirers. Those reports will obscure as well as reveal. Reports are never the same as the actual persons or events. These are the two fundamental discriminations essential to historical reconstruction.

The first requires the identification of Jesus the Galilean Jew in contrast to his neighbors and contemporaries. The second calls for setting Jesus of Nazareth off from the pictures painted of him in the Christian gospels. In this book, the way we will go about making the second distinction is to contrast the gospel of Jesus with the Jesus of the gospels.

Jesus the Jew

Scholars are in the habit of saying that Jesus was a Jew, as though that identification tells us all we need to know. Used without qualification, "Jesus the Jew" often means Jesus spoke and behaved like all other Jews in his time and place. There are two things wrong with this assumption. First, we don't know as much as we would like about the religion of the Second Temple (the period beginning with the construction of the second temple around 520 B.C.E. and ending with its destruction in 70 C.E.) and especially about Jewish behavior in semipagan Galilee. The temptation is to read rabbinic Judaism, which did not take shape until after the fall of Jerusalem in 70 C.E., back into Galilee in the first decades of the common era. That would be an anachronism.

In the second place, Jesus was not just another Jew. John the Baptist was not just another Jew. Caiaphas was not just another Jew. The philosophical premise underlying these assertions is that every human being is unique. That is not to suggest that Jesus was unique in every respect or that he was divine. On the contrary, it is only to suggest that Jesus must have been enough of an individual to have said and done some things that were unusual or at least distinctive. The records indicate that at least he was perceived as just such a person.

According to the gospels, Jesus was a social deviant, a charismatic teacher who attracted a considerable following. He was apparently a non-conformist, like many of the ancient prophets of Israel. He seems to have criticized the temple cult and subverted some purity codes. He was a troublemaker. So we should be able to identify him among the throngs who came frequently to Jerusalem for the holy days.

Jesus the Christ

Just as it is tempting to assert that Jesus was a Jew, it is equally convenient for Christians to conflate the Jesus of history with the Christ of the gospels and creeds. The temptation on the Christian side of the ledger is to insist that the historical Jesus is the same as the figure who is the object of adoration in the Christ cult. In addition to comparing and contrasting Jesus with what we know of other Galilean Jews of his time, it is important to compare and contrast Jesus with the picture the evangelists paint of him. As historians, scholars must take pains to segregate what we can know historically about Jesus the Galilean from the profile of the Christ produced by each of the evangelists. We know there is a difference if for no other reason than that each of the gospel writers presents us with a different profile of Jesus. We can be sure that the dozen different images of Jesus created by a dozen different gospels in the first century cannot all be entirely accurate in what they claim about the historical Jesus.

Additional Warnings

It is fashionable these days to belittle the historian's craft as "a cover for a theologically tendentious agenda." The historical method is "fatuous," we are told, or "an ideology posing as science." The goal of historical reconstruction, we are warned, is to create a picture of early Christianity that ignores claims to the divine authorship of its sources, substitutes observable causes for the miraculous, and applies the most rigorous tests of date, authorship, tendency, and historical accuracy to all extant sources. These, please note, are *criticisms*. The product of this faulty method is "a kind of paper-chase" that is essentially sterile: it does nothing but frustrate members of the churches and the students who enter university classrooms looking for spiritual sustenance.[1]

There is a little truth in all of these extravagant charges, and a lot of truth in some of them. I have a large helping of misgivings about the integrity of biblical scholars, some of which were expressed in the preceding chapter. But the best antidote for such histrionics is more, not less, history. The only correction I know for extravagant claims not undergirded by carefully screened evidence is modest claims resting on the best evidence we can gather. Our new reconstructions will not of course be the real Jesus, now set out for the final time. It will be a reconstruction based on the best evidence currently available, submitted to the most rigorous collective and cumulative analyses, and shaped into a relatively consistent whole. It is the best we or anyone can do. It is all we can do. To propose abandoning that method because it allies itself with the sciences, traffics in empirical data, and inevitably represents the perspectives of the modern age is a counsel of despair. It is advice to return to a sheltered religious enclave and to indulge, along with the televangelists, in the rhetorical will to power. It is a long step backwards.

I see no ultimate reason to abandon hope. Scholarship is still our best bet. The church has surrendered its rightful prophetic role: it is in a survival mode and will not easily be moved to sacrifice its life for the truth, unlike its founder. Ignorance is rampant in the land. The political right has claimed a crippled and incredible creed as the platform of its campaign. There is nowhere else to go for light. As sorry as we are, even at our best, scholars who have the knowledge and the freedom and the integrity to engage in the quest must not surrender to old-time religion with its endless denominational claims and need for perpetual emotional fixes. Now is the time for all true questers to come to the aid of the tradition.

THE FUNCTIONS OF HISTORICAL INQUIRY

The first function of historical inquiry is to isolate and establish the particular. Any profile of Jesus we may assemble will be based on hundreds of specific bits of information of varying quality, significance, and reliability. The process of gathering and verifying those bits of information involves a complex set of procedures known as historical criticism. Particulars are isolated by distinguishing one thing from another, by the close comparison of reports. Particulars are established by attempting to verify each item, either by the confirmation of independent sources or by comparative evidence.

This basic function of historical investigation is not well understood by the amateur, who prefers to run the particulars of history through a possibility blender in order to amalgamate facts with fancies. The confusion begins with collapsing what is probable into what is possible. I am often asked, "Is it not possible that Jesus walked on the water?" My answer to that question can only be "Of course. Nothing is impossible, unless we exclude logical impossibilities, such as square circles." To the amateur, however, to grant that something is possible is immediately taken as verification of a canonical report. For the skeptic, on the other hand, walking on the water is impossible; therefore Jesus did not do it. The historian accedes to neither generalization. Possibilities (and impossibilities) do not and cannot establish facts. Historians insist on looking every report in the face and judging its reliability independently of theoretical possibilities.

The second function of historians is to group the particulars into arrays or constellations—to put things together that belong together. Having insisted on discrete particulars, historians then turn around and create bunches of things.

One brief example: Scholars spend considerable effort in distinguishing Matthew from Mark and Mark from Luke and Luke from John. Having done so, they then group Mark, Matthew, and Luke together as synoptic gospels because they have a great deal in common, in contrast to the Gospel of John. Further, the four narrative gospels in the New Testament differ in marked ways from the Sayings Gospel Q (a lost early compendium of Jesus' sayings now embedded in Matthew and Luke) and from Thomas (another collection of the sayings of Jesus). This distinction yields a group of narrative gospels and a group of sayings gospels. There are still other types of gospels. Particularizing and grouping—those are the basic functions of historians.

A third function is to assemble comparative evidence. It is necessary for the historian to compare what he or she finds written about Jesus with what was written about other teachers and charismatic figures of his time, such as Apollonius of Tyana, Hanina ben Dosa, Honi the Circle Drawer, and Eleazar the exorcist described by Josephus. Again, the goal is to isolate as many particular facts as possible about persons who belong to the same general group. It is revealing to know that there are other stories of miraculous births; that other charismatic figures healed people of their afflictions and exorcized demons; that Jesus was not the only one who criticized the temple cult; that other teachers said things that were similar to what Jesus said.

A further aspect of the historical task consists in arranging arrays in strata. And stratification leads to the chronological ordering of sources and documents. It is important to establish the sequence of reports and their relation to each other. It was, for example, an extremely important step when the Gospel of Mark was identified as the earliest of the narrative gospels. It was equally important to establish that Matthew and Luke were dependent upon Mark for their narrative framework. Scholarship took one huge step forward in adopting this hypothesis: we now know that where Matthew and Luke overlap with Mark, their reports do not constitute independent sources for those events.

A fifth function of historical investigation is to study the literary vehicles of transmission. This function is the special province of form criticism. Anecdotes, for example, were commonplace in the oral culture to which Jesus and his contemporaries belonged. An anecdote is a brief story told for the sake of a witty remark or adage. Anecdotes followed a prescribed format. The historian will want to ask: To what extent did the format of this type of oral story circumscribe what was remembered and rehearsed about Jesus?

By cataloguing the types of stories found in the narrative gospels, form critics have learned much about what kinds of information such verbal vehicles could encode about Jesus of Nazareth and, correlatively, what kinds of information they were not likely to have retained in the telling and retelling. Since the stories of which the gospels are made once circulated independently of each other, we are fairly certain that their sequence in the narrative gospels provides us with virtually no chronological data for the public life of Jesus.

A sixth aspect of the task of the historian is to bring a broader perspective to a particular subject. In the case of Jesus, to what trends or currents in late antiquity did he belong? Did his views reflect the cultural crosscurrents that were blowing across the Roman world? Was he caught up in Jewish dissatisfaction with Roman hegemony? Was he critical of the temple aristocracy that controlled the politics and wealth of the people? Why did Christianity eventually succeed in capturing the Roman Empire? These and many other general questions demand the assembling of a wide range of data.

The seventh function of the historian is to analyze how the role of the observer affects the observed. The observer always interferes, to a greater or lesser extent, with the data being observed. Consequently, the carefully constructed research project regularly begins with a history of interpretation that seeks to answer two questions. First, what were the limitations or mistakes of previous historical work? Second, how can the results of predecessors be corrected or improved? Investigators are always looking for ways to overcome the deficiencies perceived in their precursors' work. They also know that they, too, are unknowingly making mistakes that their successors will eventually have to correct. The important thing is to make some advance in knowledge, however small. And to recognize that the achievements of scholarship are properly cumulative. For this reason, scholars worthy of the name shun those who claim they have the truth, the whole truth, and nothing but the truth.

The sources for information about someone who lived so long ago and so far away culturally will provide data in categories alien to modern industrialized societies. Historians need to determine whether their modern categories skew the data provided by their sources. If so, they must make some adjustment to allow for the distortion.

Finally, we will also need to take note both of how the prior interests of scholars influence the kind and range of data selected and of how that selection nuances the reconstruction.

OLD AND NEW QUESTS

The first quest ended with the publication of Albert Schweitzer's famous work, *The Quest of the Historical Jesus,* in 1906. This was followed by a long period when the quest was dormant as a consequence of the domination of neo-orthodoxy. Neo-orthodox theologians held that it was impossible to recover the real Jesus owing to the nature of the gospels. They also believed that it was theologically illegitimate to base Christian conviction about Jesus on historical data, inasmuch as those data are never finally fixed: historical scholarship, they argued, can produce only relatively assured results, but the Christian faith requires absolutely reliable foundations. The faith, they insisted, rests on the first confessions of Peter the fisherman and Paul the tentmaker rather than on anything Jesus said or did. And that, they concluded, is the best we can do.

The neo-orthodox framework was supplied by Karl Barth, the well-known Swiss theologian who produced a mammoth *Church Dogmatics* (Vol. I appeared in 1932). His New Testament ally was Rudolf Bultmann. Unlike Barth, Bultmann believed that ancient formulations of the gospel were "mythological," inextricably bound up with aspects of the premodern worldview that were no longer tenable. He proposed "demythologizing" the gospel in a provocative essay that appeared first in 1941.[2] By that he meant translating the mythological features of the old formulations into modern concepts and language. As the receptacle of that demythologizing process, he chose the existential philosophy so popular in the period just before and after the Second World War.

Several of Bultmann's students launched a new quest immediately after the war. The legitimacy of a new quest was proposed by Ernst Käsemann in 1954[3] and articulated by James M. Robinson in *A New Quest of the Historical Jesus* in 1959. The Bultmann circle suggested that the self-understanding implied by the teachings of Jesus should be compared with the self-understanding inscribed in the early Christian proclamation. The comparison of the two amounted to a new quest, they reasoned, and was legitimate under neo-orthodox guidelines. But this approach failed to take root. The time for renewal had not yet come.

The cycle represented by the period of no quest and the brief life of the new quest came to a close around 1975. The inauguration of the parables movement and allied new trends spelled the end not only of the demythologizing program of Rudolf Bultmann but also of the supporting neo-orthodox framework supplied by Karl Barth and others. Neo-orthodoxy limited the significance of Jesus to his death and resurrection and thereby made his life prior to Easter irrelevant to the inauguration of the Christian faith. With the collapse of neo-orthodoxy and the failure of demythologizing, the hegemony of the classical or creedal Christian solution began to disintegrate. But the way to a renewal of the quest was now open.

The collapse of creedal and traditional theological formulations was a momentous event. It was precipitated by the times—by the breakdown of the old symbolic universe—rather than by anything theologians or biblical scholars did. In addition, there was the coincidence of seemingly unrelated yet epoch-making events, such as the discovery of the Nag

Hammadi library and the Dead Sea Scrolls and the inception of the nuclear age. The renewal of the quest was actually set in motion by numerous factors and impulses, some of which appear only indirectly related to the focus of the quest. I will sketch them later in this chapter.

The recent quest has many players. The number increased geometrically in the two decades beginning about 1975. As in the sporting world, it is important to have a program guide to the players, to the positions they play, to their special skills, to their frames of reference, and to their parentage. Here it is possible only to categorize them generally and without detailed documentation.

Broadly speaking, there are two categories of players in the current quest. For reasons to be suggested momentarily, I am calling one group the "pretend questers," the other the "reNEWed questers." (I capitalize the "NEW" to indicate that the precursor of this quest was the new quest of the 1950s.) Assignment to a category depends on the answers each quester gives to three basic questions.

The first test concerns whether or not the quest gives credence to the distinction between the historical Jesus and the Jesus of the gospels. If the quester does not want to distinguish the two or refuses to do so, that quester belongs to a rear guard attempting to cover the retreat from neo-orthodoxy. After all, it can be no surprise that the demise of neo-orthodoxy would generate strident responses on the part of those who sense both the old and new orthodoxies slipping away.

On the other hand, those participating in the renewed quest will seek to discriminate authentic from inauthentic material in the canonical gospels. In that case, the first task is to sort out the sayings, parables, and deeds of Jesus into two groups: those that stem from Jesus of Nazareth and those that belong to the Christian overlay added by the gospel writers. If a quester is unable or unwilling to identify anything in the canonical gospels that does not reflect the historical Jesus, we may be confident he or she is privileging the New Testament gospels merely because they are in the New Testament.

A second criterion concerns the sources. What sources does the quester make use of in gathering data? If the quester is willing to employ sources other than the New Testament gospels, that scholar is engaged in the renewed quest. If the quester discredits all sources except those found in the New Testament, we can again be certain that he or she is fighting a rearguard action. Questers in this category are probably clandestinely defending the canon and hence what they suppose is the decision of some ancient church body or council. The question of what books belong to the New Testament will be explored in Chapter Six.

One should also take note, in passing, of the opposite extreme. There are those who doubt that there is more than a shred of evidence we can use to reconstruct the existence of Jesus of Nazareth. Skeptics on this side of the spectrum doubt that there is anything left in the sources other than a name and perhaps a place. In their case, the quest has lost its point, except as an exercise in futility.

The third and final criterion concerns whether anything is at risk in the quest. Are any of the Christian claims about Jesus immune to historical investigation? The scholar for whom nothing in the creed or in church dogma is at issue is a pretend quester.

Fundamentalists and many evangelicals belong to the pretend group. They refuse the distinction between Jesus and the Christ, or refuse to credit it with any force. These questers collapse the historical Jesus into the creedal Christ and insist that the two are the same thing. The point of their quest—to the extent that it can be called a quest at all—is to demonstrate that the canonical gospels are completely or essentially reliable while denying that the non-canonical texts tell us anything significant about Jesus. As a consequence, the Jesus of the gospels does not differ in any essentials from the gospel of Jesus. The two are identical for all practical purposes.

In taking this line, these questers in fact make the historical Jesus subservient to the creedal Christ. These questers are in fact apologists for traditional forms of Christianity, although many of them do not belong to churches whose origins antedate the Protestant Reformation or, in some cases, even the Second World War. They seek to prove that orthodox Christian convictions rest on historical fact.

"Third questers," as N. T. Wright calls them, grant the distinction between the historical Jesus and the creedal Christ but express no real interest in, or regard for, the Jesus of history beyond historical curiosity. The Christian faith was born, for them, with Peter's confession, or at Easter, or at Pentecost, or at Nicea. The holy spirit is its author. This is the position of various forms of orthodoxy, including neo-orthodoxy.

For third questers there can be no picking and choosing among sayings and acts as a way to determine who Jesus was. Instead, one must present a theory of the whole, set Jesus firmly within first-century Judaism, state what his real aims were, discover why he died, when the church began, and what kind of documents the canonical gospels are.[4]

The third questers, like Raymond E. Brown and John P. Meier in the United States, take critical scholarship about as far as it can go without impinging on the fundamentals of the creed or challenging the hegemony of the ecclesiastical bureaucracy. In their hands, orthodoxy is safe, but critical scholarship is at risk. Faith seems to make them immune to the facts. Third questers are really conducting a search primarily for historical evidence to support claims made on behalf of creedal Christianity and the canonical gospels. In other words, the third quest is an apologetic ploy.

The renewed questers distinguish the historical Jesus from the Jesus of the gospels and the Christ of the creeds. They are aboveboard in identifying a database derived from the sources for determining who

Jesus was. They make critical use of all the surviving sources in compiling such a database. They take historical reconstruction seriously. For them everything is at stake. No Christian claim is immune to review and revision.

THE RENEWED QUEST

There are actually two questions to be answered regarding the renewed quest. The first is: What has set the renewed quest in motion? The second: What reasons do we have for thinking that the renewed quest will succeed in displacing the old picture of Jesus with a new and more credible portrait?

The factors precipitating the renewed quest and undergirding its success are intertwined in the sketch that follows.

The End of an Era

Perhaps the paramount factor precipitating the renewed quest is that we came to the end of a cycle about three-quarters of the way through the century—the cycle that began with Schweitzer nearly a century ago. That cycle was dominated by the picture of Jesus as an eschatological prophet who anticipated the end of the age in his own lifetime.

In his book *The Structure of Scientific Revolutions,* Thomas S. Kuhn postulates that scientific theories move in cycles: a revolution in data and theory is followed by a period of relative tranquillity in which a set of data and a dominant theory are accepted by the majority of scientists. During this period, dissenters are ignored or marginalized. Then comes another eruption prompted by the introduction of new data, or a theoretical shift, or both. For a time, leading players in the scientific game struggle among themselves for ascendancy. Eventually a new orthodoxy prevails and a new period of tranquillity descends. Kuhn adds: At each revolutionary shift there emerges a new gestalt—a new configuration of, or perspective on, the field as a whole.

In the field of New Testament studies, a basic shift began to take place beginning about 1975. A struggle ensued between the revolutionaries and those who wanted to maintain the prevailing orthodoxy. It was not clear then—and is not yet settled—just what the new gestalt will be. Nevertheless, it is clear that a revolution is under way.

A New, Secular Mode of Biblical Scholarship

Scholars of the Bible have sought, since the Enlightenment, to break free of the stifling tyranny of ecclesiastical control. The first blush of excitement in the rarefied air of rationalism in the seventeenth and eighteenth centuries produced the rejection of authority—the authority of the church and the authority of the Bible. The struggle to win and maintain that freedom has been long and at times bitter.

It was not until the middle of the twentieth century that biblical scholars began to exit ecclesiastical precincts—church colleges and seminaries—in large numbers and to stake out homes in secular institutions. At the same time, the church reduced its support—and its control—of many colleges and universities.

That exodus and the secularization of institutions of higher learning created the context, for the first time in two millennia, for scholars to pursue their research without religious constraints—indeed, without being driven primarily by theological concerns and restrictions.

Departure from the church was often not enough. Many of us have felt that the modern secular university is no less confining than the church. S. Warren Carey, in his book *Theories of the Earth and Universe*—with its more than provocative subtitle, *A History of Dogma in the Earth Sciences*[5]—maintains that universities are no place to breed new ideas. Academies are dominated, he argues, by intellectual orthodoxies that are self-perpetuating. Professional scholars tyrannize their students and each other. If you want to think new thoughts, he says, go out into the wilderness. Like Carey, I found myself playing the role of an academic John the Baptist—in my case, withdrawing first to a real Montana wilderness and then to an urban California wilderness, but no less a wilderness for that.

A New Ecumenism

The exit from cloistered precincts meant the end of narrow denominationalism. A new ecumenism became pervasive in the new secular academic milieu. Just when denominations are multiplying like rabbits in a warren, scholars are shedding their old parochial skins—for the most part. Aside from the extremes—some Roman Catholics in their cloistered cells and a few Southern Baptists led by the "pope of Houston," as Harold Bloom has dubbed Judge Paul Pressler—one can no longer identify the players by their views on this or that topic. The loss of meaningless and mindless denominationalism is to be applauded. It is a pity the mainline churches have not awakened to that development and imitated it.

The End of the Christianized Age

The Christianized age has come to an end, and with it the colonialism and imperialism of the Christian West. We now inhabit a global village. In that village those of us with Christian or Jewish heritages must compete with gods and goddesses of other ancient and powerful religious traditions. We cannot smugly equate our technological superiority —which is fast fading—with a cultural superiority. Our claims will have to compete in a world marketplace of ideas and claims. We will have to match Jesus with the Buddha, with Lao-tzu, with Confucius, with Gandhi, and others named and nameless.

We have come to the end of the Christian age in which missionary endeavor meant the conversion of everyone in the inhabitable world to the Western point of view. Modern societies are becoming permanently pluralistic—in spite of efforts by Islamic and other fundamentalisms to reinstate monolithic constituencies.

The Rediscovery of the Parables

Changes in context do not of themselves produce new ideas. We do not know for sure how new configurations come about. Knowledge may be thought of as having the shape of a gigantic sphere of unknown dimensions. On the circumference of that balloon, from time to time, for unknown reasons, a new fact or theory produces a small bulge or nodule. As the sphere rotates, the flexible circumference adjusts to accommodate the bump. The result is a new configuration. A single intrusive element will somehow produce a fresh gestalt, a new constellation, with a different organizing principle.

All of that is highly figurative, I realize. Yet something like that is what happened with the rediscovery of the parables of Jesus. The Jesus of the parables differed from Jesus the apocalyptic prophet—the Jesus that had dominated the theological scene since Schweitzer.

Of course, scholars had always known about the parables, but they did not come to the center of attention until the late 1960s. They were often treated as allegories—as encoded theologies—in traditional interpretation. Or they were moralized: they were taken to offer moral advice or admonitions. In both of these views, the story form was considered marginal decoration for a theological or moral point that could have been made by other and less dramatic or decorative means. In the new view, they came to be understood as literary and aesthetic entities in their own right, with their own integrity and with new interpretive potential. That discovery changed everything.

The parables, and to a lesser extent the aphorisms, came to be understood as speech forms characteristic of Jesus. In the case of the parables, it was a form Jesus had not borrowed from his predecessors and a form not easily replicated. Very few sages have achieved the same level of creativity with this particular genre of discourse. Franz Kafka and Jorge Luis Borges are among the few who have mastered the form.

The parables are ostensibly about the kingdom of God or God's domain, but in fact they are pictures and stories about baking, dinner parties, shrewd managers, vineyards, lost sheep and sons, and other everyday topics. (But none about carpentry, which makes one wonder about the historical reliability of the legend that Joseph was a carpenter.) Jesus did not explain to his listeners how these stories were related to God's imperial rule; he left it to them to figure that out for themselves. As a consequence, the parables are enigmatic: it is difficult to specify what they mean, what they actually teach.

The discovery that the parables were metaphorical or nonliteral or figurative softened the historian's interest in the historical holy land of fact and awakened interest in the metaphorical, poetic, and nonliteral features of the Jesus tradition. The scholarly landscape began to change. As enigmatic literary constructions, the parables suddenly became open-ended vehicles of a gospel that could not be specified once and for all.

Of the twenty-odd parables that are probably authentically from Jesus, the strange thing is that not one says anything about the end of the world or the apocalyptic trauma that is supposed to accompany that event (the authentic parables of Jesus are catalogued in an appendix and discussed in Chapters Eight through Eleven). And this body of Jesus lore is by volume the largest part of the surviving Jesus tradition. Did Johannes Weiss, the German scholar from whom Schweitzer borrowed his thesis, not notice that this significant part of the Jesus tradition was not apocalyptic at all? Or were scholars of that period more interested in developing a critique of nineteenth-century liberalism than they were in exploring the full extent of the gospel tradition?

With the rediscovery of the parables, scholars awakened to the fact that their intellectual attics were filled with mementos of a bygone age. The contrast between the parables and the reigning views of Jesus' teaching was shocking. Scholars became nostalgic about the old contents; they didn't want to give them up, but they found it essential to have a housecleaning. The parables, followed by new work on the aphorisms, provided the basis for developing rules of evidence to guide the renewed quest.

The Rediscovery of the Wisdom Tradition

The Jewish scriptures, which Christians call the Old Testament, consist of three major divisions: the law, the prophets, and the writings. The law—the five books of Moses—became the basis and special province of the priestly class connected with the temple in Jerusalem. The second division has two subdivisions. The first is the "former prophets," which are really historical works that cover the history of Israel from Joshua through the beginning of the Exile. The second subdivision consists of the "latter prophets," a collection of the oracles of the great prophets of the eighth and seventh centuries B.C.E. The latter prophets include such names as Amos, Isaiah, and Jeremiah, who were critics of the temple cult.

The third division of the scriptures, the writings, which consists largely of folk wisdom, was not given much attention by scholars until recently. Yet the wisdom books—Proverbs, Ecclesiastes, Job, Wisdom of Solomon—were probably the part of the Israelite scriptures best known by ordinary folk.

Jesus has often been compared with or identified as a Moses or as one of the prophets by scholars searching for an ancient model. With the rediscovery of the wisdom tradition, scholars began to see that Jesus may well have been a wisdom teacher—a sage. That possibility was enhanced by the presence of hellenistic philosophers and teachers in Galilee during Jesus' life. Now we know that many things Jesus said had parallels in the lore taught by Cynic philosophers he may have heard as a youngster in hellenized Galilee. A whole new paradigm for understanding Jesus suddenly presented itself. This new paradigm is the subject of Chapters Eight through Eleven.

The Discovery of New Sources

The rediscovery of the parables and aphorisms of Jesus was accompanied—actually preceded—by the discovery of wonderful new ancient sources. It is amazing what has come to light in this century through archaeology and happenstance. In addition to hundreds of new manuscripts of the New Testament (to be discussed in Chapters Five and Six), brand-new sources have appeared.

THE DEAD SEA SCROLLS   The best known of the many sensational discoveries of the twentieth century are the Dead Sea Scrolls. The scrolls were hurriedly hidden in eleven caves along the Wadi Qumran, just above the Essene settlement at Khirbet Qumran (the ruins of Qumran), located on the shores of the Dead Sea. They were the property of the Essene community in all probability, secreted away just prior to the time the Romans arrived in the Jordan valley in 68 C.E. and destroyed the settlement.

Shepherd boys stumbled into the first cave in 1947. That cave eventually produced seven leather scrolls. Additional caves were located between 1947 and 1956. Other discoveries made subsequently in other wadis along the western shores of the Dead Sea further expand our knowledge of the period stretching from the Maccabean revolt in 167 B.C.E. to the second Jewish revolt in 132–135 C.E. But the primary interest has remained focused on the documents connected with the Essene community at Qumran.

Complete scrolls were found in caves one and eleven. Over thirty thousand fragments of more than five hundred documents were unearthed in cave four alone, much of that material still unpublished—after almost fifty years. Scrolls and fragments of every book of the Hebrew Bible, with the exception of Esther, have been found in the caves.

The scrolls were produced and treasured by the Essenes, a sectarian community that had withdrawn from society to prepare itself for the final days. John the Baptist and Jesus must have known of the community; indeed, the Baptist's movement bears some affinities to the Essene group.

The Qumran sectarians expected two, possibly three, messiahs: a lay king messiah in the line of David and a priestly messiah, a descendant of Aaron, the brother of Moses. There is also mention of a prophet-messiah, perhaps Elijah returned.

The group, like many other groups and movements, believed that history was drawing to a close. They regarded the Jerusalem temple and its establishment as hopelessly corrupt. They and they alone were the true custodians of the ancient faith. The community at Qumran appears, however, to have been a contemplative group, given not to revolution and insurgency but to prayer and devotion, to the study of the law, and to strict discipline.

Claims that the Essenes of Qumran were linked to Christianity have been thoroughly discredited. Nevertheless, the thought that both John the Baptist and Jesus may have known of the community, and perhaps even visited it, prompts endless speculation. While the scrolls provide detailed information about one sectarian movement contemporary with John and Jesus, thus far there is no evidence to link it with them directly.

THE NAG HAMMADI LIBRARY   Another remarkable discovery preceded the Dead Sea Scrolls. That was the unearthing of the Nag Hammadi library in upper Egypt in 1945. Fifty books gathered originally into twelve codices, plus two additional tractates, all of which can be dated to the fourth century, formed the library, which, like the Dead Sea Scrolls, had evidently been buried by its owners.

The Nag Hammadi texts have greatly enhanced our knowledge of the rivalries in the church of the first four centuries between those who eventually established themselves as orthodox and those who lost out as heretics. For the first time, we have ample actual documents produced by the so-called heretics, rather than reports about them written by their accusers. The picture has begun to come back into focus, and the resulting knowledge prompts us to reopen many questions once thought entirely settled.

Of stunning importance for the study of Christian origins was the appearance of a complete text of the Gospel of Thomas. Three Greek fragments of "an unknown gospel" had been published in 1897 as Oxyrhynchus papyri 1, 654, and 655. When Coptic Thomas was discovered at Nag Hammadi, those fragments were recognized at once as part of the same gospel. Coptic Thomas is a fourth-century manuscript; the Greek fragments can be dated about two hundred years earlier, thus placing them among the very earliest fragments of any of the gospels surviving from antiquity.

Thomas is a collection of 114 sayings of Jesus. There is minimal dialogue and virtually no narrative. Thomas lacks a passion narrative; it has no appearance stories, no birth and childhood stories, and it provides no narrative context for the various sayings and dialogues. Indeed, Thomas looks very much like the hypothetical Sayings Gospel Q, now embedded in Matthew and Luke. There is an approximately 40 percent overlap between the sayings found in Thomas and those found in Q. Many of the Fellows of the Jesus Seminar believe that Thomas represents an early version of Jesus' sayings that is independent of the canonical gospels.

Another gospel found among the books of the library was Secret James. The alleged author of Secret James is the brother of Jesus. In a framing letter, James states that Jesus appeared to his disciples 550 days after his resurrection, took Peter and James aside, and "filled" them with secret knowledge. This, James claims, is the Lord's final and definitive teaching. The body of the work consists of sayings, parables, prophecies, and rules governing the community. Jesus then ascends to the Father. None of the words ascribed to Jesus in Secret James originated with Jesus, although some sayings have affinities with other, authentic words of Jesus.

The primary content of the Dialogue of the Savior, a third gospel, consists of an exchange between Jesus and three disciples, Judas, Mary, and Matthew. The form of these dialogues parallels conversations found in the Gospel of John. The Dialogue also contains a creation myth, a list of elementary substances, and an apocalyptic section. This gospel was probably created in the middle of the second century, but it incorporates older traditions. The Fellows of the Jesus Seminar identified only one saying in it that might have originated with Jesus: "I say to you, those who have power should deny it and change their ways."[6] The basis for thinking it authentic was that it comports with other things Jesus may have said. The Coptic manuscript is the only known copy of this document. Unfortunately, it is in a very fragmentary condition.

Three other gospels were found in the library. The Gospel of Truth is a homily on the subject of "gospel." The Gospel of Philip is a loose collection of theological assertions and interpretive traditions about the sacraments. It was probably composed in the third century. The last of these documents bearing the gospel label is the Gospel of the Egyptians, of which there are two versions in the library. It is to be distinguished from another lost gospel of the same title, of which only fragments have been preserved by some early Christian authors. The Gospel of the Egyptians depicts the mythological origins of the gnostic system. These three Nag Hammadi texts are gospels in name only. There are, of course, many other kinds of books among the fifty-two tractates comprising the Nag Hammadi library.

OTHER GOSPELS   Other gospels, all fragmentary, have come to light in the last one hundred years.

The Gospel of Mary is another sayings gospel. Mary is usually listed among the Nag Hammadi codices, but it was actually known prior to the Nag Hammadi find from two Greek fragments and a Coptic version. Papyrus Rylands 463 was found in 1938; Papyrus Oxyrhynchus 3524 was published in 1983; and the Coptic text, Berlin Papyrus 8052,1, was made accessible in 1955.

Mary also consists of a dialogue between Jesus and his disciples. Mary of Magdala, it seems, understands the teachings of Jesus better than Peter and Andrew, as the result of a vision she has had of Jesus. Mary proceeds to expound her understanding of the gospel to the others. Only about half of this gospel has survived, partly in Coptic, partly in the two Greek fragments. Mary was probably originally composed early in the second century.

The Gospel of Peter appeared first in 1886, although it did not then attract much attention. A Greek fragment was published in 1972 as POxy 2949, and another Greek fragment was published more recently as POxy 4009. Peter is a fragmentary passion gospel that begins with Pilate washing his hands and ends with Peter and Andrew going fishing. While it does not extend the gospel story beyond the perimeters established by Mark, it does add new perspectives and details to the story of Jesus' burial and resurrection.

The Gospel of Peter almost certainly went through more than one edition, which is true of nearly all of our gospels. An early version of Peter could be dated to the beginning of the second century.

Gospel Oxyrhynchus 1224 contains some very fragmentary sayings of Jesus. The fragments belong to a codex that originally contained this otherwise unknown gospel. The fragments can be dated to the late third or early fourth century, although the form of the sayings suggest that it originated at a much earlier time, perhaps as early as the Sayings Gospel Q.

The Egerton Gospel consists of four fragments catalogued as Papyrus Egerton 2; a fifth fragment turned up in Germany and is known as Papyrus Köln 255. Egerton can be dated to the middle of the second century, making it almost as old as P^{52}, a tiny fragment of the Gospel of John that can be dated to about 125 c.e. Egerton contains the healing of a leper, a controversy over payment of taxes, a miracle performed by Jesus at the Jordan River, plus two tiny segments closely related to the Gospel of John. The Egerton Gospel is a narrative gospel that has some affinities with both the synoptics and John, although it is probably dependent on neither.

Gospel Oxyrhynchus 840, another fragmentary narrative gospel, was discovered about 1900 (the exact date is unknown). It consists of a single leaf that can be dated to the fourth century. It contains a dialogue between Jesus and his disciples and a controversy over purity between Jesus and a Pharisaic priest in the temple court.

Secret Mark was discovered in 1958 at Mar Saba, a monastery in the Jordan valley, by Morton Smith, a well-known scholar of the Bible. The few verses, written on the flyleaf of another book, allegedly belonged to a secret version of Mark. The manuscript itself has since disappeared. However, a photograph of the text exists and was published soon after its discovery. Secret Mark is probably an earlier version of the Gospel of

Mark included in the New Testament; the first version of Mark was composed sometime after the fall of Jerusalem in 70 C.E.

These fragmentary documents provide only a small amount of information not found in the gospels for which a more or less complete text has survived.

In addition to these physical remains, scholars in this century have attempted to reconstruct the Sayings Gospel Q, using the double tradition in Matthew and Luke. There are several excellent editions of Q now available for general use. These reconstructions and synopses began with the work of Adolf von Harnack in 1907.[7] They have continued most recently with the work of four Fellows of the Jesus Seminar, James M. Robinson, John Kloppenborg, Arland Jacobson, and Leif Vaage.[8]

Attempts have also been made to isolate a Signs Gospel that underlies the Gospel of John. Robert T. Fortna, also a Fellow of the seminar, has been a leader in this research.*

The End of Canonical Imperialism

The discovery of all these new sources, the end of ecclesiastical hegemony over biblical scholarship, and the emergence of the comparative study of religion—inspired in part by the world exposition in Chicago in 1892—led to the end of canonical imperialism. The Bible was no longer a hermetically sealed body of scriptures to be studied in isolation from other comparable documents belonging to late antiquity (roughly the six hundred years from Alexander the Great to the Emperor Constantine).

We are still in the middle of this massive remapping of our territory. We have yet to create the new reference and study instruments we need to be able to comprehend this vast literature and its archaeology with the same precision that we apply to the narrower selection of canonical books.

The Collapse of the Symbolic Universe

In addition to these sweeping changes, we are faced with the collapse of the old symbolic universe. That symbolic world has been in collapse since the Renaissance and especially this side of the Enlightenment. Astronomy, astrophysics, physics, geology—to mention only a few contributors—have proposed a wholly different kind of cosmos from the one imagined at the time the gospels were created. The earth, Stephen Hawking explains, is a minor planet in a galaxy that is approximately one hundred thousand light years across; our galaxy is one of another hundred thousand million galaxies that can be observed by means of scientific instruments; and each of those galaxies contains something like a hundred thousand million stars. Such a universe taxes the imagination

---

*All of these gospels have been freshly translated into English by the Fellows of the Jesus Seminar and gathered into *The Complete Gospels,* edited by Robert J. Miller.

beyond its limits. We can scarcely pick up the daily newspaper without reading of some new observation about the physical universe that shakes the old views to their foundations.

The images currently connected with Jesus, in the popular mind and among traditionalists, tend to be linked to aspects of the worldview that prevailed in late antiquity—the Graeco-Roman age. That worldview was made up of a three-tiered cosmos: an earth in the shape of a pancake, flat, with arching heavens overhead and fiery regions below. The mountains at the edge of the earth functioned as pillars to hold up the skies, and beyond those mountains lay utter darkness, on one side, and perhaps the Elysian Fields, on the other (see Figure 2 below).

When freed from these notions of the design and location of heaven and hell, of a geocentric and anthropocentric universe, of a God located somewhere above the highest heaven, Jesus begins to escape from the symbolic world into which he was taken up by his admirers. For his part, judging by his authentic words, Jesus had little or nothing to say that is tied to his symbolic world. But those who formulated their convictions about him did so in language imbued with this cosmology.

The resistance to Bultmann's demythologizing program and the correlative popularity of fundamentalist views indicate how deeply entrenched the old symbolic world was and is. In the modern industrialized

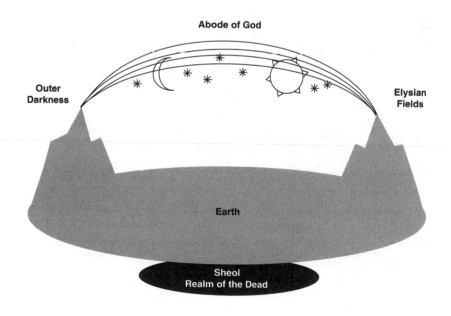

FIGURE 2: THE THREE-TIERED COSMOS

West, the old worldview was very much alive until midcentury. We haven't gotten over it yet. Galileo's telescope was only the beginning. Einstein's theory of relativity ($E = mc^2$) was a fatal blow to the old symbolic universe. We now know there are no fixed points in space and time; everything is relative to everything else.

New or Revised Methodologies

To cap it off, biblical scholars have been faced with having to master new languages, new methodologies, new bodies of knowledge, in addition to the staggering requirements of the earlier, more defined curriculum. There are so many that I can only mention a few of these new demands here.

In addition to the biblical languages—Greek, Hebrew, and Aramaic —we have had to learn modern scientific languages, French and German, in order to read the work of other scholars. Of course, Latin was also required as the traditional theological language. New Testament scholars now have to master Coptic if they want to be able to work in the Nag Hammadi texts.

Many of us discovered that we had to get inside literary criticism if we wanted to apply the same techniques to the interpretation of biblical texts that were being utilized on other literary texts. That meant learning another body of scholarly lore and engaging in its practice.

The twentieth century has witnessed a revolution in linguistics. Older grammars and lexicons have had to be reconceived and revamped to reflect the newer understanding of how language works—and to take into account all the new texts that have come to light in this century. And, of course, the advent of the computer has revolutionized the way scholars compile and sort large bodies of data. It is now possible to search all the extant literary Greek texts down to about 800 C.E. on one CD-ROM.

The social sciences have become necessary ancillary disciplines for biblical scholars. Cross-cultural anthropology, sociology, the sociology of knowledge, and other specialties are being increasingly utilized in understanding the Mediterranean cultures in which Christianity took its rise.

Archaeology has ceased to be treasure hunting and has become a field science in this century. Biblical scholars have to be able to read and interpret archaeological evidence even if they haven't had field experience.

These staggering requirements mean that few scholars are able to master them all. The demands have led to more and more specialization, which makes collaboration among specialists the order of the day.

These ten factors have precipitated the renewed quest of the historical Jesus—they have made it necessary. But they are also the reason scholars are in a much better position to recover reliable information about Jesus of Nazareth than were our predecessors during the first quest a century ago.

Chapter Five

TRANSLATION AND TEXT

THE LANGUAGES OF THE BIBLE

The original languages of the Bible are Hebrew, Aramaic, and Greek. The Old Testament was written in Hebrew, with a few sections in Aramaic. The New Testament was composed entirely in Greek, so far as we know.

Alexander the Great played a decisive role in preparing the Mediterranean world by setting a stage on which Christianity could flourish. His conquests in the fourth century B.C.E. introduced Greek ways and customs into many lands around the Mediterranean, as well into territories lying farther to the East. Greek colonies were established everywhere. Greek became the common tongue. Commerce developed more freely where merchants could understand each other. Alexander had founded cities, like Alexandria in Egypt, which later became centers of Greek culture and learning. A great library was created in Alexandria. Unfortunately, part of its treasures were burned in Roman times; the balance of the library was lost when the Arabs invaded in the seventh century C.E.

The spread of Greek led to the translation of the Old Testament from Hebrew into Greek. The Greek version of the Hebrew Bible, known as the Septuagint, was produced in Egypt by Jewish scholars over a period of a century or more. It was begun under Ptolemy Philadelphus in the third century B.C.E. and completed in the first century. It became the Bible of Greek-speaking Jews living around the Mediterranean world under the Pax Romana. According to legend, the Septuagint (often cited as the LXX, because Septuagint means "seventy") was produced by seventy-two scholars working in pairs for seventy-two days. Like other legends it makes a good story but lacks foundation in fact. No one knows how the seventy-two got reduced to seventy in the label LXX.

The LXX was the Bible Paul and the other early Jewish Christians knew and used. It was the Bible of the gospel writers and early scholars of the church. It was the basis of several other translations as well. It remains the first half of the Bible of the Greek church to this day. In spite of the dominance of Latin as a theological language, Greek continued to be the main biblical language for many centuries in the Western tradition, as the plethora of Greek manuscripts of the Bible, both Old and New Testaments, demonstrates.

The Hebrew Bible was translated into Syriac, a dialect of Aramaic, at an early date. Christian scriptures also found their way into Syriac sometime around the middle of the second century C.E. The Syriac version is accordingly one of the oldest translations into a regional language.

The transition to Latin was under way by the middle of the third century. The Old Latin version was made for Latin-speaking Christians living in North Africa. The Greek LXX was the basis of this early Latin translation. The famous biblical scholar Jerome (346–420 C.E.) was the principal creator of a new Latin version to be known as the Vulgate. Jerome at first translated from the Greek Old Testament; later he retranslated the Jewish scriptures from Hebrew and Aramaic. The New Testament books were of course translated from their Greek originals. The Vulgate became the official Bible of the Latin church.

Other early translations were made into Coptic, Ethiopic, Armenian, Gothic, Slavic, and Arabic. Scholars who are specialists in the textual history of the various books of the Bible must be able to work in most or all of these languages. We will return to the subject of early versions of the scriptures in the next chapter, when we consider the formation of the New Testament canon of scriptures.

WHAT LANGUAGES DID JESUS SPEAK?

Dylan Thomas, the Welsh poet, once remarked that he could speak three languages: English, BBC third program, and saloon. Jesus also spoke three languages: Aramaic, Greek, and *basileia* (ba-si-láy-ya), which is the Greek term for kingdom or domain. The only one of this trio of languages about which there has been controversy is the middle one, Greek.

Jesus' native tongue was undoubtedly Aramaic, a Semitic language related to Hebrew. A few words or phrases are preserved in Aramaic or Hebrew in the gospels. The term *rabbi*—meaning "lord, master, teacher"—is used once to address John the Baptist,[1] more frequently to address Jesus. In the Gospel of Mark, Jesus once addresses God as *Abba,* "Father,"[2] although the evangelists elsewhere substitute the Greek term *Pater*. Paul also uses this form of divine address.[3] Mark has Jesus employ Aramaic words in raising Jairus' daughter and in the cure of the deaf-mute.[4] Neither Matthew nor Luke adopts these terms when rewriting Mark. Jesus is reported to have quoted Psalm 22:2 while hanging on the cross, either in Aramaic or Hebrew.[5] Bystanders thought he was calling on Elijah because "My God, My God" in Hebrew *(Eli, Eli)* sounds similar to the name Elijah. These words and phrases are not original with Jesus.

In any case, they do not constitute substantial evidence that the Jesus tradition took shape in Aramaic (or Hebrew).

At all events, apart from the few words mentioned in the previous paragraph, all the gospels have survived only in Greek or in languages that are clearly translations of a Greek original. It is increasingly dubious that the gospels were composed in Aramaic.

For a long time scholars were inclined to the view that Jesus spoke only Aramaic; they concluded that his words had been translated into Greek at an early stage and their original Semitic form lost. There is now mounting archaeological evidence that Greek was widely employed in semipagan Galilee, in hellenistic cities like Sepphoris, only four miles from Jesus' native Nazareth. There is powerful evidence, furthermore, that the parables and aphorisms recorded in the gospels were formulated originally in Greek: assonance, resonance, rhythm, and repetition with wordplay reflect a poetic mind rather than the belabored prose a translator often produces. It thus seems likely that Jesus was bilingual and that he formulated his wisdom in his second language, much in the same way Franz Kafka, whose first language was Czech, wrote in German, and Samuel Beckett, whose native tongue was English, in French. Jesus was not, of course, the only Jew who mastered Greek in the first century; Josephus and Philo come to mind, along with Paul of Tarsus and the author of the Wisdom of Solomon, a first-century work written, in all probability, by a Jew living in Alexandria, Egypt.

Jesus attempted to teach his disciples to speak *basileia*. They had difficulties learning that tongue. They were not adept at it, so they settled, fortunately, mostly for repeating what Jesus himself had said—to the extent they could recall his words. They did not, of course, hesitate to modify, adapt, and rearrange what they could remember. Occasionally they managed to imitate his rhetoric. For the most part, however, they permitted his talk of God's kingdom to be domesticated—assimilated to the common understanding—and institutionalized. They soon invented their own language in which Jesus himself became the topic and focus, rather than the domain of God that Jesus had initially taught them.

THE BIBLE IN MODERN LANGUAGES

The translation of the Bible into modern languages is an amazing story in itself. The process of translating the Bible into modern tongues was stimulated by the invention of the printing press. The Gutenberg Bible, also known as the Mazarin Bible, appeared in 1456 and was the first full book to be printed. It was an edition of the Latin Vulgate. But translation into other languages surged with the new opportunity to print identical multiple copies of a book. The Protestant Reformation was inaugurated by Luther's translation of the Bible into German. The first part of his translation appeared in 1522. One major issue in the Reformation was whether the Bible was to be made accessible to the general population or whether it was to remain the private province of the clergy. Luther's translation marked a radical departure from the Latin tradition and put the Bible within reach of any literate lay reader. His translation had one other major consequence: It provided the German people with a single, unifying language for the first time in their history.

English translations actually preceded Luther's German version. Parts of the Bible had already been put into Anglo-Saxon as early as the eighth century. John Wycliff, with the help of associates, produced a version in Old English based on the Latin Vulgate in the fourteenth century. But it was William Tyndale who first created an English translation derived from Hebrew and Greek. His New Testament first appeared in 1525. Tyndale's work was followed in quick succession by other translations and revisions prior to the authorized version that was to come a century later.

It is an article of faith among many of the uninformed that the King James Version is an inerrant translation of the original Bible. This so-called authorized version was published in 1611 C.E., more than fifteen hundred years after the first gospels were composed in Greek. It put the English church on a firm political and cultural footing. The King James Version helped canonize Shakespearian English as the literary norm for English-speaking people everywhere.

The beauty and cadence of the King James Bible retarded any interest in replacing it with a more accurate rendering. Theological conservatism also functioned as a retarding factor, since many cardinal points rested on the English vocabulary of that version. However, even the elevated English of the King James Version could not thwart progress forever. Towards the close of the nineteenth century, new English translations and revisions began to appear in abundance. The flood grew in the twentieth century.

The English Bible tradition has been firmly established. Many English-speaking people are not even cognizant that the original languages of the Bible were Hebrew, Aramaic, and Greek. The biblical languages are now in use primarily among scholars and a decreasing number of clergy. Many seminaries no longer require candidates for ordination to learn a biblical language. As a consequence, the English Bible has rapidly become the only version of the Bible known to most speakers of English. Translation has become a necessity.

Revisions of translations are required as the target language evolves and words and idioms shift in nuance. New translations are also occasioned by the discovery of new textual evidence, archaeological data, and additional information about ancient languages. As the Bible's role in society is diminished, enhanced, or relocated, new study instruments, including translations, are created to accommodate those shifts. In the present cultural context, the Bible's role has greatly diminished in the mainline churches, while it has grown among newer, sectarian movements. At the same time, the Bible has become more of a secular cultural artifact than a document of the church. Consequently, scholars of the humanities now study the Bible for the role it has played in Western societies in general and the American tradition in particular. These changes are reflected in the rise and fall of translations.

THROUGH THE HAZE OF TRANSLATION

Translation as Betrayal

Every translation is a betrayal: it is misleading in some respects. But every translation is also a revelation. Members of the translation panel of the Scholars Version—a new translation produced by members of the Jesus Seminar—testify to the same experience: the challenge of putting the Greek gospels into English has called attention to problems and issues unnoticed in our regular reading of the Greek text. Translation has convinced most of us that the grammars and dictionaries prepared originally in the nineteenth century but still in use are seriously out of date. It has also enhanced our sense that ecclesiastically sponsored translations are attuned to contemporary liturgical, catechetical, and theological purposes rather than to the style and nuances of the original. It has persuaded us that traditional translations in general prefer archaic and artificial English to living idiom.

The first barrier to understanding the origins of Christianity is a lack of appreciation of the semantic and cultural distance that separates modern translations into English from the original Greek texts. The initial step in overcoming that barrier is to defamiliarize the words of, and stories about, Jesus. To defamiliarize means to employ fresh, vibrant language wherever possible, while remaining faithful to the sense and style of the original. If we do not defamiliarize, we will read right over the words. The King James Version lulls the reader to sleep; although beautiful, the language is archaic, and the meaning is ensconced in sonorous cadences and Shakespearian phrasing. The Scholars Version, along with some other modern translations, is designed to wake the reader up. When Jesus once again becomes a stranger to the modern temper, he will be able to command a fresh hearing.

It's All Greek

The New Testament is in Greek, along with most other early Christian records. It is the task of translators to interpret the sounds, words, sentences, and other features of Greek for those who do not speak and read Greek. In the case of the scriptures and other classic texts, that is an awesome responsibility. But even modern translators, no matter how well trained and experienced, cannot bring the full range of the original nuances and overtones to their work. Even when we think we see or hear them in a Greek text, we cannot always reproduce them in English. It is easier to illustrate than generalize.

The semantic range of words in different languages is never entirely congruent. Put more simply, one Greek word never has precisely the same range of meaning that some corresponding single term in English has. Translation is therefore an art as well as a science. The best dictionary for translators is a concordance. A concordance of Greek permits the translator to scan hundreds of examples of words in the context of the phrases and sentences in which they were originally used. Those examples exhibit the semantic range of a given term. As a consequence, it often requires an array of English terms to translate a single word in Greek.

In *A Brief History of Time,* Stephen Hawking reports a warning he received from an editor: the use of mathematical formulas will drastically reduce your readership. He decided to risk including a single formidable equation: Einstein's famous summary of the theory of relativity. I aspire to be no less bold. A one-word Greek lesson is perhaps worth the sacrifice. I have selected a simple term that is ubiquitous in Greek texts.

The beginning student learns that the Greek word καί (pronounced like the *ki* in "kite") is a conjunction used to link words and phrases together and that it means *and*. Because the gospels are written in Koine Greek, a simpler version of classical Greek spoken and written by a large non-Greek population, *kai* appears much more frequently than it did in classical usage. Indeed, its use by the evangelists is so frequent as to be monotonous. The question immediately arises for the translator: Is *kai* to be represented everywhere by the English word *and*? Is it important to let the reader of English know where and how often it occurs?

Here the seasoned translator invokes two rules: First, one English word never exhausts the meaning of one Greek word. *Kai* does not merely mean *and*. *Kai* has a different semantic range than *and*. In addition to meaning *and,* it also means, depending on the context and construction: *also, then, at this (that) point, so, next, but, yet, nevertheless, in spite of that, and then, and so,* and many similar and related expressions in English. The second rule is this: A translation should not be a pony to the Greek text (a pony is a literal line-by-line translation for use in learning a foreign language). A literal, word-for-word translation makes the source language primary, when a translation should follow the natural lines of the target language. A pony translation, in other words, is serviceable only for those who are learning Greek.

We can illustrate the same problem without citing the underlying Greek word.

The dictionary meaning of another Greek term is given as *just, righteous*. These are high and serious terms that bear a great deal of semantic freight in English, especially when found in the Bible. But those English words don't always fit the context where the Greek term appears and hence don't always represent the most accurate meaning of the Greek. In the following sentences, note the italicized words that translate the same Greek term, for which the dictionary meaning is *just, righteous:*

> Since Joseph her husband was a *decent* man and did not wish to expose her publicly . . .[6]

> After all, I did not come to enlist *religious folks* but sinners![7]

> You go into the vineyards too, and I'll pay you whatever is *fair*.[8]

> [Judas to the ranking priests:] I have made the grave mistake of turning in this *blameless* man.[9]

> [Pilate's wife to husband:] Don't have anything to do with that *innocent* man.[10]

The English words *just, righteous* are possible but wooden translations in the passages cited. And yet they are the dictionary definitions for the Greek term used in all of these sentences. Translators are advised to select terms that express in English the nuances of the Greek in the original context. A brief dictionary definition is not always the best way to represent a Greek term with a different semantic range.

Good translation, I would insist, should not be a pony to the Greek text. The translation of words and phrases should be context sensitive rather than dictionary driven. In translation, consistency is not a virtue; the accuracy of nuance is. The final test of a good translation is this: Can you forget, while reading it, that it is a translation at all? Of course, it is not a good translation unless it represents in the secondary language what the words meant in the original.

There is another little word in Greek that presents a challenge to the translator. Its dictionary definition is given as *behold,* and that is the way it is rendered in traditional translations. *Behold* strikes the contemporary ear as "biblical" and therefore as archaic English. There are many English alternatives that work better: *look, listen, see here, wait, hold it, now look, look now, just a minute, wait a minute, hey! hold on!,* to mention only a few. The translator's art is to pick the one that suits the context. If we were translating into French, the precise equivalents would be *voilà* or *voici*.

The Greek noun from which the English words "ethnic" and "ethnicity" are derived has two basic meanings: nation or people, and foreigner. For Judeans in Jesus' day, everyone who was not a Judean was a foreigner or a gentile—but even foreigners belonged to some nation or people. The proper translation depends on the context in which the Greek word is used.

Contexts in the Gospel of Luke will exemplify the necessary variation. When Jesus is arrested, he will be turned over to *foreigners,* meaning the Romans.[11] Food, drink, and clothing are things the world's *pagans* seek; others seek God's domain.[12] At the end time, *nation* will rise up against *nation*.[13] The coming of the messiah, according to Luke, will be a revelatory light for *gentiles* and glory for Israel.[14] Yet the same term may also refer to Israel and the Judeans: The Roman officer whose daughter Jesus healed, we are told, built a synagogue for our *people,* meaning the Jews.[15] The English words in italics all translate the same Greek noun.

Sense over Words

It is wise as a general rule not to translate anything we do not understand. Only in that rare case where we can make no sense of the original should we translate the words literally and woodenly. Ordinarily, it is best to determine the meaning of the original word or sentence and then to put that meaning into current English idiom. The sense should take priority over the literal meaning of words.

There is an expression attributed to Jesus that the Scholars Version translates in this way: "Anyone here with two good ears had better listen!" Ed Beutner, a Fellow of the Jesus Seminar and one of the translators, proposed this English equivalent: "A wink is as good as a nod to a blind horse." That witty remark in English is an excellent way to represent the sense of the Greek original. It is an excellent translation. But it is not very close to the underlying Greek vocabulary. The translators searched for some expression that was closer to the Greek vocabulary yet carried the necessary warning with it in English. We thought of what mothers (sometimes our fathers) said to us as youngsters: "You had better listen." "Listen" preserves the Greek idiom accurately. In addition, however, there is assonance in the Greek expression (assonance is the succession of similar sounds). We endeavored to capture a hint of that sequence of sounds with "here . . . ear."

When John the Baptist sees the Pharisees and Sadducees coming out to hear him at the Jordan, he addresses them thus in the King James Version: "O generation of vipers."[16] The old Revised Standard Version modified this in 1946 to "You brood of vipers!" Other modern English translations have stuck to the traditional rendering. The Scholars Version panel of translators decided that John's mode of address was not given its real ring by those traditional translations.

The snake or viper is a symbol personifying evil or Satan. John was referring to these hypocrites, as he viewed them, as offspring of Satan. At the suggestion of a schoolteacher who learned of our problem, we adopted "You spawn of Satan!" as our version. "Brood" became "spawn" and "viper" was transformed into its better-known image. Spawn is used in English of the offspring of aquatic animals produced in masses. Spawn is also slimy—a subtle nuance that applies also to snakes in the common perception, even though snakes are not actually slimy. The match seemed excellent.

However, we had discussed another possibility that further illustrates the quest of translators for the right match. In the context, John advises his listeners, "Don't even think of saying to yourselves, 'We have Abraham for our father.' Let me tell you, God can raise up children for Abraham right out of these rocks."[17] This context, together with the expression, "brood of vipers" in Greek, suggested the translation: "You slimy bastards!" "Slimy" captures that quality of snakes that makes them repulsive to handle (in the popular imagination), and "bastard" picks up and reinforces the note John introduces about the descendants of Abraham. But translators of the Bible tend, in spite of high resolve to the contrary, to walk on the conservative side. "Spawn of Satan" won out.

It is important to capture, if possible, the style and texture of the original. In the case of the Jesus tradition, that entails making aphorisms sound like witticisms and not like flat platitudes. "Since when do the able-bodied need a doctor? It's the sick who do"[18] has the right ring to it. "What you treasure is your heart's true measure"[19] sounds more like a proverb than "For where your treasure is, there your heart will be also" (Revised Standard Version). "Those who promote themselves will be demoted, and those who demote themselves will be promoted"[20] strikes a note close to the modern ear, in contrast to "For everyone who exalts himself will be humbled, and he who humbles himself will be exalted" (New International Version), which sounds a little quaint, in addition to the sexist "himself" and "he who." "Congratulations, you poor! God's domain belongs to you"[21] goes straight to the heart of the matter in English; "Blessed are you who are poor, for yours is the kingdom of God" skirts the issue with archaic language and too many words. When someone has been especially favored by circumstances, we do not say "blessed are you" in English idiom, we offer them congratulations. In aphoristic speech, brevity, brilliance, and tone are essential.

Right Names for Things

It is also important in translating to select the correct labels for things. The King James translation has "Foxes have holes," a mistake repeated in the New Revised Standard Version and the New International Version.[22] Foxes do not have holes, they have dens (a "foxhole" is a military term, not a place where foxes live). The term "temple" suggests a building to most users of English. Because the temple was a relatively small building that sat in the middle of a huge space some thirty-five acres in extent, one should translate "temple" as "temple area," to avoid the impression that the building was always intended. "Disciple" has perhaps lost its root sense for those familiar with the English Bible. A disciple is a student, a learner, or a follower of a teacher (teachers were often itinerant, so students followed them around—or, in the style of the peripatetic, teachers walked around as they taught).

But the right name for things doesn't always work. Very few contemporary farmers know what a "winnowing fork" is. In the Scholars Version, the panel decided to translate the Greek term as "pitchfork." This also presents problems, since English readers will not know that the Greek word denoted an instrument used to toss grain into the air so the breeze could blow the chaff away. A pitchfork cannot serve that function. "Centurion" seems a little technical for the average reader; "Roman officer" is a reader-friendly counterpart. Most Americans know what "yeast" is; very few could tell us what "leaven" meant. Yet we could not bring ourselves to change the parable of the leaven to the parable of the yeast. The Middle English term "tares," employed in the parable of the weeds,[23] was modernized as "weeds." And the "denarius" became the "silver coin," since it is not particularly illuminating to know the ancient names of coins.

The old "talent" of Matthew's parable[24] has become simply "money." The talent varied in weight and value in the hellenistic world. In addition, to most English speakers, talent refers to a special aptitude or gift for a particular activity. In the event an amount is mentioned in the text, it is appropriate to transpose that amount into some relevant counterpart. The nobleman or master in the parable of the entrusted money entrusts thirty thousand silver coins to one servant in one version; in another it is only one hundred silver coins. In the story of the enslaved manager who is unable to cancel a paltry obligation owed him, the manager is in debt to his master to the tune of a million dollars; the obligation owed the manager is ten dollars. The amounts are not exact, of course, but the dollar figures reflect the degree of discrepancy specified by Jesus.

Troublesome Terms

There are troublesome terms that resist ready translation. In one story, a "leper" comes up to Jesus. Or was it really a leper? The Greek term refers to someone with a skin lesion of some kind—eczema, psoriasis, or a kind of dermatitis, but not Hansen's disease, which is what we know as leprosy. How shall we translate the malady to reflect the original accurately? "Someone with a skin rash comes up to Jesus . . ." takes the edge off the story. For those who major in miracles, such a translation would appear to demean the account, yet that is probably what the term meant in Jesus' day. On the other hand, skin diseases were much more serious matters in that society because they carried a powerful social stigma. While not medically correct, "leper" best conveys the gravity of the affliction.

Jesus is reported to have shared a common table with "toll collectors and sinners" and thus associated with social outcasts. One member of the inner circle of followers, named Levi, is supposed to have been a toll collector. Toll collectors were petty tax officials who were hired by official tax collectors, usually higher local officials or wealthy foreigners, to gather excise taxes or transportation tolls. Because they were at liberty to levy at rates higher than the official rates and because they were in the service of foreigners, they were usually hated by indigenous populations. The picture of Levi, or Matthew as he is called in Matthew 9:9, sitting at a toll booth collecting tolls (Mark 2:14)—and the conjunction of this figure with prostitutes and sinners—make me wonder whether "toll collector" is a good English equivalent each time I cross the Golden Gate Bridge. Accuracy is not the issue—the persons in question were undoubtedly toll collectors—appropriateness is the question. Should we substitute something like "petty tax official" or "self-serving IRS bureaucrat" or "bill collector" to catch more of the nuances of the original? It is a difficult decision.

In Jesus' society few people could read and write. Among the few who could were the "scribes"—the traditional translation for the Greek term. It is perhaps better to call these people "scholars" for two reasons: the term "scribe" is not an everyday label in use in English today; the term "scholar" catches some of the nuances of the original—scholars are those who can read and write and interpret written documents—and it mirrors a bit of the arrogance and pride of the scribes of Jesus' time.

Thomas 42 is translated (from Coptic) as "Be passersby." The meaning of this term is unknown, or cannot be determined precisely. There is no context that helps narrow down the possibilities other than the Gospel of Thomas itself. Thomas scholars have wondered whether the term should not be translated as "Be itinerants" or "Be transients," since that is what Jesus himself was. However, caution is in order. The use of "itinerant" or "transient" may merely echo academic empathy for our own rootless age and thus suit the scholarly penchant for political correctness. Translation difficulties are occasioned as often as not by the nuances and uses of words in the receptor language as by problems with the original.

Translators of the Bible have long struggled with terms for the Israelites and their descendants. It has been customary to use the term "Jew" for all descendants of Abraham during the period of the Second Temple—from its rebuilding in the sixth century B.C.E. to its destruction in 70 C.E. "Jew" is of course derived from Judah, one of the twelve sons of Jacob, and from the territory presumably allotted to Judah—namely, Judea, with its principal city Jerusalem. The difficulty with this equation is that "Jew" is anachronistic for the period of the Second Temple, since Judaism in its modern form was not inaugurated for decades after Jesus' death around 30 C.E., until after the destruction of the temple in 70 C.E.

In the interests of historical accuracy, the Scholars Version decided to use "Israelite" for this people for the time period up to and including the first temple built by Solomon and to employ "Judean" for the same people when the reference is to the period of the Second Temple, but to limit the use of the term "Jew" to refer to the people and religion only after the inauguration of Judaism late in the first century. This vocabulary also avoids the unfortunate and sometimes disastrous implication that Jews were responsible for the death of Jesus. The people involved in the death of Jesus were admittedly some Judean authorities, who played a subordinate if complicit role to the Romans, whose descendants are the Italians, including those who now reside in Vatican City.

Jesus speaks frequently of something he calls "the kingdom of God." That phrase was adopted by early translators of the gospels as the appropriate equivalent of the royalty they knew in their time. It seems less appropriate in modern democracies and perhaps smacks too much of rascally King James with whom the King James Version is associated. In Jesus' speech, the phrase sometimes refers to a place or locale, at other times to an activity or relationship of God to a people or land. The Scholars Version panel adopted a variety of renderings, including "God's domain" or "God's estate" when a locale is intended and "God's imperial rule" when the reference is to God's sovereignty. The term "imperial" was intended to suggest the absolute character of God's reign. "Empire" was suggested by the analogy of the Roman "Empire" in Jesus' time and by the tyrannical counterparts in the empires of Japan and Germany in the twentieth century.

Some members of the panel objected strenuously to the use of "empire" and "imperial" because their connotations seemed antithetical to the irenic landscape of God's domain in Jesus' teachings. It has been extremely difficult to find terms that accommodate both the absolute character of the divine reign and the pacific disposition of Jesus. This problem still awaits solution.

Translating the Grammar

Until recently scholars have not been altogether clear about how to handle narrative tenses in Greek. Events that were reported as typical, recurring activities in Greek were often historicized: the verbs representing those events were translated as simple past tenses as though they referred to something that happened only once, on one particular occasion.

In Mark 2:13 it is reported:

> Again he went out by the sea. Lots of people used to gather around him and he would teach them.

In the Revised Standard Version the second sentence is translated:

> The whole crowd gathered around him, and he taught them.

People frequently gathered around Jesus, and he would teach them on those occasions. Older English translations make it sound as though this activity were a single incident. Typical, recurring activity is indicated again in 4:1 and following:

Once again he started to teach beside the sea. An enormous crowd gathers around him, so he climbs into a boat and sits there on the water facing the huge crowd on the shore.

He would teach them many things in parables. In the course of his teaching he would tell them:

At this point Mark gives the parable of the sower.

And as usual he said: "Anyone with two good ears had better listen."

These scenes are typical; they are stereotyped scenes in the public life of Jesus rather than reports of specific historical incidents. Yet modern English translations have tended to treat them as specific historical events. That practice has led readers of the English text to assume that Jesus spoke the long discourse in Mark 4 on a single occasion and that the sermon on the mount in Matthew 5–7 was a speech delivered on a particular occasion, like the Gettysburg address of President Lincoln. In fact, Mark has formed a compendium out of parables spoken, in all probability, on many different occasions, and Matthew has assembled disparate teachings in the great sermon, the structure of which is probably the work of Matthew or some scribes prior to Matthew. Moreover, the admonition to pay attention, appended occasionally to parables or aphorisms of Jesus, is also represented, in Greek, as a typical rather than a specific practice of Jesus.

Levels of Meaning and Ambiguities

Among the more difficult translation problems is how to represent levels of meaning and how to handle double meanings (double entendres), ambiguities, and irony. Out of many examples, I have chosen a few to illustrate the issues involved.

In Jesus' conversation with Nicodemus in the Gospel of John, Jesus says to Nicodemus, "No one can experience God's imperial rule without being reborn from above."[25] This awkward rendering seems necessary in order to translate a single Greek term that has two distinct meanings: *again* and *from above*. Most translations simply elect to put one in the translation and assign the second to a footnote.

The point of the exchange is that Jesus uses a standard Greek term capable of two interpretations; Nicodemus takes the literal sense and thus misunderstands; Jesus reprimands him for choosing the wrong meaning and provides him with the correct interpretation. Jesus did not intend, the author reminds us, for Nicodemus to think that a person could enter a second time into his mother's womb and be born again. Rather, Nicodemus should have perceived that Jesus meant him to understand that the new birth was a birth from above. Well, actually, the deception was intended. The author of the Fourth Gospel wants the reader to understand that a second birth is required (born again) but that this birth is of the spirit (from above). So the literal sense is an ingredient in the real or spiritual sense. It is extremely difficult to represent that kind of play on a word with two senses in the target language.

In the Sayings Gospel Q there is preserved this trio of lines:

> Foxes have dens,
> and birds of the sky have nests,
> but the son of Adam has nowhere to rest his head.[26]

The question is to whom does the phrase "son of Adam" in the third line refer. There are three possibilities. The definition of "son of Adam" given in Psalm 8 is the first possibility:

> When I consider your heavens,
> the work of your fingers,
> the moon and the stars,
> which you have set in place,
> what is man that you are mindful of him,
> the *son of man* that you care for him?
> You have made him a little lower than the
> heavenly beings
> and crowned him with glory and honor.[27]

"Son of man" in the sixth line translates the Hebrew phrase *ben adam,* quite literally, as the son of Adam, the progenitor of humankind. The same verse could as readily and more accurately (for English speakers) be translated:

> what are human beings that you should regard them,
> the offspring of Adam that you should respect them?

In other words, the reference is to descendants of Adam and Eve, the mythical parents of the human race.

If we take this meaning of the phrase as our guide, we could translate the words of Jesus as J. Dominic Crossan does:

> Every fox has a den.
> Every bird has a nest.
> Only humans are homeless.[28]

A second possible interpretation is provided by Jesus' alleged instruction to his disciples concerning his own death:

> The *son of Adam* is being turned over to his enemies, and they will end up killing him. And three days after he is killed he will rise![29]

In this context, "son of Adam" appears to be Jesus' oblique way of referring to himself. "Son of Adam" is the equivalent of "I." If that is the sense, we could translate:

> Foxes have their dens,
> birds of the air have their nests,
> but this mother's son has no place to call home.

We are of course translating the exact same Greek words in this version as we did in the first.

There is a third option. The Book of Daniel offers a different way of understanding the phrase "son of Adam":

> As I looked on, in a night vision,
> I saw one like a *son of Adam* coming with heaven's clouds.
> He came to the Ancient of Days and was presented to him.
> Dominion and glory and rule were given to him.
> His dominion is an everlasting dominion that will not pass away,
> and his rule is one that will never be destroyed.[30]

In his dream Daniel has a vision of a heavenly figure who will come in the future in the form of a human being. This "son of Adam" is to be appointed by the Most High, the Ancient of Days. The figure in Daniel seems to be the same figure that Mark has Jesus speak of in his gospel:

> If any of you are ashamed of me and my message in this adulterous and sinful generation, of you the *son of Adam* will likewise be ashamed when he comes in his Father's glory accompanied by holy angels![31]

If the third definition of "son of Adam" is allowed to prevail, the translation would be the more traditional one:

> but the *son of Adam* has nowhere to lay his head.

An ideal translation would be one in which all three possibilities were latent. Translating literally as "son of Adam" is one way to preserve that range of options. Yet that option was understood by the evangelists as a messianic title for Jesus, as the one who will return in the future with clouds of heaven. And that is the way the average Christian reader, ancient and modern, will take it. It is an almost certain way to limit the range of possible meanings. On the other hand, it seems equally likely that Jesus understood it as an oblique reference to himself. As an itinerant sage, he had no place to call home. If we translate it as Jesus probably used the phrase, we would select the meaning "I." Yet taking the phrase in the sense of any human being, the first option, is also quite possible on the lips of Jesus. The translator's dilemma is whether to translate at one particular level of understanding—say, the level at which Jesus understood it—and cover the other possibilities in a footnote, or to preserve the ambiguity and allow the modern reader, perhaps with the aid of a footnote, to stumble on the truth. The use of a footnote to cover the deficiencies of a translation is a counsel of despair. But there are moments when the translator founders on despair.

It is interesting to observe that in the Epistle of Barnabas, a treatise written perhaps towards the end of the first century, Jesus is said to be not a "son of Adam" but the son of God.[32] The author of this document evidently understood "son of Adam" to refer to Jesus' human side. Early in the second century, Ignatius, bishop of Antioch, while on his way to Rome where he would suffer martyrdom, wrote a letter to the church at Ephesus in which he described Jesus both as "son of Adam" and as son of God, by which he meant both human and divine.[33]

Son of Adam and Lord

Translation problems are compounded when two troublesome terms appear in the same context. This pronouncement of Jesus is recorded by Mark:

> The sabbath day was created for Adam and Eve,
> not Adam and Eve for the sabbath day.
> So, the son of Adam is lord even of the sabbath.[34]

The phrase "son of Adam" occurs in the same sentence as the term "lord," spelled here with a lowercase "l." As in the case of "son of Adam," the term "lord" was also immediately caught up in ambiguities when used as a title for Jesus.

The term here translated as "lord" is a common Greek word *(kyrios)*. It can denote a person of property, such as an owner of a vineyard or slaves. It can refer to a husband, since in ancient societies a wife was considered property. It can also be used as a form of polite, respectful address to males, the equivalent of "Sir" in English. But the Greek term also came to be applied to deified rulers, such as Roman emperors. Because of a curious overlap with usage in the Old Testament, it was also commonly used to refer to God. The simple term "Lord" is often used of God. In addition, the phrase *Lord God* is a translation of a Hebrew combination of the proper name for the God of Israel with the generic word for God. Since the Israelites and later the Judeans were forbidden to pronounce God's real name (represented in English translations as Jehovah, more recently as Yahweh), the Greek translators of the Hebrew Old Testament substituted the combination "Lord God." As a result, "Lord" with a capital "L" was employed as a common term for God.

In offering this explanation I have relied on English capitalization. That distinction was not observed in Greek manuscripts; Greek was regularly written without a special form for capital letters. One must therefore rely on context in Greek to determine which sense was intended.

The word "lord" has a semantic range similar to that of the Greek term. It can mean, according to the *Oxford English Dictionary,* a master or ruler, a chief, prince, or sovereign, a feudal superior as in "lord of the manor," and it can also be used as a designation for God and a title for

Jesus. "Our Lord" for many speakers of English denotes Jesus. As in Greek, "lord" is employed as a term of polite address for one deemed of superior social standing. It often suggests the social rank of a nobleman. There is also a verb, "lord," which means to exercise dominion over.

With all these possibilities in mind, the translator's dilemma can be observed in many passages in the gospels. (Italics in the following examples denote the same underlying Greek term. Note how the context can alter the meaning.) A leper comes up to Jesus and says, "*Sir,* if you want to, you can make me clean."[35] The leper, who was not a Christian, used it as a term of polite address. Matthew, who cites the word, no doubt understood it as a christological title. A Canaanite woman says to Jesus, "Have mercy on me, *sir,* you son of David." Later, she pleads, "*Sir,* please help me."[36] By "son of David" she probably meant only to imply that he was a descendant of David and Solomon, the healer and sage. But Christian readers soon understood "son of David" as another messianic title. They probably also read "sir" as "Lord."

In another context, the same term can be translated "master":

> Students are not above their teachers,
> nor slaves above their *masters*.
> It is appropriate for students to be like their teachers
> and slaves to be like their *masters*.[37]

Students have teachers and slaves have masters. But Christians understood themselves as both disciples and slaves of Jesus, their teacher and "Lord." The Scholars Version elected to translate what was probably the original level of meaning, the meaning the term had on the lips of Jesus, rather than the meaning it had as his followers understood it. The original King James Version translated "lord" with a small "l"; only with the Revised Standard Version of 1946 was "lord" changed to "master" with a small "m." The trend in these cases has been away from the Christian reinterpretation back in the direction of the original sense.

A few stories in the gospels play on the ambiguity between "sir" and "master." In the account of the woman at the well, Jesus is first addressed as "mister," then a little later as "sir." After a moment of recognition, Jesus becomes "master." Although the woman uses the same term in each instance, her regard for her discussion partner steadily increases.[38] The translator must have a good storyteller's ear to catch such nuances.

Isaiah is quoted in the opening lines of the Gospel of Mark:

> A voice shouting in the wilderness:
> "Make ready the way of the Lord,
> make his paths straight."[39]

Isaiah was referring to God; Mark of course means that John the Baptist—the voice in the wilderness—is preparing the way for Jesus, a different lord. This kind of confusion led to the transition from "lord" as a polite address to "Lord" as a title of divinity. Jesus is reported to have said, "I praise you, Father, *Lord* of heaven and earth,"[40] where the term obviously refers to God. In his letters, Paul frequently writes of the "Lord Jesus Christ." For Paul "Lord" is clearly an elevated title, although, when used of Jesus, it has not yet been equated with God.

In the passage with which we began, the question arises: How are we to understand the expression "son of Adam" and the term "lord"?

> The sabbath day was created for Adam and Eve,
> not Adam and Eve for the sabbath day.
> So, the son of Adam is lord even of the sabbath.[41]

The parallelism between the two lines suggests that son of Adam and lord are to be taken as references to human beings—to descendants of Adam and Eve. God established the sabbath for the benefit of humankind, not the other way around. That is the way Jesus probably understood his aphorism.

When Matthew comes to this point in editing Mark, however, he omits the first line and includes only the second: "Remember, the son of Adam is Lord of the sabbath."[42] Luke follows suit.[43] They have edited out the original sense and retained only the Christian overlay. The translator's dilemma, once again, is to figure out how to handle this bundle of ambiguities.

WHICH IS THE INSPIRED TEXT?

The original manuscripts of the books of the New Testament have disappeared. The earliest fragment of any part of the New Testament is a scrap from a papyrus codex of the Gospel of John. It has been variously dated from 125 to 160 C.E., roughly one hundred years after the death of Jesus. More substantial pieces of papyrus manuscripts have survived from the end of the second century, but the earliest surviving copies of complete gospels come from the third century. And we have no copies of the complete Christian Bible that can be dated earlier than the fourth century. To put the situation in a nutshell, we can say that, in all probability, only a very few ever read the original of one of Paul's letters or of one of the gospels—copies were made almost immediately as the letters and gospels were circulated among congregations; meanwhile, the originals wore out or were lost.

To add to the problem, no two copies of any of the books of the New Testament are exactly alike, since they were all handmade. It has been estimated that there are over seventy thousand meaningful variants in the Greek manuscripts of the New Testament itself. That mountain of variants has been reduced to a manageable number by modern critical editions that sort, evaluate, and choose among the myriad of possibilities. The critical editions of the Greek New Testament used by scholars are in fact the creations of textual critics and editors. They are not identical with any surviving ancient manuscript. They are a composite of many variant versions. Specialists select the best reading from among variants and print that as the main text. They also list important alternative readings in footnotes so that our scholars can make their own judgments regarding the best text. It is unlikely, of course, that any surviving ancient manuscript is identical with the autographs—the originals—of the books, or portions of books, that it contains. Translators and interpreters are thus twice removed from those originals.

It has been suggested that scholars should work with an actual version of the gospels—one taken, for example, from the Codex Sinaiticus, a fourth-century manuscript. At least that would be a *real* text as distinguished from a *reconstructed* text. Yet Sinaiticus contains errors of unknown magnitude, some of which were later corrected by scribes in the margins of that manuscript. Were scholars to work with Sinaiticus directly, the question arises: Should they use the underlying text or adopt the corrections that were made in ancient times to that copy? And if they adopt the corrections rather than the original text, should they also make other obvious corrections of misspellings and the like? In making these relatively minor decisions, scholars would have already begun to produce a "critical" text, a text based on the "critical" judgments of scholars.

It was once the exclusive aim of textual critics to attempt to reconstruct the original text of the documents comprising the New Testament. The goal, then, was to determine what had originally been *written*. That aim has been modified to a certain degree by the recognition that it is equally important to recognize what was *read* by various scribes and interpreters in different periods and at different localities. In other words, it has become a part of the science of textual criticism to chart the history of variant readings and use that history to understand how the text was variously interpreted.

We are fairly confident, for example, that the scribes who made copies of the New Testament (the gospels in particular) tended to modify the Greek text to match the orthodox views that were emerging. The opening line of the Gospel of Mark, to cite one example, reads "the good news of Jesus Christ" in several ancient manuscripts. Other manuscripts have amended this to "Jesus Christ, son of God." The tendency of scribes was to expand titles and labels in accordance with the practice current in their times. Those expansions, while of interest to the historian, also obscure earlier practice and usage. And historians have an interest in those earlier traditions as well. Indeed, there remains a strong interest in establishing the text at every stage of its history.

This question arises for scholars who make use of critical editions of the Greek gospels: Should we consider all the significant variants and versions preserved by all manuscripts, or should we be selective and limit our analyses to those readings that are closest to the original? For those who believe the Bible is the word of God, which is the inspired text? Critical editions such as the Nestle-Aland New Testament in fact print numerous variant readings at the bottom of each page.[44] The editors have also made decisions about which readings to print as part of the continuous text. In recent years, those editors have included more and more of the variant readings in the continuous text, although they have indicated that the variants are dubious by putting them in square brackets.

Among the many interesting textual problems facing the scholar, none is perhaps more intriguing than the story of the woman caught in the act of adultery. It is usually printed in modern translations as a part of the Gospel of John and is versified as 7:53–8:11.

This charming account appears in only a few ancient manuscripts at this point in John. In other manuscripts it appears after Luke 21:38; in still others, after John 7:44; and in the Armenian version, at the end of John after 21:25. Because it appears in various locations it is known as a "floating pericope" (a pericope is a narrative segment).

Scholars agree that the vocabulary and grammar of the story do not comport with the style of the Fourth Gospel. It clearly was not composed by the author of John. Nor does it belong to the Gospel of Luke. Indeed, the first three verses indicate that it is a fragment, perhaps a single page of a codex that belonged originally to a gospel whose name and contents are now lost. The introduction can be translated as follows:

> Then everybody returned home, but Jesus went to the Mount of Olives. Early in the morning he showed up again in the temple area and everybody gathered around him. He sat down and began to teach them.

John 7:53–8:2

There is no connection between this introduction and what precedes it in the Gospel of John. If one skips from 7:52 to 8:12, the flow of John is uninterrupted. This is further evidence that the story did not belong originally to John. The setting suggests that the incident took place during passion week, when Jesus was in Jerusalem teaching daily in the temple but returning to the Mount of Olives at night. It could well have belonged to a gospel, now lost, that contained other stories assigned to the final week of Jesus' life.

The Fellows of the Jesus Seminar, like many other scholars, have described this fragment as an orphan story, without a home in a known gospel. Like other critical scholars, they hesitate to regard it as a report of an actual incident in the life of Jesus. Yet they recognize that it is congruent with what is otherwise known of Jesus of Nazareth. They have excluded it from the database of stories that they think reflect the historical Jesus, but they have done so reluctantly. I see no good reason myself not to take it as a fragment of a lost gospel that may well tell us something important about Jesus. But in this I am at odds with many of my colleagues.

The translation from Greek to English and the reconstruction of the original text together form a formidable bridge that must be crossed on the way back to Nazareth. We have assumed that these two tasks apply to a well-defined body of literature, a collection of documents known as the Bible. However, critical scholars are not inclined to regard the limits of the canon—those books that have traditionally been included in printed Bibles—as limits imposed on historical inquiry. The next bridge to be crossed accordingly calls for an answer to the question: Which books belong to the Bible?

Chapter Six

TESTAMENT

AN ORTHODOX BRIDGE
TO THE PAST

THE NEW TESTAMENT AS BRIDGE

The collection of ancient documents we know as the New Testament privileges twenty-seven documents—gospels, acts, letters, epistles, plus one apocalypse—as the basis for defining what authentic Christianity is. Within that larger collection, the four canonical gospels were selected to undergird and propagate a standard—orthodox—picture of Jesus.

In contrast to the large number of sources that were available in antiquity, the New Testament itself provides a relatively narrow bridge to cross on the road to the origins of Christianity. The four narrative gospels of the New Testament can also deflect the search for the historical Jesus. The tendency has been, especially in the popular mind but also among scholars working within traditional guidelines, to look no further than the New Testament for information about Christian beginnings. Critical scholars of the Bible, on the other hand, have long since widened and modernized that canonical bridge. And I number myself among them. Since our interests extend beyond one orthodox version of Christianity, we have decided to take into account all the information from all the surviving ancient sources about Jesus of Nazareth and the events that produced the Christian movement. Indeed, our oaths of office as critical scholars and historians require that we investigate and weigh every document, every artifact, in reaching particular historical judgments. As historians, we are interested in the wide variety and complexity of the whole early Christian movement, rather than merely in one narrow, prescriptive account.

If canonical boundaries are meaningless from the perspective of the critical scholar, has the time not come to reopen the question of what books belong in the biblical canon? Is it not time to think of adopting a new New Testament?

The process of forming the first New Testament lasted for centuries. The uninformed tend to view that process as though it happened overnight. For them, the New Testament took shape around 1611, when the authorized edition was promulgated in England by James I. Many people assume that the English Bible fell out of heaven complete. As a consequence, the King James Bible is erroneously regarded as inerrant and infallible. The popular mind has simply invented a myth to confirm what it wishes were true. But the task of the serious scholar is to segregate fact from wishful thinking.

In reviewing the very complex process of forming the Bible, we must lay aside preconceived notions and gather the raw data. In order to limit the quantity of information to be considered, we will here confine our investigations to the New Testament.

BOOKS AND BOOKMAKING IN THE ANCIENT WORLD

The physical evidence for the books of the New Testament consists of manuscripts produced between the death of Jesus around 30 C.E. and the sixteenth century, the effective end of manuscript production. (I cannot bring myself to write "handwritten manuscripts" since manuscript means "written by hand.") The discussion of the evidence to follow will be easier to comprehend if we preface those remarks with a modest primer of terms and categories. The three principal areas to consider are (1) types of writing materials, (2) writing styles, and (3) book formats.

Types of Writing Materials

Manuscripts of the New Testament are customarily classified in three broad categories based on the kind of writing material. There are three types of writing materials: papyrus, parchment or vellum, and paper.

PAPYRUS   The earliest manuscripts were written on papyrus. Papyrus was made from the Egyptian papyrus reed cut into strips laid adjoining each other on a flat surface to form sheets. A second layer of strips was superimposed on the first but at right angles, so that the fibers in the papyrus ran at right angles to each other on opposite sides of the page. The side with horizontal fibers is called the recto, the side with vertical fibers is termed the verso.

PARCHMENT   Parchment and vellum were also used as manuscript material. Both parchment and vellum were made of animal skins—sheep, goats, or calves—scraped clean of flesh and hair and then cured. Parchments, in other words, are leather sheets. Vellum is of a higher quality and is therefore a more expensive form of parchment.

PAPER   The earliest New Testament manuscript written on paper dates to the ninth century. The Chinese had actually produced paper as early as the first century C.E. However, paper was not introduced in the West until much later and was not widely used until the twelfth century. About 1,300 of the 5,487 surviving manuscripts of the New Testament, or portions of the New Testament, are written on paper. To be sure, the early types of paper imitated the look and feel of parchment, just as expensive papers today do (diplomas and awards are still printed on imitation parchment to indicate the antiquity of the traditions under-lying them).[1]

Writing Styles

Manuscripts are further classified by the types of handwriting. There were two types of hand, generally speaking: a book hand used for literary works and a cursive script employed for ordinary purposes such as contracts, bills of lading, deeds, receipts, and personal correspondence. Later a special cursive style was created for books as well.

THE UNCIAL BOOK HAND In the book hand, letters are formed ele-gantly and discretely, each letter of approximately the same height and width. Letters are printed rather than written, in imitation of the style found on inscriptions, where letters consisted of straight lines and angles made by the stonemason's chisel. The book hand, which tended to round the more rigid style of the inscription, is customarily called uncial (mean-ing letters "one inch" high). In uncial manuscripts the text is written continuously, without word spacing or paragraph breaks and by filling up each line with letters without regard to word breaks. In early manu-scripts there is virtually no punctuation. The uncial style was employed in the production of literary texts, including the Bible, for approximately fifteen hundred years, beginning in the fourth century B.C.E.

CURSIVE AND MINUSCULE A more efficient form of writing, called cursive, was in general use for the creation of nonliterary texts of various kinds. In the cursive style, letters are frequently joined to one another without lifting the quill from the page. Combinations of letters were developed, called ligatures, to speed up writing and copying.

At the end of the eighth or the beginning of the ninth century C.E., a new book hand emerged; it was smaller than the uncial script and adopted the cursive style. The smaller size led to its being termed "minus-cule," which is what biblical manuscripts written in this style are called. Minuscules were prepared on a variety of writing materials.

Book Formats

Another way to classify manuscripts is by how the "book" is formed. There are two types: (1) the scroll or roll, which consisted of sheets of papyrus or leather glued together in a continuous strip and rolled up on a wooden, bone, or metal dowel, and (2) the codex, which consisted of sheets folded in two and fastened together on one side. The codex is the precursor of the modern bound book. Scrolls were normally written on one side, codices on both sides, of the sheet. As a consequence, we can tell whether even a tiny fragment is from a scroll or a codex by whether there is writing on one or both sides of the sheet.

Dates

The earliest of the papyrus manuscripts of the New Testament can be dated to the second century C.E., the latest to the eighth. Papyrus manuscripts are almost always written in the uncial hand. The parchments in uncial script range in date from somewhere between the second and third to the eleventh centuries. The earliest of the parchment minuscules can be dated to the ninth century, the latest to the sixteenth. Handwritten minuscules continued to be produced even after the invention of the printing press around 1454 C.E.

To judge by the surviving evidence, Jewish copies of the scriptures in ancient times were always produced on leather or parchment in scroll form. The codex was not used for Jewish literature until the eighth century. Pagan literary texts also retained the scroll form until the late third or early fourth centuries; the transition to the codex had virtually been completed by the beginning of the fifth century. In contrast, Christian writers seem to have adopted the codex form almost from the beginning of Christian manuscript production in the late first or early second century. Scholars are uncertain why this happened. One explanation is that Christian writers wanted to distinguish their texts from both Jewish and pagan authors. The real cause is more probably less ideological; Christians may have adopted the codex in order to accommodate longer texts or collections of texts under one cover. The collection of texts bound together was simply not possible in a scroll format.

Evaluation

Papyrus manuscripts of the New Testament are considered the most valuable of the three groups. Their value lies in the fact that they are the closest thing we have to the original texts, called "autograph" copies (written or signed by the original authors), of the New Testament documents, none of which has survived. But they do not in themselves tell us much about the formation of the canon, which was just getting under way in the early papyrus period.

Some of the early parchments in uncial script are also considered very valuable, not only for their textual evidence but also because they were formed into thicker codices and thus reveal which books were being included in larger collections of important, perhaps even sacred, documents.

Minuscules or cursives come relatively late in the development of the text and canon of the New Testament. As a result, they were thought by textual critics not to be as important and, as a consequence, have not been given the close attention the earlier manuscripts have received. That is a deficiency that eventually needs to be rectified for one simple reason: later manuscripts may actually be copies made from much earlier texts, to which they are therefore immediate, rather than intermediate, witnesses. The date of the manuscript does not always indicate the age of its text.

THE NEW TESTAMENT AS CANON

Formal Definitions of Canon

The New Testament is a canon of scripture. What does that mean?

The term canon means "a critical standard or criterion." In the case of the New Testament, the canon includes those books accepted as genuine and inspired scripture by the community forming the canon. But that is a purely formal definition. What we will need subsequently is a historical definition, one that depicts how and when an authoritative collection of sacred writings was actually formed.

According to Bruce Metzger, an authority on the history of the canon, the term canonical designates documents that were produced while the apostolic tradition was still alive.[2] Such a definition is intentionally vague: apostolic tradition was "alive" well into the second century and is a suitable qualifier for many documents that were not included in the New Testament. If we were to use that definition as a guide, we would have a New Testament of seventy-five or a hundred books rather than the customary twenty-seven.

Another definition is this: canonical means accepted and used by the church or churches at large.[3] In the early centuries, what was considered "canonical" varied from region to region and was actually determined largely by regional ecclesiastical officials rather than by popular assent: most members of the Christian movement would not have possessed copies of any of the books, and manuscripts of a complete Bible did not yet exist. Consequently, they would not have been able to form independent judgments about the merit of individual books. In any case, this definition would exclude the Book of Revelation from the New Testament: it was never universally approved by the churches before being included in printed Bibles.

The canon comprises books that conform to the rule of faith, according to yet another definition.[4] It is not clear from this way of putting the matter whether documents included in the New Testament conform to some rule of faith previously established—let's say, by one or the other of the creeds—or whether the New Testament was meant to be the basis for establishing some new rule of faith. Churches differ widely in how they interpret this definition.

Finally, the New Testament can be understood as a list of books adopted or approved by some ecumenical or denominational ecclesiastical council. Modern defenders of the canon seem to prefer this definition. Yet if we adopt this definition, we can only say that the Roman

Catholic Church did not officially close its canon until the Council of Trent meeting in 1545, and many Protestant bodies have never taken official action. And, as we shall see, the Eastern churches have established canons of scripture quite at variance with those of the Western churches.

The Canon as Historical Process

As preparation for addressing the canon question, we need to consider how and when the New Testament we now have was formed. I propose to consider that process under three rubrics: the canon as a physical collection of books; the canon as an authoritative list of books; and the canon as scriptures selected and arranged for public reading—as a lectionary.

The notion most contemporary Bible users have is that of a physical collection of books assembled under one cover. Modern readers are accustomed to the codex book created out of a stack of sheets sewn or glued together on one side; they have very little practical acquaintance with the book as a scroll. The prevailing idea of what constitutes a Bible is therefore physical and palpable: the Bible is a bound book.

Prior to the invention of the printing press and the advent of the codex, a canon would have consisted of a list of books recommended for reading. The recommendation would have come from a bishop or other ecclesiastical leader. In the absence or unavailability of bound collections, the list would have served as a table of contents of a hypothetical book. A canon would be something like a bibliographic syllabus prepared by a college instructor for a course, say, in English literature or the French Revolution.

Canon can also refer to the reproduction of selected texts intended for public reading on some liturgical schedule. Compendia made for this purpose are called lectionaries. A lectionary is a kind of anthology designed for use in worship, study, and meditation. Of the 5,487 manuscripts in the inventory at the Institute for New Testament Textual Research (Münster, Germany), 2,280 are lectionaries. We will return to their significance subsequently.

Scholarly Myopia

As a residue of habit, modern scholars tend to view the history of the canon from the perspective of the finished product. Since physical copies of codices containing a large number of sacred books did not exist before the fourth century, considering the Bible, or the New Testament, as a physical book was not an option. Scholars have depended, consequently, on *lists* of books quoted by early Christian authors or compiled by ecclesiastical officials. In addition, scholars have searched for fragments of earlier evidence to support decisions actually made at a later time, rather than looking for clues about how the process took place. In other words, they have made decisions taken in the sixteenth century or later retroactive. As a consequence, the data we have in the scholarly literature are often not complete or reliable. We learn in inventories whether a given manuscript contains fewer than the standard number of books, but when it contains more than the usual number, that fact may not be noted. It will take some time to expand our database so that we have full and accurate information about the contents of the surviving codices and scrolls.

It was not until the printing press was invented that the modern book could readily accommodate the volume of pages required to reproduce the entire New Testament or the whole Bible. Even though it was physically possible to create huge codices containing many books, it was not often done for the simple reason that it was very expensive. A relatively small codex required the hides of fifty to sixty sheep or goats; the hides of more than 360 animals were needed to create a codex the length of Sinaiticus, the famous fourth-century copy of the Bible. Only kings and those who could afford a king's ransom could fund bookmaking of this magnitude.

An extensive collection of books the length of the New Testament, copied onto a single *scroll*, was not physically possible. Papyrus Harris 1, a chronicle of the reign of Ramses II, is 143 feet in length. Other hieroglyphic burial scrolls ran to fifty feet or more, but these were monumental documents not meant for ordinary use.[5] The Isaiah scroll found at Qumran is twenty-eight feet, but this too is an unusually long roll. The Qumran temple scroll is slightly longer than the Isaiah scroll at twenty-nine feet. The maximum length of a usable scroll was said to be about thirty-five feet. However, most Greek rolls were shorter and contained a single book or segment of a book.

The division of ancient works into "books" suggests that divisions of works corresponded to the average length of the scrolls on which they were written. The *Antiquities* of Josephus in twenty books meant that this work would have occupied twenty scrolls. Philostratus' life of Apollonius of Tyana occupied eight books or scrolls. Homer's *Iliad* is a work that required twenty-four scrolls.

The Greek name for Bible is *ta biblia,* "the books" or "the writings." Modern usage prefers the singular "book" in contradiction to the Greek plural "books." The difference undoubtedly reflects whether a work consisted of plural "books" or whether a work consisted of a single "book." "The scriptures," which could be translated literally as "the writings," is perhaps a better English equivalent of *ta biblia.* A "bible" in the first century C.E. would have consisted of a storage jar containing a number of scrolls. The Latin name for a scroll is *volumen;* each volume carried a tag, called a *syllabus,* that identified the content of that roll.

The books found at Qumran, dated between approximately 200 B.C.E. and 68 C.E., are all in scroll rather than codex form. In contrast, the fourth-century C.E. Nag Hammadi library was entirely in a codex format.

Most Christian codices of the second and early third centuries were one-document books. That may be due to the fact that early Christian writers at first created books only of single-scroll length. Initially it seems that the codex was made in a single-quire format: a stack of the required number of sheets was folded once in the middle to form the entire book. As a consequence, when the codex was trimmed, the inside pages were much shorter than the outside pages. This practice mitigated against forming large codices. With some important exceptions (P⁴⁶, P⁴⁵), it was not until the fourth century that codices were made of smaller quires or signatures (sets of sheets folded in the middle) and then assembled into one codex by sewing them along the spine, as shown in Figure 3 (p. 140). Because huge codices were expensive and because the scroll format continued to be used for both pagan and Jewish publications, the list of sacred writings played an important role in the formation of the biblical canon.

Books of the New Testament first circulated individually; they were later collected into related groups. In the second century C.E. we begin to see two-document codices. Multidocument codices begin to appear in the third century. It is only in the fourth century C.E. that the first great parchment or vellum codices appear. At Nag Hammadi, in the fourth century C.E., fifty tractates (or "books") were collected into twelve codices. Comprehensive codices containing many books continue to be rare for the next millennium—to such an extent that Bruce Metzger concludes that very few Christians could ever have owned, or even seen, a copy of a complete New Testament, judging by the small number of surviving copies.[6]

The more than two centuries from the invention of the printing press to the beginning of the Enlightenment were tumultuous. Johann Gutenberg is believed to have printed the first Latin Bible, Jerome's Vulgate, sometime between 1452 and 1456. The Greek New Testament did not appear in print until between 1514 and 1517. Martin Luther tacked his ninety-five theses to the door of the church at Wittenberg on 31 October 1517. The Council of Trent acted on the canonical question on 8 April 1545 for the Roman church, in reaction to the reformation inaugurated by Luther. The reaction in part was to Luther's low regard for the Book of Revelation and the Epistle of James in the New Testament. The first edition of the King James Bible appeared in 1611, complete with the extra books that appear in Catholic but not Protestant Bibles. Galileo was warned of his heresy in 1616 and condemned in 1632. John Locke published his *Essay Concerning Human Understanding* in 1690, which signaled the beginning of the Enlightenment. The Enlightenment broke out in full force in the following century.

Those were momentous times. And those were the times in which the formation of the canonical New Testament entered its final stage. Those events mark the watershed that separates the Middle Ages from the

TABLE 1

PAPYRUS MANUSCRIPTS OF THE SECOND CENTURY c.e.

P^{52}	ca. 125	a tiny fragment of the Gospel of John
P^{66}	ca. 200	the Gospel of John
P^{46}	ca. 200	the letters of Paul
P^{90}	ca. 175	a fragment of the Gospel of John
P^{98}	2nd cent.	a fragment of Acts
P$^{64, 67}$	ca. 200	fragments of the Gospel of Matthew

NOTE: P^4, a fragment of Luke, may belong to the same codex as P$^{64, 67}$.

modern period. In the midst of that maelstrom, publishers were the ones, for the most part, who settled which books belonged to the Bible; for the first time they printed Bibles by the score for distribution to everyone who could read and had the price of a book. It was the invention of the printing press and the modern multisignature book that finally settled matters. Even so, these developments did not settle the status of the so-called deuterocanonical books, also known as the Old Testament apocrypha—the intertestamental books such as Tobit, Judith, the Wisdom of Solomon, and 1 and 2 Maccabees. New editions of the Bible often include that disputed group of books, although other, more conservative editions continue to omit them. The final resolution of their inclusion or exclusion is still pending.

We cannot imagine, from the distance of the twentieth century, how earthshaking the events were that took place between 1450 and 1700. Nor can we imagine how unsettled the Bible as a collection of books was prior to the printing press. But we can discipline our imaginations by gathering some minimal facts about the Bible as a physical book, about lists, and about lectionaries.

THE BIBLE AS BOOK (CODEX)

Papyri

Very few papyrus manuscripts of the canonical books can be dated to the second century. The six that qualify are listed in Table 1. In scholarly treatises and inventories, papyrus manuscripts are preceded by a "P" to indicate the kind of writing material; the "P" is followed by an inventory number assigned to each manuscript or fragment indicating the order in which they were discovered.

If we examine the physical evidence provided by the New Testament papyrus manuscripts, mostly fragmentary, that survive from the period

TABLE 2

CONTENTS OF THE LONGER EARLY PAPYRUS CODICES

P^{13}	3rd/4th cent.	Hebrews
P^{45}	3rd cent.	Four gospels and Acts
P^{46}	ca. 200	The letters of Paul
P^{47}	3rd cent.	Revelation
P^{66}	ca. 200	John
P^{72}	3rd/4th cent.	1 and 2 Peter, Jude
P^{75}	3rd cent.	Luke, John

NOTE: The inventory numbers indicate the order in which the papyri were discovered, not their age.

prior to Nicea (325 C.E.), we learn that the preponderance of fragments are from single-document codices. Among the papyrus manuscripts known to scholars from the entire papyrus period (second to eighth century), only nine contain ten or more folios and thus about forty pages (a folio is a sheet folded in two to make four pages, counting both sides of each resulting page). The contents of seven of these nine early codices are summarized in Table 2.

As Table 2 indicates, from prior to 325 C.E. there have survived only four papyrus manuscripts that contain more than one biblical document—none of the whole New Testament, none of the entire Bible. The discovery of the Chester Beatty Papyri in the 1930s produced the two most extensive documents in the list above, P^{45} and P^{46}, both of which can be dated to the end of the second or beginning of the third century.

There are now ninety-eight known papyrus manuscripts of New Testament books. They span the period from the second to the eighth centuries C.E. A catalogue of the contents of all the surviving papyrus manuscripts, many of which, it will be recalled, contain only a few words or verses, reveals that most of them contained only a single book, so far as we can tell. Such a catalogue also indicates the popularity of various books, if we may judge by the number of surviving copies. The catalogue is provided in Table 3.

Among the twenty-seven books in the standard New Testament, 1 and 2 Timothy are not represented among the papyrus fragments.

In general, most papyrus manuscripts were copies of single books. Eventually books were arranged in larger groups as the capacity of the codex was expanded. The earliest compendia consisted of books that had something in common: the gospels were grouped together, as were the Pauline letters. Acts, the story of the early church, tended to be linked to the so-called catholic epistles, like Hebrews and James, which were presumably addressed to the church at large rather than to a particular

TABLE 3
CONTENTS OF ALL PAPYRUS CODICES

CODICES OF SINGLE BOOKS		CODICES OF TWO BOOKS	
John	16	Luke, John	2
Matthew	14	Matthew, John	1
Acts	10	Mark, John	1
Luke	7	Matthew, Acts	1
Romans	6	John, James	1
Hebrews	5	1 and 2 Corinthians	1
Revelation	5	1 and 2 Thessalonians	1
1 Corinthians	4	Ephesians and	
James	3	2 Thessalonians	1
Mark	1		
1 John	1		
Philippians	1		
1 Thessalonians	1		
Titus	1		
Ephesians	1		
Galatians	1		
Philemon	1		
1 Peter	1		
Jude	1		

CODICES CONTAINING THREE OR MORE BOOKS

P45	3rd cent.	Matthew, Mark, Luke, John, Acts
P46	ca. 200	Romans, 1 and 2 Corinthians, Galatians, Ephesians, Philippians, Colossians, 1 Thessalonians, Hebrews
P61	ca. 700	Romans, 1 Corinthians, Philippians, Colossians, 1 Thessalonians, Titus, Philemon
P72	3rd/4th cent.	1 and 2 Peter, Jude
P74	7th cent.	Acts, James, 1 and 2 Peter, 1, 2 and 3 John, Jude

congregation. Revelation remained in a class by itself as the only independent apocalypse in the New Testament. It was rare for more than one of these clusters to be included in a single papyrus codex (P45, which contains the four gospels and Acts, is the sole surviving exception).

Parchments (Uncials)

Two hundred ninety-nine parchment manuscripts of the New Testament have survived from antiquity. Of that number, only four originally contained major portions of the entire Bible, both Old and New Testaments. Yet two of these codices, Sinaiticus and Alexandrinus, have New Testaments with twenty-nine books rather than the customary twenty-seven. The two additional books in Sinaiticus are the Shepherd of Hermas and Barnabas, two works included among the so-called Apostolic Fathers—a collection of books written by authors who lived in the "apostolic age," roughly prior to 150 c.e. The two additional items in Alexandrinus are the two Epistles of Clement. Codex Ephraemi Syri Rescriptus, the third great codex, is defective in that 2 Thessalonians and 2 John are missing, although it may originally have included them.

The fourth parchment manuscript, Vaticanus, now lodged in the Vatican library as its name indicates, is defective from Hebrews 9:14 on. Professor Kurt Aland maintains that Vaticanus probably also contained some documents from what we now know as the Apostolic Fathers.[7] If Aland is correct, then we have four codices containing the twenty-seven books of the later New Testament, plus additional writings of the Apostolic Fathers.

The other 295 uncials lack one or more books. However, the data given in most lists preclude determining whether additional documents were once a part of any of these uncials. The earliest of these uncials are 0189, a fragment of Acts dated to the second or third century, and 0212, a third-century fragment of Tatian's Diatessaron (a harmony of the four canonical gospels). The latest of the uncials is dated to the eleventh century.

None of the papyrus or uncial codices contains precisely the contents of what was eventually to become the New Testament. Two of the codices have twenty-nine books in their New Testaments, and two are defective. The New Testament as a physical book had not yet been born.

Minuscules

The minuscules continue the saga of the papyri and uncials. The surviving minuscules date from the ninth to the sixteenth centuries. Aland claims that fifty-six of about 2,800 minuscules contain the whole of the New Testament.[8] It is difficult to know how much of this generalization is based on firm empirical evidence. The minuscules have yet to be adequately examined for their contribution to textual criticism and to the formation of the canon. However, the twenty-seven books that came to be part of the New Testament were being increasingly collected into single codices, judging by the scattered evidence presently available to us. But even by the sixteenth century, the limits of the New Testament had by no means been finally fixed.

THE NEW TESTAMENT AS LIST

Because early evidence for the New Testament as a physical book was lacking or incomplete, scholars have depended on lists of authoritative or recommended books as a guide to what was considered a part of the New Testament canon.

Lists have been understood in two senses. In the first sense the reference is to a separate list of documents, such as a bishop might provide for his parishioners. In the second sense, "list" can be understood to be an index of scriptural quotations and allusions found in a particular author's work. Quotations and allusions are customarily taken as an author's approval of the books being cited, unless the author specifies the contrary. The two kinds of lists should be kept distinct. In what follows, I will explore the first kind of list and refer to the second type only in passing.

What do we learn from the lists? We can do no more than sample the possibilities.

Marcion

Marcion, a wealthy shipowner who organized his own Christian sect, gathered into his Bible only those scriptures that supported his theological position. After coming to Rome from Pontus in Asia Minor (ca. 140–150), Marcion promulgated a collection of "scriptures" consisting of the Gospel of Luke and ten letters of Paul, all heavily edited. The lesson was not lost on the later church. Both Marcion and the church excluded books if they were deemed to deviate from desirable doctrine or practice. The Puritans and Presbyterians adopted this strategy in forcing the publishers of the King James Version in the seventeenth century to drop the Old Testament apocrypha from their editions. The British and Foreign Bible Society added its weight to exclusion in the nineteenth century by refusing to print and circulate Bibles with the Old Testament apocrypha in them.

Marcion is also known to have taken scissors and paste to the documents he chose. He cut out parts of Luke and the Pauline letters that he didn't like. We do not know how often that same approach was used prior to the fixing of the text in the fourth and fifth centuries. Many scholars now believe canonical Mark is an edited text in its own right. Mark was certainly edited by Matthew and Luke in the process of creating their own gospels; they also edited Q, to judge by the results. And there is good reason to believe that Thomas went through more than one edition.

Exclusion and editing constituted one strategy. Expansion and combination formed another. We know the Pauline corpus was expanded by letters and epistles written in the name of the apostle. Marcion probably did not know the Pastoral epistles (1 and 2 Timothy, Titus); in fact, the pastorals may not have been composed by Marcion's time. The epistles of Peter and Jude are also pseudographs—writings incorrectly attributed to those authors—that made it into official lists, although not without difficulty.

Irenaeus

It is well known that Irenaeus, a heresy hunter who flourished towards the close of the second century in Gaul, insisted on the fourfold gospel. His argument—that since there were four winds and four cardinal directions there should be four gospels—was specious, of course. Yet the principle he was enunciating proved to be important: the narrative gospels, he reasoned, should not be reduced to a single witness, as Marcion had done. Irenaeus believed, probably for the fanciful reasons he adduced, that multiple witnesses were essential to the health of the tradition. Tatian (second century C.E.), a scholar of the Syriac church, made another attempt to reduce the four witnesses to one; he combined the four gospels into one harmonized version in the Diatessaron. The Western church eventually rejected his work. It was apparently considered illegitimate to conflate the four gospels into one harmonized account. The production of harmonies, suspended in antiquity, was resumed in modern times when scholars began to create the first critical study instruments. Today the synopsis or gospel parallels is the standard format: the gospels are arranged in parallel columns for ready comparison, often with matched lines. Modern scholars have decided that "harmonizing" the gospels produces an arbitrary sequence of events that obscures the lack of real chronological information in the texts themselves.

Irenaeus did not propose a formal list of approved writings beyond his list of the four narrative gospels. He cites a number of other documents, however, that he may have regarded as authoritative. We cannot be sure. In any case, Irenaeus refers to twenty-one or twenty-two books as though they were "scripture." However, within this group, the letters of Paul had not yet attained the same status for him as the gospels; he also includes the Shepherd of Hermas in his "canon."

Muratorian Canon

The so-called Muratorian Canon, an annotated list of authoritative books, was first published in 1740 on the basis of an eighth-century manuscript. Some scholars think it may have originated as early as 200 C.E. The language is Latin, although it may have existed at one time in Greek. The text is fragmentary and must have begun originally with Matthew. It now begins with Mark, who is identified as probably not an eyewitness; the author of the Gospel of Luke was certainly not an eyewitness, according to this canon. The Gospel of John, on the other hand, was taken to be based on the testimony of all twelve apostles. The anonymous author of this unusual document obviously regarded the Fourth Gospel as the most valuable of the four.

The fragment alleges that the epistle to the "Laodiceans," which may be a reference to the epistle now known as Ephesians, and the epistle to the Alexandrians, an unknown work, were falsely attributed to Paul and should not be regarded as authoritative. The fragment includes the Wisdom of Solomon among authoritative books, along with both the Book of Revelation and the Apocalypse of Peter.

The approved books in the Muratorian list include the four canonical gospels, the thirteen letters of Paul (including the Pastoral epistles), Jude and two epistles of John (we don't know which), together with the Wisdom of Solomon, and the Book of Revelation and the Apocalypse of Peter. The Muratorian Canon rejects the Shepherd of Hermas, Paul's letter to the Laodiceans and to the Alexandrians. Hebrews, 1 and 2 Peter, and James are not mentioned.

Montanism

A certain Montanus, like Marcion before him, began a movement in the late second century C.E. that produced a strong adverse reaction on the part of orthodox theologians. That reaction has had consequences for the formation of the New Testament canon.

Montanism was an apocalyptic movement that originated in Asia Minor but spread rapidly throughout the empire. Two women, Prisca and Maximilla, were closely associated with Montanus. According to the story, Montanus fell into a trance after his conversion and began to speak in tongues, which he took to be the fulfillment of the promise made by Jesus to his disciples in the Gospel of John that he would send the Paraclete (the Spirit). He and his associates believed the world would soon come to an end. In response to this conviction, the Montanists developed a rigorous ascetic discipline.

The orthodox reaction to the Montanist movement was to distrust apocalypticism and to reject pentecostalism (new outpourings of the spirit). The apocalypse of John, already under suspicion, became a steady target of rejection in the Eastern wing of the church as a part of this reaction. The Montanists themselves also rejected the Epistle to the Hebrews because it asserts that a second repentance is impossible. Even the Gospel of John came under fire by orthodox leaders because of its association with the Montanists.

Montanism indicates that a definitive collection of Christian texts had not yet been determined at the end of the second and the beginning of the third centuries. But the backlash created by Montanism contributed to a hardening of the orthodox position and gave new impetus to the creation of a theologically orthodox collection of scriptures.[9]

Athanasius

Athanasius (296–373) was the bishop of Alexandria beginning in 328 C.E. His festal letter of 367 C.E. is frequently cited as the first unalloyed list of the twenty-seven books that eventually became the New Testament of the Western church. In that letter he lists the books he commends to his parishioners for their edification. Athanasius was an untiring opponent of Arianism, the view that Christ was not coeternal and coequal with God; he stoutly defended the full deity of the second person of the Trinity.

The fact that his letter is so frequently cited as evidence for the early determination of the New Testament canon calls attention to the reverse perspective from which canonical issues are often viewed: With a bow to Marcion, scholars look, as it were, for data to confirm what is taken to be the final decision, rather than assembling the widest possible collection of data to illuminate the historical process, which took place over a long period of time and was disjointed and uneven at best.

Eusebius

Eusebius was the bishop of Caesarea and a principal participant in the Council of Nicea. In Eusebius' time (260–340 C.E.), sacred books were still being divided into three categories: accepted, disputed, and rejected. That should hardly surprise us. But we would give a lot to know which books Eusebius, who wrote the first surviving history of the church after Luke, actually included in the fifty copies of "the Bible" Constantine ordered him to produce. His lists have survived; in them the accepted books include the four gospels, Acts, the letters of Paul (number not specified), 1 John, 1 Peter, and the Apocalypse of John, which is also listed in the second category. Among the disputed books he lists James, Jude, 1 Peter, 2 and 3 John, the Acts of Paul, the Shepherd of Hermas, the Apocalypse of Peter, Barnabas, the Didache, and the Gospel of the Hebrews. The disputed list indicates which books belonging to the authoritative list were still being debated in the fourth century. As heretical books, Eusebius names the Gospel of Peter, the Gospel of Thomas, the Gospel of Matthias, along with other gospels, the Acts of Andrew, and the Acts of John.

THE NEW TESTAMENT AS LECTIONARY

Lectionaries (anthologies of selected texts arranged for liturgical use) are in a class by themselves. There are about 2,280 of them extant, although the Nestle-Aland Greek New Testament cites only five of them in indicating variant readings in the New Testament. The Byzantine lectionary system did not arise until the seventh or eighth century. One generalization can be made immediately: The Book of Revelation was never included in the Byzantine lectionary. Furthermore, regional churches developed their own lectionary systems in the early period. There is great variety in the surviving lectionary manuscripts.

THE NEW TESTAMENT IN OTHER TRADITIONS

We have been speaking as though the Greek tradition has exclusive claim to the attention of scholars interested in the question of scripture. In fact, much of what has been said derives from the Latin church. The shift to Latin in the West had already begun with Tertullian, an early African Christian theologian, around 200 C.E. and was more or less complete by 250 C.E. But we have failed to notice what was going on in the East.

Syrian Church

The Peshitta version of the Christian scriptures contained only twenty-two writings. The Peshitta was the Bible of the Syriac-speaking church. It is believed to have originated in the fifth century C.E. The five books that would have brought the number of the New Testament books to twenty-seven include 2 Peter, 2 and 3 John, Jude, and the Apocalypse of John. The Peshitta effectively closed the canon for the Syrian church since it separated itself from the rest of the church at the Council of Ephesus in 431 C.E.

Ethiopian Church

The Ethiopian church, which legitimately claims that its tradition dates to the fourth century C.E., has a canon of eighty-one books, of which thirty-five comprise the New Testament. The notion of what is canonical is regarded more loosely here than in other church traditions. In addition to the twenty-seven known to us, the Ethiopian canon includes the Synodos (a church order), the book of Clement, The Book of the Covenant (a church order followed by a resurrection gospel known as the Testament of the Lord), and the Didascalia.[10] The authorities of the Ethiopian Orthodox Church have never claimed that their Bible was complete.

The Syrian and Ethiopian canons are enough to remind us that the tradition in the West is not the only tradition.

American Churches

A final word must be reserved for the canon in the American tradition.

The contents of the New Testament and the entire Bible were not fixed for the Roman Catholic tradition until 8 April 1545, when the Council of Trent took action as a part of the Counter-Reformation. But that Roman Catholic decision had the Latin version of the Bible, known as the Latin Vulgate, as its object; the Vulgate included the Old

Testament apocrypha. Luther's translation of the Bible into German was printed in 1522. Because Luther did not regard four books highly (Hebrews, James, Jude, and Revelation), he placed them in an appendix. For English-speaking Protestants, on the other hand, the preeminent act was the publication of the King James Version in 1611, first with, and then later without, the apocrypha. That event was so decisive that the Discipline of the Methodist Episcopal Church included this statement as a result of an action taken on 24 December 1784, at Baltimore, Maryland: "All the books of the New Testament as they are commonly received, we do receive and account canonical." By this date it was no longer necessary to list the twenty-seven books. It should be noted, however, that this resolution on the part of the Methodist Church does not constitute an independent act and scarcely reflects a considered reevaluation of the possible contents of the New Testament.[11]

A number of movements in the United States have expanded the canon with additional revelations set down in writing. Prominent among them are the Church of Jesus Christ of Latter-Day Saints with the *Book of Mormon*. The Christian Science movement recognizes Mary Baker Glover Eddy's *Science and Health with Key to the Scriptures* as part of its authoritative canon. Similar remarks could be made of the Seventh-Day Adventists and other groups claiming the Christian appellation but expanding the base of their received revelations.

A NEW NEW TESTAMENT?

So far as we know, none of the original followers of Jesus wrote books. Those ascribed to the first disciples or to relatives of Jesus are actually pseudographs—documents written by unknown authors but attributed to known persons. The genuine letters of Paul of Tarsus, penned in the fifties of the first century C.E., have the strongest claim to antiquity, to apostolic authority (on the basis of his Damascus road vision), and to originality. In addition, Paul was the founder of a great part of the Greek-speaking church and is perhaps the one most responsible for the shape Christianity eventually assumed. It is difficult to conceive a collection of basic Christian writings that would not include most or all of what Paul wrote (Romans, 1 and 2 Corinthians, Galatians, 1 Thessalonians, Philippians, Philemon).

The Pauline school wrote and circulated letters in the name of Paul. Most scholars have concluded that the Pastorals (1 and 2 Timothy and Titus) belong to a generation or two subsequent to Paul and therefore were not written by him. Ephesians is almost certainly not from the hand of Paul; it may have functioned as an introduction to the first collection of Paul's letters. Many scholars regard Colossians and 2 Thessalonians as letters composed by Paul's successors and attributed to him. In a revision of the New Testament canon, it will be necessary to reconsider the status of each of the letters attributed to Paul but not written by him.

The same may be said of the so-called catholic epistles, presumed to have been addressed to the church at large, the catholic church (with a lowercase "c"). The catholic letters are Hebrews; James; 1 and 2 Peter; Jude; and 1, 2, and 3 John.

The letter of Clement, allegedly bishop of Rome, to the church at Corinth is dated by most scholars to about 95 C.E. It was written in response to a disturbance in the church at Corinth and rehearses the basic tenets of the Christian faith as though heresy were at issue. It deserves consideration along with other early letters. The seven letters of Ignatius, bishop of Antioch, who was probably martyred in Rome in the second decade of the second century, are worthy of close consideration. Since Ignatius knew he was on his way to his execution, he wrote letters to seven churches with whom he had had contact; they are, in fact, his last will and testament. He sums up the gospel as he had come to know it through the letters of Paul. The letter of Polycarp, bishop of Smyrna, addressed to the Philippians, was written later than Ignatius' letters. Polycarp provides insights into the situation in Greece in the middle of the second century.

Gospels constitute a basic ingredient in any collection of documents that purports to represent the beginnings of Christianity. The gospels recognize the pivotal role of Jesus of Nazareth, who is usually assumed to be the founder of the Christian faith. The gospels have preserved a body of teaching and a record of deeds that can, after careful sorting, be traced back to Jesus himself. The earliest of these records are the Sayings Gospel Q and some hypothetical early version of the Gospel of Thomas. In a revised collection of gospels, the narrative gospels should be preceded by a reconstructed Q and a selection of parallel materials from the Gospel of Thomas. A selection of what are considered the authentic aphorisms and parables of Jesus could conceivably form a preface to Q and Thomas. Most scholars agree that the first of the narrative gospels is Mark; Mark ought, therefore, to come first in the sequence of the four narrative gospels. Mark should be followed by Matthew and Luke, who based their narratives on Mark; they supplemented their stories with materials from Q and with stories of the appearance of the risen Jesus to select disciples, along with accounts of Jesus' miraculous birth and childhood.

A new New Testament, however, should consider other early gospels. In *Ancient Christian Gospels*, Helmut Koester has written:

> For the description of the history and development of gospel literature in the earliest period of Christianity, the epithets "heretical" and "orthodox" are meaningless. Only dogmatic prejudice can assert that the canonical writings have an exclusive claim to apostolic origin and thus to historical priority.[12]

TABLE 4
PHYSICAL EVIDENCE FOR THE EXISTENCE OF GOSPELS

100–150 C.E.

Gospel of John	P52
Egerton Gospel	PEgerton 2

150–225 C.E.

Gospel of Matthew	P64, 67, 77
Gospel of John	P66, 90
Gospel of Thomas	POxy 1
Gospel of Peter	POxy 2949, 4009

THIRD CENTURY

Gospel of Mark	P45
Gospel of Matthew	P1, 45, 53,70
Gospel of Luke	P4, 45, 69, 75
Gospel of John	P5, 22, 28, 39, 45, 75, 80, 95
Gospel of Thomas	POxy 654, 655
Infancy Gospel of James	PBodmer V
Gospel Oxyrhynchus 1224	POxy 1224
Gospel of Mary	PRylands 463; POxy 3525

The physical evidence for the existence of gospels as old as those that were eventually included in the New Testament is impressive (Table 4). And the content of several of these documents makes them worthy of review. The Gospel of Thomas is not the only candidate. The time has come to end the orthodox bias that has caused these documents to be ignored.

The Gospel of Peter offers an alternative version of the trial and execution of Jesus and for that reason should probably be evaluated for inclusion in any new canon. Unfortunately, Peter is fragmentary. In addition, we now have part of the text of the Gospel of Mary, which ought to be seriously considered for inclusion if only because it is unique among early Christian documents in giving a central place to a woman close to Jesus. This century has brought to light fragments of three other previously unknown gospels—Egerton, and gospels 840 and 1224 found at Oxyrhynchus in Egypt. The fragmentary story about a woman accused of adultery, usually attached to the Gospel of John but almost certainly a piece of another unknown gospel, deserves review along with the other fragments.

If an apocalypse (a revelation, usually in a dream, of events connected with the end of history) is to be included, we should consider adding at least one more to the Apocalypse of John. The Apocalypse of Peter might be a suitable candidate. There are over a hundred other apocalypses to choose from, so popular was this particular literary genre.

If other types of literature are desirable, we might think of the Didache (Teachings of the Twelve Apostles), which is an early Christian church order or discipline. And there are still other documents that belong to the formative years of Christianity that might be evaluated for inclusion.

If it is desirable to expand the boundaries of the New Testament, we should develop a list of viable candidates among treatises of the post-apostolic age (roughly 150–300 c.e.), subject them to extensive review, and then decide whether they contribute materially to the history, variety, and definition of Christianity.

In any case, by any of the criteria used to isolate "sacred" Christian scriptures in antiquity, the present canonical limits of the New Testament call for review and reassessment. Scholarly practice ignores canonical boundaries, yet critical scholars do not accord every early Christian writing the same weight among the plethora of sources available.

Uppermost in any review of the canon must be the practical limits of what a literate person might be expected to read and understand. If we include too many documents, readers will be put off by excessive demands. If we embrace too few, we may slight one or another of the strands of early Christian development. Practical limitations preclude what many scholars would prefer: a New Testament that includes *all* the surviving documents from the first two or three centuries. While such a New Testament might be no larger than the Old Testament, it would still present formidable dimensions to the average student of the Bible. Julian Hills, in private correspondence, has suggested that the selection should be as large as possible but no larger; that it should be as small as possible but no smaller.[13] Another way of putting it is to say that the canon should have both inside and outside limits. That is sage advice.

The reconsideration of the canon ought to be an ecumenical enterprise. It should not be driven by the same motives that marked canonical decisions in the early church. The canon of the New Testament was developed, along with the creeds, as a way of excluding political enemies, so regarded because they deviated from institutional opinion or practice; the primary interest was to build a fence around right doctrine and hierarchic privilege. This also had the effect of consolidating ecclesiastical power. The scholars of the Bible in the twentieth century—at least those who call themselves critical scholars—should have as their aim the desire to lay bare that process. The power we seek is the power of information that we can share with a literate readership. We should endeavor to include rather than exclude. We might, for example, want to defend rather than condemn Arius, who, in defense of monotheism, argued that the Christ was not truly God. In any case, our canonical boundaries ought to be flexible, limited only by the requirements of literacy and the ability to master a body of literature. It is just possible that we should return to the time-hallowed practice of publishing the Bible in pieces.

Whatever else we do, we must move beyond the traditional canonical limits in the construction of databases, research tools, and study instruments. The perpetuation of artificial canonical boundaries still cripples our endeavors in textual criticism, papyrus and parchment inventories, concordances, and similar instruments. Above all we need a handy compendium of original-language texts that explodes the boundaries of the standard Greek New Testament. The horizons of biblical scholarship have expanded far beyond the limits of the canonical sources.

A new New Testament will be promulgated not by the church or churches but by some publisher or publishers. I believe we will find it necessary to continue the use of the terms *New Testament* and *Bible,* with or without qualifiers, if we are to achieve that goal. Publishers and Bible societies established the terms for the current canon; Bible publishing is a special domain in the publishing world. But new publishers and seminars can reset the terms for a new stage in the history of the canon.

If we have taken these steps, we will have made the major moves. However, there remains another herculean task: we will need to explain to interested parties what a revised canon means. That task may turn out to be the most difficult of all.

Chapter Seven

THE GOSPELS

Enter by the narrow door.

THE CREATION OF NARRATIVE GOSPELS

Sometime after the fall of Jerusalem in 70 C.E., an unknown Christian author created the first narrative gospel. The author made Jesus the chief player in a drama that begins with his baptism at the hands of John the Baptist and ends with his death and the subsequent discovery, by his followers, of an empty tomb on Easter morning. In his study of the infancy gospels, Ronald Hock has observed that the creation of the first story in which Jesus of Nazareth played the leading role was a momentous step in the history of the Christian movement.[1]

Prior to this moment, Jesus had been the subject of such things as odes borrowed from other traditions and revised, embryonic creedal formulations, prayers, and letters to and from churches and individuals. In addition, his teachings had been collected into oral clusters and written compendia without narrative settings; his words were being gathered and recorded but not his acts. Only with the creation of the Gospel of Mark did Jesus become the protagonist of a story plot, in which words and actions were combined into a continuous story.

Mark's innovative narrative was soon revised and expanded. A decade or so later, first Matthew and then Luke adopted Mark's story as the basis of their own, new versions. In doing so, they revised Mark's anecdotes and augmented his materials in various ways. The largest single change they made was to work a written collection of sayings into the framework of their gospels. That collection was the Sayings Gospel Q. Q apparently did not satisfy the definition of gospel as the orthodox view emerged and eventually ceased to be copied as an independent document.

Mark's gospel had ended with some women disciples finding an empty tomb. Matthew and Luke extended Mark's narrative by adding accounts of Jesus' appearances to his disciples after his death. Matthew set those appearances in Galilee; Luke confined them to Jerusalem and

Judea. Luke, however, carried the revision even further: he wrote a second volume, the Acts of the Apostles, which narrated the first several years of the new movement. After depicting the ascension of Jesus, Luke's principal champions of the new movement in Acts were Peter the fisherman in the first half and Paul of Tarsus in the second half.

Matthew and Luke also added birth and childhood stories at the front end of their gospels, stories that preceded Mark's account of Jesus' baptism. Mark's narrative begins just as Jesus leaves Galilee and goes down to the Jordan, where he joins the baptist movement of John. Shortly thereafter, following the imprisonment of John, Jesus launches his own public ministry in Galilee. Jesus is adopted as God's son in the baptismal scene: the divine spirit descends on Jesus in the form of a dove and a voice from heaven makes the adoption announcement.[2] While repeating (and modifying) this story, Matthew and Luke begin the story further back—with Jesus' birth. They both narrate, though in very different ways, how Jesus came to be God's son. They are, in effect, stories about Jesus' parents, Mary and Joseph, and the events that surrounded the birth of Jesus.

In the second century, other gospel writers were to take up this particular set of themes and expand them. Interest in Mary, Jesus' mother, was developed in the Infancy Gospel of James. In that gospel are stories about Mary's parents, her birth, and upbringing, themes only touched on by Luke.[3] A second gospel, the Infancy Gospel of Thomas (to be distinguished from the Gospel of Thomas found at Nag Hammadi), tells stories about the miraculous deeds of the precocious child Jesus, another theme only briefly discussed by Luke.[4]

The beginning of the gospel story was extended even further back by the Gospel of John. In the prologue, the author of this gospel takes the story back to the beginning of time: the divine word and wisdom—the logos—was present with God at the creation and only later took on the form of a human being and accepted the conditions of finite existence. The author of the Fourth Gospel, as it is also called, expands the story after the death of Jesus. He, too, relates stories about the risen Jesus appearing to his followers in Jerusalem. Later, a second author, or an editor, added other appearance stories located in Galilee as an appendix in John 21.

FRAMING THE NARRATIVE GOSPELS

The narrative gospels have five principal components (listed in their probable order of composition) and a sixth component supplied by the Book of Acts:

1. The public acts and teachings of Jesus (all four)
2. The story of Jesus' passion and burial (all four)

3. Appearance stories (Matthew, Luke, John)
4. The birth and childhood stories (Matthew and Luke only)
5. A prologue (John only)
6. The acts of the apostles (Luke only).

The basic component as well as the earliest segment of the narrative gospels consists of the first item in this list:

| 1 | ACTS AND WORDS OF JESUS |

To this part was affixed an appendix treating the plot against Jesus, his arrest, trial, execution, and death:

| 2 | PASSION |

As the gospels developed, appearance stories were appended to the body of the story by each of the evangelists independently of the others. Because there was no common tradition, these appearance reports diverged widely in terms of witnesses and detail:

| 3 | APPEARANCES |

In addition, Matthew and Luke prefaced their gospels with birth and childhood stories, which again cannot be easily reconciled with each other:

| 4 | BIRTH AND CHILDHOOD |

John lacks the stories relating the birth of a divine child and substitutes a prologue in the form of a poem to Logos—the word and wisdom of God:

| 5 | PROLOGUE |

Finally, Luke adds his version of the acts of the apostles:

| 6 | ACTS OF THE APOSTLES |

When these parts are assembled in their story order, they form the first five books of the New Testament. The numbers in the blocks indicate the order in which the components were created.

| 5 | 4 | 1 | 2 | 3 | 6 |

Scholars view the gospels from the perspective of how they were composed and assembled. The earliest gospel narrative was created by the author of the Gospel of Mark; it consisted of the public words and acts of Jesus. Mark framed his story with opening and closing events—the baptism of Jesus and his arrest, trial, and crucifixion. Mark's frame was enlarged by Matthew and Luke, who added birth and childhood stories and appearance stories. The Gospel of John expands the frame even more with its prologue and additional appearance stories. There is a succession of ever larger frames. The additional frames move farther and farther away from the history of Jesus the itinerant teacher, healer, and exorcist. The larger the frame, the more likely that frame is out of touch with the actual events of an earlier time.

SAYINGS GOSPELS

Mark was the first narrative gospel. The first written gospels were apparently not narrative gospels but collections of the sayings of Jesus the teacher or sage. One such collection was Q, the written compendium both Matthew and Luke made use of in creating their expanded versions of Mark (discussed at length later in this chapter). It is virtually certain that Q was a written source because Matthew and Luke often quote it word for word. The two evangelists move Mark back in the direction of the historical Jesus by incorporating sayings material from an earlier source. Mark itself is relatively thin in parables and aphorisms. In this one respect, Matthew and Luke are correcting the "gospel" tradition stemming from Paul, for whom it was necessary to recite only the bare outline of the death and resurrection of Jesus to have a complete message to proclaim, which he could also refer to as a "gospel."

The existence and shape of Q was reinforced by the recovery of another sayings gospel at Nag Hammadi in the form of the Coptic Gospel of Thomas. That gospel also consists of a collection of sayings without a narrative framework. About 40 percent of the sayings and parables recorded in Thomas are paralleled by similar words in Q; the two collections were no doubt drawing on a common fund of oral tradition, but the evidence indicates that neither borrowed directly from the other.

There were of course other sayings gospels, as we learned in the survey of new discoveries in Chapter Four. Gospel Oxyrhynchus 1224 is a fragmentary sayings gospel. The Gospel of Mary, Secret James, and the Dialogue of the Savior are also predominantly sayings gospels. The last two appear to be extensions of the kind of traditions reflected at a much earlier stage in the Gospel of Thomas.

THE CHRONOLOGY OF THE GOSPELS

If we put this fund of information into a chronological frame and include the other gospels catalogued in Chapter Four, the sequence looks something like this:

Stage 1: 50–60 C.E.

    Sayings gospels Q and Thomas

    Gospel Oxyrhynchus 1224

Stage 2: 70–80

    Gospel of Mark

    Egerton Gospel

Stage 3: 80–90

    Gospels of Matthew and Luke

Stage 4: 90–100

    Gospel of John

Stage 5: 100–150

    Gospel of Peter

    Gospel of Mary

    Infancy Gospels of James and Thomas

    Secret James

    Gospel Oxyrhynchus 840

    Dialogue of the Savior

The watershed in the emergence of early Christian literature is the fall of Jerusalem and the destruction of the temple in 70 C.E. With the end of the temple cult and its accompanying bureaucracy, Judaism found a new mode of existence and underwent a rebirth. The rabbinic tradition that was to become the foundation of Judaism began to form. The new Jewish sect, the Jesus movement, also had to adjust to new conditions, among which was the resurgence of apocalyptic expectations inspired by the destruction of Jerusalem. The apocalyptic fervor was inflamed again towards the close of the first century as a result of the persecutions under Domitian (81–96 C.E.). The New Testament gospels were probably created in the decades immediately following the fall of Jerusalem. During the second century the Christian movement acquired its literary legs and began to produce literature at a rapid rate.

The first step for critical scholars is to thread their way back through the history of the narrative gospels. Much of this process is hypothetical, to be sure. There are anomalies in even our best theories, and unresolved questions plague our reconstructions. Yet the broad outlines are clear and command a substantial consensus among critical scholars. We begin with the most recent of the narrative gospels, the Gospel of John.

THE GOSPEL OF JOHN

The Gospel of John was probably the last of the narrative gospels to be created. John did not make direct use of any earlier written gospels in creating his own version, although this point is disputed. In any case, John does not make use of his predecessors in the way Matthew and Luke made use of Mark and Q. John goes his own independent way; he shares only a few anecdotes with the other narrative gospels and records no parables and aphorisms of the type found in the other gospels.

John presents a very different sketch of Jesus than the synoptics (Mark, Matthew, and Luke). In the synoptics Jesus speaks frequently in parables and aphorisms; in John, Jesus is a lecturer given to extended monologues. In the synoptics Jesus speaks about God's domain; in John, Jesus speaks mostly about himself and his relation to the Father. In the first three gospels, Jesus performs exorcisms; in John, Jesus performs "signs."

John presupposes but does not narrate the baptism of Jesus. He does not include a temptation narrative. There is no confession of Peter at Caesarea Philippi to the effect that Jesus is the messiah. The transfiguration is lacking. Gethsemane and the last supper have been entirely recast.

There are also discrepancies in chronology when John is compared with the synoptics. There are three Passovers in John, only one in the synoptics. The temple incident occurs at the beginning of Jesus' public activity in John, at the beginning of passion week in Mark. The crucifixion takes place on Passover eve in the Fourth Gospel, just at the time the Passover lamb was butchered; it occurs on Passover day in the synoptics. Jesus begins his public work when John the Baptist is arrested in the synoptics; in the Fourth Gospel Jesus begins his public work while John is still active.

While John overlaps with the synoptics at certain points, its versions of common stories diverge markedly. One may compare the account of the paralytic in Mark[5] with the lame man at the pool in John;[6] the two versions of the miracle of the loaves and fish for five thousand;[7] the two accounts of walking on the sea;[8] the two versions of curing a blind man;[9] and the two widely divergent stories of raising a person from the dead.[10] This series of miracle stories may well have derived from a source common to John and Mark, but if so, the two evangelists have treated their source with great liberties.

The Fourth Gospel supplies stories that are unique to it: the sign at Cana, where Jesus transforms water into wine at a wedding feast; the dialogue with Nicodemus, in which Jesus teaches that to experience God's imperial rule one has to be born a second time "from above"; the conversation with the Samaritan woman at the well, who has come to draw water and then learns that there is water that will quench one's thirst forever; and the response to the Greeks who come looking for Jesus. In addition, John provides numerous lengthy discourses on a variety of themes that have nothing in common with the Jesus of the synoptics.

It was once fashionable to attempt to harmonize John with the synoptics by weaving them together. That practice is currently out of favor: there is no way to determine the original order of events at those points where the gospels disagree.

In the Gospel of John, Jesus is a self-conscious messiah rather than a self-effacing sage. In John, Jesus seems to have little concern for the impoverished, the disabled, and the religious outcasts. Although John preserves the illusion of combining a real Jesus with the mythic Christ, the human side of Jesus is in fact diminished. For all these reasons, the current quest for the historical Jesus makes little use of the heavily interpreted data found in the Gospel of John.

THE STRUCTURE OF MARK

For the most part, Matthew and Luke do not represent independent witnesses to what Jesus said and did. They borrow extensively from Mark and the Sayings Gospel Q. For that reason we can set them aside temporarily. We will return to them subsequently and consider the acts and words for which they are the sole witnesses.

The Gospel of Mark consists, as observed earlier, of two major parts: an account of Jesus' arrest, trial, and execution; and a collection of anecdotes and teachings. We will examine the first part, the passion narrative, in detail in Chapter Twelve. To preview the results of that examination: The story of Jesus' arrest, trials, and execution is largely fictional; it was based on a few historical reminiscences augmented by scenes and details suggested by prophetic texts and the Psalms.

For a long time scholars were inclined to the view that the first thirteen chapters of Mark preserved a chronological sketch of the course of Jesus' public ministry. That view disintegrated as scholars learned more about the oral transmission of anecdotes. Those who have specialized in folklore have taught us that the Jesus traditions took shape as short, independent segments suitable for telling and retelling in a variety of contexts. These were oral units—anecdotes unconnected to other anecdotes, for the most part, or parables (which were themselves short stories), or memorable sayings, often in poetic form. Scholars began to see that the body of the Gospel of Mark was in fact made up of such individual units organized into groups based on form, or on common theme, or simply hooked together by the association of key words. We will note several of these groups in due course.

This analysis of Mark made it evident that behind Mark lay several decades when stories about Jesus were circulated orally—told and retold in varying sequence and combination. Stories about Jesus continued to be transmitted orally well into the second century. The written gospels did not at first displace the "oral gospel." Indeed, many valued the oral tradition more highly than the written tradition. One practical reason for the preference was undoubtedly that many early converts could not read, and those who could may not have been able to afford papyrus manuscripts or did not have access to written versions. In any case, the gospels exhibit many traces of their oral ancestry.

These traces are of two kinds. The first consists of the tendency to group materials having the same or similar form as an aid to memory: one anecdote about a controversy Jesus had with his opponents reminds the storyteller of another similar incident; one parable reminds the speaker of a second; and so on. By clustering controversy stories or parables together, the author of Mark indicates that he did not know the context in which that story or parable belonged. Scholars have concluded that Mark was no historian: he was not interested in the sequence of events or had no knowledge of chronology. The second trace is the freedom with which Matthew and Luke rearrange the materials they find in Mark and assign them to new contexts. They obviously did not regard Mark's placement as indicative of a fixed order of events.

There is a third feature to note: Mark's gospel, like the other three canonical gospels, is essentially a travel narrative. Jesus moves about from place to place as he performs deeds and makes pronouncements. The travel narrative was the simplest way for ancient storytellers to turn a series of anecdotes into a connected tale: change in locale was accompanied by encounters with different persons, and this elementary connection provided a minimal continuity. Yet that continuity, or that sequence, was not necessarily regarded as the order in which events actually took place, as evidenced by the fact that other storytellers could tell the same stories in a different order or sequence.

All four narrative gospels are basically travel narratives. The Book of Acts is a travel narrative. The life of Apollonius of Tyana, a contemporary of Jesus, is a travel narrative. The *Odyssey* of Homer—the most widely known story in late antiquity—is a travel narrative. And there are many other examples.

After its initial scenes depicting the baptism of Jesus and his temptation, Mark presents a purported typical day in the life of Jesus.[11] When John is thrown into prison, Jesus returns to Galilee and announces his gospel. He then calls the first two pairs of disciples as he is walking along by the Sea of Galilee. Next we are told he goes to Capernaum, teaches in the synagogue, and exorcizes an unclean spirit. Upon leaving the synagogue, he goes to Simon Peter's home and cures his mother-in-law of a fever. At evening, on that same day, they bring all sorts of sick and demon-possessed to him to be cured (here Mark begins to generalize without giving the reader particulars). Jesus gets up the next morning and retreats to an isolated place. His followers find him, and they then set off on a preaching tour around Galilee. At some point on this tour, presumably, a leper comes up to Jesus and asks to be healed. Jesus obliges him.

This series of events is not based on the memory of an actual sequence; it is what Mark imagined a typical day in the life of Jesus to be like. It is a sampler of the kinds of things Jesus did. The individual stories were told originally as isolated incidents prior to their incorporation into Mark. In some cases Mark (or Matthew or Luke) has invented the incident, often as the duplicate of an older tale.

Scholars have analyzed the stories Mark records and grouped them into types. One type is called the anecdote or pronouncement story. These are brief narratives that provide a setting for something Jesus said. Some anecdotes relate controversies with Jesus' critics; others are dialogues attached to miraculous cures, exorcisms, or other incidents. There are thirty-two anecdotes of this type in Mark alone. This type of narrative was common among storytellers in the ancient world. Vernon K. Robbins and a team of scholars have collected hundreds of them from other literature of the period for comparative study.[12]

Mark also records a number of miracle stories. These are of several broad types. There are healing stories and exorcisms; it is often difficult to tell one from the other, since in Jesus' day deformities and illnesses were usually thought to be the result of demon possession. There are also nature wonders, such as walking on the sea, stilling the storm, and multiplying the loaves and fish. And, finally, there are epiphany stories. An epiphany is an appearance or revelatory manifestation of a divine being, such as an angel or saint. The transfiguration—Jesus talking with Moses and Elijah—is an example of an epiphany story. Altogether there about twenty of these different types of miracle stories in Mark.

THE BUILDING BLOCKS OF MARK

Out of the oral stories available to him, Mark fashioned his gospel. By examining the ways in which the materials are put together, we can reconstruct much of the process by which he did so.

Part of the process had already taken place in the oral period. Some single sayings of Jesus had already been turned into compounds (two sayings joined together) and clusters (three or more sayings joined). Mark may have known and incorporated a chain of miracle stories that had already been assembled in an earlier source. We cannot always tell whether stories were joined together by Mark's predecessors or whether Mark himself is responsible for their connection.

Mark relates a series of controversy stories one after the other in 2:1–3:6. There is a collection of parables in Mark 4. Mark has created a compendium of sayings related to discipleship in the ninth chapter. The thirteenth chapter is known as the "little apocalypse" because in it are assembled sayings having to do with the events preceding the final holocaust. Another group of anecdotes of the same type is gathered in 11:27–12:37. These examples indicate that Mark grouped stories and sayings by their form and theme. He did not know the order in which events occurred, and he had no idea of the original occasion on which a saying or parable might have been spoken.

Philip H. Sellew has demonstrated that Mark has also created what may be called didactic scenes.[13] In a didactic scene, Jesus teaches in public and is later interrogated privately by his closest followers, who need help understanding his teaching. Mark has assembled a different kind of complex in the third chapter: Jesus' relatives come to get him and take him home because they think him mad—in other words, they think him controlled by demons. Meanwhile, Jesus has an exchange with some critics about whether he is in fact demon-possessed. Finally, he tells his audience that his true relatives are those who do God's will, suggesting that his blood relatives may not be true relatives.

Additional narrative techniques of Mark are visible in his gospel. Mark is noted for inserting one block of material into another. One example is where Mark embeds one healing story in another, as we find with the healing of Jairus' daughter and the woman with a vaginal flow.[14] There are seven other examples of this literary device. Mark has also apparently created doublets: he twice has Jesus feed a crowd in the wilderness, perhaps in imitation of Moses;[15] he twice restores sight to a blind man;[16] he twice sends disciples into Jerusalem to make advance arrangements.[17] Mark has also interspersed his narrative with asides. For example, he translates Aramaic words for his readers; he explains unfamiliar customs; at one point he explains why Jesus' mother and siblings come to get him in an aside: "You see," he writes, "they thought he was out of his mind."[18] Mark has also composed numerous transitions to provide connective glue for his gospel.

The stories Mark employs to frame his gospel appear at the beginning, middle, and end of his tale. These stories appear to have been composed by the author specifically to provide an interpretive frame for his gospel (Table 5).

One set of framing stories narrates Jesus' connection with John the Baptist, his baptism by John, his decision to part company with John, his wilderness test, and a summary of Jesus' message as Mark understood it. This group forms Mark's introduction to his gospel.

A second group of stories forms the turning point of his narrative. Jesus three times predicts that he will die in the fulfillment of prophecy. In addition, Jesus appears transfigured with Moses and Elijah, two great heroes of Israel. In that scene Jesus is recognized by a heavenly voice as God's favorite son—obviously a Christian motif that Mark has used to interpret the scene.

A third cluster of stories forms the spine of the passion narrative. Mark has gathered episodes related to Jesus' passion into this section: a woman's anointing of Jesus, Judas' pledge to betray Jesus, Jesus' cele-

TABLE 5

FRAMEWORK STORIES IN MARK

	MARK
Voice in the wilderness	1:1–8
John baptizes Jesus	1:9–11
Jesus is put to the test	1:12–13
Jesus proclaims the good news	1:14–15
Who do people say I am?	8:27–30
Son of Adam must suffer	8:31–33
Jesus transformed	9:2–8
Son of Adam will die and rise	9:30–32
Son of Adam will die and rise	10:32–34
Passion story	14:1–15:47
Empty tomb	16:1–8

bration of Passover, Jesus in Gethsemane, and Peter's rash oath. The use of tales that circulated in oral form prior to Mark ceases with the beginning of Mark's account of the passion, which reaches its climax, of course, with Jesus' arrest, trial, and crucifixion. Most of these elements are products of Mark's narrative imagination, although he may be drawing on historical reminiscence in a few instances. We will examine the passion story in detail in Chapter Twelve.

MATTHEW AND LUKE: SPECIAL SOURCES

Matthew and Luke preserve an array of miscellaneous materials not found in either Mark or Q. As a kind of shorthand for these items collectively, scholars have called Matthew's special materials "M" and Luke's unique contributions "L." Whether "M" and "L" were written or oral sources is difficult to determine. Matthew and Luke may have created these materials themselves, or they may have known miscellaneous items that had either survived or been created in the oral tradition. Oral storytelling was still very much alive at the time Matthew and Luke composed their gospels, towards the end of the first century.

Matthew records a few narrative incidents not found in Mark or the other gospels. They include the remarks about giving Peter the keys of the kingdom[19] and the story of the coin Peter is to find in a fish's mouth with

TABLE 6
SPECIAL MATTHEAN PARABLES

	MATTHEW
Sabotage of weeds	13:24–30
Treasure	13:44
Pearl	13:45–46
Unforgiving slave	18:23–34
Vineyard laborers	20:1–15
Two sons	21:28–32
Wedding celebration	22:2–13
Ten maidens	25:1–12
Money in trust	25:14–30
Last judgment	25:31–46

which he is to pay the temple tax.[20] Matthew, of course, also has unparalleled material in the birth and childhood stories, in the passion narrative, and in his postresurrection reports. These narrative supplements are most likely the inventions of Matthew. Scholars are inclined to be skeptical of narrative incidents that are dependent on a single source. Even if these stray reports were based on historical reminiscence, they add very little to our fund of significant information.

In addition, Matthew records several compendia of teachings not paralleled elsewhere and a number of parables unknown from other sources. The compendia include a series on murder, adultery, divorce, and swearing; these are a part of the great sermon, known traditionally as the sermon on the mount.[21] There is also a complex on alms, prayer, forgiveness, and fasting, incorporated into the same sermon.[22] A third group, consisting of harsh sayings directed against scholars and Pharisees, has some incidental parallels in Q and Luke, but several of the pronouncements are unique to Matthew.[23] These sayings must all be evaluated individually, although evaluation is a more speculative task when there are no parallels to assist in reconstructing the history of the materials.

Other sayings can be approached with more confidence, however. Matthew has been thought by some scholars to have had an independent collection of parables at his disposal (Table 6). The bulk of these are parables or parable-like sayings. That in itself is revealing. We now know that the sabotage of weeds, the treasure, and the pearl have parallels in the Gospel of Thomas. The wedding celebration is probably an edited version of the dinner party found in both Luke and Thomas.[24] The parallel

	LUKE
Sermon at Nazareth	4:16–30
Miraculous catch of fish	5:4–11
Widow of Nain's son	7:11–17
Women disciples	8:1–3
Samaritan incident	9:51–56
Return of seventy-two	10:17–20
Mary and Martha	10:38–42
Crippled woman	13:10–17
Herod Antipas' threat	13:31–33
Man with dropsy	14:1–6
Ten lepers	17:11–19
Zacchaeus	19:1–10

in Luke suggests that it came originally from Q. The money in trust, similarly, is found in Luke, although in a different version.[25] Again, Q probably contained some form of this parable. The remaining parables are unique to Matthew. As in the case of the sayings, the unique parables must be evaluated individually.

The Gospel of Luke is rather richer than Matthew in both unique narrative incidents and unparalleled sayings. The so-called "L" narrative segments in Luke are listed in Table 7. Some of these are alternatives to incidents reported in Mark; others appear to duplicate similar events recorded by Mark and appearing elsewhere in Luke. For example, the account of the cure of the ten lepers is an elaborate retelling of the cure of the leper in Mark, which Luke has already borrowed and repeated in his gospel.[26] All of them appear to have been created by Luke or his community, with perhaps a few exceptions. They cannot be used as the basis for major innovations in reconstructing the activities of Jesus.

However, Luke records a number of sayings and parables that—while unknown from other sources—exhibit features reminiscent of the early Jesus tradition (Table 8). Again, most are parables, parable-like segments, or aphoristic sayings. These are Jesus' primary speech forms. Exceptions to those forms, such as apocalyptic predictions, laments, "I am" sayings, and the like, are of little value in determining the content of Jesus' teachings, since those forms did not originate with him. On the other hand, several of these "L" sayings, especially the parables, are to be

TABLE 8

"L" SAYINGS AND PARABLES

	LUKE
Saying about looking back	9:61–62
Good Samaritan	10:30–35
Friend at midnight	11:5–8
Truly blessed	11:27–28
Rich farmer	12:13–21
Galilean sinners	13:1–5
Sayings about conduct at table	14:7–14
Lost coin	15:8–10
Prodigal son	15:11–32
Shrewd manager	16:1–8a
Rich man and Lazarus	16:19–31
Worthy servant	17:7–10
Corrupt judge	18:1–8
Pharisee and toll collector	18:9–14
Lament over Jerusalem	19:41–44

considered an authentic part of Jesus' teaching. Nevertheless, each item has to be assessed separately in relation to other elements preserved by other sources.

To sum up, Matthew and Luke record quite a number of miscellaneous items, unknown from other sources, some of which are valuable in determining who Jesus was. Bits of oral tradition may well have survived apart from Q and Mark (or Thomas) and been captured in writing only later by Matthew or Luke.

SAYINGS GOSPELS: Q AND THOMAS

Matthew and Luke record a substantial number of sayings and parables, with an occasional anecdote, that they did not take from Mark. The words, phrases, and even sentences are often identical or very similar. It is difficult to believe that they did not have a written text in front of them. In 1838 Hermann Christian Weisse proposed to account for these non-Markan agreements by positing a source, now lost, from which both Matthew and Luke borrowed. The word for "source" in German is *Quelle;* the proposed source was later dubbed "Q" for short, and the designation stuck.[27]

The Q hypothesis has had its dissenters. The argument for a long time consisted in the observation that a collection of sayings without a narrative framework could not constitute a gospel. Then in 1945 came the discovery of the Coptic version of the Gospel of Thomas. As it turns out, three Greek fragments of the same gospel had been discovered earlier, but scholars were unable to identify them except as pieces of an unknown gospel. The Greek fragments can be dated to about 200 C.E. These fragments come from an edition of Thomas that differs substantially from the Coptic version. Thomas was obviously known in more than one version. With the discovery of Thomas, a second sayings gospel had been unearthed, one that overlapped extensively with Q.

Sayings Gospel Q antedates Matthew and Luke, since they both make use of it. Q specialists are inclined to date Q to about 50 C.E., thus making it the earliest written record of the words of Jesus. What about Thomas? On the theory that Thomas went through several editions, some Thomas specialists have proposed dating a hypothetical first edition of Thomas also to the decade 50–60 C.E.

The startling insight this hypothetical scenario brings with it is that collections of Jesus' sayings, without narrative setting, preceded the creation of narrative gospels. Q and Thomas lack any reference to Jesus' death; they lack resurrection stories; they do not have any birth or childhood stories; and, even more significantly, they do not provide narrative settings that might place Jesus' utterances in some historical context.

It suddenly becomes possible to speculate that the Christian overlay found in the New Testament gospels may be just that—an overlay. The original, or at least an original, gospel probably consisted only of a collection of pronouncements attributed to Jesus, in which his birth, death, and resurrection played no role at all. In retrospect, it is intriguing to discover that this possibility had been opened up by Hermann Samuel Reimarus (1694–1768), the first critical scholar of the gospels, when he observed that who Jesus was and what he said may have differed from what the New Testament evangelists report he said and did. From the time of Reimarus, a series of further insights, aided by the discovery of new documents, has further widened the gap between the reality of Jesus and the canonical gospels' description of that reality. One observation has led to another. New evidence has prompted scholars to review and revise earlier judgments. The process seems to know no end.

It is possible that Q also went through more than one edition. There appear to be layers of tradition in Q. If reconstructions of the history of Q are not wide of the mark, the earliest layer of tradition reveals a Jesus who functioned mostly as a secular sage. The material in the Gospel of Thomas supports that suggestion. But whether or not the layering of Q and Thomas is certain, both gospels have been of inestimable help in reconstructing the history of the Jesus tradition.

Identifying Characteristic Speech Forms

The rediscovery of the parables in the 1960s and 1970s made it possible to identify a significant speech form characteristic of Jesus. The parable as Jesus used it is virtually unknown in the Old Testament, and it was rarely successfully imitated in Christian lore. When the Jesus Seminar began its work in 1985, it started with the parables. It did so because several of the Fellows of the seminar had produced pioneering works on the parables. The identification of a speech form distinctive of the historical Jesus gave the seminar the initial impetus it required. The parables lent a positive note at the outset; to a degree, the parables offset the skepticism about the reliability of the tradition that had prevailed among gospel scholars up to that time.

Innovative work on the parables was followed by equally pioneering analyses of the proverbs and aphorisms. True proverbs are folk sayings or maxims that function authoritatively but anonymously within the culture—they do not require a specific author. It is unimportant to know who first said, "An apple a day keeps the doctor away." Such adages are public property. They are general observations about human experience that are taken to be more or less self-evident. An aphorism, on the other hand, is a subversive adage or epigram: it contradicts or undermines folk wisdom. Like the proverb, the aphorism is a witticism: it says as much as possible with as few words as possible. Oscar Wilde is reported to have said, "We wouldn't be so concerned about what people thought of us, if we realized how seldom they did." That is an aphoristic witticism. The presence of aphorisms in the legacy of Jesus tells us that his wisdom ran counter to proverbial folklore, at least in some respects. Folklore, or proverbial wisdom, reflects the regnant sensibilities of a people. Aphorisms contravene that sensibility and endeavor to replace the old perceptions with new. When Jesus remarked, "Leave it to the dead to bury their own dead," he was rebuking those whose hearing had grown dull and infringing the code that insisted on respect for the deceased at the same time.[28] *Anesthesia* is the deadening of all sensibilities; under an anesthetic one is without feeling. Proverbs are deadening: they crystallize the sensibilities one has inherited. Aphorisms take away the deadening effect by opening up a new *aesthesia*—a new perception of the world, of things, of others.

With the parables as a base, the Fellows of the Jesus Seminar were able to sort through the aphorisms looking for features that paralleled the techniques Jesus had used in creating the parables, such as hyperbole and paradox. The initial test of authenticity for aphorisms was thus formal coherence with Jesus' own parable tradition.

During this same period, scholars began a fresh investigation of the anecdote in hellenistic sources. The anecdote or pronouncement story was a form widely used by hellenistic rhetoricians. It appears to have been adopted by the Jesus movement as a part of its oral repertoire. A brief narrative anecdote provides the setting for an exchange between a sage and a student or a sage and a critic. Demonax, a Cynic sage, has this exchange with a student:

> One of his students said,
>> "Demonax, let us go to the Asclepium
>> and pray for my son."
> To this Demonax replied,
>> "You must think Asclepius so deaf he
>> can't hear our prayers from here."

The point of the story is of course to highlight a witticism or clever reply by the sage. Anecdotes were employed as the vehicle for some of the most notable one- and two-liners of Jesus.

The investigation of these speech forms led the Fellows of the seminar to begin their search for the authentic words of Jesus among the many parables, proverbs, aphorisms, and dialogues recorded in the various gospels. It made for a promising beginning.

Sorting Through the Sources

Progress in one area often means progress in another. It is remarkable how seemingly unrelated discoveries and trends converge to form a new cycle in a scientific discipline or sphere of understanding. In the case of the gospels, the discovery of the Coptic Gospel of Thomas at Nag Hammadi triggered a new era in the investigation of the Sayings Gospel Q, with the consequences already discussed. In a nutshell, at the very time scholars were identifying the characteristic speech forms of Jesus, the parable and aphorism, there was a successful attempt to isolate in Q an early layer of Jesus' wisdom that contained mostly aphorisms, proverbs, and parables. The convergence was electrifying. Then came the realization that the overlap between Q and Thomas gave scholars a fresh perception of the history of these sayings: By comparing the versions in Q with those in Thomas, one could often see relatively clear patterns of development. It soon became clear, thanks to the pioneering work of young scholars like Stephen J. Patterson, that Thomas was not a revision of Q; none of the characteristics of the Q tradition reappears in Thomas.[29] On the other hand, it was equally clear that Q was not a revamping of Thomas. Suddenly, scholars were blessed with clarity about two sources, one of them entirely new, that converged with the isolation of the parable and aphorism as speech forms of Jesus.

Now, for the first time, the work of James M. Robinson, John Kloppenborg, Arland Jacobson, and others made it possible to speculate that the earliest layer of Q, together with the parallels in Thomas, provided questers with a source, or sources, that antedated the Gospel of Mark by a decade or two. It appears that Q and some early version of Thomas were created at approximately midpoint between the death of Jesus (about 30 c.e.) and the composition of Mark (70–80 c.e.). The decade 50–60 c.e. became the decade of choice to which to assign the first form of these profoundly important documents.

Establishing Criteria of Authenticity

Success with speech forms and sources prompted Fellows of the Jesus Seminar to formulate other criteria for testing individual parables and sayings.

Foremost among these was the coherence test. Parables had to cohere with other parables in form and content. That was the beginning of the process. Aphorisms were then tested for their coherence with the authentic parables, both in rhetoric and in content. Finally, the acts of Jesus were compared with his words: Did his behavior comport with his teachings? Of course, it is no secret that the acts and words of human beings are not always entirely consistent with each other. That may well have been the case with Jesus. Yet if Jesus had not been reasonably consistent with himself, he would have many faces, and we would have to abandon any effort to isolate that single face in a Galilean crowd.

Scholars noticed other features of the Jesus tradition that helped in the sorting process. Words and deeds that were an embarrassment to the Christian community were not likely to have been invented by that community. There are a number of sayings and deeds that fit this category; they serve no observable apologetic purpose or function for either the evangelists or the Christian community. The baptism of Jesus by John disconcerted the Christian community—of what did Jesus need to repent? And his crucifixion—a very unmessianic thing to have happen— also appears to satisfy this criterion. But even if the messianic hope was not the expectation of Jesus' original followers, they probably were not surprised that new prophets would be persecuted and killed.[30] These two events are thus presumed to be authentic.

Difficult or hard sayings of Jesus tended to be reinterpreted and softened as time went by. We can see that process at work in the gospels. Christians often attributed sayings—and deeds—to Jesus in their admiration for him. They sometimes made him talk like a Christian, to echo their own convictions and beliefs. These and similar rules of evidence assisted the Fellows of the Jesus Seminar in their evaluation of hundreds of items preserved in the gospel records.[31]

There are also negative rules, or rules designed to exclude. Speech of Jesus that belongs solely to the fabric of stories—including words like "hello" and "good-bye"—has probably been supplied by the storyteller. In most such cases, context-bound speech does not consist of actual quotation but reflects the storyteller's idea of what Jesus (or others) might have said on a particular occasion. Hundreds of words were bracketed out by the Jesus Seminar for this reason alone. For example, to the person with a crippled hand in the synagogue, Jesus is made to say, "Get up here in front of everybody."[32] At the lakeshore, Jesus says to his disciples, "Let's go across to the other side."[33] More frequently than not, such words would contribute nothing significant to the content of Jesus' speech, even if they were authentic.

Then, too, as a matter of principle, no words or thoughts ascribed to Jesus when no auditors were present to hear and remember them were accepted as authentic. His prayers in the Garden of Gethsemane, for example, went unheard except for God. His disciples had fallen asleep. The arrest and the flight of his friends followed immediately. How could the evangelist have known what he said on that occasion?

The rigorous application of these criteria, along with others to be described in Chapter Eight, has made it possible to compile an inventory of data on which to base a picture of the historical Jesus. In the search for the bedrock of this tradition, it is wise to give skepticism rein—to enter by the narrow evidential door. If there is serious doubt, exclude. The base will be narrower but more reliable. The database I am utilizing (detailed in the Appendix) in this study comports for the most part with the conclusions reached by the Jesus Seminar. I have added nothing and subtracted nothing that alters the substance of the picture of Jesus that emerges.

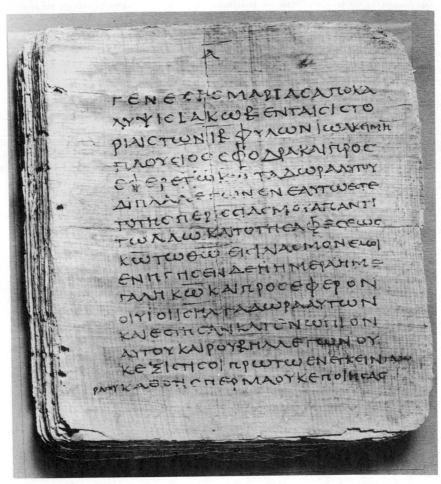

FIGURE 3

Papyrus Bodmer V is a fourth-century C.E. papyrus codex of the Infancy Gospel of James. The codex is the precursor of the modern book. The holes at the left margin indicate that the sheets were sewn together to form a book. Photograph courtesy of the Bibliotheca Bodmeriana, Geneva, Switzerland (see discussion of page 106).

PART TWO

The Gospel
of Jesus

Chapter Eight

THE SEARCH FOR
THE RHETORICAL JESUS

PROCEDURES OF THE SEARCH

Jesus did not say everything ascribed to him in the ancient sources. There are over fifteen hundred variations of the more than five hundred sayings attributed to Jesus. How is it possible to distinguish what Jesus really said from what he is alleged to have said?

We showed how this process was inaugurated by scholars in the previous chapter on the gospels. There we indicated that the earliest sources portray Jesus as a teacher of wisdom, a sage. We identified the parable, proverb, and aphorism as characteristic speech forms of Jesus. And we listed a number of basic criteria for distinguishing materials in the sources. That process must now be expanded by asking four additional questions:

What did Jesus talk about?

How did he talk about it?

What kind of knowledge or wisdom did he communicate?

Did his behavior match his words?

The first question concerns both the theme, the overarching metaphor, of his discourse and the actual topics he discussed, the subjects that he mentioned. The second is a question about his rhetoric—what rhetorical devices did he use in his speech? The third focuses on the content of his knowledge, the kind of wisdom he intended to communicate. The wisdom of Jesus, on close inspection, turns out to concern a kind of knowledge that is different from, although related to, the topics he discussed. The fourth question raises the issue of his character: Were his words translated into action? Was he a student of his own teaching? Did he integrate words and deeds?

In order to make the quantity of data more manageable in our search for the rhetorical Jesus, we will confine ourselves to the catalogue of more than one hundred authentic sayings and actions identified by the Jesus Seminar and compiled in the Appendix. Many of these items are found in the earliest strata of the gospels. They are the speech forms (and acts) most characteristic of Jesus in the memories of his followers. To judge by the content of the Sayings Gospel Q and the Gospel of Thomas, Jesus was remembered for his striking and memorable speech, which often took the form of parables and aphorisms, and for certain acts, which were often parabolic in character.

These materials enable us to establish patterns of Jesus' speech. A good deal of work has already been done on both the parables and aphorisms, so we in fact have a pretty good idea of how he talked. As it turns out, the subject matter of the parables and aphorisms exhibits a remarkable consistency. About both style and content we can make some surprising generalizations. These generalizations provide the means for evaluating other forms of speech Jesus is reported to have used. The same generalizations also enable us to distinguish the core of Jesus' pronouncements from interpretive insertions and additions. They also help us to differentiate Jesus' speech from the interpretive contexts in which the evangelists often located those pronouncements, such as the framing question and answer provided for the parable of the Good Samaritan.

The traits we can observe in his language represent in a general way the "brush strokes" of his style as a word artist. Taken together they provide a kind of voice print. They are the ingredients of the quest for the rhetorical Jesus. When listed as particular features and then generalized, they form the rules of evidence that make it possible to distinguish the authentic speech and behavior of Jesus from what is imitative and derivative.

Distinguishing Jesus from the interpretive overlay provided by the authors of the gospels is a mature, established procedure among gospel specialists. It has been practiced for more than two centuries. We can observe tendencies of the unfolding tradition as it passed from oral speaker to oral speaker and from written source to written source. Those tendencies reveal the directions in which the tradition was developing. Moreover, developmental trends can also be traced in reverse, in the direction of the original, underlying form and content. Isolating those tendencies and trends enables scholars to create a profile of typical Christian ways of reporting and interpreting the words of Jesus.

These procedures make it possible to refine the results of the initial observations and both expand and contract the base of potentially authentic materials.

We will endeavor to exemplify this complex process later in this chapter. Before we do so, however, we should consider some of the criticisms made of this method.

PROBLEMS WITH THE PROCEDURES

Some scholars have found fault with the criterion of dissimilarity. The criterion of dissimilarity has been used as a way of identifying the genuine words of Jesus by contrasting them with both Jewish and Christian lore. In other words, Jesus' sayings were confined to those that are "dissimilar." The criticism, for which there is some real justification, is that such a restrictive maneuver would distort the true picture of Jesus: he would not have said anything that comports with either his Jewish ancestry or his contribution to the emergence of the new Jewish sect called Christianity.

More recently scholars have modulated the term "dissimilar" into "distinctive" to soften the contrast. Jesus may have developed a style that was his own and yet have borrowed some or many features and content from other sages and the wisdom of Israel. Similarly, Jesus may have contributed to the style and content of the message proclaimed by his first followers, in which case they will sometimes sound like him.

Burton Mack has argued that the criterion of dissimilarity is based on a prior assumption that Jesus was a unique individual, one of a kind, by which he intends to suggest that scholars employing this criterion begin with the view that Jesus was divine, God's son, the messiah, or something similar.[1] But that is not necessarily the case. It is undoubtedly true that some Christian scholars do think Jesus must have said novel things because he was the messiah. For them, "dissimilar" may well be a theological rather than a historical category. But it is not a theological ploy to attempt to distinguish the actual words of Abraham Lincoln from what he is alleged to have said. Mack doesn't hesitate to differentiate Paul of Tarsus from his imitators. If the evidence warrants, there is no reason to avoid the historical judgment that Jesus' speech was characterized by certain distinctive features, without implying any underlying theological claims.

Several scholars have expressed outrage at one of the early conclusions reached by the Jesus Seminar—namely, that Jesus was not an eschatological prophet who expected history to come to an end in his own time. Frankly, the Fellows of the seminar were a bit surprised at their own discovery.

The reason the seminar came to that conclusion is simple: The characteristic parables and aphorisms of Jesus proved, on close scrutiny, to be non-eschatological. Indeed, a couple of his sayings indicate that Jesus was critical of the kind of dire warnings made by other prophets, such as John the Baptist. Furthermore, apocalypticism was widely embraced and endorsed in Jesus' day, while Jesus' view of things may have been odd or unusual. The best explanation for this discrepancy between what Jesus said and what his disciples said he said is this: Many of his followers were originally followers of John the Baptist; John was an eschatological prophet, to judge by the sayings attributed to him in Q; after Jesus died, his disciples, who had not understood his sophisticated notion of time, reverted to what they had learned from John and assigned that same point of view to Jesus. This appears to be the best explanation for the contradictory evidence provided by the gospels.

TENDENCIES OF THE UNFOLDING TRADITION

The ways in which Jesus' words and deeds are reported and interpreted as the gospels develop betray certain trends. Observations on these trends provide material assistance in isolating and identifying features of Jesus' discourse. In some cases, such tendencies are relatively obvious. In others the modifications take place slowly and subtly. Three examples will suffice to illustrate the types.

According to an anecdote recorded in Mark, John's disciples and the Pharisees were in the habit of fasting.[2] That is historically plausible since John the Baptist is said to have led an ascetic life with a restricted diet and uncomfortable clothes. He also lived in the desert, presumably to avoid contact with the compromises necessary in urban societies. The Pharisees, for their part, almost certainly advocated fasting. So disciples of John and the Pharisees come to Jesus and ask, "Why do the disciples of John fast, and the adherents of Pharisaism, while your disciples don't?"

The scene as Mark depicts it is undoubtedly contrived. First of all, at issue is the behavior of Jesus' disciples rather than that of Jesus. It seems odd that Jesus' own practice is not mentioned. Second, it would have been an unusual occasion indeed for disciples of John and the Pharisees to join in posing this question to Jesus. After all, the Pharisees were among those "spawn of Satan" who went out to the Jordan to hear John preach. For these reasons, we may be confident that the scene is a fiction as presented. Yet evidence scattered through the gospels makes it all but certain that Jesus did not advocate or practice fasting himself.

On the other hand, we also know that the Christian community resumed the practice of fasting as it began to form its own social agenda during the first century. An early second-century manual of teaching called the Didache instructs Christians to fast on Wednesdays and Fridays rather than on Mondays and Thursdays, when Jews fast. The behavior of Jesus is sandwiched between John the Baptist and the Pharisees, on the one side, and early Christian practice, on the other. The fact that Jesus contrasts with both is solid evidence that he did not fast, at least not as a general rule. Rather, he celebrated life by eating and drinking, as many of his parables attest.

To return to Mark's contrived scene: in response to the question posed to him, Jesus replies, "The groom's friends can't fast while the groom is around, can they? So long as the groom is around, you can't expect them to fast." Jesus apparently thought of life as analogous to a wedding celebration, which was one of the times the peasant world ignored its limited resources and celebrated.

To Jesus' response, however, Mark adds this notice: "But the days will come when the groom is taken away from them, and then they will fast, on that day." This predictive addition betrays the time when Christians had, in fact, resumed fasting and wanted to justify the practice by having Jesus authorize it. The addendum is a piece of self-justifying Christian overlay.

The contrast between the behavior of Jesus and his predecessors and successors is a decisive argument for the reliability of the report that he did not fast: Jesus was convivial, festive, given to celebration, which involved eating and drinking in all kinds of company. At the same time, the reversal tacked on at the end of this scene in Mark indicates that Jesus' behavior was later rejected as a model of Christian practice, and the old ways were reinstated.

A second example illustrates the early Christian tendency to mitigate the harshness of Jesus' aphorisms by softening them. There are three versions of a single saying, with subtle but significant variations:

1. "The last will be first and the first last."[3]
2. "Many of the first will be last, of the last many will be first."[4]
3. "For many of the first will be last, and will become a single one."[5]

The terms of the first example are absolute: the first will be last, the last first, with no exceptions. In the second version, however, the edge is taken off the saying by adding "many." In the third version, the pattern last/first, first/last has been broken and a typical Thomas expression substituted for the second part. When compared with other aphoristic formulations of Jesus, the absolute version must be the original form, since Jesus seems to have preferred uncompromising pronouncements. That is what made them memorable and repeatable. The first version, derived from Q, is probably the original form.

A third example, also derived from Q, is rather more elaborate because it involves the creation of a trio of lines, which is then repeated:

Ask—it'll be given to you;
    seek—you'll find;
    knock—it'll be opened to you

    Rest assured:
    everyone who asks receives;
    everyone who seeks finds;
    and for the one who knocks it is opened.[6]

In this complex, the poet has created a trio of lines, using a different verb in each line. Then a second trio forms the second stanza; the same verbs are repeated. The same grammatical constructions are utilized in each of the lines in the first triple set; in the second group, a different pattern is used in the first two, then Jesus the poet employs a variation in the third as a climax to the series. It is virtually impossible to read these lines in either Greek or in translation without doing so with some rhythm or cadence. It is not certain that the triple verse originated with Jesus, but it probably did, as the development of the tradition suggests.

Thomas preserves a version with only two lines:

One who seeks will find;
for one who knocks it will be opened.[7]

This probably represents a truncation of the original triple form. That suggestion becomes more plausible in view of how the tradition develops: the verse with "ask" gets split off from the other lines and interpreted in connection with prayer:

Trust that you will receive everything you pray and ask for,
and that's the way it will turn out.[8]

Thomas records yet another version:

Seek—and you will find.
Yet what you asked me about in former times
and which I did not tell you then,
now I do desire to tell,
but you do not inquire after it.[9]

In this instance, the "seek" verse is detached from the series of three and given a gnostic setting: the special knowledge that the living redeemer did not give the disciples earlier is now available, but they are unwilling or unable to inquire for it. This is yet another example of the disciples' lack of comprehension, a frequent theme in several gospels.

The Gospel of John knows the "ask" saying but elects to turn it into prose:

Ask whatever you want
and it will happen to you.[10]

The author of the Fourth Gospel probably knew the prayer context reported in Mark, but he doesn't make that explicit in its new context.

We cannot be sure, but the original context for Jesus was his itinerant life: ask, seek, knock, and you will find hospitality wherever you go; God is gracious and will provide. As the Jesus movement became more settled, that original context faded into the background, and the "knock" part of it was lost because it was no longer relevant. The "ask" and "seek" parts could be reinterpreted as requests made in prayer—which preserves echoes of the original context—and as the desire for knowledge. A change in context from Jesus to the Jesus movement led to the modification of the internal structure of the saying and to the reassignment of its meaning.

With these observations in hand, we are ready to return to the four questions posed earlier.

VOICE PRINT

What did Jesus talk about?

Theme: The Kingdom of God

Scholars are universally agreed that the theme of Jesus' discourse was something he called "the kingdom of God," to use the traditional English translation. In the Scholars Version we have translated it as "God's domain" if a place is intended or as "God's imperial rule" when an activity seems to be required by the context. In Jesus' vision, God's domain was that region or sphere where God's dominion was immediate and absolute.

How did Jesus talk about the kingdom of God or God's domain? We can begin to answer that question by observing what kind of language he used.

The Rhetorical Strategies of Jesus

When Jesus talked about this wonderful place, God's estate, he always talked about it in terms drawn from the everyday, the mundane world around him. The language of Jesus, consequently, was concrete and specific. The scenery of his parables and aphorisms consisted entirely of everyday events and topics, of ordinary times, places, and persons. He spoke of dinner parties, of travelers being mugged, of truant sons, of corrupt officials, of a cache of coins found in a field, of poor peasants, of precious pearls, of the hungry and tearful, of lawsuits and conscription, of beggars and lending, of birds and flowers, of purity and defilement, of the sabbath, of wealth, and occasionally of scholars. He also referred to common concerns for food, clothing, and shelter, of parents' gifts to children, of a speck in the eye, of true relatives, of sowing and planting, of jars with broken handles, of evil demons, of doctors and the sick, of crushing debt, of vineyard workers, of weeds and gardening, and of wedding celebrations. He talked about camels and needles, about friends and enemies, about priests and levites, about shrewd managers and persistent widows. His images were drawn from the scene he and his neighbors experienced directly on ordinary days. The landscape and cast of characters he depicted in his parables and the figures of speech he employed in his aphorisms were thus realistic and palpable.

Much to the surprise of the modern reader, he did not develop major themes on the basis of the Hebrew scriptures. He did not cite and interpret scripture. For the most part he did not interpret fine points in the law, and when he did, he tended to parody the legal process. He rarely spoke directly about the temple, the priests, and the sacred ceremonies. His parables and aphorisms did not recount the epic events of Israel's past. He did not borrow concepts from the world of ideas. There are no theological statements and no philosophical generalizations among his formulations. He did not say things like:

I believe in God the Father Almighty

or

God is love

or

Everyone has sinned and fallen short of the glory of God

or

I think; therefore I am.

He began his stories with things like "Suppose a friend comes to you in the middle of the night,"[11] or "Someone has a hundred sheep and one wanders off. . . ."[12] He could and did talk about the healthy who don't need a doctor, or lamps that shouldn't be put under a bushel basket, and rich people who can't find the door to God's domain.

There was, however, an anomaly at the base of his speech. While he spoke unceasingly in mundane terms, his listeners must have perceived that he always had some other subject in mind, to judge by their reported reactions. His basic metaphor, as we observed, was God's reign or God's estate, but he never spoke about it directly. He regularly compared it to something else, without telling his followers how the two things were alike or related. As a result, his language is highly figurative. It is non-literal or metaphorical.

We know that the parable of the leaven is not about baking bread. The parable of the dinner party has nothing to do with social etiquette or with seating patterns at the table. The mustard seed and the sower are not advice about gardening. His admonition on lending has no relevance to banking practices. His advice to give no thought for clothing is not an anti-fashion statement. And so on through dozens of similar examples. It is clear that his ostensible topics—the things he actually mentions, like baking bread—did not constitute the real subject matter of his discourse.

To speak of God's rule—something not immediately observable—in tropes or figures of speech drawn from the sensible world around him is to speak obliquely or indirectly. We know that this was his strategy because his followers remember him warning them about misunderstanding his words ("If anyone here has two good ears, use them"). But we are also certain that he adopted this style because he laces his discourse with tension in a variety of forms.

Tension is a kind of stress or strain that Jesus builds into his speech. He does so in three forms. He makes use of opposing poles or nodes within his speech forms themselves. He builds in a contrast between the expectations of his listeners and the frustration of those expectations in his stories. And he sometimes combines the two when the opposition between characters in his stories matches differences in his listeners. These forms of tension overlap, spill over into each other, and resonate with each other at several levels.

In order to appreciate Jesus' rhetorical strategies and to observe how extensively he employs them, we need to explore those tensions at greater length.

INTERPLAY BETWEEN THE LITERAL AND THE NON-LITERAL   The first form of tension in Jesus' speech consists of the interplay between the literal and the nonliteral. The literal functions effectively as a vehicle for the nonliteral because internal tensions within the literal make it impossible to take the literal merely literally. It is literally implausible, for example, that a Samaritan would stop and render aid to a Judean. It is equally unlikely that an employer would pay all his laborers, no matter how long they worked, the same wage. We will subsequently probe this principle in detail in studies of the good Samaritan and the prodigal son (Chapters Nine and Ten).

ANTITHETICAL COUPLETS   A second form of tension is the contrast between lines in antithetical couplets. An example that may not have originated with Jesus but that he is likely to have quoted is this saying:

Since when do the able-bodied need a doctor?
It's the sick who do.[13]

That may have been Jesus' response to criticism that he associated with social outcasts. In a second example, the second line again contrasts with the first:

What goes into you can't defile you;
what comes out of you can.[14]

In the context of purity regulations concerning kosher foods, the second line stands in tension with the first. It also involves a radical reversal: the wrong food or foods improperly prepared were thought to defile when ingested; Jesus reverses the direction and states that only what comes out can defile. He is probably indulging in a bit of humor. Excrement, which comes out, is defiling, as everyone knows; but there are other things that come out of another aperture in the body—namely, the mouth—that also pollute the social atmosphere.

In other similar reversals of conventional lore, Jesus creates such antithetical couplets as these:

> The sabbath day was created for Adam and Eve,
> not Adam and Eve for the sabbath day.[15]

and

> Foxes have dens, and the birds of the sky have nests;
> but this mother's son has nowhere to lay his head.[16]

Then there is the antithetical pair expressing a paradox:

> Whoever tries to hang on to life will forfeit it,
> but whoever forfeits life will preserve it.[17]

These are all forms of tension built into the fabric of his speech.

Of course Jesus also quoted or composed lines in which the second line repeated, in paraphrase, the thought expressed by the first:

> Figs are not gathered from thorns,
> nor are grapes picked from brambles.[18]

Here is another example:

> Students are not above their teachers,
> Nor are slaves above their masters.[19]

This type of couplet is called synonymous parallelism. Couplets with parallel synonymous lines are often proverbs. We are much less certain that proverbs of this type originated with Jesus because they were so common and so widely quoted. The authenticity of specific examples depends on whether scholars can imagine a plausible historical context in which Jesus might have quoted them. In any case, proverbs do not tell much specifically about Jesus. Since we do not know their original contexts, we cannot be sure of what they meant on his lips.

EVERYDAY LOGIC AS WEAPON   In another strong rhetorical ploy, Jesus turns couplets embodying everyday logic against his critics. For example, Jesus has been accused of being in league with Beelzebul, the head demon, when he exorcizes demons. To this charge he responds with a threefold rhetorical ploy. He begins with a rhetorical question:

> How can Satan drive out Satan?

As a means of getting under or around the logic of his critics, Jesus begins with the obvious as he responds to his own question:

> a If a government is divided against itself,
> b that government cannot endure.
> a If a household is divided against itself,
> b that household cannot survive.

To these self-evident truisms Jesus adds a conclusion:

a If Satan rebels against himself
a′ and is divided,
b he cannot endure
b′ but is done for.[20]

In this series, the first two couplets (governments, households) are synonymous. The third couplet (Satan) functions as the climax. In the climax, Jesus has two *a* clauses and two *b* clauses, corresponding to the two clauses of the first two couplets, but they are much shorter than their earlier counterparts. In other words, the third form is climactic as well as emphatic, but builds on the first two preceding versions that are self-verifying. This rhetorical structure involves repetition, contrast, rhythm, and assonance (the repetition of certain sounds in each clause).

Governments and households torn by division do not last. These assertions are self-authenticating. That creates the expectation that the third example will be equally self-authenticating. But in the third Jesus turns the logic against his interlocutors: If I drive out demons by force of a conspiracy with Beelzebul, then Satan is finished. So whether I do it with or without the assistance of Satan, by your own logic Satan is done for.

Jesus employs a similar rhetorical strategy in many of his narrative parables.

TYPIFICATION, CARICATURE, AND REVERSAL   Jesus trades in other ways in the simplicities of ordinary language. He begins drawing on stereotypes that everyone knows and accepts. He overstates those stereotypes —exaggerates them, caricatures them. And then he detypifies them by reversing the anticipated destinies of players in his dramas.

This is how it works.

The language people employ on an everyday basis is filled with typifications: teenagers are impolite, the wealthy are arrogant, pastors are pious, the government is corrupt. Jesus' language assumes the platitudes of his day: village laborers are indolent and expect more wages than they deserve; justice is not blind because judges are corrupt; sons are ungrateful and wasteful; priests and levites are indifferent to suffering. But he overstates those characterizations—he exaggerates, makes sweeping generalizations, inflates, just enough to bait the listener.

As soon as the hook is set—as soon as the audience is nodding its collective head in approval—Jesus introduces an unexpected twist into the story. His stories are laced with surprise. As with all good jokes and stories, one cannot anticipate the outcome. His listeners did not anticipate that everyone would be invited to the dinner party. They did not expect those hired last to be paid the same as those hired in the morning. They didn't believe things would turn out well for the shrewd manager.

In other words, Jesus detypifies, he defamiliarizes common perceptions. He says the unexpected. He confounds by contradicting what everybody already knows, by reversing those commonplaces his audience has just endorsed with their assent to his opening lines.

Jesus employs repetition in his stories first to confirm and then to undermine habituated perceptions. In the story of the good Samaritan, not one but two clerical parties ignore the victim in the ditch; that reinforces what common people thought of the clergy.[21] In the parable of the dinner party, three guests in succession refuse to come to the party.[22] In the story of the vineyard laborers, the owner hires all day long, right up to the final hour of a twelve-hour workday.[23] These parables begin by building on ordinary expectations, often in exaggerated form, but then they smash those expectations by a surprising turn of events.

This is the means Jesus uses to challenge the entrenched, self-evident facade of the received world. Things, he avers, are not what they seem. He forms his challenge by lampooning what others take for granted. His parables and aphorisms bring to the surface the homespun features of the everyday in order to poke fun at them.

A Pharisee and a toll collector go up to the temple to pray. The first thanks God for the model role he has played in life in contrast to the fellow standing at his side. The second confesses his unworthiness and asks God for mercy. The behavior of the two is caricatured: Pharisees are not that hypocritical, and toll collectors are certainly not that humble. But the story elicits responses from Jesus' audience that contradict the kind of response they might have given had they had their fairness caps on. Jesus' listeners were induced by the parable, perhaps intimidated by it, to give the kudos to the character they would normally have regarded as a sinner and then to scorn the Pharisee.[24] That is a devastating rhetorical device. We will also subsequently explore this strategy at work in the parables of the Samaritan and the prodigal.

PARADOXES   In another form of tension, Jesus indulges the paradox. "Love your enemies"[25] is a contradiction in terms: by definition enemies are the hated. The paradox gave Jesus' original listeners pause because it contradicted their ingrained impulses. For the modern reader, who has heard the aphorism quoted numerous times, its paradoxical bite has been dulled by a leveling familiarity.

In speaking of acts of charity, Jesus advises, "Don't let your left hand in on what your right hand is up to."[26] And elsewhere he asserts you can only save your life by losing it.[27] These are strange pieces of advice, meant to challenge the listener but not meant to be taken literally.

CASE PARODIES   In a series of aphoristic admonitions derived from Q, Jesus makes use of what may be termed case parodies:

When someone slaps you on the right cheek,
turn the other as well.

If someone sues you for your coat,
Give him the shirt off your back to go with it.

When anyone conscripts you for one mile,
go along for two.[28]

These admonitions give the appearance of being a series of particular cases that call for corresponding legal precedents. But, in fact, they parody case law and legal reasoning.

A blow to the *right* cheek would require a left-handed slap, which would be intended not to injure but to humiliate. The left hand was not used publicly in Jesus' society, since it was used for unclean tasks. At Qumran to gesture with the left hand was punishable by ten days of penance.[29] So a backhanded slap to the right cheek was an insult delivered from a superior to an inferior, as Walter Wink has so brilliantly shown: master to slave, husband to wife, parent to child, Roman to Jew. Its message: Get back in your place. Don't put on airs.[30]

To turn the other cheek under the circumstances was an act of defiance. The left cheek invited a right-hand blow that might injure. The master, or husband, or parent, or Roman would hesitate. The humiliation of the initial blow was answered with a nonviolent, very subtle, but quite effective challenge. The act of defiance entailed risk; it was symbolic, to be sure, but for that reason appealed to those who were regarded as subservient inferiors in Jesus' world.

A coat was often given as surety for a loan or debt. The poor could lose their coats under such circumstances, but only during the daylight hours; at night, according to Deuteronomic law, the coat had to be returned since the truly destitute might have nothing else for warmth.[31] Jesus' injunction was to give up both coat and shirt. In a two-garment society, that meant going naked. Nakedness was frowned on, to say the least. Again, according to the Manual of Discipline, one of the Dead Sea Scrolls, accidentally exposing one's nakedness when taking one's hand out of one's robe called for thirty days of penance. Exposing oneself to a companion needlessly drew a penalty of six months.[32] Jesus combined humor with a call for a serious infraction of the social code.

Roman soldiers were allowed to commandeer Judeans for a mile's march to assist with gear. More than that was forbidden. To comply with a conscriptive order meant subservience; to refuse meant rebellion. Imagine the consternation of the Roman soldier when confronted with a Judean offer to carry the pack a second mile.

These examples all refer to real problems, real circumstances. The responses, however, are not prescriptive; they are suggestive of behavior that undermines the intent of the initial act. They prompted Jesus' listeners to think of other cases, other circumstances, in which a comparable response went beyond and undercut the primary aggression. For that reason, they are best thought of as case parodies.

They accurately reflect Jesus' style: he was not a teacher of practical wisdom; he was not an expounder of the fine points of the law; he didn't formulate commandments that governed behavior. He constantly pushed beyond the limits of legal prescriptions and proscriptions into virgin territory.

THE PARODY OF SYMBOLS   Concomitant with the parody of cases was the parody of symbols. To discredit the symbols that support the world under attack was to introduce a new sense of reality. God's domain was a new reality for Jesus. Replacing the old symbolic world could be achieved by understanding those prevailing symbols in something like their opposite sense or by creating a burlesque of them. In a burlesque one gives a serious subject a frivolous or comic twist, or treats a trivial topic as though it were deadly serious. Jesus parodies three symbols: the leaven; the mighty cedar of Lebanon; and an unending supply of meal.

The parable of the leaven turns the symbol of leaven on its traditional head:

> Heaven's imperial rule is like leaven that a woman took and concealed in fifty pounds of flour until it was all leavened.[33]

Leaven is of course nothing other than the yeast that causes dough to rise. In ancient Israel yeast was banned on sacred days:

> You are to observe the feast of unleavened bread, since on this very day I brought your people out of the land of Egypt. . . . For seven days no leaven is to be found in your houses; for if anyone eats what is leavened, that person will be expelled from the congregation of Israel.[34]

Yeast was prohibited in connection with sacrifices and meal offerings as well.[35] In Paul's first letter to the Corinthians, he associates yeast with malice and evil, the unleavened with sincerity and truth.[36] He does so because he was steeped in the tradition that understood yeast to stand for corruption, the unleavened to refer to the sacred.

The parable is about yeast that is "concealed" in fifty pounds of flour. Elsewhere Jesus likens God's domain to a treasure "hidden" in a field. In addition, God "hides" wisdom from the wise and understanding. For Jesus, God's imperial rule is "hidden" from the eyes of the world. Here, too, the new symbol for the sacred, the one that subverts the established tradition, is "hidden."

Fifty pounds of flour translates "three measures" in the Greek text. When Abraham is visited by God at the oaks of Mamre in Genesis 18, he instructs Sarah his wife to make cakes from "three measures" of flour for the occasion. Fifty pounds of flour is enough, it has been estimated, to serve about one hundred souls. Just about the right amount to celebrate an epiphany!

In the span of a single sentence Jesus combines a new symbol, yeast, with mystery and an epiphany to signal God's domain. By so doing he creates a burlesque of the old standard—the unleavened—that used to be associated with the sacred. Now it is what is leavened that is connected with the sacred. To invert the images of the sacred in a society is to subvert its sacred institutions. His word-act was thus understood as an attack on the temple and the temple cult in place in his day.

The parable of the mustard seed parodies the mighty cedar of Lebanon as the symbol of Israel's Davidic hopes. According to the prophet Ezekiel, God will take a twig from the lofty heights of the mighty cedar and plant it on the dizzy heights of Israel.[37] That twig will grow into a mighty haven for birds of every feather, coming from every cardinal direction, who will flock to the shade of its branches. Thus will Israel be exalted. The new, divinely implanted cedar became a symbol of the apocalyptic hope that the Davidic kingdom would be restored.

In contrast, Jesus compares God's domain to the mustard weed, which is short-lived, an annual, and a pain in anyone's garden. Nevertheless, we know it replaces the mighty cedar on the mountain because the birds of the sky come to roost in its branches. It is a very modest tree by comparison with Ezekiel's tree.

Jesus parodies the mighty cedar by turning it into a weed. It retains its ancient function: the birds gather under it for shade and seed. But it is now only a miniature of the expected Davidic restoration. Jesus must be poking fun in a deadly serious vein.

There is a story about Elijah, the great prophet, and a widow of Zarephath.[38] In this story, the widow and her son are starving. She has only a handful of meal in a jar and a little oil in a cruse or cruet. But Elijah is sent to her anyway and told that she will feed him. When Elijah arrives, she is gathering fuel to cook her final meal before she and her son die. She does as Elijah instructs and makes cakes for the three of them. In accordance with the instructions of Yahweh, the meal is not depleted, the oil does not give out, and the three of them eat for many days.

A new Jesus parable came to light in the recently discovered Gospel of Thomas. In this story, called the empty jar, which reiterates many features of the Elijah legend, Jesus caricatures that early tale. A woman is carrying a jar full of meal on her head. As she walks along still some distance from home, a handle on the jar breaks and the meal sifts out through the hole onto the road behind her. She is unaware of what has happened. When she reaches her house, she sets the jar down and finds it empty.[39]

Jesus' parable subverts the tradition that God is powerfully present and at work in the world; he substitutes for it the mystery of God's ostensible absence. Again, Jesus achieves his purpose by comic inversion.

GLOBAL INJUNCTIONS Jesus also creates tension by formulating admonitions that, if carried out, would bring the system crashing down:

> Give to everyone who begs from you.[40]

This injunction endorses the Mediterranean mandate to perform charitable acts. But to respond positively to every beggar in a society in which beggars are ubiquitous would produce financial ruin even for the most affluent.

Another global admonition found in the newly discovered Gospel of Thomas is equally financially disastrous:

> If you have money, don't lend it at interest. Rather, give it to someone from whom you won't get it back.[41]

Jesus appears to have been critical of both banking and the legal system. Injunctions of this type are designed to undermine the system.

HUMOR AND THE CONTOURS OF GOD'S DOMAIN

Jesus was a comic savant. He mixed humor with subversive and troubling knowledge born of direct insight. That was also the technique of Mark Twain and Will Rogers, who might also be described as comic savants. A comic savant is an intellectual—better, a poet—who is redefining what it means to be wise. That is the real role of the court jester: tell the king the truth but tell it as a joke. Jesters consequently enjoyed a limited immunity for their jokes. New truth is easier to embrace if it comes wrapped in humor.

Economically and socially Jesus was a peasant. He was also probably technically illiterate—he may not have been able to read and write. Yet by virtue of his linguistic skills he belonged to the wisdom aristocracy. He could therefore be compared to David and Solomon in the popular culture: he is referred to as a son of David, and there is a Q saying to the effect that Jesus is wiser than Solomon.[42] Attributions of this type eased the way for the transition from Jesus the sage to Jesus the messiah. His rhetorical skills bordered on the magical—he was a word wizard. The combination of his style with the content of his discourse marked him as a social deviant. That may be the reason his mother and brothers thought him daft.[43] It was certainly one of the reasons he was both feared and adored.

What are the characteristics of comic savants?

Avoid Practical Advice

Maxims and platitudes played a significant role in everyday life then, as they do in modern societies. Ordinary and not-so-ordinary people live by epigrams and anecdotes. A comic savant trades in this propensity but then subverts his or her own role by mocking it. Refuse to give practical advice. Or rather, give what appears to be practical advice but what on closer consideration turns out to be useless. As a result, moralisms are foreign to Jesus' authentic pronouncements. Unlike Benjamin Franklin, who coined and quoted many memorable proverbs embodying common wisdom, Jesus would not have said something like

> God helps those who help themselves

or

> Early to bed, early to rise,
> makes a man healthy, wealthy, and wise.

Many of Franklin's proverbs appeared in *Poor Richard's Almanac,* published in 1757. Such statements would have been entirely uncharacteristic of Jesus.

Very few of Jesus' pronouncements constitute practical advice. They have to do, rather, with something that is not stated: namely, how one is disposed to the things that really matter, to what one considers to be the ultimate. Here it is necessary to pause and explore the significance of this feature of Jesus' discourse.

The knowledge most of us have and use daily consists of formulas for performing routine tasks. We know where to go to buy a loaf of bread; we know how to do our job at our place of employment; we can start the car and drive to Aunt Nan's; we know a doctor to consult when we get sick; we routinely prepare and eat meals; we can go to bed without the advice of experts. Knowing how to do all these things and countless other tasks like them is called *recipe* or *procedure knowledge.* Human beings also possess the ability to recall episodes, which is the basis of storytelling. Episode memory and knowledge are not our immediate interest here.

Behind and beyond our recipe knowledge lies a vast region that is dark to most of us. We may have heard of primitive tribes living in the Philippines, seen a TV documentary on life at the bottom of the ocean, read about the Milky Way, and seen diagrams of the structure of the atom. But these regions of knowledge are only vaguely accessible to most of us and are known in detail only by highly specialized scientists. Above all, the nature and purpose of the universe is something we do not regularly ponder. This dark region lies far beyond our ken unless we pause, turn aside from daily cares, and give special attention to such matters.

The topics Jesus discussed in his parables and aphorisms were persons and events in the everyday world. In spite of that fact, and in seeming contradiction to it, Jesus taught his disciples nothing about the performance of routine tasks. His words offer no recipes for achieving mundane goals. His disciples were often puzzled by his lack of interest in pragmatic knowledge. They looked to him for advice they could use in accomplishing routine tasks. He offered them none. In the history of the Jesus tradition, especially in modern times, interpreters have occasionally attempted to extract recipe knowledge from Jesus' teachings, but these efforts have been mostly futile. Jesus' teachings are thin in recipe knowledge.

Because Jesus was concerned with a different kind of knowledge, knowledge that lies beyond the practical, he gave no practical advice, refused to be explicit, and avoided endorsements. His attention was riveted on his Father's will, on the order and purpose of creation, on the way things really are rather than the way they seem to be.

Refuse to Be Explicit

Jesus steadily refuses to be explicit. Explicitness is characteristic of an established world, of habituated society, where patterns of behavior are settled. In Jesus' own vision of the world, everything is in flux because its inhabitants are departing, crossing over to a new time and place. When Jesus is asked whether to pay the tax, he tells his listeners, "Pay the emperor what is due the emperor and pay God what is due God." He advises them to set their own priorities; in sum, he refuses to answer the question for them.

When asked about keeping kosher, he responds, "It is not what goes in that pollutes but what comes out." He then leaves it to his audience to decide which human orifice he has in mind.

The kingdom of God for Jesus was always beyond the here and now; it was the world being created anew. It was always outstanding. About that world one can never be entirely explicit. All one can say is this: If you think you know what it is, you are mistaken. That future will be a perpetual surprise. If it were not so, human beings would trust themselves and not God.

Avoid Endorsements

The new language Jesus is creating, like the new world, is tenuous, subject to revision at any moment. It is order being formed in the face of chaos. It is advanced playfully, without external endorsement or sanction. It is announced and allowed to commend itself for what it is. Jesus does not attempt to impose his views on others. His Father is not a cosmic bully. Jesus himself was not a moralist—he does not advise people how to live or how to behave.

Jesus advises his followers to avoid lawsuits. If someone sues to acquire one's outer garment for unpaid debt, he advises that person to give the litigant the shirt off one's back to go with it. He suggests settlement with one's adversary on the way to court.[44] That advice, if taken literally, undercuts the legal system. The judge has no cases to try and the lawyers go unpaid. Ordinary folk like suggestions that defeat the legalists and undermine the pomposity of the law. But commoners hesitate to adopt radical solutions. Jesus was not endorsing revolution; he was recommending compliance with the law, but with a wink at the defendant.

Create a New Fiction

The first step in crossing the Jordan into the promised land is to transform the habituated world in fantastic ways. Jesus makes a Samaritan the hero-rescuer of a Judean;[45] he has a landowner pay day laborers in the vineyard the same wage for twelve hours as for one hour of work;[46] those who could not have expected an invitation to a state banquet are swept into the royal hall;[47] the wayward son is given an extravagant welcome home to the dismay of the older son.[48] Jesus' narrative parables are the primary vehicles of the new fiction.

Act on That Fiction

Jesus associated with petty tax officials. He is seen in public in the company of women and engages in serious exchange with them. He welcomes children, the chattel of Mediterranean society. He belittles reality experts, like Pharisees and scholars, by calling attention to their need for recognition and privilege. He asks nothing for himself, other than bread for the day. He takes no thought for clothing or shelter. He has no place to sleep at night. He forgives everyone. He loves his enemies.

To make sure it is all real, ritualize, ritualize, ritualize. To ritualize means to celebrate, to solemnize with appropriate rites. It also means to refrain from ordinary business, and to memorialize in new and exalted language and rites.

Jesus' discourse and deeds are filled with celebration. A woman celebrates the recovery of a lost coin;[49] a shepherd ritualizes the finding of a lost sheep;[50] a father solemnizes the return of a prodigal son.[51] A royal dinner party is given for the homeless and destitute.[52] Jesus himself reclines at public table with toll collectors and prostitutes in defiance of the social code.[53] His initial public meal took place at a wedding, according to the Gospel of John;[54] his final meal was a celebration with his intimate followers.[55] Jesus acts in accordance with the contours of his own vision.

Jesus employs language at the level at which word and act cannot be clearly distinguished. His pronouncements are often tantamount to acts, and his acts often "say" something striking.

A leper comes up to him and says, "If you want to, you can make me clean." Jesus responds, "Okay, you're clean."[56] The fact is an integral part of the pronouncement. Whether Jesus actually altered the physical condition of the leper, we cannot say, but it is certain that he altered the social status of the sufferer.

To the paralytic who was lowered through the roof into Jesus' presence, Jesus says, "My child, your sins are forgiven."[57] With that the paralytic is cured.

To his audiences Jesus remarks, "Congratulations, you poor! God's domain belongs to you."[58] That assertion redefines their status.

Jesus awards God's domain to the destitute, he cures paralysis by forgiving sin, and he awards a leper a clean bill of health, all with his words.

There is a profound difference between a new theory of reality and a new reality: in the first, the distinction between word and act are maintained; in the second, that distinction is blurred. In theories of the real, the old self that goes with the old reality is preserved, while the new reality is entertained as an "idea." When a new reality is truly actualized, the old self is transformed into a new self that corresponds to the new reality.

Jesus inhabited the world of his aphorisms and parables: in him word and deed were congruent.

FEATURES OF THE CHRISTIAN OVERLAY

The rhetorical tactics of Jesus reveal that he spoke with a fresh authority. He did not quote proof texts from the scriptures to prove his points. There are no "footnotes" in his discourse; he does not cite other authorities to endorse his claims. He does not look to Moses or the prophets or the sages of Israel for his wisdom. He does not invoke precedents. His knowledge is born of direct insight. He appeals directly to his audience, to their world, to their perceptions of their world, to the logic inherent in what he takes to be the true order of things. To him, the requirements of God's domain are obvious and endorse themselves. Jesus' vision of God's estate provides the standard by which all truth is to be measured.

It is virtually axiomatic for interpreters to say that Jesus was proclaiming a message. He did indeed do that. But it is more important to observe that he was also receiving a message. Jesus told his parables as though he were hearing them. He gave expression to the vision of which he himself was the recipient. The demands of that vision were demands made on him. Rather than making assertions about the world, about God, about himself, he allowed himself to be claimed. The kingdom of God was announcing itself. He was transfixed by a vision that both captivated and liberated him, as Ed Beutner puts it. He was the victim, eventually, not primarily of the civil and religious authorities but of his own vision. It is very difficult to remember this reversal of roles—Jesus as listener rather than Jesus as speaker—when reciting the creed. We will return to this crucial point in the epilogue, where we will observe that the story plot of the creed overwhelms and effaces the Jesus of the parables and aphorisms.

It is unthinkable, in view of the parables and aphorisms, that Jesus said many of the things he is reported to have said. He certainly did not make claims for himself. To have done so would have contradicted his fundamental disdain for arrogance and hypocrisy and run counter to his rhetorical strategies, such as the reversal of roles so common in his parables. Sayings like those we find in the Fourth Gospel could not have originated with Jesus:

I am the light of the world.[59]

As God is my witness, I existed before there was an Abraham.[60]

I am the way, and I am truth, and I am life. No one gets to the Father unless it is through me.[61]

Furthermore, he seems not to have been given to summary judgments of others. A saying like another found in the Gospel of John is atypical of the Jesus of the parables and aphorisms:

You are your father's children all right—children of the devil.[62]

Since he was not an eschatological prophet like John the Baptist and since he was not a moralist, he probably did not call for repentance in view of some impending judgment. We may then conclude that Mark 1:15 is a formulation of Mark, or of the community prior to Mark, rather than a reflection of something Jesus said:

The time is up: God's imperial rule is closing in. Change your ways, and put your trust in the good news!

Jesus may have called for trust in the good news, but the balance of this summary probably originated with Mark rather than Jesus, as many scholars have concluded.

All of this makes it very unlikely that Jesus would have predicted his own death and resurrection, as reported in Mark:

The son of Adam will be turned over to the ranking priests and the scholars, and they will sentence him to death, and turn him over to foreigners, and they will make fun of him, and spit on him, and flog him, and put him to death. Yet after three days he will rise![63]

Had Jesus anticipated his own resurrection, it would have made a mockery of his suffering and death: had he known that his life would not end, his death would not have been the sacrifice Christian interpretation has alleged. These passion predictions in Mark conform to newly acquired Christian convictions about Jesus, convictions so powerful they are read back into history and placed on the lips of Jesus as prophecy. Unfortunately, they also partially obscure the underlying memories of the humble sage from Galilee.

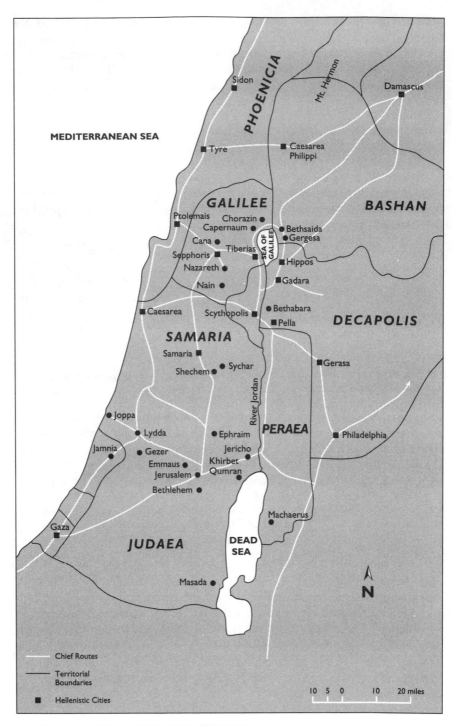

FIGURE 4: PALESTINE IN THE TIME OF JESUS

Chapter Nine

IN THE BEGINNING
WAS THE PARABLE

IN THE BEGINNING

In the beginning was the parable. The parable, for Jesus, was a window on the world: through that window Jesus looked out on familiar scenes —a harvest of grapes, dinner parties, mustard growing in a field, a woman baking bread—and saw these common realities in an entirely new light. For him, the logic of life had been radically revised. Jesus' parables and aphorisms are doors opening on to an alternate construal of reality. The vista through those doors takes one back to the dawn of time, to chaos giving way to order. Parable is genesis. Parable is creation.

Jesus names this new logic God's imperial rule, or, in traditional language, the kingdom of God. In that realm, in God's domain, people and things do not behave in expected ways. In Jesus' imagined world, normal, everyday expectations are regularly frustrated.

For Jesus the everyday perception of the world was false, deceptive, misleading. For most other people, the ordinary world was the only world there was. In fact, according to Jesus, the habituated world obscured the real world, where his Father, God, had absolute dominion. That is why he called it "God's domain." For the ordinary person, the everyday was solid, stable, and unrelenting: it would not go away, no matter how much one wished it to do so, except, perhaps, at some future date, when the whole earth would be consumed by fire and creation transformed. People like Jesus who thought there was another reality already present, one the average Judean did not recognize, were to be regarded as mad and dangerous, possibly possessed by an evil demon. According to the Gospel of John, that is precisely what Jesus' critics thought of him:

> The Judeans replied, "Aren't we right to say, 'You're a Samaritan and out of your mind'?"[1]

It is bad enough to be put down by your critics, but when your own family joins in the chorus of accusations, it becomes a threat to self-identity in a society based on honor and shame, in which the status of individuals was determined by what their relatives and neighbors thought of them:

> Then he goes home, and once again a crowd gathers, so they could not even grab a bite to eat. When his relatives heard about it, they came to get him. (You see, they thought he was out of his mind.)[2]

The charge that Jesus is demented indicates that the world Jesus had in view as he spoke was organized quite differently from the world his friends and neighbors took to be certified by everyday experience. We should explore that difference in a preliminary way before engaging the parables themselves.

GOD'S IMPERIAL RULE: NOW OR LATER?

In conventional lore among pessimists, ancient and modern, God's dominion prevailed prior to the fall of Adam and Eve in the garden and is to be restored at the end of the age when a line will be drawn across history and a new era inaugurated. The innocence that prevailed prior to the fall will be restored at the end of time. Between the times, evil and hostile cosmic powers, together with rebellious humankind, will thwart the will of God in one way or another.

For this-worldly optimists, on the other hand, God's kingdom had prevailed during the time of the Israelite monarchy under David and Solomon, and it had returned briefly under the Maccabees in the second and first centuries B.C.E. with the renewal of the temple in Jerusalem and the expulsion of foreign powers. Yet "God's reign" had been interrupted during the exile, which began for the northern kingdom in 722 B.C.E., when Israel fell to the Assyrians, and for the southern kingdom in 586 B.C.E., when the Babylonians captured Jerusalem and relocated many Judeans to Mesopotamia. It was suspended again when the Romans arrived in Jerusalem in 63 B.C.E. in the person of Pompey. In Jesus' time the earthly reign of God under Judean rulers was as remote as ever.

For Jesus, God's domain was not a royal or political kingdom such as the Israelites had under David and Solomon. Nor was God's rule to be established apocalyptically. So it was not something for which he and his neighbors had to wait in the age to come, after ordinary history had come to an end. Jesus' talk about the reign of God did not refer to a geographical area or a political entity but to a set of relationships that actually obtain, or should obtain, between creator and creatures, between God and the world.

In Jesus' vision, the old age was ending and the new age beginning right there and then. It is difficult for the modern mind to imagine how profoundly this conviction altered the landscape of Jesus' everyday world, how radically it modified his notion of how to behave and think. And it did so in new and unusual ways. He apparently did not require a David or a Judas Maccabeus as a divine agent to reinstate God's domain. And he did not seem to anticipate the appearance of the son of Adam coming with clouds—clouds indicate the divine presence with their luminous brilliance, yet they also veil the deity—to restore God's order.

The first and most difficult point for us to grasp is that this change had *already* taken place for him. He did not need to argue for it, he did not cite prophecy that it was to take place, he did not calculate the day or hour when it was to arrive. For him the furniture of the world had already been rearranged. God's estate was present everywhere; it was just difficult to detect its reality with habituated eyes. To catch sight of it, one had to see with naked eyes and hear with unobstructed ears. Jesus seems never to have doubted that the kingdom of his vision was more real than the deceptive landscape taken for granted by others. God's rule was an evident if inexplicable fact to which he could only submit.

When asked why its reality was not obvious to others, according to the Gospel of Thomas, he replied:

> God's imperial rule will not come by watching for it. It will not be said, "Look, here it is!" or "Look, there it is!" Rather, the Father's imperial rule is spread out upon the earth, and people don't see it.[3]

Another version of this saying is found in Luke:

> You won't be able to observe the coming of God's imperial rule. People are not going to be able to say, "Look, here it is!" or "Over there!" On the contrary, God's imperial rule is right there in your presence.[4]

In spite of these pronouncements, Jesus' interpreters, ancient and modern, have often said and still do say that Jesus predicted that God would intervene in the near future and put an end to history. They claim he endorsed the widespread apocalyptic expectation so prevalent in his day. This claim is based on sayings like these found in the Gospel of Mark:

> But in those days, after that tribulation, the sun will be darkened, and the moon will not give off her glow, and the stars will fall from the sky, and the heavenly forces will be shaken! And then they will see the son of Adam coming on clouds with great power and splendor. And then he will send out his messengers and will gather the chosen people from the four winds, from the ends of the earth to the edge of the sky! . . . I swear to you, this generation certainly won't pass into oblivion before all these things take place![5]

Other scholars, including many Fellows of the Jesus Seminar, believe that such predictions were not characteristic of Jesus but expressions of the message of John the Baptist and his followers. If we take his parables and the kingdom sayings that we have quoted from Thomas and Luke as the true index to his views, Jesus was certain that God's rule was already present—people just couldn't see it. For him the future was fused together with the past in the intensity of the present moment to such a degree that he did not distinguish the past, present, and future as modes of time. In the company of other seers and poets, he experienced the confluence of the tenses in his vision. He stood there in Galilee, back again at the moment of creation, so to speak, and, at the same time, he was also there at the end of time in his vision of God's imperial rule. There is no other way adequately to explain his words and his behavior.

Jesus took his own ability to expel demons as evidence that God was directly at work in the world restoring creation: the old cosmic powers were being defeated. When asked for evidence that the creator's control of creation was being renewed, he referred to the defeat of these contrary forces:

> But if by God's finger I drive out demons, then for you God's imperial rule has arrived.[6]

When accused of being in league with Satan, Jesus responded that whether he was or not, Satan's reign was done for.[7] Jesus' world was demon-infested. He believed that he was out from under the power of these evil spirits and was in a position to help others gain liberation from their control. Yet it was to be another millennium and more before the Western world would begin to recognize the fall of Satan from heaven. Indeed, even under the spell of the empirical sciences in the modern world, many continue to ignore their sway and pay homage to the spirits and stars that allegedly control human destiny. Nevertheless, it was the rise of a strict monotheism that opened the way for the advance of the scientific spirit. Jesus of Nazareth was a distant precursor of this revolution.

If such generalizations do in fact represent Jesus' views, he can hardly have shared the apocalyptic outlook of John the Baptist, Paul, and other members of the early Christian community. The apocalypticism of the Book of Revelation is entirely foreign to Jesus' convictions about God's rule. We can understand the intrusion of the standard apocalyptic hope back into his gospel at the hands of his disciples, some of whom had formerly been followers of the Baptist: they had not understood the subtleties of Jesus' position, they had not captured the intensity of his vision, and so reverted to the standard, orthodox scenario once Jesus had departed from the scene.

On the whole, Jesus was not directly critical of the visions of Ezekiel and Daniel. He simply did not develop the prevailing line of thought either positively or negatively. He devoted his discourse rather to describing the terrain of this divine domain beyond the frontiers of the everyday —just beyond the end of the average nose. It was as though he were looking across the Jordan of his imagination to the promised land. He spoke of this fantastic country in figures and tropes that were not always understood by his followers. As a consequence, they had difficulty remembering what he had said. They were hard of hearing because they were hard of seeing. He used to say, "Anyone here with two good ears had better listen!" as though one could easily see what he saw. Instead, they—and others centuries later—are held captive by eyes that see not and ears that hear not.

THE KINGDOM AS FRONTIER

In the gospel of Jesus, God's domain is understood as a frontier beyond which there was a new but unobserved region. Like Abraham, Jesus was embarked on a journey to the holy land, and, like Moses, he was leading an exodus. He was on the way out of Egypt, prepared to cross the inhospitable desert before entering the promised land. In his vision, human beings all begin on the near side of that fabulous frontier: crossing it is a task to be repeated again and again as the mundane world closes in and obscures the view.

A *frontier* is a dividing line between civilization and the wilderness. It separates settled country from unsettled territory, the known, inhabited, and reliable from the unknown, uninhabited, and unpredictable.

A frontier is a hypothetical line of demarcation. It is a movable marker. The American frontier, for example, moved from the Atlantic to the Hudson River, to the Appalachians, to the Mississippi, to the Rocky Mountains, and then jumped later into space. The true line of demarcation between settled, civilized country and unexplored and unoccupied territory is in the mind. True frontiers are not on any map; they are in the head.

Because a frontier marks off civilization from wilderness, it is something across which there is conflict. Pioneers cross frontiers in order to tame—domesticate—the wild country beyond. Among pioneers there are heroes who become mediators for those who come after. A mediator is needed to interpose between regions at variance with each other. In the myth of the American West, the mountain man was the mediator between settled towns and a hostile wilderness filled with wild beasts and savages. The cowboy succeeded the mountain man when the frontier was redefined as the line between open, unfenced cow country and fenced, cultivated farmland.

The parables of Jesus mark the frontier of a new reality. They mediate that reality by helping those on this side of the frontier cross over to the world beyond. That "beyond" is an alternative reality, a country strangely familiar but also frighteningly new. Those who glimpse that far country are both charmed and repulsed; they are simultaneously attracted and repelled.

The parables are doors opening onto that reality just as doors open onto rooms and houses. The parables function both as an entrance and as a guide to the contours of the new territory. They are also an invitation to cross over.

For those who choose to cross over, there will be conflict. The conflict arises out of the clash of the old, the familiar, the comfortable, with the new, the innovative, the strange. Jesus is a heroic figure because he has ventured through the apertures of his own parables and aphorisms. But the invitation extended by his parables to join the exodus from the inherited world of the everyday offers the new reality only on its own terms. Jesus does not promise that the parabolic domain can be effortlessly occupied, that it will be settled easily without a wrench.

It is time to explore one parable in quest of its metaphorical frontier. I have chosen the so-called good Samaritan because it is paradigmatic both of the potential of parables and of the moralistic misinterpretation that obscures what parables are about. For millions over the centuries, good Sam has been a good neighbor. The rest of his name has been buried under an avalanche of familiarity. We have to allow his name to evoke the hostile response it did originally.

GOOD SAM

The parable of the Samaritan is traditionally taken as an example story illustrating what it means to be a good neighbor. This interpretation goes all the way back to Luke the evangelist, who recorded the parable out of special tradition preserved by him alone. On the lips of Jesus, however, it was probably intended to introduce the listener to the contours of the world as Jesus saw it under the direct rule of the God he called Father. In this case, to say that Jesus saw the world in such and such a way is also to say that he inhabited a world of just those dimensions. The shape of the world in Jesus' parabolic vision was his *life world*—the world within which he actually lived. Luke's (mis)understanding of the Samaritan as an example story is a moralizing interpretation, which, in fact, robs the story of its parabolic character. But that is to anticipate how the parable itself provokes the listener or reader to understand it. We should begin with the parable itself; here it is in a fresh translation:

THE GOOD SAMARITAN

This guy was on his way down to Jericho from Jerusalem when he was waylaid by thieves. They robbed him, beat him up, and ran off, leaving him for dead. By chance a priest was on his way down that road; when he spied the victim, he went out of his way to avoid him. Similarly, when a levite came to the place, he, too, took one look at him and passed by on the far side of the road. In contrast, there was this Samaritan who was also traveling that way. When he came to the place where the victim lay, he was moved to pity at the sight of him. He went up to him, treated his wounds with oil and wine, and bandaged them. He hoisted the fellow onto his own animal, brought him to an inn, and cared for him. The next day he took out two silver coins, which he gave to the innkeeper with these instructions, "Look after him, and on my way back I'll reimburse you for any extra expense you've had."

Gospel of Luke 10:30–35; Scholars Version revised

The parable opens with a man, undoubtedly a Judean (Judeans were the ancestors of the Jews), jogging down that lonely and treacherous road from Jerusalem to Jericho. (The Roman road today remains a lonely and treacherous road, passing as it does through a desolate wilderness.) He gets waylaid, just as those of us in Jesus' audience familiar with local roads and bandits expect, and, because we are sympathetic listeners and Judeans, we assume the perspective of the victim in the ditch. In other words, the listener (Jesus was an oral teacher) adopts the point of view suggested by the story and awaits further developments.

First the priest and then the levite pass by. If we are anticlerical, as many common folk in those days were, we are delighted to have our opinions confirmed—the priestly clan that ran the Jerusalem temple operations are a self-serving lot. But those associated with the temple and its many social, economic, and religious functions will want, as the story unfolds, to pause and debate whether there were good and sufficient reasons to pass on without stopping. As religious leaders, we want to exercise good judgment and consider the situation from all angles. But the storyteller ignores the inclination to debate the issues and the story moves ahead.

Parable interpretation for Jesus is allowing oneself to be drawn into the story as the story line dictates, and then to face the choices the plot presents. At our great remove from the original context in which the terms of the story resonated with meaning, we must allow ourselves to step back and fill in the missing nuances. In that process, it is as important to note what the story does *not* say as to focus on what it does say.

Developments as portrayed in the text have opened up a preliminary division in the audience—or so we imagine. On the one side are the common folk who side with the victim; they agree that the Jericho road is no place to travel alone, and they are modestly bemused by the behavior of the clerics, whom they know to have a callous indifference to such ordinary occurrences. On the other side are the chagrined priests and their lay assistants, the levites, who immediately stiffen when the story makes them out to be unseeing and uncaring. Into the tension between these two segments of Jesus' society rides the Samaritan astride his ass. It is difficult to exaggerate the negative response a Judean audience would have given to the appearance of a sympathetic Samaritan (we will explore the reason for this hostile response later). The resistance of the clergy now becomes open revolt, as this hated interloper appears on the scene. And the ordinary folk, "the people who belong to the land," as they are called in Hebrew, begin to desert the ditch they initially shared with the victim: they like the intrusion of this foreigner even less, especially when he is given the hero's role to play.

In all of this, of course, I am imagining the way in which those in Jesus' audience must have responded. I am being guided by clues taken from the story itself and from what we know historically of the four characters who appear in the narrative.

We should linger for additional observations on the story itself. This will help avoid the mistake frequently made in popular biblical interpretation: the interpreter, in a rush to get to the moral of the story, forsakes the text prematurely and hastens to some point previously determined, usually without reference to the story itself. The story then becomes merely the occasion for the interpreter to affirm some conviction previously ascertained on some other basis. Much popular biblical interpretation is of this sort.

There are several things to notice about this story. It is very brief. It contains a minimal amount of information. The parsimony of information suggests that the narrator mentions only the details that are significant. We should therefore pay attention to specifics. This parable, like other narrative parables of Jesus, follows the law of three, so common in folktales the world over: there are three responses to the victim in the ditch, and those responses are narrated in three scenes. The stage is set with the beating and robbery. Then the responses of the first two travelers are reported in two extremely brief scenes.

The Samaritan is introduced in a more leisurely way, his reaction and action are described in considerable and vivid detail, and the third scene is drawn out with the trip to the inn. Then, with the audience now seething with rage, the listeners are made to spend the night and observe more of the exaggerated goodness of this hated alien the following morning. The structure of the narrative—two abbreviated negative responses and one elaborate positive response—conveys its own subtle message.

Jesus was evidently given to caricature and exaggeration. His parables function something like modern cartoons that exaggerate the features of a person or event for the sake of immediate and humorous recognition and to make a point.

The plot is simple: two travelers ignore a robbery victim on a desolate and dangerous road that runs down the steep grade from Jerusalem to Jericho in the Jordan valley, while a third, a Samaritan, who could not have been expected to assist a Judean victim, stops and renders aid. The story does not provide information about the background or character of the individuals, beyond their basic identification as priest, levite, and

Samaritan. Each is made to stand for what is taken as the "typical" behavior of the entire group. Priest and levite, of course, are members of closely related groups devoted to temple service. As a consequence, the contrast in behavior is between clerical religious leaders, on the one hand, and the half-breed Samaritan, on the other. In spite of its brevity and minimal detail, the parable sets up powerful tensions to which those in Jesus' audience would have responded without prompting. Why would two religious leaders deliberately ignore this unlucky victim? Why would a foreigner without any affection for Judeans stop and assist? Does not this combination of events make the tale simply unbelievable?

Indeed, we do not know whether the story mirrors an actual event or whether it is pure fiction. It is not important to decide. What we can determine is that the narrative is a caricature—a ludicrous exaggeration —of what average, ordinary people took to be the case in that day. The normal Judean did not think highly of Samaritans (the Samaritan woman at the well is surprised that Jesus, a Judean, would ask her for a drink). The Judean listeners probably doubted that there was a Samaritan in the world who would help a Judean victim. The religious authorities certainly thought highly of themselves, but it would immediately have occurred to them that contact with blood or with a dead body would defile them and render them ineligible for temple service. There were thus good and sufficient reasons not to stop. Undoubtedly, some in the audience would have nodded their heads in silent approval at the depiction of the priest and levite as completely engrossed in their own importance and safety, to the exclusion of other concerns. The story herds listeners into separate social corrals of their own devising. Why did Jesus concoct the tale in just this way?

The answer lies in Jesus' rhetorical strategy: he constructs the story so as to catch the listener offguard. C. H. Dodd, a great British scholar of the New Testament, defined a parable this way:

> The parable is a metaphor or simile drawn from nature or common life, arresting the hearer by its vividness or strangeness, and leaving the mind in sufficient doubt about its precise application to tease it into active thought.[8]

Dodd might have written that the parable arrests the hearer by its caricature, hyperbole, or satire, and he might have said that it provokes the listener to adopt a position, rather than simply teasing the mind. Dodd makes the parable a more cerebral operation than is appropriate to the elusive nature of Jesus' style. Nevertheless, his definition characterizes the parables as subtle constructions that develop in such a way that the listener is trapped before he or she realizes it.

There are very few parables in the Hebrew scriptures that approximate Jesus' technique. However, Nathan the prophet is credited with a parable that he narrates to King David. It runs like this:

Two men lived in this city. One was rich, the other poor. The rich man possessed large flocks and herds; the poor man had nothing except a young ewe that he had bought. He raised it like one of his children, sharing his food with it and allowing it to drink from his cup. The ewe would lie in his lap; it was like a daughter to him.

It so happened that a traveler arrived at the rich man's house just then. The rich man was unwilling to slaughter one of his own flock to satisfy the law of hospitality, so he seized the poor man's ewe and prepared it for the stranger.

2 Samuel 12:1–4

When David heard this story it made him angry. He took it literally, of course, and told Nathan that the man who had done such a thing ought to be put to death. Nathan said to David, "You are that man." This cleverly disguised accusation succeeded in evading David's wariness by baiting it with an incident that evoked moral outrage. Jesus employed similar techniques in his parables.

LITERAL FOUNDATIONS

The Samaritan works as a parable because it is loaded with heavily freighted literal, social, political, and religious terms. The Jericho road was a lonely and dangerous road. The priests were powerful upper-class authorities governing the temple cult, and the levites were the priests' associates, providing music, incense, sacred bread, temple curtains and adornments, and administration for a national business that included "kosher meatpacking" and banking. The importance of the cult for the economic well-being of Jerusalem cannot be overestimated. Herds and flocks were in constant demand for sacrificial offerings, and the influx of pilgrims at festival times required money changing and banking. Priests and levites were known to have quarters in the Jordan valley near Jericho where they retreated from the beehive of activity surrounding the temple on ordinary days, to say nothing of feasts. The opulence of the priestly class was an irritant for the ordinary Judean, in spite of his or her devotion to the law and the sacrificial system.

The initial face of the story invites the reader to take it in its everyday and literal sense. In other words, the narrative gains the assent of the listener by affirming everyday reality, the world as everyone knows it. The story thus rests on a stock of images that are current, concrete, and cogent.

The everyday and literal sense of the narrative, however, is also laced with barbs. What would have incensed the listeners is the brusque treatment of the priests and levites and the complimentary picture of the Samaritan. Indeed, it is the Samaritan who turns the story into a parable.

The Samaritans were a bastard race by Judean standards. They were presumably descended from Israelites who had remained behind when the Assyrians deported the leading families of the region following their conquest in 722 B.C.E. The Israelites remaining behind intermarried with foreign settlers brought in by the Assyrians in the years that followed, although the Samaritans—the new ethnic group—continued to regard the Torah as their law. They erected their own temple on Mount Gerizim, just outside Shechem (modern Nablus), at a time when there was no temple in Jerusalem. John Hyrcanus, a Maccabean ruler, destroyed that temple during his reign (134–104 B.C.E.) and so raised enmity between the Judeans and Samaritans to a new level of intensity. In Luke, Jesus is made to refer to the grateful Samaritan leper as an alien, a foreigner.[9] To call someone a Samaritan was a term of insult; in John, Jesus is called a Samaritan and a madman.[10] The two epithets were taken as synonymous. Samaritans were regarded by Judeans as gentiles, as outside the scope of God's chosen people, in spite of the fact that Samaritans claimed Moses as their teacher and ancestor. In fact, the Samaritans claimed they were descended from the patriarchs, Abraham, Isaac, and Jacob.

Galilean pilgrims on their way to Jerusalem for festivals often went through Samaria, which separated Galilee on the north from Judea to the south. The only way to avoid transit through this hostile territory was to cross the Jordan south of the Sea of Galilee, journey south through Transjordan or Perea, and then recross the Jordan at Jericho, to ascend to Jerusalem along the Jericho road. (Consult the map on p. 164 for a layout of the land.)

Josephus records one incident that illustrates the enmity between the two groups. In 52 C.E., a group of Galilean pilgrims was attacked and some of them were killed after they crossed the border into Samaria at the village of Jenin. In retaliation, Judean guerrilla forces from Jerusalem raided some Samaritan villages, slaughtered the inhabitants, and burned the towns. The Romans intervened; they crucified or beheaded numerous notables on both sides of the conflict and delivered one of their own tribunes, who had bungled his job, over to the people of Jerusalem. They then dragged him through the streets behind a horse and had him beheaded. It is thus understandable that the labels *Samaritan* and *Judean* stood in considerable tension with each other.

Those who listened to Jesus tell the parable of the Samaritan, as good Judeans, would have expected the third person along that road to be a Judean. The hero of the story would naturally have been one of them. How shocked they must have been when that figure turned out to be a hated Samaritan. At the mention of the Samaritan, Judean listeners would have bristled, rejected the plot, and quit the story, in spite of their initial inclination to give it a sympathetic hearing.

Those who refused the narrative were those who identified themselves literally with participants in the story. Some Judeans, priests, and levites took themselves literally and so were offended. There were probably no Samaritans present. Had there been, they, too, would have suffered indignity at the thought of giving such profuse assistance to a Judean.

METAPHORICAL PROCLIVITIES

The narrative of the Samaritan trades in the full ugliness of the everyday world. It is precisely that specificity, when taken literally, that offends. We must now ask whether there are clues in the story that inhibit the listener from taking it merely literally. Are there any clues in the story that suggest it should not be understood as a moralistic admonition to be a good neighbor?

The first suggestion derives from the semantic organization of the plot. As already noted, the first response on the part of the Judean audience would have been to affirm the everyday features of the tale: the Jericho road was known for its robberies, so it would have been natural to identify with the victim in the ditch. The appearance of the priest and then the levite would have caused the audience to divide over the issue of the clergy: some would have protested, others would have smiled, depending on whether they were pro- or anticlergy. Jesus introduced this preliminary tension into the story in order to heighten the real tension still to come. With Jesus' audience divided on what will eventually prove to be a secondary issue, the Samaritan, an enemy of both parties, intrudes. This narrative strategy sows additional confusion in an audience already divided.

The confusion of roles in the story was designed to teach the listener a lesson: be wary of easy identification with characters in the parable. You may be sorry. The parable instructs the listener to be circumspect in taking sides.

The second suggestion is less subtle. There are no warrants for the behavior of the Samaritan. Historically, the Samaritans were something less than hospitable to Judeans. The story provides no real motivation for the action of this alien traveler. The behavior of the Samaritan contravenes normal, everyday expectations. As a consequence, the parable takes on the character of a fairy tale. The Samaritan acts in an altogether unexpected way. The peasant listener in the audience would no longer be an innocent victim in the ditch but the object of Samaritan mercy. That is a role no self-respecting Judean wanted to play. To be sure, no self-respecting Samaritan wanted to play the role of the helping hand either. The priest and levite, on the other hand, must have believed they had been shortchanged, thinking, in retrospect, that they should have been given the role of the hero. And some lay listeners would have objected that the hero should have been an ordinary Judean. The story thus promoted the transposition or the migration of social roles. The biggest movement of all was called for by the appearance of the Samaritan.

Who in the audience wanted to let himself or herself be helped by a Samaritan? This is the primary challenge because the appearance of the Samaritan makes sense on no other basis. Had the victim in the ditch been a Samaritan and the hero an ordinary Judean, then the question would have been reversed: who in the Judean audience wanted to play the role of a hero to a Samaritan victim? Further, the role of the victim is the inferior role, the role of the helper the superior one. Listeners would have found it more congenial to adopt the role of the helper as their own than to accept the status of victim. The role of helper gives one the initiative, puts one in charge, so to speak, of the outcome. The role of victim is passive, helpless, subject to initiatives taken by others. It is not the perspective of the helper that dominates the story—no, it is the perspective of the victim that provides the narrative focus.

Among Jesus' listeners, those who would have responded positively to this story were those who had nothing to lose by doing so. Note that the victim in the ditch has nothing to do or say. The victim's inability to resist the Samaritan's ministrations is a weak form of consent, but it plays an essential role in the story: God's domain is open to outcasts, to the undeserving, to those who do not merit inclusion. In other words, all who are truly victims, truly disinherited, have no reason and are unable to resist mercy when it is offered. The despised half-breed becomes the instrument of compassion and grace—Judeans would have choked on that irony. It has occasionally been suggested that there is an auto-biographical element in the parable of the Samaritan. After all, Jesus was a lowly Galilean peasant, only slightly higher on the social scale than the Samaritan. Was he thinking of himself as an instrument of his Father's grace? This suggestion is farfetched, in my judgment, although it does square with Jesus' view that salvation will come from unexpected quarters.

The Samaritan is made to behave in a way that runs counter to expectations. The parable greatly exaggerates his willingness to help. Exaggeration and atypicality add an element of fantasy to the story: listeners could no longer believe their ears; their normal sense of reality was being called into question. In the world of the parable, things run the other way around, as they do in Alice's looking glass: the proud Judean is a helpless victim; the hated Samaritan is the hero helper; the clergy and the cult of the affluent are overtly depreciated.

Once it is understood that the parable is a fantasy—a fantasy about God's domain, an order of reality that feeds on but ultimately overturns the everyday world—it is but a short step to the view that the story is not about a stickup on Jericho boulevard at all. It is about a new order of things, a new reality that lies beyond, but just barely beyond, the everyday, the humdrum, the habituated. Then the parable is understood as an invitation to cross over. The ability to cross over will depend, of course, on both the tenacity with which one holds to the inherited order of reality, the received world, and on one's willingness to cut the ties to comfortable tradition. The parable is pitted against the power of the proven. Making the transition under such circumstances does not come easily. But, then, Jesus never suggests that it is easy—only that it is obvious.

THE DOMESTICATION OF THE PARABLE

Luke, the author of the third gospel, the only source for this parable, is known as a physician and companion of Paul the apostle. Luke's historic position as confidant of Paul and medical doctor has steadily eroded. It is said of Henry J. Cadbury, a renowned New Testament scholar and Quaker, that he gained his doctor's degree by depriving Luke of his. Many New Testament scholars now doubt that Luke ever knew Paul, and they have been convinced by Cadbury that Luke had no more medical knowledge than the average educated writer of hellenistic times. Cadbury demonstrated that the so-called medical terminology of Luke was known to and used by other, nonmedical writers of the period.

That information, along with many other data, has caused gospel scholars to be wary of interpretive settings given to the parables and aphorisms of Jesus by Luke (and the other evangelists). The gospel setting is often secondary and misleading. Luke's interpretation of the Samaritan is but one example.

In a context where the loaded terms of the parable have lost their original strong values and have been replaced by terms with zero or faded values, the fundamental tensions of the story have been released. By the time Luke edits this parable for his gospel, much has changed. Judeans and Samaritans no longer hate each other. For Luke, the Samaritan is just another gentile, who fits nicely into his geographical plan for the march of the gospel from Jerusalem to Samaria (the next closest territory) and then to the ends of the earth. The temple and its priests and levites are gone (the temple was destroyed in 70 C.E. and with it the function of the priestly guild). The Jericho road has become any Roman roadway. And Luke's audience is made up not of Judeans but of gentiles; in fact, Luke makes no mention of Judeans in the story at all. Gone, too, is the inclination of Jesus' original audience to identify with the victim in the ditch, and the Samaritan's fantastic behavior has been replaced by an image of him as a good neighbor. An entirely new story has emerged. It is now the story of good Sam.

As Luke understands the story, there is a nameless victim in some ditch or other. Two parties ignore the silent appeal for help. A third notices and is compassionate. The third is incidentally called a Samaritan, who, because of his act of mercy, is now called good. The story is told to commend this kind of behavior. In this later version of the story with the same text, roles in the parable have been generalized as victim, passersby, helper. Readers are surprised not at the generosity of the Samaritan but at the callousness of the clergy. That part of the story is transferable because everyone in every time and place knows who priests are. Readers view the story objectively: they listen without being drawn into it, without suffering the stringent claims placed on the original hearers. There is no urge to switch social roles. A moralizing admonition is now appended as the interpretive conclusion: "Go and do the same yourself." This reading of the parable is derived, of course, from the context given the parable in the Gospel of Luke, and it is the reading adopted by countless interpreters who have followed him.

AUTHENTICITY

The parable of good Sam has been preserved only by the Gospel of Luke. That reduces the level of probability for its authenticity. But the context and interpretation given the parable by Luke contradict the content of the parable itself. That raises the level of probability back up: we can be confident that the parable is older than the evangelist's interpretation of it. Since the earliest members of the Jesus movement were Judeans, they might not have been eager to transmit a story so pointedly critical of themselves. That may account for its lack of wider attestation in the sources. A final judgment regarding authenticity depends, however, on the coherence test—does the parable square with other elements in the authentic Jesus tradition?—and on *the critic's ear*—can one hear the voice of Jesus in it? Does it exhibit the characteristic features of the rhetorical Jesus?

Scholars of the gospels, most of whom have been trained as textual critics and historians, are frequently tone-deaf. Preoccupation with words may in practice deaden the ear to the resonances of a text, to its oblique poetry, to its subtleties. That makes it difficult to detect the faint echoes issuing from a story overlaid with centuries of obfuscating interpretive debris. Once that debris has been penetrated, however, the echoes become stronger. I think they are unmistakable in the parable of the Samaritan.

This parable also passes the coherence test. Jesus steadily privileged those marginalized in his society—the diseased, the infirm, women, children, toll collectors, gentile suppliants, perhaps even Samaritans—precisely because they were regarded as the *enemy,* the outsider, the victim. The Samaritan as helper was an implausible role in the everyday world of Jesus; that is what makes the Samaritan plausible as a helper in a story told by Jesus.

The parable, however, is not about Samaritan helpers. It is about victims. No one elects to be beaten, robbed, and left for dead. Yet in this story the way to get help is to be discovered helpless. The parable as a metaphor is permission for the listener to understand himself or herself in just that way. There were many in Jesus' society who could identify with that possibility without strain. Others could not imagine themselves being helped by a Samaritan. That is where the difference lay: how his listeners understood themselves. In the parable only victims need apply for help.

The meaning of the parable cannot be made more explicit than that. Listeners may respond to the parable as they wish. They may accept help, or they may refuse it. The story is not tyrannical: it does not dictate. But it does set the terms. Those religiously privileged do not need help, so they don't stop and help. Religious outcasts know they need assistance, so they can stop because they have nothing to lose—they have already been excommunicated. They are the ones who recognize the victim in the ditch.

It is possible to transpose the message of the parable into another key, to state its meaning abstractly. If we were to do so on the basis of the reading just given, the result would be quite unlike the traditional interpretation assigned to the parable by Luke and subsequent exegetes. But there is risk. In any restatement we must remember to retain something of the metaphorical quality of the parable itself. That suggests two propositions:

1. In God's domain help comes only to those who have no right to expect it and who cannot resist it when it is offered.
2. Help always comes from the quarter from which one does not and cannot expect it.

We might reduce these two statements to one:

In God's domain help is perpetually a surprise.

Chapter Ten

PROFLIGATE
AND PROPER SONS

THE PRODIGAL AS ALLEGORY

The parable of the prodigal son is traditionally understood as an allegory. The father in the story is presumably a model of behavior for God the Father, whose love embraces the younger son upon his return. The prodigal stands for the gentiles, who are foreigners and sinners. The older son, of course, represents the Judeans, specifically the Pharisees, who object to the treatment God the Father extends to the godless gentiles.

This way of reading the parable has been customary ever since the evangelist Luke incorporated the story into his gospel. Yet modern scholars have been virtually unanimous in rejecting the allegory as a christianization of the parable. The interpretation of the story as the history of salvation from a Christian perspective was possible only because the Christian movement had already established its own version of biblical history and simply superimposed it on this parable, as it did on other parables. Early Christian interpreters knew what the parable meant because they had previously decided on the truth; the parable was adjusted to their truth, rather than their truth to the parable.

THE PLOT OF THE PRODIGAL

The parable of the prodigal consists formally of two episodes, each of which consists of two scenes. In the first episode, scene i, the younger son takes his inheritance and leaves home. He returns at the end of the scene. In scene ii, the younger son receives an elaborate welcome home by his father.

The second episode also consists of two scenes. In the first, the older son hears music and dancing and asks one of the servants what the noise means. In the second scene, the older son and his father exchange views. We may imagine the shift in scenes as occasions in a stage drama when the curtain is momentarily lowered and the stage setting changed. All readings and interpretations of the parable take this structure as their point of departure.

This is how the parable goes in a modern translation:

THE PRODIGAL

Once there was a fellow who had two sons. The younger of them said to his father, "Father, give me the share of the property that is coming to me." So the father divided the estate between the two boys.

Act I, scene i
Not long after that, the younger son gathered his belongings together and departed for a distant country, where he squandered his inheritance by living extravagantly. Just as he began to run out of funds, a severe famine swept through the land and he had to do without. So he went and hired himself out to one of the citizens of that country, who sent him out to his farm to feed the pigs. He was reduced to satisfying his hunger with eating pig's food because no one gave him anything to eat.

He finally came to his senses and said to himself, "Lots of my father's hired hands have plenty to eat while I am dying of starvation! I'll return to my father and I'll tell him, 'Father, I have sinned against God and I have wronged you. I don't deserve to be called your son. Treat me like one of your hired hands.'" And he acted on his own resolve and returned to his father.

Act I, scene ii
His father saw him coming while he was still some distance off and his heart went out to his son. He went running out to meet him, threw his arms around his neck, and kissed him. And the son said to him, "Father, I have sinned against God and I have wronged you. I don't deserve to be called your son."

His father commanded his slaves, "Quick! Get our finest robe and put it on him; provide him with a ring for his finger and sandals for his feet. Fetch the fat calf and slaughter it. Let's have a feast and celebrate. After all, this son of mine was dead but has come back to life; he was lost but now has been found." And they started to celebrate.

Act II, scene i
Now the older son was out in the field at the time. As he got closer to the house, he heard music and dancing. He called one of the servant boys over and asked him what was going on.

The boy told him, "Your brother has come home and your father has slaughtered the fat calf because he has come back safe and sound."

Act II, scene ii
The older son was angry and refused to enter the house. So his father came out and began to plead with him. But he said to his father, "See here, all these years I have slaved for you. I never once disobeyed your orders. Yet you have never once provided me with so much as a kid goat so I could celebrate with my friends. But when this son of yours shows up— the one who squandered your fortune with prostitutes—for him you slaughter the fat calf."

To his son the father replied, "My child, you are always at my side. Everything that's mine is yours. But we just had to celebrate and rejoice because this brother of yours was dead but has come back to life; he was lost but now has been found."

Luke 15:11–32

The key events in the first act may be identified as *leavetaking* and *homecoming*. More will be said about this interpretation of the plot later.

Act I, scene i contributes two clearly marked aspects of the story. The account of the younger son trades in the everyday world as Jesus and his contemporaries knew it; the plot and details feature the ordinary, the concrete, what everybody takes for granted. In a word, it majors in the literal.

The second aspect is exaggeration or hyperbole. The younger son asks for and receives his share of the estate *before* his father dies, which was not the normal practice. The lad runs away from home to a foreign land, where he indulges himself without restraint. He spends his entire fortune. A famine sweeps through the land. This upper-class lad hires himself out as a day laborer. He must feed the pigs in violation of the laws of purity that are honored by his people. He eats the food meant for swine. One can hardly imagine a greater string of improbable misfortunes! There is comic exaggeration in these developments.

Then the listener (reader) is asked to believe that this young upstart actually repents. He comes to his senses. He sees that he is not worthy to be called a son and so is willing to settle for the role of slave on what remains of his father's estate. He returns home in contrite humility. Another string of fantastic, scarcely believable events!

This general sequence of events—inheritance, leavetaking, misfortune, homecoming—is nevertheless perfectly plausible; indeed, it is just what everybody thinks quite probable on the part of the ungrateful young. The parable is thus a literal caricature of everybody's opinion of undisciplined children.

In Act I, scene ii, the scene in which the father welcomes the lost son home, the hyperbole continues. The father runs out to meet this wayward son who blew his fortune, throws his arms around the neck of the boy, and kisses him. The father then orders a ring for his finger, a fine robe for his back, and sandals for his feet (we learn belatedly that the boy was barefoot—not unusual for a slave—but the gifts of the father all represent the elaborate reception ordinarily extended to an oriental potentate). The fat calf is slaughtered and the celebration immediately begins. Once again, there is nothing in this general sequence that parents in the audience would not willingly affirm: yes, they agree, after taking a deep breath, that's how we have treated our wayward children. They rob and impoverish us, but we take them back time after time. Nevertheless, the overstated behavior of the father would have brought a wry smile to the teller's face—all this is good clean fun.

LEARNING TO READ

How are we to understand the first act?

We must let the story itself teach us how to read it. We must do so for two reasons. First, the initiative belongs to the story, not to the interpreter. If the interpreter takes charge, the parable will once again fall prey to domestication: it will either be made to conform to some established paradigm of meaning in the mind or community of the interpreter, or it will be reassimilated to the everyday outlook of the first listeners. Biblical scholars are inclined to invoke the ancient everyday outlook as the interpretive frame, as a consequence of their allegiance to the social sciences; ministers and priests regularly assign a pre-determined Christian meaning to the parable.

In the second place, the story itself warns us against taking it "at face value." It alerts us to the perils of a literal reading. It does so by caricature and exaggeration. The plot is believable, we think, because as parents we know how wasteful and ungrateful our children are, or because as children we know what our parents should be like—indulgent. But the elaboration of the story is a riot of the improbable. That constitutes a subtle hint in the story itself: Beware of swallowing the tale as a morality play applicable to fathers and sons.

While the first act borders on the fantastic, the second act is straightforward and sober. The proper son pouts a bit, to be sure. But he is justified. His father has never given him the recognition he is due. Not only did he not get a calf or a lamb, he didn't even get a goat. The old man has been partial to the baby all along. The understatement of Act II suggests that it is satire.

REDISCOVERING THE PARABLES

The allegorical interpretation of the parable dominated Christian interpretation for centuries. In fact, it held sway until Adolf Jülicher published his mammoth work on the parables in 1888 and 1899 (a work that has not been translated into English). According to Jülicher, the parables were not to be read as allegories but as stories with a single point of the broadest possible application. In spite of Jülicher's influence, the allegorical way of reading the parables has remained entrenched, to a greater or lesser degree, in the work of many scholars in the twentieth century.

The work of another German scholar, Joachim Jeremias, is an example of this tendency. Jeremias wanted to rename the prodigal as the parable of the Father's love (note that Father is capitalized) in his book, *The Parables of Jesus*.[1] That is because Jeremias wanted to understand the father in the story quite literally as God. Jeremias rejected allegory in principle, but in practice he retained it in reduced form. How did he manage this strategy?

Jeremias held that the father is the central figure in the story and functions as a paradigm for God's love for sinners. Further, he believes that the parable is a vindication of the good news Jesus proclaims for sinners in the face of critics, who in Jesus' day, he thinks, were the Pharisees. The older son of course stands for these critics, who object to the warm welcome Jesus gives to sinners, represented by the prodigal son.

Notice the close fit of the figurative and the literal. The father in the story, although a *figurative* representation of the Father, quite *literally* represents the way God behaves. The close, exhaustive identification of the father with the Father means that for Jeremias the father is *literally figurative*. This is also the case with the older son: the older son acts and behaves just the way Pharisees are alleged to act when God offers salvation to the undeserving gentiles. The older son is identified with the unbelieving Judeans. But Jeremias is more guarded in the way he treats the "meaning" of the younger son: the younger son is not literally the model for Christian deportment, since as a Christian he cannot recommend that kind of behavior as something to be imitated. Moreover, the younger son was, after all, also a Judean and not a gentile outsider. There is some slippage, some discrepancy, in the way the younger son is interpreted, in contrast to the clear and unequivocal meaning assigned to the first two characters.

How can we account for this "Christian" discrepancy?

As we look back on how early Christians understood the parable and how Jeremias interprets it, the problem lies with the definition of a sinner. According to the gospels, a sinner is someone (1) who leads an exaggerated form of the immoral life (for example, an adulterer, prostitute, or swindler) or (2) who follows a dishonorable vocation (for example, a toll collector). The prodigal fits this definition: he squanders all his property in loose living among whores and winds up feeding swine in violation of his religious heritage. Now if the father in the story represents God and the older son stands for Pharisaic intransigence, why is the younger son not also taken as a literal model for the sinner and hence for the Christian?

The answer lies in the literalizing proclivities of the community transmitting this tradition. What does it mean to take something literally?

The literal meaning of a word, to begin with, is its original or etymological sense. Scholars like to say that the Greek verb for "to sin" literally means "to miss the mark." That is its etymological sense, although it is never used in that sense in hellenistic Greek.

Literal may also refer to the descriptive sense of a term. *Descriptive* in ordinary usage means things as they are commonly perceived and thus is a way of portraying things—so it is assumed—as they really are: common perceptions for common perceivers are the really real. The literal reading may accordingly be defined as the confirmation of normal, unstudied, habituated expectations. The literal confirms how everybody understands the world and his or her place in it.

The literalizing proclivities of the Jesus movement led that community to assign its own understanding of itself and the world to the parable. A literal interpretation, even if it is figurative, is a way of controlling the meaning of the story. The parable can mean only what it has already been taken to mean. The literal reading serves the interests of the controllers. Those controlling the parable insulate themselves from the critical reach of the parable.

The result is an interpretive principle that protects the interpreters: they privilege themselves in the story so they are shielded from the critical tensions in the text. The parable is now aimed only at *outsiders;* insiders are safe within the community of God's love by virtue of the haven of a fixed, favorable, protective interpretation. This tendency can be expressed in another way: The hardening of the terms goes together with a hardening of the heart—neither the terms nor the heart are open to the message of the parable. The hardening of the heart permits the controlling interpreter to overlook or ignore features in the story that, if taken into account, would undermine the safe reading.

Now to repeat: the Christian community was quite willing to understand the father in the story as God and the older son as the Pharisee, but it did not want to understand itself literally as the younger son. The younger son was not to be commended as a role model for Christian "sinners." (Marcus Borg reports that Krister Stendahl, once dean of the Harvard Divinity School, remarked that Christians are indeed sinners but think of themselves only as "honorary sinners.") This is an unbalanced or, in kinder language, an asymmetrical way of interpreting the central players in the story.

AMBIGUITY AND POLYVALENCE

The moral posture of the three figures in the parable was originally ambiguous.

The older son, who always behaves properly but who always gets the short end of the stick, is not rejected; the father commends him for his loyalty and reminds him that the estate actually belongs to him. The older son is the only one in the parable who acts in an entirely reasonable and sane manner. But he is a homebody.

The doting father is permissive and excessive in his relations to the spoiled brat of the family. From a distance his behavior is perhaps commendable. Yet if we were the older son, we would probably want to challenge the father's division of the estate in court. He certainly has not given the proper son the recognition due him.

We have to admit that the younger son is irresponsible: he does everything wrong except repent. He is a rebel without a cause. As listeners we are a little piqued that he has the audacity to return home to live off the remainder of the estate.

The inclination to read the parable in accordance with patterns of behavior already adopted as normative by the interpreter's community tends to ignore these dissonant and uncomfortable aspects of the story. This same bent tends to brick over the structural ambiguity of the parable. If the parable is structurally ambiguous, one might expect it to be subject to more than one reading. To be susceptible to more than one reading makes the parable polyvalent: it stands for more than one set of values, or it has more than one legitimate meaning. To be blind to that ambiguity restricts the possibilities of the parable, robs it of its interpretive potential, its parabolic impact, in new and altered contexts.

The prodigal is usually taken as a story in which two sons give opposite responses to their father. One son, the younger, is taken back into the family in spite of his irresponsible behavior; the other is both affirmed and chastised because of his petulant although proper demeanor. According to this reading, the story turns on the relationships of the two sons with their father (see page 190).

It may be cogently argued, however, that the central figure in the story is not the father but the younger son, in relation to whom the father and the older son give contrasting responses (see page 190). Viewed this way, the reader (or listener) is left to be drawn into the story on one side or the other: he or she may wish to empathize with the prodigal father (who is prodigal in his love for the younger son), or with the loyal son, or with both at different times.

The role of the father in the prodigal corresponds to the role of the Samaritan in the parable of the Samaritan. Just as the Samaritan would not have been expected to come to the aid of the Judean in the ditch, so the father would not be expected to respond to the younger son as he does. From the perspective of the older son, the old man has been beset by senility or something worse. But crystallized familiarity—the standard, sentimental interpretation—has fixed prodigal love as the property of the father, who stands for God the Father, so that the actual details of the story are not allowed to interfere with that sense. The literalizing reading is what Frank Kermode calls "the shrine of the single sense": interpreters long to enter that shrine and abide there.[2]

The fundamental structural ambiguity has been resolved by the single sense that Luke attached to the parable, and the details have been buried under an avalanche of familiar meaning, so that risk has been eliminated from the role of the father, who, after all, plays the role of God. In this traditional reading the father is no longer prodigal and senile; the younger son is no longer a rascal; and the older son is not viewed as reliable and dependable. With that interpretive overlay, the parable loses its parabolic character, and the tensions set up by the metaphorical functions of the father and his two sons are released.

Reading the parable as parable involves risk—the risk of violating the parable itself and the risk of catching a glimpse of oneself in the mirror of the parable. The risk is to imagine some proximate background against which the story is to be understood, some imagined constellation of issues suggested by the story itself understood as metaphor. If we hold the story at arm's length—get it out from under the urge to moralize it or interpret it religiously—we can perhaps see that it has to do with a leavetaking and a homecoming. I make this suggestion on the basis (1) of other parables and sayings in Jesus' repertoire, and (2) of the everyday world Jesus appears to reflect in his pronouncements and stories. Put in a nutshell, my suggestion is this: The younger son leaves home in order to come home. He is unable to appreciate his patrimony until he has forsaken it and squandered it. He cannot know his father as parent until he turns his back on home. The immoderate behavior of the lad and the exaggerated welcome on the part of the father suggest a momentous event in their lives, a turning point: a son cannot know the joys of return until he has suffered a departure. But, of course, all this has to be understood entirely figuratively.

The parable of the prodigal can be viewed against the background of a tradition rich in instances of leavetaking and homecoming.

At the beginning of the Gospel of Mark, John the Baptist has forsaken his community and gone out into the desert to prepare the way of the Lord. John may have had in mind a new crossing of the Jordan, a fresh invasion of the promised land, as the next step in his program. A leavetaking was to be followed by a promised homecoming.

Abram, who was to become Abraham, is instructed to quit his country, leave his relatives and his family, and go to a land as yet unspecified.[3] Upon arrival, he would father a great nation.

The Israelites, who were in servitude in Egypt, were commanded to depart, to wander in the wilderness for forty years, so that eventually they would possess a homeland.[4]

These are powerful symbolic stories. They are stronger and more durable than stories that consist only of arrivals. There can be no homecoming without a leavetaking. To come home, one must leave home. Life is not a good place for homebodies. This, incidentally, is a way to read the second episode of the parable of the prodigal: the older son is a homebody—he cannot come home because he has not left home. He is unable to party even in his own home. Homebodies are the norm, the accepted, the safe, the role to be recommended. Leavetaking is painful, traumatic, risky. But the road to maturity leads through trials in a strange land, in the forest of our nightmares, in contests with alien forces. True arrivals are preceded by true departures.

The prodigal mirrors the journey of Jesus; it has autobiographical overtones. This aspect of the parable leads one to suggest that Jesus was at risk when he told the parable: he ventured to risk leavetaking in order to comprehend the bliss of homecoming. He may not always have been certain that this was his best move, the necessary move. Yet the gospels preserve sayings and stories that confirm his willingness to take the risk. Jesus forsook his family to join the Baptist movement in the Jordan valley. Later he turned his back on John and reentered urban Galilee with a revised gospel. He had already abandoned whatever possessions he may have had to become an itinerant—actually a homeless person, although many today would find that label offensive because of the stigma attached to it. He no longer practiced his trade as a carpenter, if that was, in fact, his legacy. He seems to have quit his ethnic traditions, those that identified him as an Israelite in a largely pagan environment. Eventually he seems to have been prepared to leave life behind, almost as readily as he abandoned family and mentors.

PLAYERS AND PLOTS

A narrative parable is a story with at least three major participants and two scenes. In counting participants, groups are treated as one if they act in concert, as do the priest and levite in the good Samaritan, for example. Subordinate characters are not counted. The scale on which participants are viewed may change during the course of a narrative. In the parable of the vineyard laborers, a group of workers hired early in the day is represented by a single voice at the end. Changes in scale do not increase or decrease the number of participants.

There are ten narrative parables that meet these basic criteria:

The good Samaritan	Luke 10:30–35
The prodigal	Luke 15:11–32
The vineyard laborers	Matt 20:1–15
The dinner party	Thom 64:1–11
The money given in trust	Luke 19:13, 15–24
The leased vineyard	Thom 65:1–7
The unforgiving slave	Matt 18:23–34
The shrewd manager	Luke 16:1–8
The ten maidens	Matt 25:1–12
The rich man and Lazarus	Luke 16:19–31

Of the three characters appearing in each of these stories, one sets the stage for the drama to follow. Often that person is an authority figure, but not always. In the good Samaritan, it is the victim in the ditch; in the ten maidens, it is the bridegroom. The key participant determines the situation or the circumstances within which the action develops: the vineyard owner goes to the village to hire laborers to harvest grapes; a host plans a dinner party; an aristocrat gives money in trust to three of his slaves.

The functions of the other two participants in the story and the plot prompt us to separate the narrative parables into two categories. In one category, two persons or groups respond to the situation in different and contrasting ways. In the second category, one person responds to the initial situation, and his response becomes the focal point to which a second person responds. The two plots can be represented diagrammatically. In the first, B and C respond to A, or the situation determined by A:

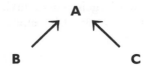

In the second kind of plot, B responds to A, and C responds to B:

$$A \longleftarrow B \longleftarrow C$$

Eight narrative parables belong to the first group:

> Good Samaritan
> Prodigal
> Vineyard laborers
> Dinner party
> Money in trust
> Leased vineyard
> Ten maidens
> Rich man and Lazarus

Two narrative parables belong to the second group:

> Unforgiving slave
> Corrupt manager

The law of stage duality, universal in folklore, is in force in the narrative parables. That law stipulates that only two persons (or groups) may speak or act at one time. A further simplification also applies to the parables, which are forms of folktales or discourse: only two of a possible three sets of relationships are developed in any one story. Thus B and C may interact with A, but B and C may not interact with each other. Similarly, B may interact with A, and C may interact with B, but then C does not interact with A. This limitation ensures the simplicity of the plot.

If the destiny of a participant turns upward, in a good or salutary direction, during the course of the story, the shape of the plot is said to be comic, according to Aristotle. If the destiny of a participant turns downward, in the wrong or evil direction, the shape of that plot is said to be tragic. The terms *comic* and *tragic* refer to the formal features of the story rather than to humorous or sad aspects of the plot.

The story line or plot of the narrative parables exhibits some constant features. In the first category, the destiny of one character, or group of characters (B or C in the diagrams), turns downward or tragic; the destiny of the other participant, or group of participants, turns upward or in a comic direction. As we have already observed, in the case of the Samaritan, the priest and levite ignore the victim in the ditch, while the Samaritan, who could not have been expected to stop and help, does what he is not thought capable of doing. Those hired first in the parable of the vineyard laborers expect to be paid more for working the entire day but are given the standard wage; they complain. Those hired during the last hour don't expect the regular wage and are surprised by the owner's generosity. Once again, the two destinies move in opposite directions. Three guests are invited to the dinner party at the outset; they refuse for good reasons. The host then gathers in the homeless and outcasts from the streets. The first group is excluded; the second group is ushered into the banquet hall, much to their surprise. In the case of the prodigal, the contrasting responses are those of the father and the older son; or, on another reading, the two responses are represented by the two sons.

In the second group of narrative parables, the corrupt manager is called to account by his boss. As a consequence, he allows his boss's debtors to pay off their obligations at a reduced rate. They respond favorably to this opportunity. The initial tragic direction of the parable, occasioned by mismanagement, is reversed when his boss commends the manager for his boldness and the debtors stand ready to take him in after his dismissal.

The unforgiving slave has an enormous debt canceled by his master. When he is asked to cancel a trivial obligation owed him by a second debtor, he refuses. His master then reverses his initial generosity. The comic direction of the first scene becomes tragic in the second.

Reversals function as the basic plot structure of all these authentic narrative parables. Those who expect things to turn out well are disappointed, and those who cannot expect good fortune are pleasantly surprised. The plots of the parables reinforce this clean, sharp dictum: "The first will be last and the last first."

There is also an element of reversal in the parables of the leased vineyard and the money in trust. In both cases, however, christianizing elements have been added and the parables allegorized. As a consequence, it is difficult to determine the original story and thus to know for certain whether they are genuine Jesus parables. The parable of the rich man and Lazarus has also been given a christianizing conclusion: Abraham is made to say, "If they won't listen to Moses and the prophets, they won't be convinced even if someone were to rise from the dead."[5] Finally, while the parable of the ten maidens presents two groups of maidens, one of which comes prepared with oil for their lamps, the other of which does not, the fate of the two groups is not reversed. There are no surprises. One group is rewarded for its diligence and forethought, the other is excluded because it was not prepared. That scenario is uncharacteristic of Jesus. For this reason, it is doubtful that this parable stems from Jesus.

INSIDERS AND OUTSIDERS

Reversals are a standard feature of the genuine parables of Jesus. In the tragic plot, reversal results in exclusion for those who think they should be included, who do the right thing, who are justified by their own standards. In the so-called comic plot, those who have been marginalized, who are outcasts, who could not have been expected to be invited, to be paid the full wage, to be welcomed home, are surprised by their unexpected good fortune. Elsewhere in the Jesus tradition, the contrast between the comic and the tragic can be translated into the difference between insiders and outsiders. That contrast undergoes a series of subtle transformations in gospel texts, some authentic, others exhibiting the marks of domestication and later Christian self-congratulation. The contrast provides another set of criteria for distinguishing the inauthentic from the authentic sayings.

Luke reports a saying taken from the Sayings Gospel Q:

> Just remember, John the Baptist appeared on the scene, eating no bread and drinking no wine, and you say, "He is demented." The son of Adam appeared on the scene both eating and drinking, and you say, "There's a glutton and a drunk, a crony of petty tax agents and sinners!"[6]

The charge that Jesus associated with toll collectors and sinners is not evidence that he actually did so, of course, any more than the charge that John the Baptist was demented means that he was actually out of his mind. Nevertheless, the contrast between John the Baptist and Jesus reflects historical reality: John was perceived as and probably was a desert ascetic; Jesus was perceived as and probably was what we would call an urban partygoer. Jesus seems to have been given to conviviality; he apparently enjoyed an open table. He would probably not have had the means to sponsor an evening of scintillating conversation over food and drink—a symposium as it was called. Yet he did not hesitate to attend convivial gatherings sponsored by others.

The claim that Jesus was a drunk has nothing to do with the alcohol content of his blood on a given occasion but with how he was perceived socially. Daryl Schmidt points out that this perception is informed by whether or not he was obedient to the Law:

> If any of you has a disobedient and rebellious son, who does not respond to the instructions of his father or mother, you are first to discipline him. If he still does not heed you, you are to bring him to the elders at the gate of the city. You are to say to the elders of the city, "This son of ours is disobedient and rebellious. He won't obey us. He is a glutton and a drunk." The men of the city are then to stone him to death. In this way you will rid yourselves of this evil, and everybody else will hear about it and be afraid.
>
> *Deuteronomy 21:18–21*

"Glutton and drunk" was evidently an epithet applied to sons who were incorrigible. The information encoded in the Q saying contrasts the ways John the Baptist and Jesus were perceived. Although thought to be demented, John may nevertheless have been perceived as an obedient son of the Torah, but Jesus apparently was not.

The Gospel of Mark reports a simple scene in which Jesus attends a dinner party in the house of Levi, a petty tax official he has just recruited.[7] This party was attended by other tax agents and "sinners." When Jesus is observed at table with such people, his disciples are reprimanded by the purists—the Pharisees—who complain that he is violating kosher and other purity codes, such as eating with the unclean.

No end of scholarly ink has been spilled over trying to determine who these "sinners" were, whether there were Pharisees in Galilee in Jesus' day and, if so, what kind of persons they were. The scene as Mark relates it, moreover, is criticized by many scholars as implausible: Where were the Pharisees during dinner? Were they peeking in through a window? Can the disciples be distinguished from tax officials and sinners at this early stage of Jesus' story, or is that distinction a retrospective view? Why is the criticism directed to the disciples rather than to Jesus? Why does Jesus respond to a question that has been posed to his followers? All of these narrative inconsistencies point to a contrived, fictional scene.

There are three groups at this fictive dinner: tax officials, sinners, and disciples. The "disciples" are undoubtedly an invention of Mark, who wants, from his later perspective, to distinguish the "undesirables" at the party from authentic followers. This unobtrusive addition tells us loads about the later Christian community: by Mark's time, "the disciples" are something different from "the toll collectors and sinners" of the underlying oral tradition. This new distinction is confirmed by the explanatory addition to the parable of the sower, in which Jesus is made to say, "You have been given the secret of God's imperial rule; but to those outside everything is presented in parables"—so they won't understand.[8] Only Christian listeners, readers, and interpreters can understand what the parables mean. By the time of Luke, two decades later, it was acceptable to identify the father in the parable of the prodigal with God and the older son with the Pharisees, as we've discussed. But it was not acceptable to think of themselves as the prodigal son. That is another way of saying that Christians no longer wanted to think of themselves as "sinners," that is, as *outsiders;* by that time they had come to believe they were the saved —that is, *insiders.* Those with whom Jesus ate and drank originally, however, were all real sinners or *outsiders*—that is how they were perceived socially from the standpoint of those who adhered to purity codes and ate kosher. Sinners, outsiders in Jesus' society, included persons with a skin disease ("lepers"), the maimed, the halt, the blind, gentiles, Samaritans, as well as petty tax officials, who were Roman collaborators, and women who did not observe the social proprieties. Outsiders must have been a fairly numerous element in Galilean and Judean society.

The Pharisees in this scene, like the disciples, are very likely an invention of the storyteller. The Pharisees are those who considered themselves insiders but who, from the later, Christian perspective, were viewed as perpetual outsiders because they were unbelievers. The clue to the development of this contrast lies in how the contrast *insider/outsider* is understood.

This paradox of Jesus—outsiders are in, insiders are out—throws light on another saying: "I swear to you, the toll collectors and prostitutes will get into God's domain, but you will not."[9] Here Jesus is speaking to religious authorities of some sort—the keepers of the social codes. Again, scholars are prone to defend the reputations of the women and insist that they were not actual prostitutes. Well, perhaps. In any case, we cannot take the charge literally any more than we are forced to believe Jesus was an alcoholic. Prostitute is a code word for "women who behave in an unseemly manner in public." To become disciples of a male teacher, to follow him about in his travels and discuss matters of moral importance with him at public meals, would have been quite enough to attract the label.

Matthew records an instruction regarding how to treat members of the Christian community who have committed a wrong: "If he or she refuses to listen even to the congregation, treat that companion like you would a pagan or a toll collector."[10] Here pagans and toll collectors are clearly considered outsiders, alien to the Christian community, anti-models of behavior. In this saying, the insider/outsider contrast is reversed. Jesus could not have given such advice: pagans and toll collectors are now viewed as outsiders, whereas Jesus regularly used them as symbols of insiders. It is the same cliché—pagans and toll collectors— but as it lingers in the tradition, its meaning is turned around. It now has a new and contrary meaning. Its continued presence indicates that it is a holdover from an earlier time when it had a subversive force.

There is a pair of sayings, with alternative forms in Matthew and Luke but derived from Q, that Christian folk like to quote. First, the Matthean form: "Tell me, if you love those who love you, why should you be commended for that? Even toll collectors do as much, don't they?"[11] In Luke the toll collectors have become sinners: "If you love those who love you, what merit is there in that? After all, even sinners love those who love them."[12] Matthew and Luke provide evidence that toll collectors and sinners belong to the same social category. Are they to be understood as insiders or outsiders in this saying?

If this rhetorical question is ironic, they are insiders: "You know, as I do," Jesus tells his listeners with tongue in cheek, "that these tax people and other social misfits love only those who love them. Can't you do better than they?" To be sure, for the irony to work, there must be critics in his audience who think of themselves as morally superior to toll collectors and sinners. And they must know that Jesus has openly associated with such outsiders. On the other hand, this same saying spoken in the later Christian community would have been understood not ironically but literally: we Christians are better than sinners and other outsiders because we are known for our love of those who don't love us.

The parable of the Pharisee and tax collector contrasts the behavior at prayer of an "insider" and an "outsider."[13] (I put the terms in quotation marks again as a reminder that the tags are not to be understood literally.) Some scholars who are enamored of the social sciences dismiss this parable as "only a story." But stories mirror social reality; they reveal how people perceive each other. In fact, stories are what most of us live by because they encode how we understand ourselves and the world we inhabit. The Pharisee, who thanks God he is not like the sinner standing at his side, is of course presented in caricature, just as the tax official's piety—he asks for mercy, sinner that he is—is exaggerated. Hyperbole gives the parable bite, makes it trenchant criticism of the social world Jesus inhabited by heightening the contrast between the two figures. There can be no doubt that Jesus preferred self-effacement to exhibitions of moral superiority and plainly said so.

The parable of the dinner party likewise contrasts two groups of people.[14] Those initially invited to the banquet are the deserving—those with social standing. They missed out on the banquet because they were preoccupied with legitimate but worldly matters. The undeserving— those who could not have expected an invitation, let us say, to a banquet at the White House—are ushered into the hall much to their surprise. The parable doesn't tell us that Jesus ate with sinners, but it does tell us that he endorsed the concept.

Jesus contrasts the destiny of two groups also in the vineyard laborers.[15] Those who labored the entire twelve-hour day are paid the same wage as those who worked only one hour. The latecomers were probably the indolent, the lethargic, the lazy, those who sat around all day on their haunches gossiping in the public square. Once again Jesus endorses the outsiders and shortchanges the deserving insiders.

There is no stronger statement of Jesus' predilection for the outsider than the parable of the good Samaritan. There is no more poignant statement of his disdain for the priests, levites, and the temple than this story. The Samaritan was an undeserving, unclean, despicable outsider in the view of the average Judean. This low regard was reciprocated, to be sure. It is not that Samaritans are more deserving than Judeans. It is rather that only outsiders are admitted to God's estate. God has a preference for the lowly, the poor, the undeserving, the sinner, the social misfits, the marginalized, the humble. I doubt that there is any typification, any generalization, about the words and acts of Jesus in which we can have more confidence. At the same time, it is necessary to add: To aspire to one or more of these conditions as the means to salvation is to turn these same definitions into "insider" categories.

In a well-ordered society, people know their places. In Jesus' world the few very rich and the many very poor knew their places. The social distance between them was mediated by brokers who dispensed favors bestowed by patrons on compliant peasants and peons. In contravention of the social order, Jesus was socially promiscuous: he ate and drank publicly with petty tax officials and "sinners," yet he did not refuse dinner with the learned and wealthy. He was seen in the company of women in public—an occasion for scandal in his society. He included children in his social circle—children were regarded as chattel, especially females, if they were permitted to live at birth—and advised that God's domain is filled with them.

Chapter Eleven

THE GOSPEL OF JESUS

In the territory known to Jesus as God's domain, family and tribal circles were greatly modified and enlarged, places and spaces took on new aspects, and the times and seasons underwent drastic revision. In his gospel, Jesus was perpetually saying good-bye to the world he inherited, the world everyone about him knew and accepted as the paramount reality. The players who populate his stories and aphorisms are at odds with the traditional cast of characters. God's estate was a vortex drawing into its swirling vacuum all the elements of the conventional drama.

KINSHIP IN THE KINGDOM

Family Ties That Don't Bind

Two of the most powerful social forces, the family and kinship, were immediately drawn into the vortex of the kingdom as Jesus understood it. Kinship extended, of course, beyond the immediate family formed by marriage and procreation; it embraced those who considered themselves descended from the same ancestor or who belonged to the same clan. Contrast Jesus' vision of the family in God's domain with what went before. Here is the fifth commandment in the Mosaic code:

> Honor your father and mother that your days may be long in the land the Lord your God is giving you.[1]

This is what Jesus has to say:

> If any of you comes to me and does not hate your own father and mother and wife and children and brothers and sisters—yes, even your own life— you're no disciple of mine.[2]

How are we to account for this harsh new directive? Jesus knew of the extended family running to three or four generations living in the same house, dominated by an aging patriarch with absolute authority over the family, especially over women and children. Respect for and obedience to the family head was at the top of the traditional-values list. Yet, in these words, Jesus insists that in God's kingdom the old family ties are to be broken in favor of new liaisons and loyalties.

We should remember that many things Jesus said cannot be taken entirely literally. Yet a strong saying like this certainly cuts across the commandment to honor one's father and mother. And the attitude toward filial responsibilities to parents is underscored by another saying:

> Another potential follower made this request, "First, let me go and bury my father."
> Jesus said to him, "Leave it to the dead to bury their own dead; but you, go out and announce God's imperial rule."[3]

And when Jesus' mother and siblings come to get him for fear he has gone mad, he tells the circle around him that his true relatives are those who do his Father's will.[4] In the context of traditional family ties, it is no wonder his mother thought him demented.

The scene from the Gospel of Mark in which his family comes to take him home is abbreviated in Thomas 99:

> The disciples said to him, "Your brothers and your mother are standing outside."
> He said to them, "Those here who do what my Father wants are my brothers and my mother."

Does this saying, attested by both Mark and Thomas, reflect some conflict between Jesus and his family? We know there was conflict later between Jesus' brother James, a leader of the Judean wing of the budding Christian movement, and other leaders, especially Paul of Tarsus. This happened after Jesus' death, of course. The tension may have triggered some claims and counterclaims about the rights and privileges of blood relatives of Jesus. But it is also entirely conceivable that the tension goes back to Jesus himself, since he seems to have crossed frontiers in overriding biological barriers along with religious and social lines of demarcation as a matter of principle.

In his admonitions to Judeans coming out to the Jordan valley to repent and be baptized, John the Baptist says:

> Well then, start producing fruit suitable for a change of heart, and don't even think of saying to yourselves, "We have Abraham as our father." Let me tell you, God can raise up children for Abraham right out of these rocks.[5]

This saying suggests that John, too, made light of genealogies and perhaps passed that assessment on to Jesus. In any case, Paul certainly espouses it later on, in his letter to the Philippians, in which he brags about his lineage—an Israelite of the tribe of Benjamin, a Hebrew of pure

Hebrew ancestry—but then writes all of that off as a "pile of crap" in his new Christian garb. Paul is driven to brag about his ancestry by his critics but then recognizes that such claims are illegitimate. By Paul's time the Jesus movement had already been permeated with gentiles.

Jesus' Extended Family

Blood relationships are devalued in Jesus' idea of the family; his real family is the family of God. God's family is an extended family that embraces those on the margins of society in Jesus' time: lepers, toll collectors, women, children, Samaritans, enemies. Social quarantines— restrictions on normal participation—were in effect for these and other persons with limited rights and status.

The expansiveness of Jesus' concept of the family is extended in other directions as well. It comes to expression in the saying: "Whoever is not against us is on our side."[6] The proverb is reported in Mark as Jesus' response to the observation that others, not followers of Jesus, have also been exorcizing demons. But in gospel fragment 1224, the same saying follows the admonition to pray for enemies.

> And pray for your enemies. For the one who is not against you is on your side. The one who today is at a distance, tomorrow will be near you. . . .

Cicero, who lived in the first century B.C.E., says this of Julius Caesar:

> Though we held everyone to be our opponents except those on our side, you, Caesar, counted everybody as your adherent who was not against you.[7]

Caesar was more politically astute than Cicero. Jesus, too, seems open to support and cooperation from all quarters. He was apparently inclusive rather than exclusive.

In the tenth chapter of Joshua, Joshua is instructed by God to assault the five confederated city-states of the Amorites. He destroys the allied armies and puts the kings to the sword with the help of God, who outdoes the troops of Joshua by raining hailstones down on the enemy. On that day, the sun is commanded to stand still so Joshua can carry out the slaughter during the daylight hours. Joshua then captures the five cities and "wipes out every living thing that breathes, just as the Lord God of Israel had commanded."[8]

Nowhere in the Jewish scriptures are Israelites instructed to hate their enemies, contrary to Matthew's claim: "We were once told, 'You are to love your neighbor,' and 'You are to hate your enemy.'"[9] Nevertheless, in the Manual of Discipline found among the Dead Sea Scrolls, members are taught to love the children of light but to hate the children of darkness.[10] In tribal societies, the limits of neighborly love customarily stopped at the tribal boundary. In Joshua's time, it was acceptable to wipe out the enemy and credit God with the command to do so. In Jesus' day, Galileans and Judeans for the most part had little love for the Romans. We have observed that Judeans had little love for the Samaritans and vice versa. Hating enemies was approved behavior. In contrast, Jesus advises his followers to love their enemies—an oxymoron of the first order. That admonition is not sentimental: loving enemies does not turn them into friends, although it may later prove to be an important first step in that direction. Yet "loved enemies" are a contradiction in terms.

The Fellows of the Jesus Seminar, along with countless other scholars, have ranked the admonition to love enemies very close to the heart of the teachings of Jesus. The limits of Jesus' extended family enclose all the undesirables mentioned earlier: lepers, toll collectors, women, children, Samaritans, enemies. Oh, yes, it also included priests, levites, Pharisees, Sadducees, and the wealthy and affluent—even scholars.

PLACES AND SPACES

Zoning and Sacred Space

Sacred space for Israelites and later Judeans was defined by the layout of the temple area in Jerusalem (see Figure 5, opposite). The temple area was zoned for degrees of sacredness, which also corresponded to levels of purity. The most holy space of all was of course the holy of holies in the temple proper. Into that space the high priest alone entered and then only once a year on the Day of Atonement. That sanctuary, called the adytum, was otherwise reserved for the divine presence. The nave or central room of the temple was the second most holy region of the temple proper. In it the bread of the presence was on display, along with the seven-branched candelabra and an altar for incense. Only priests were permitted to enter and perform their various duties there.

The sacrificial altar and the giant laver for ritual cleansing stood in front of the temple in a third zone. Here the priests carried out their duties in connection with the sacrificial cult. This area was surrounded by a court restricted to male Israelites. Beyond that court lay the area reserved for Israelite women. And finally, the larger, outer court, separated from the inner courts by a barrier, was space into which gentiles were permitted to enter. Degrees of sacredness were defined in parallel zones extending out, so to speak, from the very restricted inner sanctum of the temple.

The entire temple mount covered a little more than thirty-five acres. For comparison one might imagine space for thirty-four football fields, each measuring fifty by one hundred yards. Into that space crowded thousands of pilgrims, together with sacrificial animals and money changers, during the three great festivals—Passover, Pentecost, and Tabernacles.

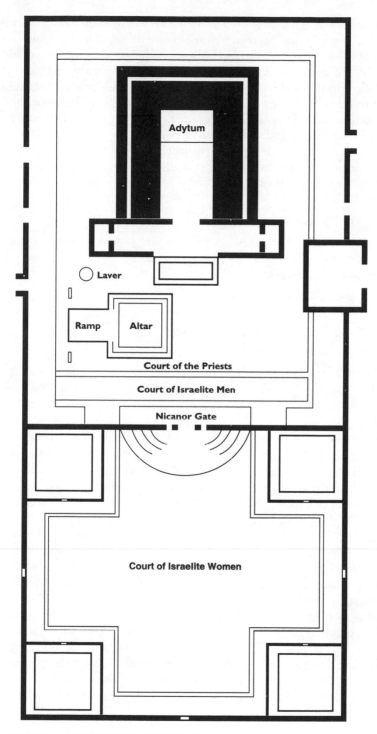

FIGURE 5: ZONES IN THE TEMPLE AREA

That set of zones reflects the structure of Judean society. Contamination occurs when persons from one zone intrude into another not intended for them. Male Israelites, even in good standing, could not invade the zone reserved for priests, and ordinary priests could not intrude into the holy of holies reserved for the high priest (and accessible even to him only once a year). Similarly, women were not permitted into the zone set aside for males, and gentiles were not allowed into any of the spaces restricted to Judeans or converts called proselytes.

The zones of the temple corresponded generally to the degrees of purity legislated for each of the categories of persons permitted in the various sacred spaces. The sanctity of persons is defined in descending order as follows:

1. The high priest
2. Ordinary priests
3. Levites
4. Israelites of pure blood
5. "Illegal" children of priests
6. Gentile converts
7. Bastards, foundlings, eunuchs
8. Those born with deformed sexual features
9. Gentiles: non-Jews.

The order is determined by the purity of the ancestral line and the ability to reproduce it. Doubts arise first with category five: the "illegal" children of priests were the product of unions involving widows, divorcees, or women who had been seduced. Gentile converts were of course Israelites only by ritual birth. Bastards and foundlings either did not know their ancestry or it was of a dubious sort. Eunuchs and those born with deformed sexual features could not reproduce and so were lower on the scale by definition. Non-Jews did not have purity status at all.

The wall around temples in the ancient Near East—called a *temenos* —defined sacred space and set it off from profane space. The temenos represented the boundary between the pure and the polluted or defiled.

Jesus routinely breached the walls and barriers that set sacred space off from profane, and he trampled indifferently on the social dividers that enforced segregation. In addition, there is evidence that he made some critical, perhaps even threatening, remark about the temple itself. This saying is reported in Thomas 71: "I will destroy this house and no one will be able to build it." "House" probably refers to the temple proper. Jesus may also have invited his disciples to take a look at the monumental buildings that adorned the temple mount: "Take a good look at these monumental buildings! You may be sure not one stone will be left on top of another!"[11]

Jesus may have believed that the temple complex would be leveled—a possible reference to the coming destruction of the Jerusalem temple, an event that actually took place in 70 c.e. Further, Jesus may have provoked a temple incident by chasing vendors and shoppers out of the temple area, along with bankers and the pigeon merchants, who were there to change money for pilgrims who wanted to pay the temple tax and to sell animals for sacrifice.[12] It could have been no more than a symbolic gesture on his part, in view of the magnitude of the space involved and the number of pilgrims probably packed into that space. Yet even such a gesture may well have been the single straw that finally broke the back of patience for authorities concerned with the orderly conduct of business, especially during the major festivals. In order to avoid a confrontation with the crowds, the authorities elected to arrest Jesus at night and privately. Within a matter of hours, before the crowds present in Jerusalem were aware of it, and almost before his friends became cognizant of the danger, Jesus had been executed.

In the vision of Jesus, the temple seemingly lacked a temenos and, had he been able to foresee the future, the church would have lacked a chancel. In his view, every person had immediate, unbrokered access to God's presence, God's love, God's forgiveness. There appeared to be no sacred places in Jesus' world: all space had become sacred. The bush burned for Jesus not just on the sacred mountain in Sinai but in the marketplace, at the public well, in every poor hovel, in the interstices of the everyday. While the story is almost certainly a fiction, Jesus advises the Samaritan woman at the well that true worshipers will worship the Father without regard to place. Neither Jerusalem nor Gerizim, neither Constantinople nor Rome, defines sacred space. That advice seems to comport with what we know of the historical Jesus.

Purity Codes

Every society has some zoning codes. A zoning code provides for boundary markers that segregate certain things and activities from other things and activities. For example, in some U.S. towns, one may not work where one lives, and, conversely, one may not live where one works. Put in different terms, industrial areas of the city are not to be mixed with residential. Similarly, it is forbidden to locate a liquor store within so many feet of a school or church. Codes segregating people by race, whether written or unwritten, are another form of zoning.

The purity system in place in Jesus' world required that he and fellow Galileans observe certain holiness codes. Israelites were to be holy because God was holy. Purity codes applied especially to the temple and the temple area, but they were also extended to the home and to the whole of the "holy land"—the land was not to be defiled because God had given it to Israel. Such codes were intended to mark off the boundaries between the sacred and profane and between the people and land of God and everyone else.

Purity could be maintained by observing the codes—by not allowing any physical, moral, or ritual contamination of persons, spaces, times, and activities. Contamination could be produced by touching, by the ingestion of certain foods, or by moral infractions. If defilement took place, there were provisions for purification: repentance, a waiting period, ritual washings, a change of clothing, the offering of appropriate sacrifices. It was the responsibility of the priests (and levites) to enforce the purity regulations.

Among the more obvious things that defiled were the touch of an unclean person, such as a "leper,"[13] or a woman suffering from vaginal bleeding,[14] or a corpse, as in the account of the widow's son[15] and in the parable of the good Samaritan.[16] There were also restrictions on the ingestion of foods deemed unsuitable for consumption, either because they were inherently unclean or because they had not been properly prepared. By extension, observant Judeans refused to share a common table with those who did not follow purity regulations, for fear of contamination. We have already noted how Jesus ignored such restrictions.

It is clear from the gospel records that Jesus was a Galilean deviant and was socially promiscuous. His deviation and promiscuity were a part of the kingdom of God, which he claimed his Father had authorized him to announce. He practiced what he preached. As a consequence, he ignored, or transgressed, or violated purity regulations and taboos.

The Gospel of Thomas preserves a saying that many Fellows of the seminar think goes back to Jesus: "When you go into any region and walk about in the countryside, when people take you in, eat what they serve you."[17] If authentic, this saying is indeed revolutionary. It enjoins Jesus' disciples to ignore kosher food regulations, to regard themselves as guests and eat whatever is offered them.

This saying is followed in Thomas by another related remark:

> After all, what goes in your mouth will not defile you; rather, it is what comes out of your mouth that will defile you.[18]

The Thomas version is a reinterpretation of the form found in Mark:

> What goes into you can't defile you; what comes out of you can.[19]

Mark's version is probably the original. In Mark, Jesus has to explain to his followers: a person is not defiled by anything that is ingested; one is defiled only by what is expelled. Jesus probably did not specify which orifice he had in mind. Feces were of course high on the list of things that defile, but Jesus may also have had the mouth in mind. That sort of ambiguity seems typical of Jesus. But Mark, too, feels constrained to interpret: Jesus meant wickedness that flows out of the heart—immorality, thefts, murders, and the like.[20] The Thomas version suggests gossip and slander, sins committed by the mouth. In either case, the witticism Jesus employed has been moralized and destroyed.

Ritual impurity is not a thing of the past, something that belonged to an earlier state of religious evolution. On the contrary, as recently as 1979 the late Ayatollah Khomeini, supreme religious authority in modern Islamic Iran, promulgated a list of the eleven things that make Shiite Muslims unclean:

1. Urine
2. Feces
3. Sperm
4. Carrion
5. Blood
6. Dog
7. Pig
8. Infidels
9. Wine
10. Beer
11. Sweat of a camel that eats unclean things.

Infidels are of course unbelievers or non-Muslims. Everything about infidels is unclean. When infidels are converted to Islam, they become clean. However, if their bodies were in contact with their clothes before their conversion, those clothes remain unclean. Similarly, rain may carry impurities from the bodies of infidels and thus defile Muslims. American soldiers serving in the Gulf region during the recent war learned the far-reaching significance of Islamic purity codes, including the meaning of alien dust or dirt (dirt imported on boots was found to be contaminating).

This is probably the significance of the admonition to the disciples that, when rejected by a community, they should shake the dust off their feet: The dust of unbelievers was believed to be polluting.[21]

Jesus is represented in the gospels as consorting with gentiles—from the Judean point of view, all the world is divided into Judeans and gentiles—which means that he suffered in a general way from ritual pollution. Repeated and intimate contact with aliens, especially at common meals, would have stigmatized Jesus in the eyes of observant Judeans.

The apostle Peter seems to have had trouble learning the lesson about kosher food, as the story goes in Acts 10–11. In his vision, Peter saw a sheet being lowered out of the sky containing all sorts of animals, clean and unclean. Peter was instructed to kill and eat. Peter refused at first, since he had never eaten anything profane or unclean. He eventually acceded. Peter's heavenly vision, it seems, was telling him that all foods were clean or nonpolluting. But the "circumcision party" in Jerusalem—that part of the community that advocated the continued observance of purity regulations—criticized Peter for associating with uncircumcised males and sharing nonkosher food with them.

Paul also ran into this debate, and he, too, found himself on the side of the freedom party—freedom from ritual constraints. At one point Paul confronts Peter over this issue because Peter had been inconsistent in his behavior. While Paul resisted the conservatism of the Jerusalem pillars, he was also willing to compromise principle, now and again, for the sake of those who were offended either by too much constraint or not enough. For example, he was willing to forgo the pleasure of meat bought at a pagan temple meat market for the sake of those who objected to eating meat that had been sacrificed to pagan deities.

Circumcision was another mark of the Judean insider. John the Baptist and Jesus were both undoubtedly circumcised, as the gospels report. Yet Jesus seems to have laid the groundwork for abandoning that religious custom by his openness to gentile inclusion in God's estate. But we cannot be entirely sure that the stories portraying that openness are based on historical reminiscence. At all events, there is a curious saying in the Gospel of Thomas on this subject:

> His disciples said to him, "Is circumcision useful or not?"
> He said to them, "If it were useful, their father would produce children already circumcised from their mother."[22]

This saying may not be authentically Jesus', although it is clear that it was not only Thomas Christians who understood Jesus to nullify circumcision as a mark of the insider. Paul also did so. Paul's companion and assistant, Titus, was an uncircumcised gentile; he was not forced to be circumcised,[23] although Luke reports in the Book of Acts that Timothy was circumcised out of deference to Jewish brethren.[24]

Ritual washing of both vessels and body were a part of purity practice. Again, Jesus appears to have been critical of ritual washing. Another saying in Thomas—"Why do you wash the outside of the cup? Don't you understand that the one who made the inside is also the one who made the outside?"—suggests that Jesus regards both surfaces of the cup as equal.[25] Why then wash only the outside as a purity gesture?

Baptism is of course another aspect of ritual washing. John the Baptist practiced it, as did the Qumran community, to judge by their many pools and baths. Jesus' criticism of the practice may be the reason he did not practice baptism—or so we are told in the Gospel of John. Gospel Oxyrhynchus 840 preserves a story of Jesus in the temple precinct, engaged in a debate about ritual washing and purity. It seems he and his disciples were in an area open only to ritually clean priests. For this he is criticized by a leading priest. In response, Jesus argues that the stagnant water of the pool of David, frequented at least metaphorically by pigs and dogs—both were considered unclean animals—would not make a priest clean. Instead Jesus is made to propose ritual cleansing in the lively, running water of Christian baptism.[26]

The gospel fragment is clearly later and looks back on events in the temple era from a great distance. The author seems not to understand clearly the rules about temple space that would have precluded Jesus and his followers from wandering around in an area reserved for priests. But, like other traces in the tradition, this one hints that Jesus may have been critical of ritual washing.

Sacred Names

Associates of the Qumran community were expelled from the group for the infraction of any regulation, even one word, of the law of Moses.[27] Members of the community in good standing were not allowed to fraternize with any one excommunicated at any level, for any reason. The boundaries of the community had to be maintained at all costs.

Excommunication was the penalty for uttering the divine name. The name of God—Yahweh in Hebrew—although it appears frequently in the Hebrew Bible, was not to be pronounced; God's name, like God, was ineffable (incapable of being expressed in words, unutterable, beyond description). Scholars and others who read from the sacred text learned that the sound of the word *Adonai* ("Lord") was to be substituted for Yahweh whenever it appeared in the text. In other words, the text read "Yahweh," but the reader was to say "Adonai." It was acceptable to pronounce the word for "God," Elohim (literally, "gods"), but enunciating the sounds of Yahweh was forbidden.

The rule in the Dead Sea Scrolls' Manual of Discipline for the community at Qumran was this:

> If any person has uttered the most sacred name, even though lightheartedly, or as a result of shock, or for any other reason whatever, while reading the scripture or praying, he is to be dismissed and not permitted to return to the community forever.[28]

That may seem like a heavy penalty for so minor an infraction—as it appears to modern Western minds. Again, however, the boundaries of sacred times, places, and things were considered inviolable. In closely regulated communities, those who violated those boundaries, who transgressed the limits, even accidentally, were no longer fit to belong to the group.

Jesus is not reported to have pronounced the Hebrew name of God in the surviving gospels. Indeed, that name never appears in extant gospel texts. Instead, Jesus is represented as employing *theos,* the Greek word for God, to replace the Hebrew *Elohim,* and he uses the Greek term *kyrios* as a substitute for both *Adonai* and *Yahweh*. Jesus uses the intimate address *Abba* or "Father" to address God.[29] This term is well attested prior to Jesus, even in some Qumran texts, but it seems not to have made a dent in the rules governing practice in conservative circles, such as those at Qumran.

The term suggests that Jesus understood himself to have a particularly intimate relationship to God. Moreover, he taught his disciples to address God in a similar fashion. He also taught his disciples to hold the name of God in reverence.[30] The use of this familiar term, however, suggests that Jesus did not observe the conventions connected with God's name but conceived of having a filial relationship to God, yet without sentimental overtones.

Jesus seems to have infringed a number of religious and social prohibitions and restrictions in his day. That earned him a considerable amount of ill will and may eventually have had something to do with his death. In any case, he appears to have been a free spirit. For Jesus the rigidities of his traditional world, of his religious and social order, exercised no hold on him. He commanded his disciples to join him in crossing over the Jordan to the promised land of new associations and liberties—to God's domain.

TIMES AND TENURES: TODAY

Celebration

Jesus initially followed his mentor, John the Baptist, into the wilderness to escape the evils of urban life and to repent, fast, and pray. As a follower of John, Jesus would have become an ascetic. John neither ate nor drank, and folks used to say he was demented. Jesus soon rejected the options offered by the Baptist. He returned to hellenized Galilee and feasted rather than fasted. His rule was not merely to simplify, simplify, simplify, like Henry David Thoreau, but to celebrate, celebrate, celebrate.

Because Jesus is confident God will provide and because he is willing to trust human generosity, he strongly recommends celebration. He congratulates the hungry and promises them a feast.[31] Jesus shows up both eating and drinking, and so people call him a glutton and a drunk, a crony of toll collectors and sinners.[32] He advises his critics that the groom's friends can't fast as long as the groom is around.[33] His parables are filled with parties—over the recovery of a lost coin, a lost sheep, a lost son—and Jesus pictures the arrival of God's rule as a dinner party. He is the proverbial party animal, as one of our colleagues in the Jesus Seminar has put it.

The standard party in Jesus' day for those who wished to discuss philosophy and traffic in wit was the symposium. (Women were rarely found at them, except in elite circles.) Jesus must have been familiar with such gatherings, since he castigates the scholars "who love the best couches at banquets." He also criticizes them for parading around in the marketplace in order to be the recipients of accolades and respectful greetings. It may have been in the context of such remarks that Jesus advises, "Those who promote themselves will be demoted and those who demote themselves will be promoted."[34] That's not the way it works in the real world.

In the parable of the Pharisee and the toll collector, the Pharisee boasts, "I fast twice a week, and I give tithes of everything I acquire."[35] That is probably an accurate description of the pious Pharisee of Jesus' day. In the Gospel of Mark we are told that John's disciples and the Pharisees are in the habit of fasting. So they approach Jesus and ask, "Why do John's disciples fast, but your disciples don't?" Jesus replies in figurative language: "The groom's friends can't fast while the groom is present, can they?"[36] The answer he expects is "Of course not."

In celebrating, one takes no thought for tomorrow. A celebration is a departure from routine existence, from normal, daily activities. A woman loses a coin, sweeps the dirt floor of her house to find it, then spends that coin and more to celebrate her good fortune. A sheep wanders off from the flock and becomes lost in the wilderness; the shepherd leaves the flock alone to search for the stray. When he finds it, he throws a party to celebrate and probably slaughters the sheep he has just retrieved. A senile old father risks the loyalty of his faithful son in order to celebrate the return of the truant prodigal. Merrymaking, Jesus tells his followers, is what follows upon the recovery of what was lost.

Celebration is appropriate for another reason: God's estate is like a very valuable pearl or a cache of coins found in a field. It is something like winning the lottery. It is not, in these cases, finding something that had been lost but stumbling on a new, unanticipated treasure. The unexpected discovery of something for which one has not been searching produces the joy that comes with surprise. Festivities are then spontaneous.

Sacred Times and Seasons

There are sacred times and seasons as well as sacred places. Jesus seems to have displaced the standard sacred times and inaugurated new ones—when something lost was found, when a treasure was unexpectedly discovered. For example, the fourth commandment states:

Remember the sabbath day, and keep it holy.[37]

Jesus responds with his own vision:

The sabbath day was created for Adam and Eve, not Adam and Eve for the sabbath day. So, the son of Adam lords it even over the sabbath day.[38]

In this saying, the phrase "son of Adam" originally referred to the progenitors of humankind, Adam and Eve, and was not a technical term meaning the Expected One or the messiah. On the lips of Jesus, "son of Adam" undoubtedly referred to any human being: human beings, he is saying, are masters of sabbath observance, not the other way around. (We discussed this phrase at length in Chapter Five.)

Understood in this way, his right as redeemer to reinterpret the commandment authorized the church to move the sabbath from the seventh to the first day of the week in order to distinguish Christian practice from that of Judaism. Seventh-Day Adventists have moved it back. Meanwhile, the original point made by Jesus has been buried under an avalanche of legal maneuvering.

For his part, however, Jesus meant to set human needs above those of the sabbath. In so doing, he was reinterpreting the creation story as well as the fourth commandment. Adam and Eve, not the commandment, take precedence in disputes over the sabbath. This seems to square with the practice of Jesus, who apparently healed and exorcised on the seventh day.

Jesus seems regularly to have broken sabbath regulations, though the particulars are far from clear. According to the Gospel of John, Jesus is criticized for telling a lame man to pick up his mat and walk around—in other words, to demonstrate that he has been cured. Of course, it was against the Law of Moses to carry one's mat around on the sabbath. So, the Gospel tells us,

> This is the reason the Judeans tried even harder to kill him: not only did he violate the sabbath; worse still, he would call God his Father and make himself out to be God's equal.[39]

Jesus probably did infringe sabbath regulations. He certainly called God his Father, as the address in the Lord's Prayer makes evident. But it is extremely doubtful that he claimed to be God's equal.

John the Baptist fasted; Jesus did not. As soon as Jesus was gone, the Christian community reverted to the practice of fasting. At a later time, when the first missionaries were being commissioned according to the Book of Acts, the community was worshiping the Lord and fasting when the holy spirit instructed them: "Commission Barnabas and Saul to carry out the task which I have assigned them." The whole assembly fasted and prayed and laid their hands on the pair; then they sent them on their way.[40]

However, as the Christian movement separated from Judaism, Christians were careful to distinguish their fasts from those practiced by Jews:

> You are not to fast in concert with the pretenders. They fast on Mondays and Thursdays. You are to fast on Wednesdays and Fridays.[41]

There is an excessive amount of posturing in this Christian admonition.

Fasting has never been popular among Americans. Even Catholics have abandoned the practice of restricting their diets on Fridays to fish only. No one can practice fasting religiously and be as overweight as Americans tend to be. On the other hand, the blue laws that once controlled behavior on Sundays have died a slow and laborious death in the United States. Some of them are still around. I can remember when stores could not open for business on Sundays, when football and basketball games were not allowed, when it was impossible to purchase beer or wine on Sunday, which people erroneously referred to as the sabbath. As the Puritan mentality waned, it became legal to have sports on Sunday so long as they didn't begin until after the noon hour (the morning belonged to the churches), and it became possible to buy beer after 10:00 A.M. These more relaxed regulations are still in force in many American communities.

This is all to say that Jesus' teaching on sabbath observance and his propensity for feasting rather than fasting were lost on the Puritans. In more recent times, Americans seem to have taken Jesus too literally and abandoned all self-restraint.

TIMES AND TENURES: TOMORROW

Anxieties: God Will Provide (Manna)

Human beings are concerned about food, clothing, shelter. Does that reflect lack of faith? Jesus seems to think so.

In God's estate, as in the Sinai wilderness of old, Jesus believes his Father will provide. What father, he asks, will give his son a stone when it's bread he's asking for? (Bread in the shape of a stone, like the pita bread we have today, was the common form.) Or, if he asks for a fish, what father will hand him a snake? (A fish perhaps in the shape of an eel so it could be confused with a snake.) If human fathers don't act that way, how much more unlikely that our heavenly Father would behave that way.[42]

Travelers arrive at a neighbor's house in the night. The neighbor comes to you and asks to borrow bread to feed them in accordance with the law of hospitality. You and your family are in bed. It is late; you don't want to get up and give your neighbor food. Yet, because you know you would be shamed by your friends and relatives if you refused to be hospitable, you will do what you don't want to do. My Father, Jesus advises, is at least as good as the law of hospitality. That has to be a hilarious understatement.

The theme of much of Jesus' discourse concerns trust in God. God is to be trusted for manna—for daily sustenance—just as the wandering Israelites trusted him in the wilderness. They subsisted on manna for forty years, we are told. But they were allowed to gather only enough manna for the day. When the sun grew hot, the rest melted. Moreover, those who gathered much had nothing left over when they had eaten; those who had collected a small amount found that they had plenty to eat. On the day before each sabbath, the Israelites were permitted to gather enough for two days.[43] Daryl Schmidt has pointed out these interesting parallels to the habits of Jesus and his wandering pilgrims, who also trusted God—and human generosity—for their daily rations.

Jesus advises one and all not to fret about food and clothing. His Father looks after the sparrows, he says, and they are a dime a dozen. God clothes the lilies of the field, so why worry?[44] God counts the hairs on human heads, Jesus avers in typical hyperbole.[45] His sayings on anxiety and on itinerancy suggest that he took no thought for shelter—he had no place to sleep, unlike the foxes and birds.[46] Without a permanent address and unemployed—so he was a vagabond sage.

On teaching excursions he depends on handouts, like a common hobo. He doesn't take a backpack, goes barefoot, and even refuses a staff for protection.[47] He recommends that his followers trust the Father for bread for one day at a time.[48] He need not plan ahead since he is convinced:

Ask—it'll be given you;
seek—you'll find;
knock—it'll be opened for you.[49]

TIMES AND TENURES: THE FUTURE

Success, Riches, and God's Domain

In the Gospel of John, there is a story about a man who was born blind. The disciples ask Jesus, "Was it this man's wrongdoing or his parents' that caused him to be born blind?"[50] Although the story may well be a fiction, the premise that misfortune was occasioned by sin was not fictive. According to the Deuteronomic history, Israel prospered when it followed divine dictates, but it suffered when it strayed from the covenant codes. In contrast, Job protests that his misfortunes were not brought on by sin; his friends chide him for challenging that sacrosanct doctrine. Jesus would have been on Job's side.

The playing field of life is level, according to Jesus.

God causes the sun to rise on both the bad and the good, and sends rain on both the just and the unjust.[51]

God does not privilege the status of the righteous and successful, in Jesus' view. The man was not born blind because of his sin or the sin of his parents.

Yet, according to Jesus, the playing field of life is not entirely level, after all. God's estate belongs to the poor, he announces, thereby reversing the old slogan that prosperity and righteousness go hand in glove. The hungry are to have a feast, and those who mourn will get to laugh. These reversals are fundamental to Jesus' notion of God's priorities.

Jesus tells his followers that it is easier for a camel to squeeze through the eye of a needle than for a rich person to get into God's domain.[52] Jesus thereby reverses the Deuteronomic rule and contradicts Pat Robertson, who televangelizes that the Los Angeles earthquake in 1994 was a punishment for the sins of Hollywood. Robertson does not tell us why God punished the innocent in the Los Angeles basin along with the guilty. Jesus reminds his listeners that it is difficult for those with money to get into God's domain.[53] And he caricatures the rich farmer and big investor who plants, sows, and reaps in order to fill granaries for which he will have no use when he dies.[54]

Jesus further advises that it is impossible to be committed to both God and the almighty dollar.[55] Although this is undoubtedly a folk proverb, Jesus may well have cited it; it is congruent with other remarks on the subject of wealth and God's estate.

Jesus apparently had little use for merchants and traders. Such people, he remarks in an addendum to the parable of the dinner party in Thomas, will not get into the places of his Father.[56]

Rewards and Punishments

In garden-variety societies, bad behavior is supposedly punished, sometimes severely, and good behavior allegedly rewarded, sometimes generously. At the mythical extremes lie heaven and hell.

It is imagined in most human societies that penalties ought to be increased as a deterrent to crime and rewards enhanced as a further incentive to virtue. Baseball players and film stars insist on the second principle, although they are not as keen on the first. Survey after survey has demonstrated that most people who believe in hell think themselves headed for heaven; people who believe in hell usually think it is for others.

Jesus, on the other hand, was not impressed with the standard schedule of rewards and punishments. In fact, Jesus did not accuse or judge those who knew themselves to be sinners. However, he was scathing in his criticism of the self-righteous and hypocritical. In this, as in other matters, he reversed normal expectations.

Reciprocity is his fundamental principle. The standard I apply to you, he suggests, is the standard that will be applied to me. As a consequence, he makes forgiveness reciprocal: "Forgive and you'll be forgiven."[57] One of the petitions he may have taught his disciples asks God to forgive only to the extent that the petitioner has forgiven others. One cannot be a recipient of forgiveness unless or until one is an agent of forgiveness. It's as simple as that and as difficult as that.

In the parable of the unforgiving slave, the slave is forgiven a debt of ten million dollars but is unwilling to cancel a paltry obligation of ten dollars. By foreclosing on the unfortunate debtor, the indentured manager forfeits the magnanimous treatment he had earlier received—he is given a taste of his own medicine by being imprisoned.[58] (Neither he nor the government and banks have learned that foreclosure trails disaster in its wake.)

Then there is the striking—and painful—figure of someone trying to extract a sliver from a friend's eye—ouch!—while a timber protrudes from his own.[59]

And in a story that may well be apocryphal, Jesus advises the accusers of the woman charged with adultery that the one without sin should cast the first stone.[60] Not many qualify, it seems, for that dubious honor.

Jesus' views of reward and punishment might be summed up this way: punishment is proximity without relationship; reward is association with intimacy.

Public Piety

It was expected in Judean society that decent folks would perform acts of charity. Okay, Jesus admonishes, "give to everyone who begs from you."[61] The global injunction does not constitute practical advice; in fact, it frustrates good intentions by making it unacceptable to discriminate among beggars. Of course, for someone without possessions it is easy to practice. And then he advises, "Don't let your left hand in on what your right hand is up to."[62] The admonition to keep acts of charity secret, even from yourself, is a paradox with a sting.

Jesus may have advised his followers about prayer. He seems to have taught them some prayer sentences, a few of which have been gathered into what is now known as the Lord's Prayer.[63] There is a core saying embedded in a cluster on prayer found in Matthew that undoubtedly expresses the view of Jesus on the subject:

> When you pray, go into a room by yourself and shut the door behind you.[64]

According to Jesus, prayer is a secret relationship between worshiper and God. He was probably critical of public posturing in any form, which is always suggestive of hypocrisy.

The Ultimate Frontier: Death

Humankind is arrogant enough to think it should be immortal like the gods. We yearn for continued existence after death, though we don't know what to do with ourselves on a rainy Sunday afternoon. Jesus did not have much to say about what lies on the other side of that ultimate temporal barrier, death. But he did say this:

> Whoever tries to hang on to life will forfeit it, but whoever forfeits life will preserve it.[65]

That surely is a paradox. How can we gain life by giving it up? Jesus does not explain. It is clear, however, that Jesus is not talking about extrinsic rewards—rewards that are extraneous to the thing for which they are the reward. For Jesus, entering God's domain, which is not a place like heaven or Disneyland, is its own reward. In the paradox about losing and gaining life, he is probably not talking about some future life beyond the veil of death but about the here and now.

The present also seems to be the time schedule in the parable of the vineyard laborers.[66] Those working the entire twelve-hour day thought they should be paid more than the idlers hired at the eleventh hour. But they were not. Rewards, it appears, are not handed out in relation to time put in or merit acquired. Nor is anything said or implied in that parable about rectifying a shortage in some hypothetical life to come.

Christianity has turned its conviction about the resurrection of Jesus into the promise of an extended existence for all believers. To be sure, the kind of existence will vary. For the believing righteous, it will be bliss in God's presence. That makes the hope self-serving. It is difficult to imagine Jesus projecting such a future for himself or for others. He asked nothing for himself, and he evidently did not promise recompense to others. At times Jesus' teaching perplexed his followers: They wondered who could actually be saved if not even the rich could get into God's domain. The answer provided by Mark is a reassuring: "Everything's possible for God."[67] Other sweeping aphorisms have also been softened. Similarly, the promise that those who have sacrificed relatives or property or wealth will receive a hundred times as much in the world to come is simply a misleading restatement of something Jesus probably promised as a reward in this life: those who forsake blood relatives will acquire hundreds of real relatives in the community of the kingdom, here and now.[68] Attempts to revamp Jesus' radical admonitions and promises usually leave traces in the surrounding verbal terrain. In this case, the aphorism that concludes this cluster—"Many of the first will be last, and of the last many will be first"—has also been modified from an absolute to a partial reversal by the simple addition of the word *many*.[69]

ENTERING THE KINGDOM

How does one get into God's kingdom? Where is the entrance? Does one need permission to cross over?

Jesus insisted that people can only enter the kingdom if they don't deserve to. The poor, the bereaved, the hungry are welcome there, but the self-righteous and hypocritical are not. Those who think they belong don't; those who are afraid they don't do. The last will be first and the first last.

The undeserving, like the prodigal, the petty tax official, the woman of ill repute and the leper, are like the homeless who find themselves unexpected guests at a mysterious banquet, as in the parable of the great supper or, as I like to term it, the dinner party.

The entrance to the kingdom, according to Jesus, is there before your nose. Just look around carefully and you will see it. Don't be misled by those who cry out, "Here it is!" or "It's over there!" They don't really know. It's actually in plain sight, but people don't see it because they are blind.

Franz Kafka created a parable we might call "The Guard." (In standard translations, it is called "The Watchman.") It goes like this:

> I ran past the first guard. Then I was horrified, I ran back and said to the guard: "I just ran through here while you were looking the other way."
> The guard looked straight ahead and said nothing.
> "I suppose I shouldn't have done it," I said.
> The guard still said nothing.
> "Does your silence mean I have permission to enter?"[70]

Permission to pass is not required. One may enter without permission; all that is required is boldness, confidence, the trust that it is acceptable to proceed. Those who need to be authorized to pass, who feel they must have permission, are not worthy of entrance.

Strictly speaking, of course, arrival in the kingdom is not even possible. Arrival is by departure only. Entrance into God's domain is the same thing as exodus. It is the quest of Abraham for a new ancestral home. It is Moses leading the children of Israel out of Egypt in search of the promised land. It is forsaking mother and father, wife and children, in order to acquire true relatives. For it no map is available. It is truly an immense journey.

PART THREE

The Jesus
of the Gospels

Chapter Twelve

THE DEATH OF JESUS

THE FOUNDING MYTHS

As Christian scholars draw closer to those stories that belong to the founding myth of Christianity, it becomes increasingly difficult for us to be critical and thus to be honest.

The Apostles' Creed insists that Jesus of Nazareth suffered under Pontius Pilate, was raised on the third day, and ascended to heaven. It also asserts that Jesus' birth was a miracle, portending the appearance of a divine child. As a consequence, it is more difficult objectively to assess the historical reliability of the passion narrative, which relates the story of Jesus' arrest, trial, crucifixion, and death. It is equally troubling to evaluate reports of the appearances of the risen Jesus and to subject the birth and childhood stories to rigorous historical analysis.

It is not that Christian scholars seek to deceive; on the contrary, it is as hard for Christian scholars to admit that some, most, or all of these accounts are mythical in nature as it is for orthodox Jews to contemplate pork roast with relish. Yet the time has come for Christian scholars to discriminate what is mythical from what is historical in the interests of their own integrity and in the interests of a reduction in Christian arrogance, a trait notably lacking in the historical Jesus.

There is nothing in the Christian story, so far as I can see, that is immune from doubt. The crucifixion of Jesus is not entirely beyond question. One ancient source stipulates that he was hanged, which may be no more than another way of referring to crucifixion. We do not know for a fact that he was buried. His body may have been left to rot on the cross, to become carrion for dogs and crows. What we have come to call the resurrection (by a kind of theological shorthand) is nowhere narrated directly, except in the highly imaginative account in the Gospel of Peter. The reports of his appearances vary so widely with respect to location, time, and witness that we cannot particularize what sort of an event those appearances were. And very few scholars believe that the birth stories are anything other than attempts to claim that Jesus was a remarkable person. Even the existence of Jesus has been challenged more than once and not without some justification. We should begin by admitting that all of these myths and legends may rest on nothing other than the fertile imagination of early believers.

We will explore the passion story in this chapter. The resurrection stories are the subject of Chapter Fourteen. Stories about the divine child will be considered in Chapter Fifteen.

The passion narrative has a slightly different status than accounts of the resurrection and the miraculous birth. The crucifixion is a painful, cruel fact. It represents a reality check of the most acute sort. It is not a claim to the miraculous. It requires no act of faith to assent to its historicity.

THE DEATH OF JESUS: THE BARE FACTS

We know very few things for certain about the death of Jesus and the events that led up to it. Most scholars agree that Jesus was executed by crucifixion on the authority of Pontius Pilate in Jerusalem, probably in connection with the Passover celebration. Yet the addition of the word *probably* even to that minimal statement indicates how precarious our historical judgments are.

It is not that crucifixion itself was an unusual practice. The Romans burned at the stake, fed their victims to lions, and crucified their enemies—wholesale. As John Dominic Crossan points out, there was not much left to bury following these forms of execution.[1] During the siege of Jerusalem under the Roman general Titus (66–70 c.e.), rebels forced to forsake the city in search of food were seized by the Romans and crucified opposite the walls of the city at the rate of five hundred each day. They were first scourged and tortured and then, in rage, the soldiers nailed their victims up in various postures to amuse themselves. Josephus tells us that their number was so great that the Romans had difficulty finding space for the crosses and sufficient crosses for the bodies.[2]

Some scholars believe the execution of Jesus took place in the fall, in connection with the feast of Tabernacles or Booths, rather than in the spring, in connection with Passover and the feast of Unleavened Bread. However, the bare facts that Jesus was executed in Jerusalem on the authority of Pontius Pilate have stood up under close and repeated examination.

Most of Jesus' followers fled during or after his arrest, but a few, especially the women, and Mary of Magdala in particular, may have witnessed his crucifixion. We do not know how their memories came to inform the creation of a passion narrative many decades later, if indeed that narrative reflects any eyewitness observations at all. We shall return to that problem subsequently.

The Fellows of the Jesus Seminar concede that Jesus may possibly have been buried in a common grave, but they doubt that his grave site was ever known. A traditional location was not identified until the fourth century. Around 325 C.E., builders working under orders from the Emperor Constantine destroyed the temple of Aphrodite that Hadrian had erected two hundred years earlier just outside the old Jerusalem wall. They discovered a cave tomb below. The architects assumed that a pagan temple had been erected over an earlier sacred place, so they turned the site into a new religious complex, incorporating the supposed place of crucifixion and the site of the tomb.[3] The story of the women discovering an empty tomb on Easter morning, which suggests that a burial site was known, was undoubtedly a literary creation of Mark.

The assertion that the Romans were innocent of, and the Jews responsible for, Jesus' death is Christian propaganda pure and simple. Such a claim was inspired by the conflict between synagogue and church late in the first century, long after the events themselves. The new Jesus movement was anxious at that time to curry favor with the Romans and to blame opponents for what happened to Jesus.

Pilate did not wash his hands nor did Judeans accept responsibility for Jesus' death, as the Gospels of Matthew and Peter report. The account of those events in Matthew is a piece of Christian fiction.[4] That bit of apologetic license exercised by the early evangelists has deeply compromised Christian integrity for many centuries and led to atrocities beyond reckoning. There is no historical or moral reason to hold Jews responsible for Jesus' death any more than there is basis to blame Italians, the descendants of the Romans, for his execution.

Jesus was probably executed summarily as a threat to public order at a time when Jerusalem was crowded with pilgrims. Passover was the most popular of the three major festivals that drew many Judeans to Jerusalem. E. P. Sanders has estimated that approximately three hundred thousand to four hundred thousand pilgrims crowded into the city and its environs for Passover.[5] Ancient guesses were higher; other scholars believe the figure to be lower than Sanders' numbers. Some pilgrims came for as long as two weeks, living in tents or staying in neighboring villages. Passover lasted for one day; Unleavened Bread, a festival of seven days, followed immediately. An extra week prior to the festival was sometimes required for the rites of purification that preceded the slaughter of the Passover lamb on Passover eve.

With so many pilgrims gathered in and around the holy city, festivals were a time of potential unrest and riot. It should be remembered that Passover was a celebration of liberation from Egyptian bondage. Caiaphas and other high priestly authorities, who were in charge of the temple cult, very probably denounced Jesus to Pilate for having created a disturbance in the temple area. But they lacked the authority to put Jesus to death. For that option, the authority of Pilate, the procurator or prefect, was required. It is not likely that a Roman trial was held; Pilate probably acted on his own authority, with the backing of Caiaphas. It is entirely probable that the trial before Jewish authorities was a fiction. The Gospel of Mark may be near the truth when it summarizes:

> And right away, at daybreak [following the arrest], the ranking priests, after consulting with the elders and scholars and whole Council, bound Jesus and led him away and turned him over to Pilate.[6]

That was probably the extent of Judean involvement.

Josephus, the Jewish historian writing late in the first century, reports that leading Judean authorities indicted Jesus and that Pilate condemned him to death. The relevant brief paragraph in Josephus' *Antiquities* has been augmented and possibly revised by Christian scribes to conform to Christian views. The works of Josephus were, in fact, copied and preserved by Christian scholars rather than by Jewish scribes. Editorial additions have been identified by modern scholars and are indicated by brackets and italics in the translation:

> About this time,* a wise man named Jesus appeared on the scene, *[if it is appropriate to refer to him as a man]*. As you may know, he performed startling feats and taught those who were eager to learn the truth. He won the allegiance of many of the Judeans and many of the Greeks. *[He was the messiah.]* He was indicted by our leaders; Pilate condemned him to be crucified. But that did not diminish the affection of his first followers for him. *[He once again appeared alive to them on the third day. The divinely inspired prophets had prophesied this and countless other marvelous things about him.]* And the clan of Christians, who get their name from him, has not died out to this day.[7]

According to Josephus, Jesus was known as a sage who performed unusual deeds. He had a considerable following among both Judeans and Greeks. Those followers continued in their devotion to him after his death and formed a movement that took its name from him, a movement that was still in existence in Josephus' day late in the first century. While providing only a paucity of details, Josephus confirms the principal features otherwise attested of the historical Jesus.

The Roman historian Tacitus, writing early in the second century but reporting events that transpired in Rome under Nero during 64 C.E., refers to Christianity as a "pernicious superstition" that had spread to Rome. Its founder, a certain Christus (or Chrestus?), had been executed during the reign of Tiberius, under Pontius Pilate, and had given the movement its name. Judea, he continues, was the "home of the disease" but it had spread to Rome, the cesspool of the empire.[8] Both Josephus and Tacitus know of the death of Jesus and both know of the movement

---

*"About this time" refers to the occasion on which Pilate precipitated a riot by robbing the temple treasury to build an aqueduct to bring water to Jerusalem.

he spawned. Both agree that the movement got its name from the term *Christ,* which they may have thought was a surname but which we know to have been a title, the Greek equivalent of the Hebrew *messiah.* Those seem to be the facts attested by sources external to the gospels.

The basic story:

Jesus was executed at Jerusalem under the jurisdiction of Pontius Pilate with the concurrence of high Judean officials.

His followers dispersed and returned to their homes following his arrest.

It was some time before Jesus' devoted followers regrouped, formed communities, organized their memories and convictions, and became a movement.

RULES OF EVIDENCE

Why do scholars find such limited conclusions plausible? Why is the passion narrative regarded with such skepticism? And why, on the other hand, do many others, including many scholars, regard the story as virtual history?

It is wise, at this juncture, to review the rules of evidence that apply to the passion narrative (and to other reports in the gospels). What prompts the historian to be cautious, to be skeptical? What are the tests that encourage confidence?

Events and characterizations that would have been an embarrassment to Jesus' followers, to those forming and relating the story of his death, and yet were preserved by them, have some claim to be historical. The lack of motivation to create and transmit unflattering details is positive evidence, especially given the infant church's strong desire not to remember—to forget—unfavorable events.

On the other hand, anything based on prophecy is probably a fiction. It is clear that the authors of the passion narrative had searched the scriptures for clues to the meaning of Jesus' death and had allowed those clues to guide them in framing the story: event was made to match prophecy.

In addition to the promptings of prophecy, we must be on the lookout for Christian propaganda. After all, the Christian movement was engaged in a battle for its existence in the Roman Empire. Under the circumstances, we might expect Christian leaders to blame others for what went wrong, and to take credit for what went right.

In every instance it is much better to have two or more independent sources for events and personnel. It is at this point that the question of sources becomes crucial. Were there two independent versions of the passion story? If so, what were they? Can we reconstruct them?

Historians frequently rely on plausibility, or verisimilitude, as a criterion. General historical plausibility is a rubber crutch. We can establish what might have been expected of the Romans, and we can, with less confidence, determine what might have been expected of the Judeans. But general plausibility is what writers of fiction all aspire to when they want to persuade us to suspend our critical judgments and accept their fictionalized version of events. Plausibility, in other words, can be little more than a negative criterion: if the storyteller does not know the place, time, and customs of the story being narrated, we can be confident that his or her tale is not history.

Occasionally historians can infer a previous event from an established occurrence. For example, if Jesus was in fact executed, he must have been arrested and taken into custody at some point prior to that event. But, as John Dominic Crossan points out, it does not follow that he had to have been buried if he had been executed.[9] Indeed, in crucifixions, exposure to the elements and scavengers was the rule rather than the exception.

Critical scholars are also wary of events and sequences that match too neatly the aims of the evangelist telling the story. Matthew and Luke rewrite and revise their source, Mark, the better to advance their own theological programs. That process is clearly in evidence in the passion narrative. Scholars are accordingly skeptical of alterations made to the Markan account by either Matthew or Luke.

THE PASSION AS STORY

We have spoken frequently of something called the passion narrative. It is time to define it more closely and distinguish it from the passion as *gospel.*

In its narrow sense, the passion consists of the agony, the suffering of Jesus during the mocking, scourging, and crucifixion. As a short, well-focused story, the passion encompasses the events that began the evening prior to his death with the common meal and concluded with his burial. Those events are narrated in Mark 14–15 and in the parallels to Mark in Matthew, Luke, John, and Peter. As a more extended narrative, the passion story is sometimes taken to refer to all the events of the passion week, beginning with the so-called triumphal entry on Palm Sunday (Mark 11–15) and ending with the resurrection.

The passion narrative assumes that Jesus was executed as a common criminal. For the historian that is the first fact to confront and assess. The passion story then endeavors to explain why Jesus was executed. That is the second major question to be addressed. And, finally, we must ask what significance was assigned to the death of Jesus by his followers. Why did they take an interest in his death? What was their motivation for telling the story?

In order to get these issues in focus, we need to consider the passion story as a whole. What is the passion narrative? What are its constituent parts? Out of what was it created? What was its history?

TABLE 9

THE PASSION NARRATIVE ACCORDING TO MARK

The extended passion narrative covers the following events:

1.	Entry into Jerusalem	Mark 11:1–10
2.	*Barren fig tree*	*Mark 11:12–14, 20–25*
3.	The temple incident	Mark 11:15–19
4.	*Teaching in the temple area*	*Mark 11:27–12:44, 13:1–37*
5.	The conspiracy against Jesus	Mark 14:1–2 and 43–52
6.	*The anointing*	*Mark 14:3–9*
7.	Judas' betrayal	Mark 14:10–11 and 43–52
8.	*Last supper*	*Mark 14:12–21, 22–26*
9.	Peter's denial	Mark 14:27–31
10.	Gethsemane	Mark 14:32–42
11.	Arrest	Mark 14:43–52
12.	Trial: Council	Mark 14:53–72
13.	Trial: Pilate	Mark 15:1–5, 6–15
14.	Mocking and crucifixion	Mark 15:16–20, 21–41
15.	The burial	Mark 15:42–47

Additions by Matthew and Luke:

16.	*The incident of the two swords*	*Luke 22:35–38*
17.	*The death of Judas*	*Matt 27:3–10*
18.	*Hearing before Herod*	*Luke 23:6–16*
19.	*The guard at the tomb*	*Matt 27:62–66*

NOTE: Italic indicates intrusive elements.

INTRUSIVE EVENTS

The first step is to identify the events that did not originally belong to the passion story. Scholars do that by differentiating segments that circulated as independent units in the oral tradition from those that are integral to the sequence of events constituting the passion narrative. Events that are reported in other contexts or that are not essential to the passion story are considered intrusive. Incidents that make sense only as part of the passion narrative are regarded as integral to that story.

In the outline provided in Table 9, the episode of the barren fig tree (item 2) appears in the form of a "parable" in Luke, which is located outside the passion narrative in that gospel.[10] It does not appear in the passion (or elsewhere) in either John or Peter. Matthew follows Mark in locating it in the passion week.

The collection of anecdotes and sayings Mark has gathered in 11:27–12:44 and 13:1–37 (item 4) do not necessarily belong to utterances made during the final week of Jesus' life. Some or all of them could as readily have been located elsewhere.

The story of the woman who anoints Jesus in the house of Simon the leper in Bethany, just outside Jerusalem (item 6) appears in Luke 7.[11] There the woman is a sinner and the dinner party Jesus is attending is being held in a Pharisee's house. This story, placed where it is in Mark, interrupts the flow of the narrative from 14:1–2 to 14:10–11; omit it and the sequence is smoothed out. John concurs in locating it during passion week, but at his hands it involves Mary and Martha and Lazarus. Mary anoints the feet of Jesus, rather than his head, and, as in other versions of the story, Judas complains about the cost. Variations in location and other details suggest that this story, too, must have circulated independently at one time, without connection to the passion. The role of Judas in it is what prompted storytellers to connect it with Judas' betrayal as the passion story was augmented.

The words spoken by Jesus at the last supper (item 8), which were to form the basis of the later eucharist, do not fit with the Passover celebration. On that occasion, the sacrificial lamb (or kid) was slaughtered on the afternoon of Nisan the fourteenth in the Hebrew calendar. The Passover meal was eaten that evening, in remembrance of the events in Egypt centuries earlier, prior to the exodus. Jesus was allegedly speaking words about his own body and blood at the moment when he should have been speaking of the Passover lamb. The breaking of bread and the common cup were elements introduced into the meal by Christian interpreters who took it as a memorial to the death of Jesus rather than as a reminder of the exodus. Paul links it to the death of Jesus in his first letter to the Corinthians.[12] The counterpart in Mark 14:22–25, in which Jesus speaks of his own body and blood as a sacrifice, is thus not a part of the original passion story.

In addition, items 16 through 19 in Table 9 were inserted into the story by Matthew and Luke. None of them is likely to be historical. These four bring to eight the total number of events that were not part of the original passion story. And there are other anomalies in the narrative to be noted subsequently.

INTERLOCKING MOTIFS

Even if we excise the intrusive oral stories identified in the preceding section, the passion narrative is relatively lengthy and involved. It interweaves five themes or motifs.

The First Motif: Jesus as a Royal Davidic Messiah

Jesus is hailed as the one inaugurating the coming kingdom of David during his so-called triumphal entry into Jerusalem riding on a colt

TABLE 10

THE PASSION NARRATIVE ACCORDING TO JOHN

The Gospel of John reports many of the same events as Mark but in different locations and order:

1.	The temple incident	John 2:14–19
2.	The conspiracy against Jesus	John 11:47–53
3.	The anointing	John 12:1–8
4.	Entry into Jerusalem	John 12:12–15
5.	Last supper	John 13:1–38
6.	Arrest	John 18:1–12
7.	Peter's denial	John 18:17–18, 25–27
8.	Hearing before the high priest	John 18:19–24
9.	Hearing before Pilate	John 18:28–19:16a
10.	Crucifixion	John 19:16b–37
11.	Burial	John 19:38–42

(Mark 11:1–10). The people greet him by spreading their cloaks on the road and waving their leafy branches while chanting a welcome taken from Zechariah and Psalm 117 (118 in the Hebrew version). That theme is not renewed until Mark 14:25, when Jesus pledges that he won't drink wine again until he does so in God's domain. In response to a query of the high priest, Jesus confesses that he is the messiah and that the son of Adam will come with clouds and restore the kingdom (Mark 14:61–62). These references are barely plausible as allusions to the theme of the Davidic messiah, but those that follow in 15:2, 9, 12, 16–20, 26, and 32 are blatant references to Jesus as the king of the Judeans and king of Israel, although many of them are in jest—the soldiers mock Jesus as a royal figure by putting a purple robe on him and crowning him with a garland of thorns. This royalty motif persists throughout the gospels, John and Peter included.

What are we to make of this theme? To understand its allure, it is helpful to get some sense of the attraction of the wilderness for messianic pretenders.

WILDERNESS   In Jesus' day the wilderness was a hotbed of messianic movements and the locale of efforts to turn the clock back to mythic time—to the time when Israel wandered in the wilderness under Moses; to visits to the sacred mountain, Mount Sinai; to the place of "the vision quest," of temptation and discipline. And the wilderness was close at hand: it included the desolate hills and deep valleys that lay between Jerusalem and the Jordan valley and the Dead Sea. It also included the desert beyond the Jordan and to the south.

Herod the Great had built a ring of fortresses in the wilderness to guard against the formation and threat of messianic movements and pretenders. Malcontents went out into the wilderness to reestablish contact with the ancient Israelite religion connected with Sinai. The ascetic and disciplined desert life cleansed the soul of the evils of civilization, particularly those associated with the cities. We Americans know about this theme firsthand: our myth of the American West has created a special place for the wilderness as the locus of the sacred. We long to recover contact with the holy when we back our RVs out of the drive on Friday afternoon and head for the mountains.

JOHN THE BAPTIST   John offered a populist alternative to the temple purification process for sin. People flocked out to him in the wilderness as he announced the imminent wrath of God amidst apocalyptic fervor and expectations of divine intervention. John the Baptist was regarded as a threat by Herod Antipas, tetrarch of Galilee and Perea, because he had a significant following. So Herod had him arrested and beheaded at Machaerus, a fortress deep in the wilderness out of reach of John's adoring crowds.

The common people undoubtedly blamed Herod for John's wrongful death because John had criticized Herod for taking Herodias, the wife of his brother Philip according to Mark, as his own wife.[13] Public antipathy directed toward Herod may have been what prompted him to spare Jesus for a time.

THEUDAS   Josephus tells of a Theudas who claimed to be a prophet. This insurrectionist led a group out into the wilderness in the Jordan valley and insisted that he would divide the river and allow his followers to pass back over on dry land, thus repeating the feat of Joshua. Fadus, the Roman procurator from 44 to 46 C.E., sent cavalry out against Theudas, slew many of his followers, and beheaded the rebel. He put his head on display in Jerusalem as a warning to other messianic pretenders.

THE EGYPTIAN   A nameless Egyptian false prophet also collected followers in the desert and then led them to the Mount of Olives. He proposed to invade Jerusalem, overpower the Roman garrison, and set himself up as tyrant. Felix, who was governor at the time, massacred many of the rebels, but the Egyptian escaped.

There have been suggestions that Jesus shared this messianic mentality. The charges brought against him at his hearings, the mockings, and the triumphal entry appear to link him with the wilderness pretenders and accordingly with the claim made on his behalf of being a royal Davidic messiah. The curious incident in which he advises his disciples in the garden of Gethsemane on the night of his arrest has perhaps lent credence to this connection. On that occasion, he reverses his earlier admonitions and advises his disciples now to take a purse and knapsack with them on their travels and, if they do not have a sword, to sell their coats and buy one.[14] Like the anonymous Egyptian pretender, Jesus is on the Mount of Olives as he says these things. Yet these clues correspond to nothing else in his behavior and certainly are at odds with the content of his aphorisms and parables. If Jesus was a rebel, he was politically naive. The worst thing that Herod and Pilate might have held against him is that his movement attracted a substantial following.

The Second Motif: The Conspiracy Against Jesus

The second of the five motifs that run through the passion story is the conspiracy against Jesus. Aided and abetted by the betrayal of Judas, this theme is introduced by Mark in 14:1–2, then continued in 10–11, after the intrusive interlude of the anointing. It is resumed in an editorial note at the conclusion of the Gethsemane episode (14:42) and in the actual betrayal in 14:43–45, signaled by the kiss. The arrest then follows. The conspiracy continues during the hearings as the priests, elders, and scholars attempt to assemble against Jesus evidence that requires the death penalty (15:1, 3, 10, 53, 55–65). The death of Judas is a legendary accretion to this basic sequence.

The Third Motif: The Temple Incident

The Romans may well have executed Jesus as a pretender to the Davidic throne, not perhaps on Jesus' own recognizance but as a result of misplaced expectations on the part of his followers and admirers. There is another, complementary reason he may have been executed: a verbal threat or hostile act directed against the temple.

Jesus is reported to have driven vendors and bankers out of the temple area (Mark 11:15–19). This incident has been moved up to the beginning of Jesus' public life in the Gospel of John (2:13–22). If this incident is historical—and many scholars think it is—it was no doubt a symbolic action. The temple area was far too large and the number of pilgrims far too great for Jesus to have done more than display his displeasure by a limited attack.

This theme comes up again much later during the hearing before the Council and again during the crucifixion. During the hearing, his accusers claim that he threatened to destroy the temple and build another not made with hands (Mark 14:58). During the crucifixion, his taunters dare Jesus to save himself from the cross since he bragged that he would destroy the temple and rebuild it in three days (Mark 15:29). Then, as Jesus dies, the curtain of the temple is torn in two, indicating that his threat against the temple has been fulfilled, at least symbolically.

These charges are plausible only if Jesus actually made some verbal threat against the temple, such as the one reported in Mark 13:2: he invites his followers to look at the monumental buildings adorning the temple mount and exclaims, "Believe me, one stone won't remain on top of another when these buildings are knocked down." That same saying is repeated in another context in Luke.[15] In Thomas 71 a similar saying is put on the lips of Jesus himself: "I will destroy this house and no one will be able to build it." "House" here can only refer to the temple. The Gospel of John interprets the saying differently. "Destroy this temple," Jesus says, "and in three days I'll resurrect it."[16] The author of the Fourth Gospel explains that "temple" here refers to the body of Jesus and that its "rebuilding" is an allusion to his coming resurrection. The charge against Jesus, according to John, was based on a misunderstanding. As in many other details, John reinterprets the tradition so that Jesus is completely exonerated.

The Fourth Motif: The Defection

The defection of Jesus' closest followers, including Peter, is introduced in Mark 14:27–31 with a prophecy taken from Zechariah: "I will strike the shepherd and the sheep will be scattered."[17] Peter takes an oath that he won't abandon Jesus, and the other disciples concur in that oath. Jesus offers a prophecy of his own: "So help me, tonight before the rooster crows twice you will disown me three times."

The prediction is followed by the inability of Peter, James, and John even to stay awake during Jesus' prayers in the garden (Mark 14:32–42). In the garden, after the arrest, the disciples all desert Jesus and run away. Even a young man wearing a shroud—otherwise unidentified—flees naked from the scene (14:50–52).

Finally, Peter, who apparently had not quit the scene entirely like the rest of the disciples, follows Jesus to the hearing before the high priest. In a painful scene in the courtyard, he three times denies that he is associated with Jesus (14:54, 66–72). In the Gospel of John, this incident is shortened but also embellished. There are now two disciples trailing along behind the arrested Jesus. One of them is known to the high priest and gets them into the courtyard. A relative of the slave whose ear Peter had cut off in the garden identifies Peter as a friend of Jesus. Peter denies that he was in the garden at the time of the arrest.[18] The addition of the slave to the garden scene and a relative of that slave to the courtyard scene are legendary accretions; storytellers cannot resist creating and elaborating fictional details such as these.

The Fifth Motif: "According to the Scriptures"

The author of the Gospel of Mark has Jesus himself announce that the son of Adam was destined to suffer; be rejected by the elders, priests, and scholars; be executed; and then after three days rise.[19] This, of course, is Mark's own formulation: it is a summary of the story he is telling, the story that culminates in the passion of Jesus. But he attributes it to Jesus, and it thus becomes a retroactive prophecy that has to come true. Mark's sketch agrees in broad outline with the one known to Paul of Tarsus, who reports his version in his first letter to the Corinthians, written in the fifties C.E.:

> Christ died for our sins
> according to the scriptures,
> and was buried,
> and rose on the third day
> according to the scriptures.[20]

Just how was "according to the scriptures" to be understood? When Mark has Jesus say, as they arrest him in the garden rather than while he was teaching in the temple area, "The scriptures had to come true,"[21] he implies his arrest couldn't have happened at any other time, even though in this case we do not know what scriptures he had in mind. In the parallel statement, Matthew has made the claim more sweeping: "All of this happened because the prophetic scriptures had to come true."[22] Events, all of them, are determined by divine providence, in Matthew's view.

The scriptures being used by these early Christian scholars were the Greek version of the Hebrew Bible. The text of that translation was still fluid, and there was more than one version available. In any case, texts were usually cited by memory, since the requisite scrolls were not immediately available to most scribes and were difficult to use even when they were accessible. As a consequence, quotations from memory were sometimes inexact, to put it kindly; in candid terms, the Greek Bible was frequently modified in order to prove a point: scripture was adjusted to correspond to its fulfillment. As we have learned from the commentaries on scripture found at Qumran, it was also quite acceptable to cite texts and then to rewrite and reinterpret them in ways considerably removed from their original sense. This technique, called the pesher method, was the means by which scripture could be kept timely and relevant.

The issues involved are complex, to be sure. The treatment of John the Baptist in the opening paragraphs of Mark will serve to illustrate the problem. The reader is told that Isaiah had written about John:

> Here is my messenger,
> whom I send on ahead of you
> to prepare your way!
> A voice of someone shouting in the wilderness:
> "Make ready the way of the Lord,
> make straight his paths."[23]

Actually the quotation is a mixture of Malachi 3:1 and Isaiah 40:3 (the first three lines are from Malachi, the last three from Isaiah). Matthew and Luke silently correct Mark's mistake, yet they retain the quotation from Malachi and use it in another context in their gospels. A little later Mark tells his readers that John dressed habitually in camel's hair and wore a leather belt around his waist. Furthermore, the reader is told he lived on locusts and raw honey. John's dress is an exact replica of the dress of Elijah the Tishbite as reported in 2 Kings: "He [Elijah] wore a garment made of hair, with a leather belt around his waist."[24] There seems to be no supporting scripture for his diet.

In the judgment of most scholars, John the Baptist did practice his craft in the Jordan valley, in the desert, perhaps in fulfillment of the oracle of Isaiah: "A voice . . . shouting in the wilderness: 'Make ready the way of the Lord, make straight his paths.'" It is also possible that he adopted the model of Elijah's dress (and diet?) as his own, although it is equally possible that the description of Elijah was later applied to John without reference to his actual practice. The motivation to do so would have been the Christian desire to identify John as a latter-day Elijah who functioned as the prophetic forerunner of Jesus. We cannot be sure whether John the Baptist was acting out scripture or whether his reporters tailored his story to the prophecy.

In the passion narrative, the situation seems to be clearer. In the absence of eyewitnesses, the delay in forming the story, and the need to explain why Jesus had been executed as a common criminal, early Christian scholars combed the ancient texts for clues. They allowed the clues to dictate the terms of their stories. After all, had not God predetermined what was to happen? Were events not dictated by divine necessity? So they permitted the prophet Zechariah, for example, to provide them with suggestions of what must have happened:

Look, your King comes to you in innocence and as a savior,
humble and mounted on a beast of burden and a young colt.

Zechariah 9:9

The Zechariah prophecy probably became the paradigm for relating the story of the "triumphal" entry: the savior, innocent and humble, enters the holy city riding on an ass. There is irony in that picture. But it appears to combine certain remembered characteristics of Jesus with a depiction of him as the promised redeemer.

Many details of the passion story were suggested by the Psalms, particularly Psalms 2, 22, and 69. Other sources include prophetic texts such as Isaiah 53 and Zechariah 9–14, together with stories of David (2 Samuel 15–17) or the suffering righteous martyr (Wisdom of Solomon 2 and 5). Christian scribes searched the Greek scriptures diligently for proof that Jesus had died in accordance with God's will.

Casting lots for the clothing of Jesus was inspired by Psalm 22:18:

They divide my clothes among themselves,
and for my clothing they cast lots.

The gall and vinegar Jesus was given to drink was suggested by Psalm 69:21:

> They gave me poison for food,
> and for my thirst they gave me vinegar to drink.

Crucifixion between two thieves was based on Isaiah 53:12:

> His soul was handed over to death,
> and he was reckoned among the sinners

in conjunction with Psalm 22:16 (21:17 in the Greek version):

> For many dogs have encircled me,
> and a host of evildoers has surrounded me.

Striking, insulting, and spitting on Jesus were prompted by Isaiah 50:6:

> I presented my back to the scourge,
> my cheeks to be slapped,
> and my face I did not turn away from the shame of spitting.

Looking on Jesus, piercing, and mourning were suggested by Zechariah 12:10:

> They shall look on the one they have pierced.

The list of such allusions and parallels is extensive. Raymond E. Brown has compiled a conservative but impressive inventory in an appendix to his mammoth study of the passion.[25]

Some of the details, such as poking and nudging, are based on the scapegoat ritual practiced annually on the Day of Atonement (*Yom Kippur*). On that day two goats were prepared, one to be sacrificed in the temple area, the other to be poked or nudged into the wilderness; the second thereby vicariously carried away the sins of the people (hence the term *scapegoat*). Disrobing and rerobing in a mock coronation were prompted by Zechariah 3:1–5. In his brilliant study, John Dominic Crossan has shown that virtually every detail connected with the passion was based on some scripture. That prompted him to conclude: We know virtually nothing about the arrest, trial, and execution of Jesus other than the fact of it.[26] The stories of the arrest in the gospels are themselves fictions; we only infer that he was arrested because we know he was executed. About the trial, or trials, we have no historically reliable information at all.

Resurrection on the third day was probably suggested by Hosea 6:2:

> [The Lord] will heal us after two days,
> On the third day we will be resurrected
> and we will live in the Lord's presence.

However, Kathleen Corley has collected the evidence to show that it was customary for women, intent on performing mourning rites and embalming, to wait three days before their visit to the grave site to make sure the deceased was really dead. Mistaken diagnosis was not infrequent in the practice of folk medicine and in the absence of a professional coroner. The third-day motif in the gospel accounts may have arisen as a part of that practice of prudent delay.[27]

GOSPEL FICTIONS

In addition to events and details suggested by scripture, the passion story contains a number of pure fictions. Judas Iscariot the betrayer is in all probability a gospel fiction. It is difficult to determine what his role as betrayer might have been, were he a real person. Did the officials need someone to identify Jesus, a relatively unknown Galilean sage? Did they require someone to provide information about where they could arrest him under the cover of darkness to avoid creating a public scene? The name of the betrayer is suggestive and probably symbolic: Jesus was betrayed by descendants of Judah—that is, by Judeans. Whatever we may think of Judas himself, Matthew's account of the death of Judas is clearly fictive.[28]

It is essential to recall that certain aspects of the passion narrative were dictated by polemics directed against the Jews: the Christian tendency to vindicate Pilate; the trial before the Council; the guards at the tomb; Judas; and the stereotyped "Jewish" opponents of Jesus in the Gospel of John.

What about other characters in the story?

Joseph of Arimathea is probably a Markan creation. Jesus lacked friends in high places, so Mark provides him with narrative support. Joseph was a respected member of the Council and someone who was also looking for God's domain. It was a perfect match. Joseph asks Pilate for the body. He takes Jesus from the cross, wraps his body in a shroud, and places it in a rock-cut tomb. A huge stone is rolled against the opening to prevent the theft of the body.[29]

Mark himself is not quite consistent in his own inventions. Earlier he had informed his readers that all the members of the Council had concurred in the death penalty; presumably Joseph was among those who agreed to the verdict.[30] Yet Joseph buries Jesus in conformity with the injunction of Deuteronomy:

> If anyone commits a crime punishable by death and is executed, and you hang him on a tree, his corpse is not to remain on the tree overnight. You must bury him that same day. Everyone hung on a tree is under God's curse. You are not to defile the land that the Lord your God is giving you as your legacy.[31]

The public display of an executed criminal was intended to bring shame on the guilty party and his family. There were restrictions, however. Under Israelite law, the corpse was not to be exposed more than one day; it was to be buried before sundown. Were it left exposed indefinitely, it would serve as carrion.

Joseph was pictured as a friend of Jesus but not necessarily a friend of the law where the other criminals were concerned. At the hands of Matthew, Joseph becomes rich and a disciple of Jesus.[32] But he is not a member of the Council. The shroud Joseph employs is "clean" and the tomb is now a "new" tomb, in spite of the fact that rock tombs were ordinarily family burial places that were used for multiple burials (old bones were cleared away and the burial niches reused). Luke corrects Mark in a slightly different direction. According to Luke, Joseph is a member of the Council but did not concur in the guilty verdict. The shroud is now made of fine linen. The tomb has not been used prior to the burial of Jesus.

In the Gospel of John, Joseph is a follower of Jesus in secret, out of fear of the Judeans. He has been given a fictive burial assistant by the name of Nicodemus. Nicodemus first appears in John 3 as a suppliant who comes to Jesus by night out of fear, as does Joseph. And, like Joseph, Nicodemus is one of the Judean authorities who warns his colleagues about condemning a man without a hearing.[33] At the burial, Nicodemus provides seventy-five pounds of spices for the anointing, enough to fill several tombs and embalm many bodies. The new, unused tomb is now located in a garden.[34] As we observe the development of the story, conditions steadily improve. The scene has become almost idyllic.

Barabbas (son of "Abba," the Father, or "son of God") in Mark 15:7 is certainly a fiction, as is Simon of Cyrene, the father of Alexander and Rufus in Mark 15:21. Blind Bartimaeus, son of Timaeus in Mark 10:46, and Jairus, a synagogue official, in 5:22 are probably also inventions. The assignment of names and the particularization of place enhance verisimilitude in fiction. Sherlock Holmes and Dr. Watson are taken by millions to have had real existence, and 221B Baker Street is an actual address in London that tourists can go see for themselves. Robin Hood and the Sheriff of Nottingham exist for many as certainly as do King Arthur, Guinevere, and Lancelot. To be sure, there may have been living models in the minds of the authors who gave fictional life to these heroes and heroines, as may also have been the case with the gospel authors, but the fictions themselves are taken to be larger than life.

INCREMENT OF LEGENDARY ELEMENTS

Among the gospels, Matthew alone reports the death of Judas.[35] According to Matthew, Judas returns the thirty silver coins he has received for his services as an informant and then hangs himself. In Acts, Luke has

Judas buy a piece of land with the money; he subsequently falls down and his guts burst out.[36] Judas becomes the subject of a great deal of legendary speculation in later documents, but the process has already begun in Matthew.

Both Matthew and Peter report the posting of a Roman guard at the tomb to make sure that Jesus' disciples do not steal his body and then claim that Jesus has risen from the dead.[37] They needed only to make the tomb secure for three days, the customary waiting period to make sure that the spark of life had in fact departed the corpse. In another resurrection story, Jesus waits until Lazarus has been buried for four days to revive him. That delay made doubly certain that Lazarus was really dead; his body had already begun to smell.[38] In the case of Jesus, the prophecy put on the lips of Jesus has to be fulfilled: Jesus had promised that "after three days I am going to be raised up."[39] Jesus' words have taken on the status of scriptural prophecies that must come true. The guard at the tomb is a Christian fiction designed to ward off the criticism that Jesus' disciples stole his body. And a good fiction makes one's opponents, in this case the Roman guard, witness to the truth.

The dream of Pilate's wife is undoubtedly a Matthean invention: She advises Pilate that Jesus is innocent because of her dream; Pilate acts on his wife's advice by washing his hands in public.[40] In Mark the curtain of the temple is split in two as Jesus dies. Matthew enhances this event by having an earthquake also split rocks and open graves; righteous ones are raised from the dead out of those graves and appear to crowds in the city.[41] These are clearly pieces of Christian apologetic and propaganda.

In the garden of Gethsemane, the unnamed disciple who draws his sword and cuts off the ear of the high priest's slave is identified as Peter in the Gospel of John, and the slave is given the name Malchus.[42] Luke embellishes with a touch of the miraculous by having Jesus restore the slave's ear.[43]

The evangelists occasionally augment the story by introducing what might be called brief edifying discourses—speeches intended for the edification of later readers of the gospels. Following on the incident of the severed ear, for example, Matthew has Jesus give a brief warning about the use of swords: "Everyone who takes up the sword will be done in by the sword." This proverb is cited also in Revelation and was known to Jeremiah.[44]

In addition to the hearings before the high priest and Pilate, Luke reports a separate interrogation by Herod Antipas, who happens to be in Jerusalem, presumably for Passover.[45] Matthew, Mark, and John seem not to know of this event, but the Gospel of Peter also has Herod in Jerusalem and in charge of the trial.[46]

The mythical as well as the fictional aspects of the story were steadily added or enlarged as the story grew. For example, Pilate is the subject of endless and often favorable speculation in later literature. One such work is the *Acts of Pilate,* a text of unknown date, which was combined with "Christ's Descent into Hell" to form the *Gospel of Nicodemus.* Pilate is also alleged to have written letters to the Emperor Tiberius detailing the marvelous deeds of Jesus. In still another tradition, Pilate's wife is given the name Procla and is regarded as a saint by the Coptic church. Another late work entitled *Paradosis* reports that Pilate was beheaded. In non-Christian sources, Pilate receives less favorable treatment.

ORIGIN OF THE PASSION NARRATIVE

What, then, is the present state of scholarly opinion about the origin of the passion story? What can we say with confidence about its history?

The four canonical accounts of the passion of Jesus, including the Gospel of John, exhibit remarkable agreement on the major events, although the reports of individual incidents vary widely in detail and their sequence is not constant. The most remarkable observation to note about the four accounts is that their agreement ends where Mark ends— with the women at the empty tomb. From that point on they go their disparate ways, without the possibility of harmonization or reconciliation. We will explore the appearance stories in detail in Chapter Fourteen.

This then is the general outline of events, omitting those that are in all probability intrusive:

1. Jesus' entry into Jerusalem
2. Temple incident
3. Conspiracy against Jesus
4. Betrayal by Judas
5. Last supper
6. Peter's denial
7. Arrest
8. Hearing before the Council
9. Hearing before Pilate
10. Mocking
11. Execution
12. Death
13. Burial
14. Empty tomb

For the fragmentary Gospel of Peter there is no text until we come to item 9: Pilate is just washing his hands in the opening scene, presumably as the hearing draws to a close. Peter then confirms the next five items.

It is strange that no source outside the five gospels knows this same sequence of events, even in outline. Paul links the death and resurrection, as we noted earlier. And he knows that on the night in which Jesus was arrested (or betrayed, depending on how we translate the Greek verb), he broke bread and shared a cup of wine.[47] But that is the extent of Paul's narrative knowledge. If the passion story were well known, it seems likely that others would have referred to it, at least in outline.

Neither the Sayings Gospel Q nor the Gospel of Thomas has a passion narrative. Indeed, they lack specific references to the death of Jesus. It is possible but by no means certain that Thomas 55—"Whoever does not hate father and mother cannot be my disciple, and whoever does not hate brothers and sisters and carry the cross as I do will not be worthy of me"—is an oblique reference to Jesus' execution. There is also a reference in Q to carrying a cross: "Unless you carry your own cross and come along with me—you're no disciple of mine."[48] This, too, could be understood similarly as a veiled reference to Jesus' death. However, in both cases, the saying may also be given a nonliteral sense: forsaking father and mother is like carrying a heavy, onerous cross to one's demise. In neither gospel has the cross symbol been interpreted as a symbol of salvation connected with Jesus' death.

Many incidents, details, and in a few cases even sequences of events, were suggested by scripture. That indicates extensive and prolonged scribal activity—scholars searching the ancient texts for clues and adapting them to a growing narrative. The Jesus movement would have required time to emerge from its peasant matrix and develop a circle of literate elites. We do not know how much time that would have required, but it probably did not occur for some years. In addition, the passion narrative betrays the incremental augmentation of legendary elements and fictions. Because the story exhibits a certain narrative coherence involving interlocking themes and motifs, it cannot be based on the oral transmission of discrete scenes loosely connected, as is the case with the rest of the gospel narrative. It was probably a written narrative from its inception. The full development of the narrative probably had to await the onset of scribal activity in earnest, which may not have begun until after the fall of Jerusalem. The longer the delay, the more likely the narrative was based on hints provided by prophetic texts and the Psalms and on speculation rather than on historical reminiscence. In its Markan form, the passion narrative is the fruit of Christian apologetics, polemics, and propaganda.

At the end of the nineteenth century, Martin Kähler argued that the gospels were passion narratives with long introductions.[49] His assessment has now been reversed by many scholars: the gospels are collections of parables and aphorisms, symbolic deeds and miraculous cures, with a passion appendix.

How are we to explain this reversal of opinion?

Scholars are hopelessly divided on a solution to the origins of the passion story. The older view was that the proclamation of the primitive

Christian community, entailing the death, burial, and resurrection of Jesus, was augmented at first with a few isolated anecdotes connected with his execution. Rudolf Bultmann thought the story in its infancy consisted of five items: arrest, sentencing, trip to Golgotha, execution, and death.[50] Following his teacher, Helmut Koester advocates an oral version of the passion story that underlies three independent written reports—those of Mark, John, and Peter.[51]

Unfortunately, scholars have not been able to isolate that sequence of anecdotes, or any other sequence, in our existing sources or to explain how such a hypothetical narrative was transmitted during the oral period.

John Dominic Crossan has advanced the thesis that some early Christian scholars created the first passion narrative in the fifties, about the same time Q was being formed. He finds that first attempt preserved in what he calls the cross gospel, a narrative embedded in the Gospel of Peter. The cross gospel is a highly mythical version: Two men descend from heaven while Jesus' body is in the tomb; the stone rolls away from the entrance by itself; the two men emerge from the tomb supporting a third between them; the heads of the two reach to the sky, but the head of the third reaches beyond the sky. Crossan believes mythical accounts tend to precede more sober, nonmythical versions, but this view has not found wide acceptance.[52]

Robert T. Fortna and others have argued that the Gospel of John is based on a passion story that is independent of its counterpart in Mark. His views have been countered by others, who think that John is dependent on Mark. There is no consensus on the source or the status of the story in John.[53]

The one relatively fixed point in the continuing debate is that Mark is the basic source for Matthew and Luke. The latter simply rewrite, correct, and extend Mark's account for their own purposes. But even here there is dispute. Some have insisted that Luke has a special source for some of his traditions. Some have proposed that Luke shared a common source with John, in addition to his use of Mark. And so the argument goes on, without resolution or even the prospect of resolution.

Prior to the Gospel of Mark, we cannot be sure that there was a passion narrative consisting of a string of events leading up to Jesus' execution. If Mark has been correctly dated to the decade of the seventies—and that seems to be the earliest conceivable date for Mark—then we have no certain evidence of such a continuous story or a series of linked events prior to that date. Matthew, Luke, and John come later, in the eighties and nineties. In the view of most scholars, Peter is an early second-century account, although, like the other gospels, it may have preserved earlier traditions. But again scholars have not agreed on what those early traditions are.

A different and promising solution has been proposed by George Nickelsburg.[54] There are several tales, it seems, in Israelite and Judean literature that have a common plot not unlike that of the passion story. The stories are found in Genesis, Daniel, Esther, and in books belonging to what is called the Old Testament apocrypha: Susanna (a story attached to Daniel), 2 Maccabees, and the Wisdom of Solomon. In these tales, generally speaking, the hero or heroine does something to provoke a *reaction;* a *conspiracy* develops against him or her; an *accusation*—false, of course—is brought forward; there is a *trial* or hearing, followed by a *sentence;* the one unjustly accused is *condemned* and may suffer martyrdom; *vindication* comes at the end. Nickelsburg reasons that Mark, or someone prior to Mark, knew such tales in outline and put together a similar tale in which Jesus was the hero.

There are differences. The older stories lack a meal as a central feature, and there is no anointing or defection of a close associate, and nothing corresponding precisely to the prayers in Gethsemane. But these are precisely the elements that many scholars identify as intrusive—out of place—in the passion story. Nickelsburg's proposal at least accounts for the string of events that forms the spine of the passion narrative. Narrative sequences of the duration of the passion of Jesus would either have been shaped initially in writing, with prophecies as guidelines, or been based on formulas known from other similar tales. It is the second option that has opened up a new way to account for the shape of the passion story of Jesus. Nevertheless, many of the events, or details of events, were suggested by prophetic texts, including the Psalms.

Nickelsburg's theory does not, however, help us determine the history of the passion story. The simplest, most reliable solution remains the view that Mark created the first version of the story and every other version is based on Mark, directly or indirectly. That solution has its problems, as we have seen. Yet it may be the best we can do until new evidence, or a new theory about the evidence we have, emerges.

Chapter Thirteen

DOMESTICATING THE TRADITION AND MARKETING THE MESSIAH

DOMESTICATING THE TRADITION

What happened to the gospel of Jesus after his death?

The tendency, from the very beginning, was to make Jesus' wisdom *conform* to popular expectations, to assimilate his vision to conventional wisdom and thus to ordinary ways of seeing and saying. In other words, his parables and aphorisms were *domesticated*.

In concert with the tendency to make Jesus' message conform, his admirers' enthusiasm led inevitably to a *shift in focus* from the vision that mesmerized Jesus to Jesus the visionary. His followers fastened on him rather than on his glimpse of God's domain. The shift in focus from vision to visionary carried along with it a shift in his followers' perceptions of themselves: they no longer thought of themselves as outsiders; as the tradition was domesticated, they became insiders.

At the same time, the believing community wanted to propagate its faith by making it appealing to others. They wanted to *market the messiah*. They did that by making Jesus do all the things other charismatic miracle workers did. In addition, they certified his stature, validated his standing, with a series of epiphanies, including appearances to themselves after his death. Finally, they set Jesus in a mythical narrative frame in which the Christ figure replaced Jesus the Galilean sage. All of this was in the interests of missionary propaganda.

The crowning development in this process was the loss of Jesus' sense of the immediacy of the kingdom, of the overpowering nature of his glimpse. The fusion of present and future in Jesus' vision was dissolved, and the future again segregated from the present. The enchantment of the kingdom was gone. God's incursion into history was again anticipated as an event of the future rather than as a fact of the present. The apocalyptic mentality reasserted itself and sealed off Jesus' naive sense of time.

That is what happened. How did it happen? The transformation took place through a series of subtle and not so subtle changes. In the first place, the rhetorical strategies of Jesus, sketched in Chapter Eight, were slowly weakened, modified, and then lost. The change in strategy produced a change in content.

The conscious decision to market the messiah to a wider audience necessitated utilizing story forms customary for that purpose: anecdotes about a rare wit, miracle stories, epiphanies, and a story plot suitable for a superhuman savior.

These tendencies of the unfolding tradition can be observed in all the gospels, in all levels of the tradition. In this chapter we can only sample the range of possibilities.

THE MODIFICATION OF RHETORICAL STRATEGIES

The Loss of Tension

The tension that pervades Jesus' parables and aphorisms is reduced and then eliminated as the Jesus tradition is passed from person to person and generation to generation. The interplay between the literal and the metaphorical is diminished and often eliminated. As a consequence, the ambiguities, the polyvalent possibilities of Jesus' original language, are replaced by specific, fixed interpretations. Once the domestication of the tradition has set in, the door is open to augment the tradition with folk wisdom, proverbs, scripture citations, and other material extracted from the cultural context. Jesus becomes the repository of all the popular lore that can be endorsed by the new community. These trends are illustrated in a variety of ways, as the following subsections show.

Spiritualizing the Literal

Jesus' genuine aphorisms and parables are filled with images of hunger and poverty, food and clothing, begging and borrowing, oppression and homelessness, corrupt officials and unhearing and unseeing religious leaders. In his use of these images, Jesus maintains a tension between the literal and the nonliteral or spiritual. In one of his beatitudes, he offers congratulations to the poor as possessors of the kingdom:

Congratulations, you poor!
God's domain belongs to you.[1]

No one really believes that Jesus meant that God's kingdom was accessible only to those who were literally poverty stricken. Matthew's gospel certainly doesn't: he expands the original Q form preserved by Luke to reflect the spiritualizing tendency:

Congratulations to the poor *in spirit!*
Heaven's domain belongs to them.[2]

Matthew's version dissolves the tension between literal and spiritual by reducing the former to the latter. Real poverty no longer has privilege. And humility is no longer nurtured by the absence of figurative economic superiority.

Jesus had utter confidence in his Father and in the essential goodness of humankind: If parents might be expected to give their children bread rather than a stone, God might be expected to do as much.[3] A piece of bread somewhat like our pita bread was a day's ration. Jesus thought it appropriate to ask the Father for that amount: "Provide us with the bread we need for the day."[4] His disciples undoubtedly gave that prayer a literal interpretation. Jesus meant it as an expression of his absolute reliance on the providence of God: never ask for more than one's immediate needs—the needs for the day. But Luke has already begun the conversion to the literal: "Provide us with the bread we need day by day."[5] A shrinking fund of trust prompts human beings to request a steady handout.

So confident is Jesus in the response of both God and neighbor that he assures his followers, "Just ask, you'll be given what you need."[6] And he then sends his disciples out to live off the land and off society by knocking on doors and requesting a loaf—in imitation of his own behavior.[7] Later, as Christian evangelists take to the road, tests are developed to help local congregations tell the difference between true and false prophets:

> A traveling emissary is to accept nothing but bread until he reaches his night's lodging. If he asks for money, he is a fake. . . . If a prophet orders a meal while under the influence of the spirit, he is not to eat it. If he does eat it, he is a false prophet. . . . An itinerant preacher is to stay no more than one day, at most two; if he stays three days, he is a fake.[8]

Those criteria are found in the Didache, an early Christian manual. The trust Jesus called for was a real test of character. For Jesus, limiting one's request to a single day was an expression of the level of trust he thought one ought to have in God. That original level was lost almost immediately as the confidence of the Christian community began to fade. In the absence of the requisite degree of trust, the community generated rules to govern the behavior of its traveling missionaries.

The temptation story illustrates how the tradition has begun to drift away from Jesus' original point. In that story, the devil says to Jesus, "To prove you're God's son, order this stone to become bread." Jesus responds, "It is written, 'Human beings are not to live on bread alone.'"[9] The response attributed to Jesus by the storyteller is taken from the Greek Bible, the LXX, as it was known.[10] The point of this incident, it seems, was to justify the fact that Jesus did not perform the miracles expected of the messiah by repeating the magic of Moses—for example, providing daily bread for the children of Israel during their sojourn in the desert. But it soon came to be reinterpreted as a warning to the faithful not to be overly concerned with food—to balance the need for physical sustenance with the more important spiritual needs of the soul.[11] Bread made from flour is being subtly displaced by bread made of spirit. That transition is easily made in a social group whose members are no longer primarily concerned with where they will get their next meal.

Luke reinforces the tendency to replace the literal with the spiritual when he reinterprets the saying about the compassion of parents:

> So if you, shiftless as you are, know how to give your children good gifts, isn't it much more likely that the heavenly Father will give holy spirit to those who ask him?[12]

The good gifts in question are bread and fish, which parents may be expected to supply needy children. But in Luke's revision, real bread has been replaced by holy spirit. The transition from one to the other was barely noticed as the community matured and prospered.

In the Gospel of John, too, people ask for bread. To their request, Jesus responds:

> I am the bread of life. Anyone who comes to me will never be hungry again, and anyone who believes in me will never again be thirsty.[13]

There is no flour in this kind of bread. And there is no Jesus left in the saying either. There isn't even a trace of holy spirit. Faith in Jesus has become the substitute for bread. When Jesus says, "And the bread that I will give for the world's life is my mortal flesh,"[14] we are on our way to the eucharist in which bread has become a symbol for the sacrificial body of Jesus that redeems one from sin when eaten.

In this progression we can observe a subtle but steady movement away from a single ration of real bread made from flour, to real bread for the long term, to spiritual bread, to the body of Christ as the symbolic bread of the eucharist. Simultaneously, the original emphasis on complete trust in God is gradually eroded.

Hard Sayings Softened

Modern readers of the gospels may find it difficult to believe that the original followers of Jesus, who formed the first Christian communities, did not hesitate to modify his sayings as changing circumstances required. To understand the process, one need only put oneself in the place of followers who wanted to take Jesus seriously—very seriously. Remember, too, that at first they had no written records to refresh their memories and then when records were made, they were not always readily available to consult. The process of transmission and interpretation was mostly by word of mouth. (Recall the last time someone gave you and a companion directions on how to get to a certain address, say, at a busy street corner, with cars whizzing by. How often have you and your companion disagreed on precisely what those directions were?) The quandary posed by a difficult saying is illustrated by how disciples responded to this injunction:

Give to everyone who begs from you.[15]

The admonition to give something to every beggar who asks is a global injunction if taken literally. How were Christians to understand that command?

As a means of adjusting this stringent injunction to the conditions of ongoing life, the Christian community soon began to hedge it about with qualifications. In this case, limitations were placed on the recipient rather than on the giver. Here is how the Didache, the first Christian handbook, handles the problem:

> Give to everyone who asks you.
> And do not demand repayment.
> For our Father wishes all to receive of his gifts.
> Blessed is the one who follows this injunction.
> That person has done no wrong.
> But let the recipient beware:
> If anyone receives ⟨a gift⟩ when in need,
> that person hasn't done anything wrong.
> But if such a person is not needy,
> he or she will have to answer for what was
> accepted and account for why it was accepted.
> Such persons will be imprisoned
> and made to answer for every deed performed.
> They won't get out until they have repaid every last red cent.

And here is another saying pertinent to the issue:

> Let the money sweat in the palms of your hands
> until you know to whom you are about to make a gift.[16]

The playful, nonliteral intent of Jesus' original injunction has been lost, and it is now being interpreted quite literally. But in order to avoid the unwanted consequences of a literal interpretation, qualifications and safeguards are erected around the perimeter. The humor of hyperbole that protected the original has given way to a blatant moralistic interpretation. And a new admonition, not derived from Jesus, has been appended to safeguard the new interpretation.

Jesus seems to be equally clear about the fate of the wealthy:

> How difficult it is for those who have money to enter God's domain!

> It's easier for a camel to squeeze through a needle's eye, than for a wealthy person to get into God's domain![17]

Such pronouncements are unequivocal. Yet the Christian tradition has labored over the centuries to blunt their edge. Fabric softeners have been applied. Some, for example, have imagined a narrow pass called the needle's eye, where it is difficult but not impossible for a loaded camel to pass through. Other compromisers have suggested a gate in the walls of Jerusalem called the needle's eye: at this gate a camel was required to squat down and wriggle through. Still others have argued that "camel" is a misunderstanding of a similar-sounding word meaning "rope." All such softening ploys are uncharacteristic of Jesus and subvert both the style and content of his wisdom.

In spite of the sharp edge on many of Jesus' sayings, the Gospel of Mark is itself given to a softening strategy: in response to the needle's eye saying, the disciples ask, "Well then, who can be saved?" Mark has Jesus respond:

> For mortals it's impossible, but not for God; after all, everything's possible for God.[18]

That assurance has the effect of pulling the punch of the aphorism. This modification reflects the struggle of the community to reassure its wealthy members that they could make it into God's domain after all. According to the traditional definition, everything is possible for God, and Jesus would agree that the wealthy can be his legitimate followers. But Jesus was not given to qualifications in his memorable witticisms. To juxtapose one with the other obscures the rhetorical strategy of the original.

A Riddle Moralized

Most critical scholars agree that this antithetical aphorism in Mark originated with Jesus:

> What goes into you can't defile you;
> what comes out can.[19]

In Chapter Eight, it was treated as an antithetical couplet: the second line contradicts the first. And in Chapter Eleven, it was interpreted as a riddle with unspecified meaning. By the time the saying gets to Matthew, the riddle itself has been revised and moralized:

> What goes into your mouth does not defile you;
> what comes out of your mouth does.[20]

This permits Matthew to explain: what comes out comes from the wicked intentions of the heart—sexual immorality, thefts, murders, adulteries, and the like.[21] That aligns it with another of Matthew's proverbs: "The mouth gives voice to what the heart is full of."[22]

The steps in this progression are three in number: in the original sense, Jesus takes a theme suggested by cultic food restrictions and attempts to refocus on larger but unspecified concerns by leaving the reference of what comes out unclear. In the second step, the saying is edited so as to be limited to dietary restrictions. This appears to be what happened in the Thomas tradition, which also knows a version with the explicit mention of the "mouth."[23] That gospel has preserved the saying in the context of Jesus' advice to his followers to eat whatever is set before them on their travels. In a third step, the saying is moralized. Rather than permit the listener or reader to determine for himself or herself how to apply the aphorism, the gospel writers feel compelled to assign a single meaning. In this case, a riddle has been turned into a moral.

Reversals Reversed

In the parable of the dinner party,[24] Jesus announces the reversal of roles in God's domain: those who expect to be included but misunderstand the nature of the invitation are replaced by those who, by definition, could not have expected an invitation. In this fantasy, only those who think of themselves as social outcasts actually find seats in the banquet hall.

Matthew has rewritten this parable and added a codicil: The slaves who go out to invite the lowly and destitute to fill the hall gather both "the good and bad alike."[25] This is Matthew editorializing. Then he adds this further scene:

> The king came in to see the guests for himself and noticed this man not properly attired. And he says to him, "Look, pal, how'd you get in here without dressing for the occasion?"
> The fellow was speechless.
> Then the king ordered his waiters: "Tie him up hand and foot and throw him out where it is utterly dark. They'll weep and grind their teeth out there. After all, many are called but few are chosen."[26]

Matthew knew that some of those who had been invited to the banquet were unworthy because the Christian community in his day was a mixture of the good and the bad. Matthew has corrected the earlier version of the parable by appending an additional scene in which the king has someone improperly dressed—someone in the Christian community who doesn't follow the prescribed social codes—thrown out into the perpetual darkness beyond the pillars of Hercules where the sun never shines. And Matthew invents an aphorism to conclude the parable to reinforce his view: out of the many invited, only a few will be allowed to remain. Matthew partially reverses the original reversal in the parable as Jesus told it.

Jesus' Wisdom Augmented

Oral tradition is elastic: it can be expanded and contracted as the occasion arises. As the wisdom of Jesus is assimilated to conventional wisdom, the fund of proverbial sayings attributed to him grows. Virtues are readily extolled. Old proverbs are attached to his name. Here are a few examples:

Congratulations to the gentle!
They will inherit the earth.[27]

Congratulations to the merciful!
They will receive mercy.[28]

Congratulations to those with undefiled hearts!
They will see God.[29]

The eye is the body's lamp.[30]

The troubles that the day brings are enough.[31]

Workers deserve their wages.[32]

Each tree is known by its fruit.[33]

These are but a few of many examples of folk proverbs or lore recorded in older sources, such as the Psalms and Proverbs, that were ascribed to Jesus in the gospels. The Fellows of the Jesus Seminar think that Jesus may have quoted some of these proverbs, but they find it difficult to determine which he did and which he did not. It is certain, however, that the fund of common lore attached to Jesus' name expanded with his reputation.

SHIFT IN FOCUS

It is crucial to recall that the genuine parables and aphorisms of Jesus are not self-referential. He does not refer to himself in his own stories. Yet he is there, on the edge of the story, as a listener who stands ready to risk the consequences of his own vision. Like other listeners, Jesus is an "outsider": he is the one who did not expect an invitation to the great supper; he is the one hired at the eleventh hour; he is the prodigal; he is the victim in the ditch.

It was not long, however, before his disciples turned him into an "insider." The focus of Jesus' words was imperceptibly but steadily shifted away from his glimpse of the kingdom to a story in which Jesus himself was the center of attention. In that story, Jesus acts as God's viceregent on earth.

When Jesus' disciples are depicted going through the grain fields on the sabbath and harvesting a handful of grain, the Pharisees complain. In response, Jesus cites the example of King David who violated the temple on the sabbath by eating the showbread. And then Jesus is reported as saying, "Yet I say to you, someone greater than the temple is here."[34] The evangelists understand Jesus to be referring to himself.

Matthew then truncates the two-line aphorism to a single line: "Remember, the son of Adam lords it over the sabbath day." In this abbreviated form, "son of Adam" can only be understood as an authority figure who is greater than the temple: he has the right to violate the sabbath. In the longer version preserved in Mark, the sabbath is made subordinate to all the descendants of Adam and Eve.[35] In the revision,

Christian storytellers have here elevated Jesus to a role he would not have claimed for himself. The focus has shifted from sabbath observance to Jesus as someone who has jurisdiction over sabbath questions.

In another gospel segment, the Pharisees are represented as demanding a sign from Jesus—some token that proves he is what he says he is. In the Gospel of Mark, Jesus takes this oath:

I swear to God, no sign will be given this generation![36]

In the parallel passage in Luke, an exception is made: the only sign that evil generation will be given is the sign of Jonah, which Luke interprets as the preaching of Jonah, to which the Ninevites responded positively.[37] In Matthew, however, this report has undergone further elaboration. The sign of Jonah is now interpreted as Jonah's stay in the belly of the whale for three days and three nights. And of course the new sign is interpreted as the son of Adam's sojourn in the tomb for three days.[38] The transition from no sign, to the sign of Jonah's preaching, to Jesus' resurrection reflects a steady movement away from Jesus' perspective to the point of view of the Christian community.

Early Christian storytellers and listeners found it difficult to picture themselves as "outsiders" in the parables and aphorisms of Jesus. They had trouble coming to terms with this limitation. They tended, as time went by and his parables and sayings became more familiar, to give themselves a central part in the kingdom. The part they assigned themselves was of course the role of "insider." They appointed themselves the custodians of the tradition—its official interpreters. The new role they assigned to Jesus, that of the ultimate authority, was the basis of their own new role. The one change produced the other. As insiders, they became the brokers of the kingdom to other outsiders, just as they believed Jesus had brokered God's presence to them. We are now two steps removed from Jesus' original vision of an unbrokered kingdom, and an intermediate chain of command has sprung up to bridge the gap.

In the great sermon in Matthew, Jesus is made to say, "You are the salt of the earth," with reference to those who had become kingdom insiders. He also tells them, "You are the light of the world." And he admonishes them, "You are to let your light shine in the presence of others, so they can see your good deeds and acclaim your Father in the heavens."[39] As salt and light they have become brokers of the kingdom.

As insiders they are also the recipients of the secrets of the kingdom, a privilege that has not been granted to anyone else. That is the reason, his followers suggest, that Jesus spoke exclusively in parables—so those outside would see but not really understand.[40] As Jesus envisioned the kingdom of God, only outsiders were in a position to respond to the invitation. Now it is only the insiders who have ears to hear. The believing community has completely reversed the references of those terms!

Pronouncement Stories

The parables and aphorisms form the bedrock of the Jesus tradition. They provide Jesus' own perspective on the world. The next step in the augmentation of the tradition about Jesus is the creation of the pronouncement story. A pronouncement story is a brief anecdote climaxing in a pronouncement of Jesus. It is therefore presumably a mixture of Jesus' point of view (the saying or pronouncement) and that of a third party (the storyteller). The pronouncement story is the narrative vehicle closest to the sayings tradition. The pronouncement stories are inherently more plausible historically since we are reasonably sure that Jesus was a teacher who taught in parables and traded in irony and wit.

In these stories, the form of which was borrowed from secular rhetoric, Jesus of course appears as the clever sage. The narrative setting is often a fiction or a fictionalized occurrence (a core event that has been embellished). In some pronouncement stories, he is represented as the same Jesus who speaks in parables and aphorisms. Yet because Jesus appears as an actor—he is the one who makes a pronouncement in the anecdote—it becomes readily possible for other storytellers to assign Jesus a messianic role even though he did not play that role in the underlying event. We will examine the cure of the paralytic with this possibility in mind. With the shift in focus from Jesus' vision of God's domain to Jesus himself—from the proclaimed to the proclaimer—Jesus becomes the one who authorizes the kingdom, who guarantees that it is God's will. In addition, he also becomes the future bringer of the kingdom that has not yet arrived (in the apocalyptic view, everyone will know when the kingdom has arrived).

The enlargement of the cast of characters and the transition from Jesus' point of view to that of the evangelist can be seen quite clearly in the story of the cure of the paralytic in the Gospel of Mark.[41]

In this story, four people bring a paralytic to Jesus but can't get close to him because of the huge crowd. In desperation, the four make an opening in the flat roof of the mud brick house and lower the mat with the lame man on it down into the interior where Jesus is presumably teaching.

Recognizing their trust in his healing powers—I suppose it would have been difficult not to notice—Jesus says to the sufferer, "Child, your sins are forgiven."

As the evangelist tells the story, it has become an opportunity not just to relate the cure but to respond to Jesus' critics. So the evangelist introduces some legal experts into the scene. They wonder, "Who has the power to forgive other than God? Doesn't it constitute blasphemy to play the role of God?"

They have not spoken their complaint aloud, but Jesus knows their every thought, according to the storyteller, so he responds to them openly and directly: "Which is easier, to say 'Your sins are forgiven,' or to say, 'Get up, pick up your mat, and walk'?"

For Jesus it was probably a matter of indifference to say, "Your sins are forgiven" *or* "Pick up your mat and go home." In Jesus' world, paralysis was taken to be the result of sin; to be paralyzed meant that the victim had sinned and that God had punished him accordingly.[42] Jesus could use either pronouncement and mean the same thing by it.

In the story as the evangelists tell it, however, the experts pounce on the effrontery of Jesus in exercising rights allegedly reserved to God. For them, only God has the right and power to forgive sin. To claim divine privilege is sacrilege and blasphemy. But this complaint also opens the door for Mark, the author of the gospel, to suggest that Jesus was in fact endowed with divine power—he is authorized to forgive sins.

By making the choice of healing words a matter of indifference, what Jesus does is prepare the way for the real explosion: he announces that all human beings—all descendants of Adam and Eve—have what it takes to forgive sin and thus to break the chain of cause and effect that links disease to sin. Mark inserts this editorial comment: "But so you may realize that on earth the son of Adam has authority to forgive sins, he says to the paralytic . . ."[43] Mark wants his readers to understand the phrase *son of Adam* narrowly—that is, to have it refer exclusively to Jesus as the apocalyptic figure of Daniel 7, a figure with divine license.

In contrast, Jesus meant *son of Adam* to be understood as a reference to all human beings. We are fairly certain that this is the case because Matthew adds an explanatory aside at the end of his version: "When the crowds saw this, they became fearful and glorified God, *who had given such authority to humans.*"[44]

This story provides us with a glimpse of the transition from one level of the tradition to another—from the way Jesus understood his words and deeds to the way Mark and later admirers understood them. Jesus expresses the view that human beings have always had the authority to forgive, and in affirming what is so obvious to him, he exposes the hubris and pretense of the prevailing restriction. Mark restricts that authority to God and God's exclusive agent. And he does so by the narrative device of adding legal experts to the scene as critics of Jesus. Mark thereby buries the insight of Jesus and restores the hubris.

This technique is of course merely another means of domesticating the Jesus tradition, of making it conform to the offices and institutions that are emerging in the primitive Christian community. Elaine Pagels would ask in her characteristic way about the political and institutional implications of this transition.[45] "Where," she might inquire, "does the development go from here?"

According to Mark, the right to forgive sins is the exclusive prerogative of Jesus. Jesus has appointed apostles to represent him following his death. The bishops of the church are successors to the apostles. The bishops have the exclusive power to forgive sins by right of succession. Here we have a monopolistic rock on which the church could be safely built.

Miracle Stories

The second (logical) rhetorical development is the incorporation of the miracle story into the gospel narrative. There are three types of miracle stories in the gospels: exorcisms, cures, and nature wonders. Miracle stories are added to the Christian repertoire to make Jesus comparable to—in fact, competitive with—other charismatic teachers, exorcists, and miracle workers. The wonder worker, or thaumaturge, temporarily suspends the processes of nature in order to perform something out of the ordinary. Jesus is presented as an alchemist, so to speak, who changes base metals into gold (perhaps water into wine), or who raises a little girl or Lazarus from the dead.

Jesus is no longer the subverter of the everyday world around him; he is now integrated into that world and represented as another of its notables. He is being assimilated to secular categories. Christians later thought the miracles of Jesus set him apart from his contemporaries, when, in fact, they actually integrated him into popular culture. They were marketing devices. The subject matter of these stories is no longer Jesus' vision but Jesus.

Miracles appear to play an increasing role as the Jesus tradition grows. Conversely, as scholars trace the tradition back, the miraculous element seems to shrink. There is but one cure in the Sayings Gospel Q—the cure of the Roman officer's son at a distance—and that belongs to the second or later layer of Q.[46] The primary point of that incident, however, seems to be not the cure but the positive response of a Roman. It is also in Q that John the Baptist sends followers to find out from Jesus whether he is the expected messianic figure or whether they are to look for another. Jesus tells John's emissaries to report to John:

> the blind see again,
> the lame walk,
> lepers are cleansed,
> the deaf hear,
> the dead are raised,
> and the poor have the good news preached to them.

This response is derived, in fact, from various prophecies of Isaiah.[47] Jesus is therefore fulfilling the promise made by the ancient prophet. Luke obliges his readers by inventing the tale of the widow of Nain, whose son Jesus raises from the dead. This story imitates a miracle performed by Elijah.[48]

In the two feeding stories related by Mark, Jesus is represented as repeating the feats of Moses in the wilderness.[49] Like Moses who provided manna for the Israelites as they wandered through the desert, Jesus feeds five thousand and then four thousand, also in the wilderness. He is thereby made to compete with the epic events of Israel's past and her great leaders, Elijah and Moses.

Jesus is also pictured as a competitor of Greek heroes and wonder workers. For example, he does everything that Apollonius of Tyana, his contemporary, does, only he does it more frequently and better. Like Eleazar, an exorcist described by Josephus, he can exorcise demons. He can also walk on the water, and this makes him a god in the class of Poseidon, who could drive his chariot across the waves with impunity. Since Homer's tales were widely rehearsed in hellenistic times, the evangelists would have known what Greek gods could do.

The tale of the Gerasene demoniac is instructive for its symbolism.[50] In this story, a demon-possessed man who lives among the tombs is so strong that no one can bind him, even with chains. He howls night and day and bruises himself on the stones. His demon is named Legion, which symbolizes the Roman presence and power. After Jesus expels the filthy spirit, the demon enters a herd of pigs, which rush into the sea and are drowned. Since pigs are "unclean," they indicate how defiled the territory occupied by the Romans really was. This story was undoubtedly told to fire the imagination of what would happen to the Romans when God got around to sending his messiah.

By Mark's time, and possibly earlier if there was a Signs Gospel or collection of miracle stories underlying both Mark and the Gospel of John, miracle stories had come to play a very significant role in the gospels. As they did so, they displaced Jesus as a simple but world-shattering sage. Because the miracle stories were intended as a means of marketing Jesus as a competitive wonder worker to a large and often mostly gentile audience, very few of them are based on actual events. It is possible that Jesus pronounced a person with some kind of skin disease cured; it is equally likely that he cured a paralytic and perhaps caused a blind person to see again. And he undoubtedly exorcised what were thought to be demons. All of these ailments can be understood as psychosomatic in nature. But miracles like the raising of Lazarus, walking on the sea, stilling the storm, and feeding crowds in the wilderness are fictions. The tendency to augment these stories in imitation of Elijah and Elisha further demonstrates the proclivities of the tradition. Jesus was originally probably only a minor miracle worker.

Epiphanies: Recognition Scenes

In the framework stories supplied by the Gospel of Mark and adopted by Matthew and Luke, Jesus is recognized initially as a special envoy of God at his baptism. A voice thunders from heaven identifying his special role. That amounts to an epiphany or a theophany (the appearance or manifestation of a divine being or God). Jesus is acknowledged as God's special son on that occasion. In a second scene, Jesus is also transfigured as a divine being before his three intimates—Peter, James, and John—on the mount of transfiguration. On that occasion, he knows and predicts that he will die on the cross and promises that he will rise from the dead. He later fulfills his own prediction. In telling these stories, Mark has Jesus confirm everything the early Christian proclamation claimed for him. The Jesus of the parables and aphorisms has now been assimilated to the primitive Christian mythological kerygma.

THE END OF ENCHANTMENT: ESCHATOLOGY AND END TIME

The mythical Christ gradually replaced the Galilean sage as the gospels grew. Jesus' fantasy of the kingdom was embedded in a larger picture that had Jesus himself as the center of attention. Jesus' vision of the kingdom became his followers' vision of him. Having given Jesus the leading role in the story, they then wrote a part for themselves into the drama. The result was the disenchantment of God's kingdom.

The enchantment that had cast its spell over Jesus meant that God's dominion was immediately and powerfully present for him. With disenchantment, that kingdom was pushed off, first into the immediate future and then into the indeterminate future. If the kingdom was to come in the future, there would be a delay, and a delay required a second coming of the messiah—of Jesus—to achieve what his first coming had not. In other words, the overpowering vision of Jesus was translated back into the ordinary apocalyptic expectations of that time: God was expected eventually to interfere directly in all human affairs. The vision of Jesus was thereby domesticated. The fantastic reality of the kingdom of God for Jesus has been reduced to something to be looked for and hoped for at some future date.

Fascination with Jesus' vision fades as realism sets in. The disciples are unable to maintain the enchantment. Time stretches out. The kingdom is no longer present; it will come, it was believed, at some future date. The chronology of the long run replaces the bewitchment of the present.

Jesus' naive sense of time was swamped by the reassertion of the apocalyptic mentality and its corresponding symbolic apparatus. The evangelists add little apocalypses to their gospels and other apocalyptic touches. This is another aspect of making Jesus conform to popular expectations, another side of the shift in focus, another consequence of the modification of rhetorical strategy.

As the apocalyptic mentality began to reassert itself, the expectation that the kingdom would arrive in the immediate future emerges. In Mark's summary of the gospel, for example, Jesus is made to say:

The time is up: God's imperial rule is closing in.[51]

At another point in Mark's story, Jesus is represented as telling them repeatedly:

> I swear to you: Some of those standing here won't ever taste death before they see God's imperial rule set in with power![52]

Such remarks as these suggest that for Mark and his community the anticipation of a prompt return on the part of Jesus was still very much alive. Yet Mark includes an abbreviated apocalypse in his gospel, which appears to presuppose a more conventional temporal scheme (not just yet; at some time in the future).[53]

The time of Jesus' return has begun to stretch out for Luke also (Luke comes another decade or two later than Mark):

> He [Jesus] said, "Stay alert! Don't be deluded. You know, many will come using my name and claim, 'I'm the one!' and 'The time is near!' Don't go running after them! And when you hear of wars and insurrections, don't panic. After all, it's inevitable that these things take place first, but it doesn't mean the end is about to come."[54]

Here Jesus seems to be admonishing his followers to be patient. The time has not yet come.

Luke provides a temporal setting for Jesus as he tells the parable of the entrusted money:

> He [Jesus] proceeded to tell a parable, because he was near Jerusalem and people thought that God's imperial rule would appear immediately.[55]

This introduction suggests that people still anticipated the end time to occur in the very near future in Luke's day. But Luke is wary of that view. The parable itself enjoins Luke's readers to do business as usual in the interim.[56]

The son of Adam will return eventually to sit in judgment on the twelve tribes of Israel, according to conventional Christian intelligence. When that happens, Christian insiders will also be seated on twelve thrones to assist in the proceedings, according to Matthew.[57] The Jesus who played no role in his parables is now featured as the cosmic judge at the end of time, and all his original followers, who were once outsiders, have been promoted to insiders with correlative apocalyptic roles.

THE GOSPELS AS COUNTERWEIGHTS

The sayings gospels and the narrative gospels both played a very important conservative role in these developments. The sayings gospels served to remind the believing community that Jesus of Nazareth was not a mythical figure from another world but the Galilean originator of the

Christian movement: It was he who articulated the vision of God's kingdom that gave rise to the Christian faith. And the narrative gospels provided the incipient creed, as formulated by Paul, with a historical redeemer, although the evangelists set that figure in a mythical narrative frame. The narrative gospels—the ones included in the New Testament —can therefore be understood as counterbalancing the mythical gospel of Paul. Yet they are also a compromise: they combine a historical figure with a mythical redeemer. Nevertheless, without them, the Christ figure might well have been conceived as entirely mythical, without any anchor in history.

The gospels were created towards the end of the first century and in the first half of the second. By the time the Christian movement arrives at Nicea two hundred years later, Jesus of Nazareth has again receded into the background. The original iconoclast—the subverter of the primary world—has been replaced by an icon who belongs to the popular expectations and hopes of that world. The enchanting immediacy of his secondary world—the kingdom of God—has been replaced by the political realism of Constantine's empire.

Chapter Fourteen

RESURRECTION AND RETURN

POPULAR PIETY AND THE ELUSIVE JESUS

When I was about to embark on theological studies at Bible college many years ago, I remember tuning, by accident, to a radio roundtable discussion on the subject of Easter. One of the panelists was a professor of religion at the University of Chicago. I don't remember his name, but I do remember what he said. When asked about the resurrection of Jesus, he replied that it would not affect his faith as a Christian if Jesus' body were to be discovered in some Palestinian tomb today and verified as his body by some incontrovertible means. The resurrection, he insisted, did not involve the resuscitation of a corpse.

His copanelists were aghast. At the time I was puzzled by his response. I didn't understand how Jesus could have risen from the dead if his body were not involved. Like many other questions in my young mind, I simply put that puzzle on a back shelf and waited for several decades for it to resurface.

The issue resurfaced, as I remember, when I read a now famous statement of Rudolf Bultmann, the pre-eminent New Testament scholar of this century, to this effect: "Jesus," Bultmann wrote, "rose into the kerygma"—that is, into the faith of the first believers.[1] Their conviction that Jesus was still with them was itself his resurrection. The kerygma, it will be recalled, consists of the first formulations of the Christian gospel: Jesus died for our sins, was buried, and was raised on the third day, all in accordance with the scriptures. That is all Christians need to know and confess, Bultmann argued. To inquire behind that faith—to ask whether the resurrection really took place—is an idle question. Besides, to the modern mind a mythical event like the resuscitation of a corpse is simply incredible.

Then, many years later, the resurrection was back on my agenda. The answer I came to give to that puzzle differs in many respects from the answers I learned along the way in my studies. And yet everything I have learned, including the Chicago professor's challenge, has contributed in some small or large way to my present perspective.

Popular Christian piety believes that Jesus' existence on earth extended beyond his death on Good Friday. I took this formulation of Thomas Sheehan as my premise and framed this proposition to test the views of Fellows of the Jesus Seminar:

The resurrection was an event in the life of Jesus.

I thought it would be a firm test of whether the members of the seminar agreed with popular views. My proposition was received with hilarity by several Fellows. One suggested that it was an oxymoron. Another compared it to a koan. Still others alleged that the formulation was meaningless, since we all assume, they said, that Jesus' life ended with his crucifixion and death. I was surprised by this response. I shouldn't have been. After all, John Dominic Crossan has confessed, "I do not think that anyone, anywhere, at any time brings dead people back to life."[2] That's fairly blunt. But it squares with what we really know, as distinguished from what many want to believe. Sheehan is even blunter: "Jesus, regardless of where his corpse ended up, is dead and remains dead."[3] What that means, for Sheehan, is the end of religion.

Scholars employ various strategies to keep the resurrection of Jesus out of reach. Some have insisted that the life of the historical Jesus ends with his death, as a way of avoiding the issue posed by popular piety. Other scholars have preferred simply to claim that the gospel records are inadequate or too ambiguous for us to draw reliable conclusions. Some deny that historians have the credentials to investigate the resurrection as an event. Another ploy is to declare that the resurrection was an eschatological event that transcended space and time, that it was an event that belongs to the end of time. As an eschatological event it is out of range for empirical and historical investigation. This strategy goes together with the insistence that affirmations of the resurrection are "theological" statements rather than historical claims. For theological one could readily substitute the term *faith*. By whatever means, there has been a tendency to privilege faith statements: since they are not subject to scientific review, they can be made on the strength of private or community conviction. Privileging the resurrection is a way of blocking access to the popular heart of Christianity.

Of this I have become increasingly certain: There is nothing we can exempt, or should exempt, from scientific and historical review either as Christians or as human beings. If we think the resurrection of Jesus was not a historical event, if we believe that a video camera would not have recorded anything on film during his appearances, we should say so. Wouldn't that help clear the air? If we think our views are informed by the evidence supplied by the gospels and Paul, wouldn't it help those seeking understanding to learn about that evidence?

The Jesus Seminar decided not to duck the issue. The Fellows reached a fairly firm consensus: Belief in Jesus' resurrection did not depend on what happened to his corpse. They are supported in this by the judgment of many contemporary scholars. Jesus' resurrection did not involve the resuscitation of a dead body. About three-fourths of the Fellows believe that Jesus' followers did not know what happened to his body.

According to this view, the empty-tomb story found in the last chapter of the Gospel of Mark is a late legend, introduced into the tradition for the first time by Mark. It was unknown to Paul. It was also unknown to the Sayings Gospel Q and the Gospel of Thomas. Evidently the empty-tomb story and the reports of appearances did not come to play a central part in the Jesus tradition until several decades after Jesus' death. John Dominic Crossan suggests that the story of the resurrection was introduced first by the Cross Gospel, an early passion gospel that is now embedded in the Gospel of Peter. Mark later based his version on Peter. But Crossan's view currently represents minority opinion. In either case, the empty tomb does not reflect the historical memory of an actual event.

The piously convicted but marginally informed will immediately cite Paul's statements in his letter to the Corinthians. Paul writes:

If there is no such thing as resurrection of the dead, then Christ has not been raised; and if Christ has not been raised, then we have been wasting our time preaching and you have believed for nothing.[4]

It is the case that Paul, like other Pharisees, believed in the resurrection of the dead. It is also true that he believed that Jesus had been raised from the dead. But that is not all there is to it. Paul goes on in this same passage to ask: "In what sort of body do they appear?"[5] He proceeds to answer his own question:

One dies in a physical body, which decays, but one is raised in an incorruptible form. . . . One dies in a physical body, but one is raised in a spiritual form. . . . It is not possible for flesh and blood to participate in the kingdom of God.[6]

Those who like to quote Paul usually fail to take the whole of his argument into account.

Paul himself claimed to have seen the glorified Jesus in a vision. And he classes his own vision with appearances to other leaders—Peter, James, the twelve, all the apostles. Yet he did not have his vision until 34 or 35 C.E., some three or four years after the death of Jesus. If Jesus had been raised physically, where was Jesus' body during that long interval? What was he doing? Those who have not asked the same questions as Paul have not thought the matter through.

Paul did not recognize Jesus in his vision on the Damascus road.[7] Mary also didn't recognize Jesus when he appeared to her at the tomb.[8]

The two on the road to Emmaus also failed to recognize Jesus, although they had known him personally.[9] The seven did not recognize Jesus immediately when he appeared on the shore of the sea.[10] Traces of doubt about the reality of the resurrection are scattered through the reports.[11]

The elusive Jesus is a standard feature in the appearance stories. Jesus is elusive because he was not flesh and blood, he was not restricted by space, and his appearances took place over an extended period. However, as time passed and the tradition grew, the reported appearances become more palpable, more corporeal. They gradually lose their luminous quality and take on aspects of a resuscitated corpse. For these reasons, the stories of the appearances need to be examined closely for clues to their history and function.

THE RESURRECTION STORIES

Gospel of Mark

The Gospel of Mark, which is probably the earliest of the gospels, does not narrate any appearances of Jesus. Three women, Mary of Magdala, Mary the mother of James, and Salome, go to the tomb on Easter morning and find it empty. Somehow the huge stone blocking the entrance has been rolled away. Inside they find a young man in a white robe—a heavenly messenger—sitting on the right. He advises them that Jesus has been raised. The women are to go and tell his disciples to precede him to Galilee, where they will see him (this Galilee appearance had already been promised).[12] But the women are fearful and don't breathe a word to anyone.

Gospel of Matthew

A decade or so later, Matthew borrows and revises Mark's story. Now there are only two women, Mary of Magdala and another Mary; Salome has been left out. An earthquake (or aftershock to the one narrated earlier)[13] heralds the arrival of a heavenly messenger, who has rolled away the stone and is sitting on it. The clothes of the angel give off a dazzling light. The messenger gives them the same instructions as reported in Mark. The earthquake is a mythical element that the author of Matthew has added to Mark's inexplicable rolling away of the stone and the angelic messenger in glistening white robes.

In addition, a scene has been inserted that doesn't occur in Mark's version. As the women hurry away from the tomb to tell the disciples, Jesus meets them. He repeats the instructions of the messenger: "Go tell my companions so they can leave for Galilee, where they will see me."[14] This is a defensive move on Matthew's part to cover the flight of the disciples and to provide official permission for something they had already done.

Matthew adds another scene to the Markan tale. Some guards, it seems, report to the ranking priests what has transpired at the tomb. The plot against Jesus continues. The priests and elders meet and offer a bribe to the soldiers: Tell everyone that Jesus' disciples came at night while you were asleep and stole his body.

In the last and final appearance in Matthew, the eleven are gathered on a mountain in Galilee (mountains are the appropriate place for epiphanies to occur, since the mountaintop is the closest spot on earth to heaven). Some worship Jesus; other are dubious (about his reality?). Jesus commissions all of them to become ambassadors to all the peoples of the earth on his behalf. The great commission, as it has been termed, was of course composed by Matthew. It does not stem from Jesus.

Gospel of Luke and Acts

There were three women in Mark; Matthew reduced the number to two. In Luke's account,[15] also written a decade or more after Mark but dependent on Mark's story, the number has grown: Mary of Magdala; Joanna, the wife of Chuza, Herod Antipas' steward;[16] Mary the mother of James; and an unspecified number of other women come to the tomb. They find the stone gone and the tomb empty, as in Mark. But now *two* angels appear and remind them of Jesus' prediction that he would die and be raised. The women depart and relate to the eleven and others everything that has happened.

The disciples refuse to believe the story of the women. Impetuous Peter runs to the tomb, peeps inside, sees nothing but the shroud, and returns home marveling at what has happened.

The first appearance of Jesus in Luke is not to the women, as in Matthew, but to two people on the road to Emmaus. They tell Jesus, whom they have not recognized, that the women found the tomb empty but nobody has seen the risen Jesus. Later they recognize him when he breaks bread and gives it to them. When the two return to Jerusalem, they tell the eleven, presumably including Peter, "The Lord really has been raised, and has appeared to Simon!"[17] Nothing in Luke's story has prepared the reader for this announcement. Peter himself must have been surprised at hearing that he had been the first to see the risen Jesus. We evidently have the careless conflation of two traditions. (Other discrepancies in Luke-Acts suggest that the end of the gospel and the beginning of Acts have suffered tampering.)

Jesus himself then appears to the eleven and the others assembled.[18] During this appearance, Jesus asks for something to eat and is given a piece of grilled fish. Some are terrified, believing that they are seeing a ghost. In Mark the women don't say a word; in Matthew some are dubious of Jesus' presence; in Luke some think he is a ghost. Apparently not everyone was equally impressed with these apparitions.

But Luke reassures the eleven: Jesus shows them his hands and feet; they are invited to touch him; and Jesus asks for something to eat. This is all offered as evidence that he is not a ghost. Jesus helps them to understand what was foretold in the scriptures and commands them to stay in Jerusalem until the holy spirit comes. Then Jesus leads them out to Bethany, on the ridge opposite Jerusalem, and ascends into the sky.

Luke repeats some of this story in the opening segments of the Book of Acts. The period from the resurrection to the ascension is forty days. Jesus continues to appear to his disciples during that period. The disciples are again ordered not to leave Jerusalem. (The repetition of the order suggests that the disciples had trouble obeying.) Jesus advises them that they will be baptized with the holy spirit in the near future (that occurs at Pentecost, fifty days later). He commissions his followers to preach the good news beginning in Jerusalem and Judea, then in Samaria, and eventually to the ends of the earth. Luke has formulated his great commission in his own language, just as Matthew did in his own idiom. The *two* angels of Luke reappear as Jesus ascends, now forty days later rather than on Easter evening, and they assure Jesus' followers that he will return in similar circumstances.

Gospel of John

The stories in the Gospel of John have to be divided into two parts. John 20 is the original ending to the gospel; John 21 is an appendix supplied by a later hand.

In the earlier chapter, Mary of Magdala goes to the tomb (the evangelists have a great deal of trouble keeping the women straight) and finds the stone rolled away and the tomb empty. She runs and tells Peter and the disciple whom Jesus loved (otherwise unnamed).

In a second scene, Peter and the unnamed disciple race to the tomb. The other disciple wins the footrace, but Peter enters the tomb first. They see that the tomb is empty and observe strips of burial cloth lying there. The unnamed disciple "believes"—what he believes is not clear, since the reader is immediately advised that neither of them had as yet understood the prophecy that Jesus was destined to rise from the dead. The two return home.

Mary, it seems, has been hanging around outside the tomb all along. *Two* heavenly messengers ask her why she is crying. She responds that someone has taken Jesus away. At that moment, Mary turns around and sees someone she takes for a caretaker. It is, in fact, Jesus, whom she recognizes when he calls her name. Mary is thus the first to see the risen Jesus. She reports her experience to the disciples.

That same evening, when the disciples are assembled behind locked doors for fear of persecution, Jesus appears. He shows them his hands and side (rather than his hands and feet, as in Luke). Jesus commissions them. He also breathes the holy spirit on them, in a kind of miniature Pentecost scene. And he gives them authority to forgive and bind—not forgive—sins.

Thomas, it seems, was not present for this second appearance, to the disciples, and is dubious that it occurred. A week later, with the doors again locked, Jesus reappears. Thomas, who is invited to touch Jesus' hands and side, now believes. Then the evangelist concludes his gospel by stating that Jesus performed many other miracles so that his followers might believe.

The appendix to the Gospel of John (the twenty-first chapter) relates an appearance of Jesus in Galilee, this time on the shore of the Sea of Tiberias. Seven disciples are present: Peter, Thomas (known as the twin), Nathaniel, the sons of Zebedee, and two others. The appearance is accompanied by a miraculous catch of fish. As in other stories, Jesus shares a meal with his followers; this time the menu consists of bread and fish.

Gospel of Peter

The only depiction of the resurrection itself is found in the fragmentary and highly mythical Gospel of Peter.

To say that Peter depicts the actual resurrection is not quite correct. What Peter describes is the emergence of a mythical figure from the tomb. Earlier two luminous figures descend from the sky with a loud noise (one is reminded of the tremor in Matt 28:2). The stone rolls away by itself. The two enter the tomb of Jesus. Three men then emerge from the tomb. Two of them, presumably the two who had just arrived from heaven—the heavenly messengers—are as tall as the sky. The third figure, whom they lead by the hand, is taller than the heavens. And a cross trails along behind them. The central figure is presumably Jesus. From the sky comes a voice: "Have you preached to those who sleep?" An answer echoes from the cross: "Yes."[19]

This all happens on the sabbath. Early on the next day, the first day of the week or the Lord's day, Mary arrives at the tomb to perform the burial rites, rites she had not been able to perform earlier out of fear of the Judeans. She is accompanied by friends. Their intention is to weep and beat their breasts, as was the custom, and to leave a memorial at the entrance to the tomb in the event they can't get in.

But they find the tomb open. A young man is sitting there in a splendid robe. He tells the women that Jesus has returned to the place he came from, presumably heaven. The women flee in fear.

Gospel of the Hebrews

A slightly different version appears in the Gospel of the Hebrews. In a fragment from that gospel, Jesus hands the linen shroud to the high priest's slave and then goes and appears first to James, his brother, who had sworn to fast until he had seen the risen Jesus. The fragment is quoted by Jerome (342–420 C.E.), the translator of the Latin Vulgate.

Gospel of Mary

The recently discovered Gospel of Mary confirms that Mary had a vision of the Lord. It is not clear whether this vision is the same thing as the appearance to Mary reported in other gospels.

> She said, "I saw the Lord in a vision and I said to him, 'Lord, I saw you today in a vision.'
> "He said to me, 'Congratulations to you for not wavering at seeing me. For where the mind is, there is the treasure.'"[20]

A discussion follows in which the question arises about the faculty with which one sees a vision. Mary thinks it may be the soul or the spirit, but Jesus replies that it is the mind, which exists between the two. The mind mediates between the soul, which belongs to the lower order, and the spirit, which belongs to the higher realm. The mind enables the lower to perceive the higher.

Pseudo-Mark

Some ancient readers of the gospels felt that the Gospel of Mark was incomplete. They may have believed that Mark was not on a par with the other narrative gospels since it lacked appearance stories. As a consequence, they devised endings for Mark, one of which reports appearances. The so-called longer ending, which is certainly not authentically Mark, relates the appearance to Mary of Magdala, to the two persons walking along in the country, and finally to the eleven while they are eating together.[21] This ending may be based on the Gospel of Luke, but it is also possible that Luke's stories are an elaboration of this outline. For convenience sake, we may refer to the long ending as Pseudo-Mark.

The Apostle Paul

Paul does not describe any resurrection stories, not even the appearance he claims for himself. But he does provide a list of those to whom Jesus had allegedly appeared. His list is given in his first letter to the Corinthians, written around 54 C.E. According to Paul, Jesus appeared

> to Cephas, then to the twelve.
> Next he appeared to more than five hundred associates all at the same time, most of whom are still alive, though some have died.
> Next he appeared to James, and then to all the apostles.
> And finally, as though to someone not born at the right time, he appeared to me. Admittedly, I am the least of the apostles—not really worthy to be called an apostle because I persecuted the church of God. But by the grace of God I am what I am.[22]

Paul appears to be giving the list in chronological order, but we cannot be certain he knew the actual order. The grouping of Cephas (or Peter) and the twelve may indicate that there was a rival group consisting of James and all the apostles. There is some evidence that Peter and James were leaders of two groups that held different views within the Jesus movement. In any case, the five hundred all at once is an anomaly. No such appearance is narrated, unless, of course, the Pentecost event, depicted in the second chapter of Acts, qualifies. On that occasion, a large number of disciples experienced the descent of the spirit. It is probably the case that the followers of Jesus would not have distinguished resurrection appearances from encounters with the spirit.

Paul is clear that he falls outside the tradition he is quoting in his letter to the Corinthians. But he is equally clear that the appearance to him carries the same weight and authority as the appearances to others who were apostles before him.

TO WHOM? HOW? WHERE? WHEN?

The historian weighing the evidence for these events will want to ask the usual questions: To whom did Jesus allegedly appear? What was the nature of the appearances? Where did they take place? When did they take place?

To Whom Did Jesus Appear?

As an initial assessment of the evidence provided by our ancient sources, it is necessary to summarize and compare the appearances. The evidence reveals a number of anomalies.

No resurrection appearances are narrated in the Gospel of Mark. In Matthew, the risen Jesus appears to two Marys and then to the eleven on a mountain in Galilee.

In Luke an appearance to Peter is reported but not narrated. Jesus also appears to two disciples on their way to the village of Emmaus. Later, in Jerusalem, Jesus appears to the eleven. In Acts, Jesus appears to the apostles over a period of forty days before the ascension. The number and identity of the recipients of such visits are not further specified.

Jesus appears to Mary of Magdala just outside the tomb in the Gospel of John. That evening Jesus appears to the disciples behind locked doors. A week later, when Thomas is present, Jesus reappears to them.

In John 21, there is one appearance, and it takes place on the Sea of Tiberias or Galilee. There are seven disciples present.

In the Gospel of Peter, two soldiers, a centurion, and some Judean elders see three figures leaving the tomb, two supporting a third.

According to the Gospel of the Hebrews, Jesus appears first to James, Jesus' brother.

The Gospel of Mary reports that Mary has a vision of Jesus. Time and place are not indicated.

Pseudo-Mark confirms the appearances narrated in the Gospel of Luke. However, it makes no mention of the appearance to Peter.

To these accounts we must add the list Paul gives in his letter to the Corinthians.

If we add all these reports up, after eliminating the obvious duplications, we get the following appearances:

To individuals:

1. Peter (Paul, Luke)
2. Mary of Magdala (Matthew, John 20, Mary, Pseudo-Mark)
3. James, Jesus' brother (Paul, Hebrews)
4. Paul (Paul, Acts)

To groups:

5. The eleven (Matthew, Luke, John 20, Pseudo-Mark)
6. The twelve (Paul)
7. All the apostles (Paul, Acts)
8. Seven disciples on the Sea of Tiberias (John 21)
9. Five hundred at the same time (Paul)

Other appearances:

10. Two on the road to Emmaus (Luke, Pseudo-Mark)
11. The second, unidentified Mary (Matthew)
12. Two soldiers, a centurion, some Judean elders (Peter)
13. Unspecified witnesses (Acts)

A critical review of the list reveals some further duplication and produces some anomalies.

References to the "eleven" and to the "twelve" probably denote the same group. In that case, items 5 and 6 refer to the same event. It is also possible that "all the apostles" is a reference to the twelve or the eleven, if the list in 1 Corinthians represents rival claims: Peter and the twelve, on the one hand; James and all the apostles, on the other. It is difficult to know whether the appearance to the seven on the Sea of Tiberias is a variant of the appearance to the twelve or the eleven. The location is a problem since appearances to the eleven in Luke and John take place in Jerusalem; the appearance to the seven is set in Galilee. Variation in the number may not be significant since we cannot actually establish a list of those who belonged to the circle of the twelve or the eleven.

On any reading, the appearance to the five hundred at one time is an anomaly. Only Paul mentions it. The appearances to the two on the Emmaus road; to the second, unidentified Mary; to the two soldiers, the centurion, and some Judean elders; and to other unspecified witnesses are likewise anomalies. These reports are not supported by more than one source. Scholars have been inclined to view them as legendary expansions without historical warrant.

The difficulties in reconciling the various reports of appearances with each other arouse suspicion that the lists and reports were compiled long after the fact and are therefore not reliable. In all probability they constitute claims made on behalf of some leader or sponsor. Attempts to reconcile the reports with each other have not been successful.

First Appearance: Peter, Mary, or James?

The identification of the one to whom Jesus first appeared (called the *protophany*) seems to have played a significant role in the development of the resurrection tradition. There are three candidates for the honor of being the first: Peter, Mary, and James.

According to Paul and Luke, Peter was the first to see the risen Jesus. In a Matthean addendum to Mark's account of the empty tomb, Jesus appears to the two Marys, one of whom must have been Mary of Magdala. Jesus also appears first to Mary of Magdala in the Gospel of John 20. A fragment of the Gospel of the Hebrews is the only source that reports James, Jesus' brother, as the first to see the risen Jesus. It is curious that Mary is not even mentioned in the list Paul provides in his first letter to the Corinthians.

The recipient of the protophany was undoubtedly to be understood as preeminent among the leaders of the new movement. Since Mary was a woman, she did not qualify to be a leader under the terms of the patriarchal society to which she belonged. The honor was thus shared between Peter and James.

There is another wrinkle in the tradition. In the story in John 20, there is a friendly rivalry between Peter and that other, unnamed disciple. It is an Alphonse and Gaston act, stumbling over each other to be the first at something. The other disciple wins the footrace, but Peter enters the tomb first. The storyteller, however, gives the nod to the other disciple who is the first to believe. It is a transparent attempt to accord that other disciple, Jesus' intimate in the Fourth Gospel, a place of honor alongside Peter.

The variations in these stories in all probability reflect the actual rivalries at work in the early Jesus movement.

How Did Jesus Appear?

The earliest reports of Jesus' appearances were of luminous apparitions—a blinding light surrounding an indistinct figure—accompanied by some auditory communication, whether real or imagined. In Matthew and in John 21, the appearances are of a more spiritual kind, as though it were the ascended Jesus who was appearing. On the other hand, the appearance to the women at the tomb, to the two on the Emmaus road, and the appearance to the eleven in both Luke and John 20 seem more physical and thus approximate a resuscitated corpse. The difference can be generalized: appearances in Jerusalem close to the burial site are more corporeal; appearances at some spatial remove less so. But the stories do not fit neatly into those two compartments. In general, based on the evidence of the canonical gospels, as the tradition grows older, the appearances of Jesus tend to become more physical and tangible and to be linked to the empty-tomb story. In a rival tradition, such as we find in Paul, the appearances tend to be more ethereal, linked less and less to the notion of the resuscitation of a corpse.

It is uncertain whether appearances of the risen Jesus can be distinguished from epiphanies—the appearance of an angel (called an *angelophany*) or the sighting of other divine beings. The transfiguration of Jesus is characterized by Mark as an event in which Jesus' clothes become intensely white, whiter than any bleach could make them.[23] (A brilliant light is a regular feature of epiphanies.) Jesus is then visualized as conversing with Moses and Elijah, two great Israelite figures of long ago each of whom experienced an epiphany on Mount Sinai—epiphanies that serve as models for the transfiguration. (Epiphanies break through the crust of time in bringing together figures who lived in widely separated eras.) Then a voice comes out of the cloud: "This is my son. Listen to him." (A verbal communication issues from heaven, from a cloud, since God cannot be pictured.) Because the transfiguration is an epiphany and because it resembles the resurrection appearances, many scholars have concluded that the transfiguration is a misplaced appearance story.

The resemblances between a resurrection appearance and an epiphany can also be observed in the two accounts of the miraculous catch of fish. One, related in John 21, is an appearance story. The other, told by Luke, is a commissioning story in its present location: it is Luke's substitute for the enlistment of the first disciples as related by Mark.[24] In Luke's tale, the disciples have been fishing all night and have caught nothing. When they lower their nets on the instruction of Jesus, they take so many fish that two boats nearly founder. Peter and the others are stunned. They immediately become followers of Jesus. The story may well be a duplicate of the miraculous catch narrated in John 21 as a resurrection story and, like the transfiguration, may be a misplaced resurrection appearance. Christian storytellers perhaps saw no reason to distinguish the two.

In Acts, Luke tells of Stephen's vision as he is about to be stoned: he sees the sky opened up and God's effulgence on display, with Jesus standing at the right side of God. Although Luke would not class Stephen's vision as a resurrection appearance that could potentially identify Stephen as an apostle, it is difficult to distinguish Stephen's vision from other appearance stories.

The vision of Stephen belongs in the same class with the vision of Paul on the Damascus road. Luke depicts this event three times in Acts.[25] While the three versions differ in details, the broad outline is constant. Paul is dazzled by a blinding light and he hears a voice. The question is whether the three accounts of Paul's vision are accurate depictions of the appearance to which Paul lays claim in 1 Corinthians.[26] Paul believes he was appointed an apostle directly by the authority of the risen Jesus; Luke, however, demotes Paul from the circle of the twelve, even though he pictures Paul as one of his heroes. For Luke, only those who accompanied Jesus during his earthly ministry are qualified to be apostles.[27] They alone are in a position to recognize him in his risen state. And the witnesses to Jesus' resurrection are those in authority.

The author of the Book of Revelation has a vision on the island of Patmos. Part of that vision is of the Christ figure.[28] That figure, according to John, the author, had on a robe, and his head and hair were white as wool can get, as white as snow; his eyes flashed like fire. (This must have been the script for Charlton Heston playing Moses.) His face was as radiant as the naked sun. His voice was like thunder. This vision shares some of the same features as the resurrection appearances of Jesus: intense whiteness and radiant light; a loud noise like thunder.

The imagery of the divine radiance derives ultimately from the Book of Daniel and other Old Testament texts. They, in turn, have incorporated themes and motifs from Canaanite mythology depicting the two gods, El and Baal, as a king and a fearful warrior god. A brief passage in Daniel has contributed much to New Testament images:

> While I was watching,
> thrones were set up
> and the Ancient of Days sat down.
> He had a snowy white garment on,
> and the hair of his head was like pure white fleece.
> His throne was a roaring inferno,
> and a stream of fire poured out from his presence.
> Hundreds of thousands stood ready to serve him,
> and he was surrounded by millions of attendants.[29]

James M. Robinson points out that the earliest appearances of the risen Jesus were visualized as luminous apparitions.[30] Both Paul and Luke make this evident. The move to replace a disembodied, supernatural figure with a more tangible, material bodily resurrection—the resuscitation of a corpse—was actually triggered by a conflict with gnostic views. Toward the close of the first century, the gnostics began to claim their own view of the resurrection as normative—the appearances as a blinding light accompanied by some revelatory communication. The divergence in the two views led not only to different kinds of appearance stories but to different kinds of gospels. The so-called gnostic gospels incorporate the instructions Jesus gives the insiders in a dialogue between Jesus and his intimates—they are, in other words, revelation gospels. Paul, for example, claims that he received his gospel directly by revelation, that he was not dependent on the Jerusalem leaders for his message. Paul's claim gives a gnostic twist to his relation to Jesus: his Jesus is exclusively the risen Christ.

The strand of the tradition that was to become the orthodox strand, in contrast, moved the special instruction Jesus gave his disciples back inside his life, prior to his death and resurrection. This move had the effect of restricting the circle of insiders to those who knew Jesus during his lifetime; that of course excludes Paul. The earlier, gnosticizing view can be observed, however, not just in Paul's claims but also in the opening chapters of Acts, where Jesus instructs the apostles for a forty-day period prior to his ascension. Moreover, the appearance stories often include a commissioning of the eleven or the apostles, which has affinities with the gnostic perspective. In other words, the two strands are intertwined in most early Christian sources.

Where Did the Appearances Take Place?

Many scholars are of the opinion that the earliest apparitions of Jesus after his death took place in Galilee, as forecast in the Gospel of Mark and depicted by Matthew (who is dependent on Mark). The reason for this consensus is that scholars are confident that the disciples abandoned Jesus and fled at his arrest. The appendix to John also reports Galilean apparitions, as we have noted. This evidence makes it difficult to believe that the appearances reported in Luke—all of which are located in and around Jerusalem—and the Jerusalem appearances recorded in John 20 are historically accurate. Indeed, Luke represents Jesus as commanding his followers to remain in Jerusalem—probably Luke's way of diverting attention from the fact that the disciples had, in actuality, forsaken Jesus during his arrest and trial and fled. The Gospel of John positions the Jerusalem appearances prior to the Galilean appearances, which is a very unlikely sequence. The Gospel of Peter breaks off with Peter, Andrew, and Levi returning to the sea and their fishing nets, undoubtedly in Galilee. Paul's list of appearances does not provide any clues regarding location, although it is plausible that Paul's vision was associated with Damascus.[31]

When Did the Appearances Take Place?

We do not know where the appearances took place. Do we know when?

No time frame is suggested by the Gospel of Mark for the appearance forecast for Galilee. However, such an appearance could not have taken place on Easter Sunday. In Matthew, Jesus appears to two women at the tomb on Easter and later (how much later is not indicated) to the group on a mountain in Galilee.

Luke is the first to confine the appearances to Jerusalem and Easter. According to the Gospel of Luke, the appearances on Easter day conclude with Jesus' ascension that evening. In Acts the ascension is delayed forty days, with appearances continuing in the interim.

John seems to stick with the Easter time schedule. But because Thomas is not present on the first occasion when Jesus appears to the eleven, Jesus repeats his appearance a week later. Then, in the appendix to John, there is an appearance later in Galilee. The sequence of appearances—first in Jerusalem, then in Galilee—is not plausible. In spite of the disciples' flight from the scene, and early stories depicting appearances in Galilee, the position of Jerusalem as the mythic center of the Jesus movement (Jerusalem is the navel of the earth for both Christians and Jews) and the legend of the empty tomb simply override history in favor of a myth of origins.

Luminous apparitions of Jesus are variously reported to have gone on for months, even years. The appearance to Paul must have taken place three or four years after the crucifixion, not in the forty days following Easter. Secret James, a gospel found among the Nag Hammadi codices, has Jesus continue his instruction of the disciples for 550 days, while the Pistis Sophia, a collection of writings originating in Egypt in the third century, represents Jesus as prolonging his instruction of certain followers for eleven years. Reported sightings of Jesus continue, even into twentieth-century America. All of these claims make it difficult to say how long the appearances continued.

RESURRECTION AS REVELATION

Reginald H. Fuller has suggested that the appearances of Jesus can best be defined as revelatory encounters.[32] The appearances are depicted visually as a blinding light. The light is accompanied by some communication—a voice from heaven, an angel speaking to a person, or perhaps the message of an inner voice. What do those voices communicate?

The appearances in many instances are nothing more or less than commissioning stories. They call someone to a task, to a vocation. Although we do not know which of the stories represents the inaugural appearance to Peter, he was widely assumed to be the first to be commissioned. Later appearances—to James, to all the apostles, to Paul— seem to be concerned with the inauguration of the apostolic mission of the church beyond Jerusalem and Judea. Paul reports his own commission in his letters to the Corinthians and the Galatians. Luke connects Paul's commission with his Damascus road experience in all three versions. It is possible, as Fuller thinks, that the appearance to the five hundred represents the establishment of the Christian community, perhaps at Pentecost. The appearance to the eleven was understood to be a commissioning story, as Matthew and Luke indicate.[33] This is the reason many scholars are inclined to the view that the recruitment story in Luke 5:1–11 involving a miraculous catch of fish is a resurrection appearance or epiphany *in function*.

The appearances are understood to authorize or appoint certain leaders, to give them authority to determine right teaching and to appoint their successors. As Jesus is made to say in Matthew:

> I swear to you, you who have followed me, when the son of Adam is seated on his throne of glory in the renewal of creation, you also will be seated on twelve thrones and sit in judgment on the twelve tribes of Israel.[34]

When Jesus breathes the spirit on the disciples in the Gospel of John, he says:

> If you forgive anyone their sins, they are forgiven; if you do not release them from their sins, they are not released.[35]

The concern over appearances as the gospel took shape has to do primarily with apostolic right and succession, or, as we would say, with empire building and office politics. Witnesses to the resurrection of Jesus were given special prerogatives in the ancient church that were destined to determine the organization of the churches.

Elaine Pagels insists that we cannot understand the doctrine of the resurrection solely on the basis of its religious content; we must also examine its practical consequences, its political implications. Why, for example, did Tertullian, a second-century Christian theologian, label everyone a heretic who did not accept the doctrine of the bodily resurrection of Jesus? Why did he link the resurrection of Jesus to the resurrection of the believer? Every believer, he argued, can anticipate the resurrection of the body just as Jesus rose bodily from the grave. He didn't do that for purely metaphysical or theological reasons; he did it because the authority structure of the church depended on it. In other words, the bodily resurrection of Jesus "legitimates the authority of certain men who claim to exercise exclusive leadership over the churches as the successors of the apostle Peter."[36] And it is Peter and only Peter who is empowered to pass his authority along to his successors—namely, the bishops, and ultimately to the head bishop, the pope.

This is how the chain of command works:

The ultimate authority—and the foundation of all subsequent authority—is Jesus, who receives his commission in his two epiphany experiences, the first at his baptism, the second at the transfiguration. Jesus assigns a leadership position to Peter in the Gospel of John, as he does in the Gospel of Matthew.[37] He does so because Peter is the first to come to the resurrection faith, expressed in the narrative as his being the first to see the risen lord. True, Peter had competitors in the primitive tradition—Mary, James, and even Paul—but the primacy of Peter was acknowledged by everyone. Only appearances to the original followers of Jesus were legitimizing appearances. The appearances to Stephen and Paul fell outside the charmed circle. The string of authorizing appearances ended, of course, when Jesus ascended to heaven. In fact, that was the function of the ascension story: to put a period to the appearances.

The original appearances did not depend on the view that Jesus rose bodily from the grave. Jesus appeared in ecstatic revelations, in visions, and in dreams. The gnostics took up this view and made it their special domain. In these experiences, the gnostics argued, they were given knowledge of the true nature of reality, of their origin and destiny. As a consequence, they did not think it necessary to turn to someone like Peter for information or authority; they had direct access to Jesus the risen one. Jesus continued to instruct them as the risen lord, and they incorporated the content of their visions into their gospels. To the orthodox church, the gnostic view undermined the claims of the Jerusalem authorities and eroded the authority of the original disciples. For that reason alone, Tertullian deemed it necessary to condemn the gnostics as heretics.

The right to ordain future leaders of the church carried with it the obligation to pass on the true teaching about such matters. The orthodox view, later to be embodied in the creeds, was the teaching that supported the ecclesiastical structure of the church. As Constantine discovered, the easiest way to achieve and maintain a consensus is to excommunicate everyone who does not adhere to the orthodox line. And so the leaders in power declared anyone who deviated from the orthodox line a heretic.

All of this is, of course, incongruent with the teachings of Jesus. It is by no means clear that he appointed anyone to anything. Access to God—in his vision of the kingdom—was unbrokered. He did not support the preeminence of an inner circle of followers but advised that those who aspired to be leaders should make themselves slaves of all. In sum, the leaders of the primitive community did just what most human communities do as they are formed and mature—they engaged in a struggle to establish a perpetual pecking order with themselves at the head. Viewed in this light, the resurrection is entirely self-serving for the leaders of the Jesus movement.

Was any other content given to the resurrection as revelation? Were there any other links between Jesus of Nazareth and the risen Christ?

In his letter to the Galatians, Paul insists that his gospel was not given to him by a human source but came through a revelation of Jesus Christ.[38] In his dispute with the three Jerusalem authorities—Peter, James (Jesus' brother), and John—he defends what he calls "the truth of the gospel," the meaning of the gospel that was revealed to him. The truth of the gospel for Paul was the truth about circumcision, kosher, and other aspects of the Mosaic law. That truth also seemed to imply an end to ethnic and gender-based boundaries. As he puts it in Galatians,

> Jew and Greek are no longer distinguished, slave and free are one, and there is no difference between male and female. All such distinctions are obliterated in Christ Jesus.[39]

Paul's understanding meant that his assistant Titus did not have to be circumcised to become a Christian. Moreover, Paul advocated open-table fellowship with gentiles—without observing kosher; Peter apparently vacillated on this point.[40] If Peter had had a corresponding revelatory encounter, such as the one Luke depicts in Acts 10, the lesson did not really sink in.

Unlike Peter's reluctance to embrace the implications of the new gospel, the Gospel of Thomas seems hospitable to Paul's perceptions. In saying 53, for example, there is a burlesque of circumcision:

> His disciples said to him, "Is circumcision useful or not?"
> He replied, "If it were useful, their father would produce children already circumcised from their mother. Rather, the true circumcision in spirit has become profitable in every respect."

Paul's liberal attitude on kosher food restrictions is endorsed by Thomas in 14:2: "Eat whatever they serve you" is the admonition. That corresponds to Paul's advice:

> If one of the unbelievers invites you to dine and you are inclined to accept the invitation, eat whatever they serve you without raising objections because of conscience.[41]

We do not know how Paul acquired his understanding of the gospel other than what he tells us: it came by revelation. Yet it is possible that Paul knew something of the sayings of Jesus, perhaps from sources similar to those underlying the Sayings Gospel Q and the Gospel of Thomas. For whatever reasons, Paul and Thomas appear at points to be closer to the historical Jesus than does the emerging orthodox position represented by Peter and James.

THE ROOTS OF RESURRECTION

Belief in life after death was a relatively late development in Israelite religion, according to George W. E. Nickelsburg, in concert with many other scholars.[42] Sheol was the dark and dusty abode of the dead, in the nether regions of the earth, where the "shades" of humans were to dwell forever, cut off from each other and from God. In the tale of Orpheus and Eurydice, which Ovid revives just about the time Jesus is active, Orpheus descends into Hades and seeks the return of his wife who had died prematurely. (The text of the story is found on p. 277.) Without life after death, God must hand out justice and retribution within this world and within the limits of human life. The Deuteronomic paradigm is the view that those who prosper in this life are righteous and therefore blessed, while those who are poor and sick are suffering from sin. Justice and retribution, to be sure, could be conceived as a collective matter, to be enacted for whole peoples or groups of people and realized through descendants. That seems to have been the import of Ezekiel's famous vision of the valley of dry bones, in which the prophet promises, on behalf of God, that the whole house of Israel will be "resurrected" from the Babylonian captivity, returned to Palestine, and the nation renewed.[43]

At some point in the history of Israel, probably prior to the return from exile under Ezra, a new development took place. Before the restoration of the people as a whole, and in the absence of justice for individuals, the doctrine of life after death emerged. The frustration of justice for both the nation and individuals prompted the introduction of this doctrine. This belief arose, in all probability, during the Exile of the Israelites in the sixth and fifth centuries B.C.E. At any rate, the literature of the third and second centuries begins to show an interest in resurrection as one response to persecution and oppression.

By the time the documents of the New Testament were written, belief in the resurrection of the body had become widespread. It seems to have been embraced by the Essenes at Qumran, by the Pharisees, and by the Jesus movement, but not by the Sadducees. The motivation for entertaining the idea was that the human sense of justice demanded that somebody, presumably God or the gods, rectify the injustices perpetrated in this life. Vindication results in recompense: those who are injured are entitled to be compensated for their suffering. Correlatively, those who have been the agents of evil in this life are to be punished in the next.

The resurrection was a particularly congenial idea for the new Jesus movement. This movement had a savior figure who was not treated as the messiah should have been treated. Jesus' fate seemed to match the fate of many, if not most, of Jesus' early followers, who were poor peasants. There was a disjunction between their experience of life and their belief that God would vindicate them. Jesus' resurrection represented vindication for the persecuted and wrongfully executed man Jesus. It was compensation for his suffering. It also positioned Jesus as a cosmic judge who would return at the end of the age and preside over the resurrection of the righteous to eternal life and the resurrection of the wicked to eternal punishment. The resurrection of Jesus was thus understood as a down payment on a future general resurrection. Justice would eventually be handed out to everyone according to merit. Resurrection was the centerpiece of a comprehensive compensatory scheme.

The resurrection is the extension of the Deuteronomic paradigm beyond the grave: since the righteous are not being rewarded and the wicked are not being punished in this life, reward and punishment will be handed out after death. Since Jesus was not vindicated in this life, he was vindicated by his resurrection. Jesus' fate becomes the paradigm for the fate of all, believers and nonbelievers alike.

There is not much supporting evidence and a great deal of contradictory evidence in the authentic teachings of Jesus for this doctrine. Jesus seems to have repeatedly suggested that only the undeserving would be eligible to enter God's domain; that those who thought they should be first would in fact be last. Insiders would be out and outsiders in. The reversal of first and last was for him the fundamental model.

A second way to judge whether the doctrine of the resurrection is consonant with what we know of Jesus' sayings is to ask whether the promised rewards are intrinsic or extrinsic. Or does reward involve compensation in another medium? Then it is appropriate to ask whether the rewards are for insiders or for outsiders. It makes me smile even to pose the question: For how many who espouse the doctrine of the resurrection are the rewards designed for others not in their group?

A final test is to ask, with Elaine Pagels, whether this system of rewards and punishments legitimizes the hierarchic structure of the church, with its claim to have the authority to remit sin and to condemn. Putting all these tests together, is the motivation for maintaining this scheme anything more than human hubris, human arrogance? Do human beings have the right to expect eternal bliss for being good or believing the right things? Conversely, does anyone really think that eternal punishment is the proper destiny of any human being?

There is, of course, the final question of whether we can divorce the resurrection from eschatology—from the notion that history will end at some future date and a new era begin. Is the resurrection of Jesus—and the resurrection of all human beings—inextricably bound up with the concept of eschatology?

The answers Jesus might give to all these questions will be the subject of the epilogue to this book, "Jesus for a New Age."

ORPHEUS AND EURYDICE IN THE UNDERWORLD

Orpheus was a Thracian minstrel whose playing and singing were so enchanting that the animals were charmed and the stones and trees followed him about. After his marriage, while his wife Eurydice was wandering in the meadows, a serpent bit her ankle and she died. Orpheus mourned her loss. He was so grief-stricken that he boldly descended through the gate of Taenarus to the river Styx, where he attempted to arouse the sympathy of the shades. He wandered among the ghosts, the wraiths of the dead, till he reached Persephone and her lord, the king of the shades. He pleaded with them by singing and playing the lyre. "I beg you," he sang, "weave again Eurydice's destiny, brought too swiftly to a close. We mortals and all that is ours are fated to fall to you, and after a little time, sooner or later, we hasten to this abode. We are all on our way here, this is our final home, and yours the most lasting sway over the human race. If you cannot extend the sojourn of my wife on earth, I do not wish to return myself."

The bloodless ghosts were in tears. The king and queen of the underworld could not refuse Orpheus. They called Eurydice, who walked slowly because of the injury to her ankle. She was given to Orpheus but only on the condition that he not look back until he had emerged from the underworld.

As Orpheus made his way up the sloping path, when they had almost reached the surface of the earth, out of anxiety that his wife's strength might be failing, he glanced back to make certain she was still there. Immediately she slipped back into the depths. Orpheus reached out to grasp her with his arms but to no avail. His arms enfolded nothing but air.

Ovid, the Roman poet, was born in 43 B.C.E. and died in 17 C.E. He was educated in Rome, where he studied rhetoric and poetry. He was exiled by the Emperor Augustus in 8 C.E. for some unspecified offense. During his life he composed numerous works, of which the best known is perhaps the *Metamorphoses*. All the stories in this collection have to do with transformations. The story of Orpheus and Eurydice is recounted in Book Ten. It is the story of a failed resurrection that is contemporary with Jesus of Nazareth. It also provides some important clues as to how the underworld was conceived.

Chapter Fifteen

THE DIVINE CHILD

There are three infancy narratives in the New Testament gospels. One tells the story of the birth of John the Baptist, two relate the birth of Jesus. In addition, the Infancy Gospel of James depicts the infancy of Mary, while the Infancy Gospel of Thomas (not to be confused with the Gospel of Thomas) features the precocious Jesus as a wonder-working child.

The infancy stories and gospels come relatively late in the development of the gospels. The birth and childhood stories that appear in Matthew and Luke were composed late in the first century or early in the second and thus stand at the greatest remove from the events they depict. They contain very little historical information.

The two infancy gospels were composed in the second century. They are entirely imaginative constructs. They contain no reliable historical data.

Yet it is important to understand why these stories and gospels were composed—to understand their function in the unfolding gospel traditions. Unless we take the trouble to come to terms with their content and function, they will continue to be the source of misunderstanding and misinformation.

HOW JESUS BECAME GOD

There are two basic ways to account for the creation of the infancy stories. One way is to observe the role they played in the gradual and retrospective enhancement of the status of Jesus, in the gradual elevation of Jesus to the role of divinity. How the person and work of Jesus as the messiah, as the Christ, is to be interpreted is known as *christology*. Christology is a subdivision of systematic theology, which includes other doctrines, such as the doctrine of God, of the church, of salvation.

A second way to account for the creation of the infancy stories is to note the function of their counterparts in conventional hellenistic biographies of famous persons. Famous military and intellectual heroes were often said to have had at least one divinity as a parent. Miraculous births in depictions of their lives were the rule rather than the exception.

In this chapter, we will pursue both perspectives, beginning with reverse christology. We will fit the infancy narratives of Matthew and Luke into the development of christology at the appropriate point.

Reverse Christology: Stage One

As nearly as scholars can reconstruct what happened immediately after the crucifixion, Jesus' disciples fled to Galilee and resumed their previous lives. Later, as Peter and others came to the conviction that Jesus was not dead but alive, they began to think of him as the son of Adam pictured in Daniel 7—the cosmic judge who would come with clouds at the end of history and set things right. Since Jesus had not acted as the expected messiah during his life, they came to believe that he had been designated son of Adam at his death and would return soon to fulfill his promise. This view, perhaps the earliest Christian affirmation, has been described as an "exaltation christology"—as an evaluation of Jesus that assigns him the role of son of Adam at his death and resurrection. Some scholars have isolated an early formulation of this view in the opening of Paul's letter to the Romans, written in the sixties c.e.:

> Christ Jesus, God's son,
> descended from David,
> appointed son of God in power by his resurrection from the dead.[1]

In this view, Jesus became, or was elevated to, son of God by virtue of his resurrection. This is how Luke pictures the earliest stage of christology:

> Every Israelite ought now to be confident that God has appointed him both lord and messiah, this Jesus whom you crucified.[2]

As lord and messiah, Jesus would return in the near future and exercise the function of son of Adam in accordance with the prophecy in Daniel and expressed elsewhere—for example, by Jesus himself at his trial:

> You will see the son of Adam sitting at the right hand of Power and coming with the clouds of the sky![3]

Although his followers certainly regarded Jesus as an eschatological prophet during his brief public life, his real function was to be exercised in the future.

Reverse Christology: Stage Two

The first stage of christology did not require the creation of a gospel because the words and deeds of Jesus were not essential to his function; the real role of Jesus was to return as the messiah in the very near future. When he did not return immediately as expected, his followers began to review what they remembered of him and decided that his life, after all, had exhibited some unusual traits. They had already collected some of his teachings into a preliminary gospel, the Sayings Gospel Q, which they had framed with the dire warnings of John the Baptist at one end and with the forecast of a final judgment, with themselves in the role of judges, at the other.[4] Now they started to fashion another version of his story in which he was designated son of God, not at his resurrection but at his baptism (this is known as "adoptionist christology"). This version has survived as the Gospel of Mark. In the opening scene, Mark depicts Jesus coming up out of the water of John's baptism:

> He saw the skies torn open and the spirit coming down toward him like a dove. There was also a voice from the skies: "You are my favored son—I fully approve of you."[5]

The designation of Jesus as God's son—and by implication as messiah—was thereby moved backwards from his resurrection to the beginning of his public ministry.

Reverse Christology: Stage Three

It was already the decade of the seventies C.E. when the Gospel of Mark was first composed. The next step in this reverse enhancement of the role of Jesus was to come with the gospels of Matthew and Luke. By the end of the century, they had moved the messianic status of Jesus back to his birth. This step was taken in conjunction with the outline of conventional hellenistic biographies of famous people. It was the merger of two interests that led to the creation of the infancy narratives. One interest was the desire to push Jesus' messianic status back farther and farther into the past to make it all the more credible. A second interest was to account for his unusual life and his noble death in terms that enhanced his comparison with other famous people. Each of their noble lives, according to reports, had been preceded by an unusual birth and infancy, so Jesus' birth and life must also have been portentous.

FAMOUS BIRTHS AND PEDIGREES

The ancient Greek biography was a stereotypical account of the military hero's life, consisting of four divisions: origins, youth, adult achievements, and death. Biographies of military heroes of course recounted their victories and heroism. But for heroes like Socrates and Jesus, adult achievements consisted of teachings and other forms of worthy behavior. Such lives were read and interpreted backwards from their deaths, usually viewed as noble. The story of their lives consisted of tales of wisdom and actions manifesting character that were considered exemplary and worthy of imitation. The biography was thus conceived as a kind of eulogy or panegyric, known to the ancient rhetoricians as an encomium, which was used in instruction. Because the encomium was an established literary form, the ancients knew the topics it was supposed to cover.

The retrospective interpretation of the hero's life from the perspective of his or her noble death was regarded as a legitimate perspective. The basis for that perspective was the view that one's destiny was predetermined or controlled by fate. What a particular individual turned out to be was determined at the outset, at birth. At the same time, one could not know what fate had in store until that life had run its course. Birth stories were considered an essential part of the biography because infancy anecdotes recounted omens that pointed to the future, a future known only from the perspective of the hero's noble death. If someone had died a noble death and had lived an exemplary life, that person must have had a noteworthy birth.

The hellenistic biography or encomium, following the model of Aristoxenus, a student of Aristotle, consisted of five elements: a miraculous or unusual birth; revealing childhood episode (or episodes); a summary of wise teachings; wondrous deeds; a martyrdom or noble death. This form of the biography was more suitable for philosophers and religious heroes, such as Socrates and Jesus. The New Testament gospels encompass precisely these five elements and are thus examples of the hellenistic biography.

Within the framework of the hellenistic biography, ancient infancy narratives were literary creations designed to fill in the obscure origins of great figures. According to Lane McGaughy, whose general outline I am following here, the full form of the hellenistic infancy narrative consisted of five parts:[6]

1. A genealogy revealing illustrious ancestors
2. An unusual, mysterious, or miraculous conception
3. An annunciation by an angel or in a dream
4. A birth accompanied by supernatural portents
5a. Praise or forecast of great things to come, or
5b. Persecution by a potential competitor.

The fifth part represents the response to the hero's birth. A positive response results in praise of the gods or thanks offered to them and the forecast of the great things the hero will achieve. A negative response to the hero's birth is manifest in the abandonment of the infant or persecution of the hero by a potential rival. The persecution motif often involves the exposure of an infant by a parent for one reason or another (the parent as enemy) and the subsequent adoption of the child by an animal or foster parents of a lower class. Sometimes a rival throne claimant persecutes the child for fear of competition. This motif is found in the story of the birth of Sargon, the great king of Babylonia in the third millennium B.C.E.; in the story of Moses; in the account of Cyrus the

Great in the sixth century B.C.E.; in the tale of Remus and Romulus, the founders of Rome; and in the yarn about the birth of King Arthur, to cite only a few examples.

These elements are constituent parts of the two infancy narratives composed by Matthew and Luke. They can also be identified in the accounts of the birth of Plato, Alexander the Great, and Apollonius of Tyana, a charismatic wonder worker who was a contemporary of Jesus. Plato was a student of Socrates, who was executed in 399 B.C.E. Plato left an enduring philosophical legacy consisting of some twenty-five dialogues, a defense of Socrates, and some letters that may not be authentic. Alexander the Great died in 323 B.C.E. after having conquered the Mediterranean world as well as lands to the east. He was a military genius, but of even greater importance, he was an ambassador for Greece and things Greek. He planted the Greek language and culture wherever he went. In the following summaries of the birth stories of these three hellenistic heroes, I have identified the five constituent elements in the hellenistic birth story by numbers in square brackets corresponding to the outline just given. For example, [1] refers to the genealogy, [3] to an annunciation, while [5b] indicates the hostile reception by a potential rival.

Before we turn to the summaries, two general observations about these stories will prove helpful. If the hero is human, as in the case of Isaac[7] and John the Baptist,[8] the miracle is that a barren woman, perhaps after menopause, conceives. If the hero is considered superhuman, as in the case of Hercules and Alexander, the male parent is a god.

In Isaac's case, God promised Abraham that he would father a son when he was one hundred years old and that Sarah, his wife, who was ninety years of age, would conceive. Sarah, the reader is told, was beyond the age of childbearing. When God, or God's messengers, made the announcement to Abraham and Sarah, they both laughed. They later regretted their flippant response.[9]

In the story of Plato's birth, it appears that Plato is both human and divine. The status of Jesus in this regard is also unclear, although later interpreters of the New Testament birth stories migrated decisively toward the view that Jesus was a god.

One further aspect of these tales should be noted. In the birth and infancy stories, a miraculous birth is sometimes followed by persecution of some sort. In stories of the death of the hero, the hero is persecuted prior to his death. The martyrdom of the hero is often followed by the apotheosis of the hero—his or her deification or elevation to the status of a god or goddess—and the establishment of a cult in his or her name. McGaughy has pointed out that in the case of the birth of the hero, persecution follows triumph, so to speak; in the case of the death of the hero, triumph follows persecution.

The births of three heroes of the hellenistic age provide the basic ingredients for comparison with their gospel counterparts.

Plato

Diogenes Laertius, an author of the third century C.E., records an account of Plato's birth that includes [1] a family tree tracing Plato's illustrious ancestors back to Solon, an Athenian statesman and reformer of note, and to Poseidon (Roman name: Neptune), god of the sea. Apparently Ariston, Plato's father, stopped making love to his wife, Perictone, because she seemed unable to conceive. Later, she gave birth [2]. Meanwhile, the god Apollo appeared to Ariston in a dream, presumably to inform him of Plato's imminent birth [3]. According to the legend, Plato was born on Apollo's birthday, considered an important omen [4]. In the paeans of praise later composed for Plato, the logic of the hellenistic birth story is made evident: How could Plato have healed the souls of mortals with speech unless he had been sired by Phoebus Apollo? Plato is therefore the son of Apollo. Asclepius, the god of healing, was a mortal, like Plato, but was also the son of Apollo and subsequently deified [5a]. At the end of an ode composed in Plato's honor, Plato is translated to the celestial realms, like Enoch and Elijah.

Alexander the Great

Plutarch composed a series of lives in the late first century C.E., one of which was the life of Alexander the Great. According to Plutarch, Alexander was said to be a descendant of Hercules on his father Philip's side; on his mother Olympias's side, he was a descendant of Aeacus, the first king of Aegina, who himself was the son of Zeus and Aegina. Alexander could not help but be great! [1]

Alexander's mother-to-be had a dream prior to her wedding night with Philip. In her dream, a peal of thunder was followed by a bolt of lightning that struck her womb. Later, Philip also had a dream. In Philip's dream, he sealed his wife's womb with a seal that bore the image of a lion. According to the seer, Aristander of Telmessus, Philip sealed his wife's womb because she was pregnant. Two different versions of Olympias' conception are reported [2]. In one version, it is said that a serpent was stretched out at Olympias' side while she slept. From that time Philip hesitated to sleep with his wife for fear she might cast a spell on him or because he thought she might have mated with a higher being. Another version has Olympias practicing unrestrained and superstitious rites involving a huge tame snake. The snake would coil itself around the wands or garlands carried by the women in these barbaric rites and fill the men with terror. In both versions Olympias is said to have been united with a higher being in conceiving Alexander.

Alexander was born on the day the temple of Ephesian Artemis burned to the ground. This was regarded as an omen of further calamities [4]. At the same time, Philip received news of a great victory over the Illyrians and news that his horse had won at the Olympic games [4]. News of these victories was interpreted by the seers as evidence that Alexander would be unconquerable [5a].

Apollonius of Tyana

Flavius Philostratus was born about 170 c.e. He wrote a life of Apollonius of Tyana, a contemporary of Jesus and an itinerant sage, philosopher, and charismatic. In a vision, Apollonius' mother was told she would give birth to a god [3], a cult was formed around his memory [5a], and a temple erected close to the spot where he was born. Yet nothing is said about a miraculous conception on the part of Apollonius' mother. His birth, however, was highly unusual and surrounded by portents of great things to come [4], [5a]. Apollonius was a truth-teller, as suggested by the water of truth that flowed from a spring close to his birthplace [5a]. Water from the spring came up cold but bubbled like a hot kettle. When drunk, this water was forgiving and sweet to those who honor their oaths, but it brought swift justice to perjurers, attacking the eyes and hands and feet so that the body swelled up and decayed. Violators of oaths were crippled as a consequence and remained close by the spring, moaning and confessing their false oaths. People believed Apollonius to be the son of Zeus (the son of God), but he himself said that he was his father's son (his father was also named Apollonius). In this he may have been combining truth and modesty in a way unusual for one so widely revered.

MATTHEW'S INFANCY NARRATIVE

The version of Jesus' birth found in Matthew is organized around predictions of prophets, in addition to standard features derived from the hellenistic stories. Matthew's tale falls naturally into six segments (Table 11).

The six segments do not correspond precisely to the five parts of the traditional infancy story although the five basic elements are all present. The flight to Egypt and the murder of the infants together form the section devoted to persecution by a potential rival in the hellenistic outline [5b]. This part of Matthew's story has been influenced by the infancy stories of the baby Moses: the Pharaoh orders the midwives to destroy all male children born to Hebrew women; the Israelites were multiplying and prospering and were becoming a threat to the Egyptians (see p. 296 for the story of Moses' birth). Each section, with the exception of the genealogy, is corroborated by a prediction made by some prophet, of which the story of Jesus' birth and infancy is the fulfillment.

The migration to Nazareth has been added by Matthew to the traditional outline to make his story conform (a) to the fact that Jesus' hometown was known to be Nazareth and (b) to the prediction of the prophet that Jesus was to be called a "Nazorean," presumably an oblique

TABLE 11
BIRTH OF JESUS ACCORDING TO MATTHEW

	MATTHEW
1. Family tree	1:1–17
2. Miraculous birth of Jesus	1:18–25
Miraculous conception	1:18
Annunciation to Joseph	1:20–21
Prediction of the prophet	1:22
3. Astrologers from the East	2:1–12
Star in the East	2:1–2, 7–9
Prediction of the prophet	2:3–6
Astrologers pay homage to the child	2:10–12
4. Flight to Egypt	2:13–15
Prediction of the prophet	2:15
5. Murder of the babies	2:16–18
Prediction of the prophet	2:17
6. Migration to Nazareth	2:19–23
Prediction of the prophet	2:23

reference to Nazareth (Nazorean is not spelled exactly like Nazarean, somebody from Nazareth) or possibly a reference to Jesus as a Nazirite. Nazirites were those who had taken a vow to be consecrated wholly to God. They had to refrain from intoxicants, not allow a razor to touch their heads, and never go near a dead body. Samson was a Nazirite.[10] Another famous Nazirite in Israel was Samuel, a prophet who anointed both Saul and David, the first two kings of Israel.[11]

The Matthean genealogy reveals Jesus' illustrious ancestors, as in the hellenistic counterparts [1]. Matthew inaugurates Jesus' family tree by identifying him as a descendant of Abraham—therefore as an Israelite of pure lineage—and of David. *Son of David* was a familiar messianic title; the messiah would be one like David who would restore the ancient glory to Israel, as the prophet predicted:

> Behold the days are coming, says the Lord,
> when I will raise up a righteous star for David,
> a king who will reign with wisdom
> and bring justice and righteousness to the land.
> In his time Judah will be liberated
> and Israel will dwell in safety.
> And by this name he will be known: The Lord is our righteousness.[12]

Yet the genealogy in Matthew contains a curious paradox: How can Jesus be the descendant of David if Joseph is not his father? Jesus' lineage, after all, is traced through his father rather than through his mother; it is patriarchal rather than matriarchal.

In addition, there is the curious mention of the four disreputable women in a family tree that is otherwise limited to male ancestors. The four women precursors of Mary are Tamar, Rahab, Ruth, and Bathsheba. Tamar was the daughter-in-law of Judah, one of the sons of Jacob.[13] When her husband died, Judah gave her to another of his sons, Onan, in accordance with the rules of levirate marriage that require a brother to perform the duties of husband for a deceased brother. Onan refused to impregnate Tamar, practicing *coitus interruptus*; God killed him for his refusal. Tamar waited for Judah to give her a third son for a husband, but in vain. As a consequence, she disguised herself as a prostitute, seduced Judah, and bore twins as a result of their union. Judah condemned her to be burned for harlotry, not realizing that he was the father of her children. Tamar had wisely exacted tokens from Judah prior to their encounter, tokens that identified him as the father. By this deception, Tamar became the mother of the royal line. According to the genealogy in the Book of Ruth, Perez, one of her sons, was an ancestor of David.[14]

The second woman is Rahab, a prostitute living in Jericho at the time of the conquest under Joshua. She assisted Israelite spies and saved them from execution, in return for which Joshua promised to spare her and her family. According to one legend, Joshua married her after she became a proselyte; she then became the mother of prophets and priests. In another version, Rahab was not a prostitute but an innkeeper. According to Matthew, Rahab married Salmon and was the mother of Boaz, the husband of Ruth, the third woman in the list. Rahab is both a heroine and a prostitute according to Hebrews 11:31 and James 2:25.

Like Tamar, Ruth was the beneficiary of levirate marriage. Her husband had died, and, when she returned to Bethlehem with her mother-in-law Naomi, she was treated kindly by Boaz, a kinsman. Under somewhat dubious circumstances—Ruth went to the threshing floor during harvest and lay at the feet of Boaz during the night—Ruth became the wife of Boaz and gave birth to Obed, the father of Jesse, who was the father of David.[15]

Bathsheba was the wife of Uriah the Hittite, an officer of King David. David saw Bathsheba taking a bath, sent for her, and raped her. She became pregnant as a result. Uriah was away at war during these events. David tried to get Uriah to sleep with his wife to cover his own cupidity, but Uriah refused to do so. David then ordered Uriah into the front lines of battle where he was killed. David then married Bathsheba, who later gave birth to Solomon.

Scholars are of dissenting judgments about why Matthew included the four women in his family tree. It has been suggested that the four women were sinners and, as such, forecast that Jesus, their descendant, would be a savior of sinners. Another theory is that the four women were gentiles. Tamar, Rahab, and Ruth were clearly not Israelites; Bathsheba may also have been a foreigner, a Hittite, as the wife of Uriah. Including gentiles in the family tree of Jesus may be a hint that Jesus was to become the savior of all peoples. A third suggestion is that the four women engaged their sexual partners in an illicit manner, but in so doing became part of God's plan for the future messiah. A final suggestion is that the four women, each of whom conceived a child out of wedlock, hint at a similar scandal surrounding the youthful Mary. Jane Schaberg in *The Illegitimacy of Jesus* has advanced the thesis that the stories of the virgin birth, in fact, were invented to counter the claim of illegitimacy. Her proposal is supported by Matthew's observation that Joseph was embarrassed by Mary's pregnancy, for which he could not claim responsibility.[16]

There are three ways to account for Mary's condition. We can say that Joseph was the biological father of Jesus, the claims of the infancy stories notwithstanding. Or we could conclude that some other man, name unknown, was the actual father of Jesus—in other words, that Mary either had been raped or had been promiscuous. The third possibility is that the holy spirit was the agent of her conception.

The suggestion that the holy spirit, acting on God's behalf, somehow impregnated Mary moves the gospel accounts into the realm of the hellenistic miraculous birth stories [2]. In those stories typically a human woman takes a divine lover in conceiving a hero. That does not seem to be the intent of Matthew, Luke, or Infancy James. And that is basically the point Jane Schaberg makes. There is no precedent in the Israelite tradition for an action of God or the spirit of God replacing or canceling natural human sexual activity. God may be said to cause a woman to become fertile, but male sperm is always involved in conception. Mary was very young and therefore not past the age of childbearing. In view of the doubts of Joseph expressed in the story and the presence of the four scandalous women in the family tree, an illegitimate conception seems a plausible explanation of Mary's condition. Later, the miraculous conception of Jesus was reinterpreted to mean that Jesus was sinless and divine, without resorting to the hellenistic device of a divine lover.

Jesus' miraculous conception is narrated in connection with the angel's reassurances to Joseph that it is entirely proper for him to take Mary as his wife [3]. Matthew's strategy is to have each major event in his story correspond to something an ancient prophet predicted. In this case, he employs Isaiah:

> Behold, a virgin will conceive a child
> and she will give birth to a son,
> and they will name him Emmanuel.
>
> *Isaiah 7:14*

The predictive portent is the star in the East, observed by the astrologers, who come to Bethlehem to pay their homage to the new king. Of course, the prophet predicted that Jesus would be born in Bethlehem, the city of David:

And you, Bethlehem, in the province of Judah,
you are by no means least among the leaders of Judah.
Out of you will come a leader
who will shepherd my people, Israel.

Micah 5:2

The same star comes to rest above where the child lies, a celestial confirmation of his status as future king [4]. The astrologers present their gifts and return home by a different route to avoid the wicked Herod, as they have been instructed in a dream.

LUKE'S INFANCY NARRATIVE

Luke has two birth stories. He devotes one to John the Baptist (Table 12), a second to Jesus (Table 13). The two stories are duplicates of each other. Luke has intertwined the two: the annunciation to Mary, Mary's visit to Elizabeth during her pregnancy with John, and Mary's hymn of praise to God for allowing her to be the mother of the savior are woven into the account of John the Baptist's birth.

The Lukan story is more complicated than the version in Matthew. Luke works with signs and omens, which are interpreted as predictions about events to come. Luke uses signs where Matthew uses visions, and Luke uses forecasts by angels and others where Matthew employs prophetic predictions from scripture.

Birth of John the Baptist

Elizabeth, John's mother, was a descendant of Aaron, the brother of Moses and first high priest, according to Luke [1]. Elizabeth was infertile, and both she and Zechariah, her husband, were well along in years, possibly past the age when they could conceive a child [2]. Zechariah received a vision while serving in the temple: his wife was to give birth to a son whose name was to be John [3]. John is to be consecrated to God as a Nazirite from the day of his birth. In this he will be following in the eminent steps of Samson and Samuel. Zechariah did not really believe the angel Gabriel when he was told about John's birth, so Zechariah was struck dumb until John was born [4].

In due course, John is born. At his circumcision, Elizabeth's friends want to name him Zechariah after his father. But Elizabeth demurs. She recalls the charge of Gabriel to call him John. Zechariah concurs but has to do so in writing since he cannot yet speak. At the moment he confirms to Elizabeth that the name of the child is to be John, his speech is restored [4]. Naming, it seems, is among the omens that portend what the child

TABLE 12

BIRTH OF JOHN THE BAPTIST ACCORDING TO LUKE

	LUKE
1. Genealogy	1:5–6
2. Miraculous conception of John	1:7–25
Elizabeth's barrenness	1:7
Annunciation to Zechariah	1:8–20
Sign of Zechariah's muteness	1:21–23
Conception of John	1:24–25
3. Birth and naming of John	1:57–79
Neighbors rejoice	1:58
Sign of John's name	1:59–66
Zechariah predicts John's destiny	1:67–79
4. Persecution	
Supplied by Infancy James	
22:5–8; 23:1–8	
5. Childhood	1:80

will be. Zechariah is then able to predict that John will become the precursor of Jesus, the promised savior [5a].

The Infancy Gospel of James, a second-century work that retells the birth of John and Jesus, extends the persecution motif to the birth of John. In that work, Elizabeth flees to the hills when Herod's agents come looking for John. Elizabeth can find no place to hide and calls out to God for help. The mountain suddenly opens, and she and her son enter the depths. They are able to see because a messenger of the Lord is with them emanating light. Zechariah is murdered in the temple area because he is unable to tell Herod where his son is hidden.

Birth of Jesus

Luke has located his family tree of Jesus after his account of Jesus' baptism and thus after his infancy narrative. He does so, in all probability, because at the baptismal scene the voice from the sky identifies Jesus as God's son. Luke's genealogy traces Jesus' lineage backwards to Adam and God [1]. Matthew had traced Jesus' ancestry only back as far as Abraham.

Just as the angel Gabriel had appeared to Zechariah to announce the birth of John, so Gabriel appears to Mary with a comparable function [3]. Her conception of Jesus is miraculous since she has not had sex with any man [2]. Mary pays a visit to Elizabeth, and the baby John jumps for joy

TABLE 13
BIRTH OF JESUS ACCORDING TO LUKE

	LUKE
1. Genealogy	3:23–38
2. Miraculous conception of Jesus	1:26–56
Annunciation to Mary	1:26–38
Mary's visit to Elizabeth	1:39–45 (sign)
Mary's hymn of praise	1:46–56
3. Birth of Jesus	2:1–7
4. Visit of the shepherds	2:8–20
Annunciation to the shepherds	2:8–14
Shepherds praise God	2:15–20
5. Dedication of Jesus and predictions	2:21–38
Circumcision and naming	2:21
Presentation in the temple	2:22–24
Simeon predicts Jesus' destiny	2:25–35
Anna thanks God	2:36–38
6. Family returns to Nazareth	2:39
7. Childhood episode	2:40–52

while still in Elizabeth's womb at the presence of Mary, pregnant with Jesus [4]: John bears witness to the savior before either of them is born. Elizabeth praises God, and Mary follows suit with her own paean of praise [5a].

While Jesus is conceived miraculously, his birth is ordinary. However, there are accompanying portents [4]. An angel appears to the shepherds as they are watching their flocks at night and announces the birth of Jesus. Then a whole troop of heavenly figures appears and praises God [5a]. The shepherds visit Mary and her child where she has laid him in a feeding trough. Mary once again praises God [5a].

Unlike Matthew, Luke does not have a persecution sequence. However, Luke includes accounts of Jesus' circumcision, naming, and dedication, followed by further predictions of Jesus' greatness. In imitation of the hellenistic biography, Luke includes one incident from Jesus' youth —his visit to the temple at age twelve. On that occasion, Jesus astounds the teachers with his wisdom.

The Infancy Gospel of Thomas fills in the period between Jesus' birth and his temple appearance with fantastic stories of Jesus' childhood. In those stories Jesus forms birds of clay and commands them to fly away; he causes other children around him to die, then raises them back to life; he baffles his instructors with advanced knowledge; he heals the sick and wounded and raises the dead; he adjusts the length of beams in his father's wood shop by magic; he carries water in his cloak as though it were a jug. Such feats excel anything he does in his public life as represented by the canonical gospels.

The Infancy Gospel of James attempts to answer the basic question: Why was Mary, of all the virgins available in Israel, chosen to be the mother of the savior? The answer suggested by Infancy James, according to Ronald Hock, was that Mary achieved a level of purity that set her above other maidens.[17] Anna, Mary's mother, turns Mary's bedroom into a sanctuary where Mary is closely guarded and never allowed to eat anything impure. Later, she is moved to the temple where she spends nine years weaving a new curtain for the temple, the very curtain that is torn in two at Jesus' death. She and Joseph are accused of improper behavior when it becomes evident that Mary is pregnant, but both of them pass the poison-drink test that proves their innocence. (They are given something supposedly poison to drink and sent into the wilderness; if they survive the ordeal they are innocent.)*

According to Infancy James, Jesus was born in a cave with the assistance of a Hebrew midwife. At the moment of Jesus' birth, Joseph sees that the stars in the sky are standing still. The movement of the clouds has been arrested, and the birds are suspended in flight. People are frozen as they eat; all are looking upward. The water in the river stands still; goats have water in their mouths but do not drink. Then, suddenly, everybody and everything goes on with what they were doing [4].

The claim is made that Mary was a virgin not only before but after she gave birth. Salome, in disbelief, enters the cave to examine Mary. As Salome inserts her finger into Mary, her hand is engulfed in flames. Salome repents and is forgiven [4].

TRACES OF HISTORY

It is impossible to blend the infancy narratives of Matthew and Luke into one consistent story. Popular Christian representations, of course, ignore the discrepancies and contradictions and forge a new narrative out of elements taken from both.

Luke's infancy stories are mostly unique to him. All of the first chapter and most of the second have no parallels in Matthew. Matthew relates nothing about the birth of John the Baptist. Matthew does not seem to know the annunciation of Mary reported by Luke. Nor does Matthew mention Mary's visit to Elizabeth or Elizabeth's greeting. Matthew does not report Mary's hymn of praise, the Magnificat.

---

*A similar test was given to women suspected by their husbands of infidelity according to Numbers 5:11–31.

There is no mention in Matthew of the journey to Bethlehem to enroll in the census. Luke's mention of the swaddling clothes, the feeding trough, and the lack of privacy at the traveler's shelter are unknown to Matthew. And there are no visions of angels and no visits by shepherds in Matthew.

Matthew does not relate the circumcision of Jesus or his presentation in the temple. The recognition of Jesus in the temple by Simeon and Anna is unknown to Matthew. There is nothing in Matthew of the return from Bethlehem to Nazareth and no story of Jesus in the temple at age twelve.

Luke, on the other hand, does not know about the visit of the astrologers who have seen the special star heralding Jesus' birth. Luke does not know of the flight to Egypt to escape Herod, nor does he tell about the massacre of the babies. Since Luke does not report a flight to Egypt, he does not tell of a return from Egypt to Nazareth. In other words, all of the second chapter in Matthew's story is unique to Matthew.

Yet the two gospels have a remarkable number of things in common. They both place the birth of Jesus in the later years of the reign of Herod the Great. They agree that Jesus was born in Bethlehem. They are in accord that his home was Nazareth. They concur in the view that Joseph was Jesus' alleged father and that he was a descendant of David. Their stories both focus on Mary. They both relate that a heavenly messenger announced the coming birth of Jesus. They agree on Jesus' name. They also have in common the affirmation that Jesus was to be the savior of the people.

They agree on several features surrounding the birth of Jesus. In both stories Mary and Joseph are engaged but not married. They both suggest that Mary was a virgin. They concur that Joseph was not involved in the conception of Jesus. They claim that Mary became pregnant through the agency of the holy spirit. They agree that Jesus was born after Joseph and Mary began to live together.

There are various ways to account for what they have in common. Two of these prominent features can best be explained as the fulfillment of prophecies. Jesus was born in Bethlehem because the prophet Micah predicted that is where the messiah would be born; both Matthew and Luke knew that prophetic text. They both claim that Jesus was a descendant of David also because the prophets said the messiah would have David as an ancestor.

Annunciations by angels and predictions of greatness were of course suggested by a long and well-known tradition of miraculous birth stories. The miraculous conception of Jesus accompanied by signs was also inspired by such tales. The genealogies of Matthew and Luke, although irreconcilable in detail, nevertheless owe their origins to well-established tradition.

That leaves very little by way of fact or historical reminiscence. What we can extract from the infancy narratives that may be grounded in history is limited to four items. Jesus may have been born during the reign of Herod the Great, although that is not certain. Scholars can find no basis for the claim that Herod murdered babies wholesale in the hope of eliminating Jesus as a rival king. Jesus' home was almost certainly Nazareth, and he was quite possibly born there as well. His mother's name may well have been Mary. And we have no reason to doubt that the child was named Jesus. These constitute the meager traces of history in the birth stories. Everything else is fiction.

We can be certain that Mary did not conceive Jesus without the assistance of human male sperm. It is unclear whether Joseph or some unnamed male was the biological father of Jesus. It is possible that Jesus was illegitimate.

Mary did not conceive parthenogenetically—that is, by herself. Corroborating evidence is provided by the birth stories of Isaac, Samson, and Samuel. The visit of Yahweh to Sarah in Genesis 21:1, for example, did not imply that God had sex with Sarah but that Sarah was made fertile by divine agency—she was past the age of conception. Abraham was the biological father of Isaac. Similarly, God blessed Mary in conceiving Jesus, but some male contributed the sperm. The hellenistic option is not a real option for the post-Enlightenment mind: Mary was not impregnated by some god masquerading as a human lover.

To be sure, there was such a person as John the Baptist. Elizabeth was probably the name of John's mother. Luke describes John as a spirit-filled desert ascetic; we think that is accurate. John was successful in attracting people to hear his dire warnings. He was probably executed by Herod Antipas. But this information is based on data derived from sources outside the infancy narratives.

CHRIST AS ICON

Reverse Christology: Stage Four

The first followers of Jesus began to think of him as the son of Adam who would return at the end of the age as the messiah. That conviction was linked to his resurrection from the dead, an event that functioned as God's vindication of his righteous servant *(Stage One)*. As the Jesus movement gathered numbers and became more confident of itself, it moved the inception of Jesus' messianic role back in time. In the Gospel of Mark, Jesus is adopted as the son of God at his baptism, at the outset of his public ministry *(Stage Two)*. Even Luke confirms the Markan view by having the voice from heaven proclaim, on the occasion of Jesus' baptism:

You are my son;
today I have become your father.

But the development does not end there. At *Stage Three*, Matthew and Luke move the messianic moment back to the miraculous birth of Jesus, as we have just seen. Now we are ready to resume this trend by tracing the messianic moment back one more step to *Stage Four*.

The fourth stage in the chronology of christology is presented in the New Testament by the prologue to the Gospel of John and by the Christ hymn in Philippians.[18] The Philippians hymn was translated in Chapter Two of this book. The relevant parts of the Johannine prologue can be translated as follows:

> In the beginning there was the divine word and wisdom.
> The divine word and wisdom was there with God,
> and it was what God was.
> It was there with God from the beginning.
>   Everything came to be by means of it;
> nothing that exists came to be without its agency.
> In it was life,
> and this life was the light of humanity.
> Light was shining in the darkness,
> and darkness did not master it. . . .
>
> The divine word and wisdom became human
> and made itself at home among us.
> We have seen its majesty,
> majesty appropriate
> to a Father's only son,
> brimming with generosity and truth.[19]

The divine *logos*, a complex Greek term here translated "word and wisdom," existed from the beginning with God. It was the agent of creation. It is also the light of humanity. That word and that wisdom became incarnate—entered the lower world of flesh and blood and made its home among mortals as the Father's only son.

In the Christ hymn quoted by Paul in Philippians, Jesus is said to be divine by nature. However, he did not cling to his status as a divinity but took on the role of servant, assumed the appearance of a mortal, and even succumbed to death. As vindication, God raised Jesus up and gave him the title *Lord,* a title that was later modulated into Pantocrator, ruler of all. It is understandable that the bishops gathered at Nicea in 325 C.E. insisted on the full equality of Christ with the Father: anything less would have put him on a par with other royal figures who could boast of one divine parent. Jesus as the Christ had to be made coequal with God for political if not for theological reasons. In that process, the iconoclast was transformed into the icon.

THE BIRTH OF MOSES

The king of the Egyptians said to the Hebrew midwives, one of whom was named Sephora, the other Phua: "When you assist the Hebrew women with their deliveries, and they give birth, if it is a boy, you are to put it to death; if it is a girl, you may let it live." However, the midwives respected God and did not follow the orders of the Egyptian king; they allowed the male children to live. The Egyptian monarch summoned the midwives and said to them, "Why have you done this? Why have you allowed the male children to live?" The midwives explained to Pharaoh how the Hebrew women were not like Egyptian women: they give birth, they said, before we get to them. So God treated the midwives well and the people multiplied in number and grew very strong. And because the midwives showed respect for God, God gave them their own families. Then the Pharaoh gave this order to everyone: "If a boy is born to any of the Hebrews, he is to be thrown into the river. Only girls are permitted to live."

There was this Levite who married a woman from the same tribe. She became pregnant and gave birth to a son. When she saw that he was a pretty baby, she kept him out of sight for three months. Since she could not continue to hide him, she got a reed basket for him, smeared it inside with tar, and put the child in it. She then placed the basket in the marsh alongside the ⟨Nile⟩ river. The child's sister kept a lookout some distance away to learn what would happen to him.

Pharaoh's daughter came down to bathe in the river while her attendants patrolled the bank. When she noticed the reed basket in the marsh, she sent one of her maids to fetch it. Upon opening the basket, she saw the handsome child and took pity on him. She speculated, "This must be one of the Hebrew babies."

The child's sister then said to the Egyptian princess, "Do you want me to enlist a nursing mother from among the Hebrew women to nurse the child for you?"

The princess replied, "Please do."

The young lady departed and engaged the child's ⟨real⟩ mother.

The princess instructed her: "Take care of this child for me and nurse him, and I'll pay you for it." The woman took the child and nursed it.

As soon as the child was weaned, she brought him back to the princess, who adopted him as her son. She called him Moses, she explained, "because I fetched him out of the water."

Exodus 1:15–22, 2:1–10 (LXX)

The story of Moses' birth has affinities with a legend about Sargon, the mythical founder of the Assyrian empire. According to the legend, Sargon's mother was a virgin; Sargon did not know his father. His mother hid him when he was born. She put him in a vessel fashioned from reeds, treated it with pitch, and dropped the baby into the river. He was retrieved from the water by a watercarrier who happened on to the baby by accident. Sargon worked for a time as a gardener before he became king.[20]

Epilogue

JESUS FOR A NEW AGE

A NEW AGE

We have entered a new age, we have crossed the threshold of a new era. By some accounts, we live in a post-Christian age. Others insist that we have launched the postmodern period. It is difficult, of course, to know whether the cultural tremors that give rise to these characterizations herald the dawning of a fresh epoch or merely mark the transition to a new millennium.

Contrary to some popular expectations, Jesus for a new age does not mean Jesus for crystals and channeling, for auras and chakras, meditation and yoga, astrology and harmonic convergences, or even holistic medicine, although Jesus may have some significance for some or all of these things. What I have in mind by a "new age" is something quite different, though not entirely unrelated.

1. The "new age" refers first and foremost to the end of the Christianized era, as suggested in Chapter Four. I am not thereby claiming that Christianity has come to an end; I am only proposing that the Christianized, industrialized West can no longer pretend to sponsor the only game on planet earth.

The "new age" also refers to a greatly altered context for biblical study and theology, another trend that gave rise to the renewed quest. The scholarship of the Bible once belonged to the churches. It has now moved out into secular institutions and functions quite apart from, and in some respects in opposition to, the denominations. The Fellows of the Jesus Seminar approach the Bible, the gospels in particular, as a cultural artifact rather than as an ecclesiastical handbook. We are interested in assessing the import of the Bible, and of the pioneers and prophets who figure prominently in its story, for society at large, rather than merely for the churches and their programs.

A further factor, mentioned earlier, is the rising tide of ecumenism. Scholars of the Bible no longer adhere to denominational lines of interpretation. My earliest memories of sessions of the professional societies are those of Jewish and Christian stalwarts in a free exchange of ideas.

Departments of religion are as likely to offer courses in Asian and African religions as in Western traditions. Christian arrogance has receded.

2. In the global arena, the symbolic world that is ingredient to traditional Christianity no longer occupies a foundational position. As the economic and technological superiority of the West fades, the symbols that attend the Christian myth will lose whatever appeal they once had. Meanwhile, in the West, the old symbolic universe is on the decline. It lingers on, to be sure, in weakened form, in many pockets where a rearguard action is being waged against the erosive and corrosive acids of the modern mind. Those who cling to the old are having increasing difficulties in assigning meaning to such biblical statements as "he ascended into heaven." Appeals to an endorsing God, to heaven and hell, to a divine redeemer, to Christ as the sole mediator between God and humankind, have begun to lose their bite and more frequently fall on unhearing ears.

Since that symbolic world is crumbling or has crumbled, the times call for a wholly secular account of the Christian faith, not just for the sake of its appeal to the third world but primarily for the sake of those who inhabit the contemporary, scientifically minded Western world. For an embattled and embittered shrinking minority—yes, that is what it is—who want to retreat into contrived mental ghettos as a way of maintaining some hypothetical past, the issue does not matter. But for the rest of us, it does: we cannot continue to traffic in sedimented theological language, or in the ancient worldview at selected, discrete levels, chosen carefully as defensible religious preserves.

I am not thereby insisting that all of us adopt the putative world of the average scientist or theologian; on the contrary, I am unwilling to give hostages to any informed, or reformed, or preformed sensibility. I insist only that we give an account, in an open court of appeal, without special pleading, of every claim we venture to make. Of course, I am also of the opinion, in the company of many others, that we live in a time when new sensibilities are being formed that will serve us as we make the transition into the new era. And it is to that prospect, with all the risk it entails, that we must now address ourselves.

Let me put it this way: If what we have to say about Jesus does not matter to those outside the precincts of traditional Christianity, it probably will not matter at all, at least not for the long term. Lest it be thought that all the concern is located in one quarter, it should be said that within the institutional churches there are many who are also looking to our real future, and I include them among the "outsiders."

3. The advent of a "new age" has brought with it the chance to start over. The quester should think of how it must have been in those first, tentative decades, in the thirties and forties of the common era, when the Jesus movement was young, amorphous, a fledgling struggling to find its wings. That is the correct perspective from which to view the present challenge. At such moments in history, then and now, anything less than

complete openness to the claims being laid on the future by the past will not serve the cause of truth.

There is nothing in the creed, in the gospels, in Christian tradition, and in the historical and scientific methodologies with which we study them that is immune to critical assessment and reformulation. We cannot put a protective shield around any part of the Christian heritage if we aspire to set Jesus free. Everything is on the table.

In the quest, the methods to be used are those employed by competent researchers in all disciplines; the data to be examined and interpreted are open to everyone on an equal footing. Faith, or belief, or conviction does not exempt anyone or anything from review.

4. In the "new age," all theology is post-Auschwitz, as a German theologian recently remarked. Theology conducted in the aftermath of Auschwitz means, among other things, that we can no longer trust the authority structure of an ecclesiastical tradition that learned, at several crucial junctures in its history, it was unable to resist the ultimate compromise. We should already have learned that from the lessons of the Spanish Inquisition. Or we might have gathered something of the American propensity to read scripture in a self-serving way as an endorsement of black slavery. Now we have the Nazi horror to look back on as well. In view of the compromises "Christian" leaders made in those and similar contexts, it is a wonder that anyone would want to claim the authority of this or that church council for the ultimate truth. From now on we must always ask whether the Christian tradition has something to teach us and, if it does, what that something is. We can no longer give Christianity prior consent without determining what we are embracing as a part of the bargain.

The renewal of the search for the real Jesus is part of this fundamental hesitation.

5. There is mounting evidence that Christian folk have, in fact, entered a "new age." The climate of conversation has begun to change in small circles and in scattered public conversations in North America and Europe. People are beginning to talk—openly, intelligently, candidly, without rancor—about the Bible, the gospels in particular, and about the Christian faith, its past and its future. And this dialogue is going on, not just in the Jesus Seminar but in both likely and unlikely places. Some of it is "underground." There is promise in dissatisfaction; there is hope in candor and honesty.

There is also negative evidence. The strident, shrill, often acrimonious, occasionally vitriolic responses to the Jesus Seminar indicate how disturbing this new conversation is to ossified Christian dogma. Denigration by nervous academics who worry that we have betrayed family secrets has contributed to the turbulence of the times. Insecurity and fear sponsor loud, troubled, and irresponsible talk. But underneath that ferment there is a serene sea of release and renewal on the part of many, within and beyond the peal of church chimes.

A QUEST DESIGNED FOR A NEW AGE

In this book we have made a giant U-turn in the history of the Jesus tradition—from Nicea to Nazareth (in Part One) and back to Nicea (in Part Three)—tracking on the outward journey how scholars get back to Nazareth and Jesus and, on the return trip, how the transition was made from Jesus to the Christ, how the iconoclast became the icon. In the middle (Part Two), we endeavored to map a profile of the historical Jesus using his authentic words and deeds. This journey has permitted us to catch sight, now and again, of the Galilean sage even as he was being transformed into the martyred righteous one or the dying/rising lord of gentile Christianity. As we draw to the close of the journey, it is appropriate to peer into our future from that past and ask what we have learned that modifies the future of the tradition inaugurated by Jesus of Nazareth. What real knowledge—knowledge of consequence for us and our time—has this thirst to know the flesh-and-blood Jesus produced? What difference could it possibly make? I propose to elaborate my answer to this question in a series of theses, twenty-one in number.

1. *The aim of the quest is to set Jesus free.* Its purpose is to liberate Jesus from the scriptural and creedal and experiential prisons in which we have incarcerated him. What would happen if "the dangerous and subversive memories" of that solitary figure were really stripped of their interpretive overlay? Were that to happen, the gospel of Jesus would be liberated from the Jesus of the gospels and allowed to speak for itself. The creedal formulations of the second, third, and fourth centuries would be de-dogmatized and Jesus would be permitted to emerge as a robust, real, larger-than-life figure in his own right. Moreover, current images of Jesus would be torn up by their long affective roots and their attachment to pet causes severed. The pale, anemic, iconic Jesus would suffer by comparison with the stark realism of the genuine article.

This forecast, I am acutely aware, stands in strong contrast to what many scholars of the gospels take the quest to be all about. Many scholars perceive the quest as primarily a historical puzzle without any real significance for other questions, especially theological issues. A quest without consequences is a legacy of older posturing born of painful struggles to come clean within the confines of the church.

This is also the legacy of neo-orthodoxy, which attempted to cordon off a small but inviolable sacred precinct safe for believers. Neo-orthodox theologians like Rudolf Bultmann and Karl Barth linked that "no trespassing" zone to a large dose of skepticism about what can be learned from the gospels. They advised us that not only should we not attempt to recover Jesus, we couldn't even if we tried.

A sterile quest was also sired by other fine niceties, qualifications, and political posturing suitable for academic pretend. That legacy will survive in an increasingly diminished form as traditional Christianity shrivels and becomes paranoid, while learning to compete in a world market. But the equivocation masking an apologetic intent has already lost much of its allure.

For other scholars the rediscovery of the Galilean sage as a historical figure forces us to confront fundamental issues. Isolating a single face in a Galilean crowd is more than a challenging puzzle. It has far-reaching implications for the Christian faith. Those implications fall into three categories, at the head of each of which are my second, third, and fourth theses.

2. *The renewed quest prompts us to revamp our understanding of the origins of the Christian faith itself.* Was that faith launched by Jesus, directly or indirectly? Does Jesus—who he was, what he said, what he did—provide the Christian faith with its essential content? If the answer to that question is positive, the initial statement of Chapter Two ("Christianity as we know it did not originate with Jesus of Nazareth") will have to be revised to read, Christianity originated with Jesus of Nazareth. In that case, Christianity needs to be reanchored in his imagination, in his vision.

Then there is the further issue: Were the decisions taken in the second to the fourth centuries, during which orthodoxy achieved its ascendancy, the only correct decisions? Must the decisions of Constantine and the voting that took place at Nicea and other councils be accepted as final?

These questions and others of a similar nature entail a huge and sweeping historical and theological agenda. They invite—indeed require—a review of the practices and beliefs of the primitive Christian communities to determine whether they are consonant with the intentions of Jesus of Nazareth. Jesus rather than the Bible or the creeds becomes the norm by which other views and practices are to be measured.

We will want to revisit Nicea and the early creeds, the Nicene Creed and the Apostles' Creed. We will find it necessary to reexamine trends that led to the identification of certain documents as orthodox and authoritative and eventually to the formation of the canonical New Testament. In addition to determining which of the stories about Jesus are based on historical reminiscences and which not, we will want to develop a criticism of the myth or plot of the foundational stories. And we will need to continue our work in evaluating the sayings tradition, sorting out the authentic from the secondary elements. This agenda takes us back to the beginnings of Christianity, to a time well before it assumed its classical form at Nicea. Just as the first believers did, we will have to start all over again with a clean theological slate, with only the parables, aphorisms, parabolic acts, and deeds of Jesus as the basis on which to formulate a new version of the faith. That is a breathtaking agenda, to say the very least.

3. *The renewed quest also has serious ramifications for how we understand the Christian life.* I am in complete agreement with Marcus Borg on this point. Borg contrasts "fideistic" and "moralistic" modes of understanding; I prefer the contrast between "creedal" and "ethical." When we speak of correct belief, the customary connotation of "orthodoxy," we have to speak of formulations of some kind, and that means, for the broad sweep of the Christian tradition, creeds or confessions or their surrogates, as well as the heresies those formulations fenced off. The noncreedal branches of Christianity, such as the Baptist, Disciple, and Congregational traditions, are not exempt; in some cases, they are far more rigid in the unwritten creeds they adopt and utilize as tests of fellowship than are the creedal traditions. Moreover, Borg's term *moralistic* has gained a belittling reputation in modern usage: it carries the suggestion that one is doctrinaire about the rules of behavior, that some privileged human beings are in a position to dictate to others how to live. Christianity at its heart is not moralistic. In its finest hours it is ethical. At its worst it is creedal—creeds are designed to exclude and expunge rather than include and nourish.

4. *The renewed quest points to a secular sage who may have more relevance to the spiritual dimensions of society at large than to institutionalized religion.* As a subversive sage, Jesus is also a secular sage. His parables and aphorisms all but obliterate the boundaries separating the sacred from the secular. He can teach us something that has nothing directly to do with what we know as Christianity or, indeed, with organized religion as such. Stated as a question: Is Jesus relevant to our society, to our time, to the world we know, apart from the role he has played in the Christian religion? Or is his story merely an interesting anecdote from a bygone age?

In the minds of many, especially those who claim Christianity or Judaism as their heritage, Jesus is inseparably connected with the topic of institutionalized religion. When the name *Jesus* is mentioned, "religion" is assumed to be the subject. But, in fact, the Jesus of whom we catch glimpses in the gospels may be said to have been *irreligious, irreverent,* and *impious.* The first word he said, as Paul Tillich once remarked, was a word against religion in its habituated form; because he was indifferent to the formal practice of religion, he is said to have profaned the temple, the sabbath, and breached the purity regulations of his own legacy; most important of all, he spoke of the kingdom of God in profane terms—that is, nonreligiously. For these reasons alone, his significance deserves to be detached from any exclusive religious context and considered in a broader cultural frame of reference.

Jesus is one of the great sages of history, and his insights should be taken seriously but tested by reference to other seers, ancient and modern, who have had glimpses of the eternal, and by reference to everything we can learn from the sciences, the poets, and the artists. Real knowledge, divine knowledge, is indiscriminate in the vessels it elects to fill. That is another way of saying that the glimpse comes to those who are open to it and does so without reference to social station, education, or political prowess. The glimpse is no respecter of theologies, theological schools, or evangelists. The glimpse blows where it will—every which way.

BREAKING THE EASTER BARRIER

Christianity, we were taught, began with the affirmation that Jesus died, was buried, and rose on the third day to ascend to his glory. The Easter event forms a barrier that separates Judaism and everything preceding from Christian faith. Christian seekers were advised that nothing of significance occurred before that. In effect, the Easter barrier turns the quest of the historical Jesus into an empty exercise.

Jesus the man is to be regarded, we are told, as the presupposition, rather than the inaugurator, of the Christian faith. The basis for Christianity consists of the confessions of Peter, Paul, and other early leaders, rather than anything Jesus did or said. Yet in identifying the risen Christ as the object of faith, believers in effect have robbed Jesus of Nazareth of any real incarnate existence and have shifted the responsibility for the faith to those who experienced his resurrected presence.

Orthodox Christianity encoded these convictions in its early creeds. Affirmations about the Christ were fenced off from information about Jesus of Nazareth. The Apostles' Creed implied that nothing worth mentioning lay between the miraculous conception of Jesus and his death on the cross. The creed left a blank where Jesus should have come. Even the information about the historical Jesus provided by the canonical gospels was ignored in setting out the essentials of the faith, which the Chalcedonian definition, formulated at the Council of Chalcedon in 451 c.e., instructs "we all teach with one accord."

Under the deconstructive effects of modern critical scholarship, neo-orthodoxy, which gained its ascendancy early in this century, reaffirmed the ancient limitations. Nothing important lies within reach of the critical historian on the far side of Easter (the virgin birth is only an apparent exception; it actually lies on the near side of Easter: it was created as a consequence, not a cause, of the Easter experience). We are cautioned not to venture beyond that boundary, for if we do we will miss the essence of Christianity, which consists of the experience of Jesus as risen Lord. In retrospect, the confessions of neo-orthodox theologians, such as Rudolf Bultmann, turn out to be breathtakingly orthodox, whereas at the time of their ascendancy, they looked shockingly modern.

Neo-orthodoxy was a powerful and subtle form of orthodoxy designed to protect against the negative effects of historical criticism and the modern scientific temper. Americans have not been very interested in the subtleties of neo-orthodoxy. What Americans know far better is popular creedalism, a simplistic version of orthodoxy that has been packaged and marketed electronically like other mass-produced products.

Popular creedalism insists on a miraculous birth, accrediting miracles, death on the cross understood as a blood sacrifice, a bodily resurrection, and Jesus' eventual return to hold cosmic court. We need only ask, Which of these doctrines derives from what we know of the historical Jesus? Which of them depends on Jesus' authorization? Or are they part of the mythological overlay invented by Jesus' early admirers employing categories they knew and borrowed from other religious traditions? And have they been isolated and formulated in modern times to suit the demands of high-profile evangelism? In a similar vein, what does the Christ of the ancient creeds, and of modern neo-orthodoxy, have to do with Jesus of Nazareth?

The initial observation to be made is this: the popular forms of Christianity we now have do not require—indeed, do not even permit—Jesus to endorse them. Creedalism is a religion that supersedes Jesus, replaces him, or perhaps displaces him, with a mythology that depends on nothing Jesus said, or did, with the possible exception of his death.

I am a spiritual descendant of Rudolf Bultmann and Karl Barth, Reinhold Niebuhr and Paul Tillich, and the neo-orthodox movement they sponsored. I am deeply indebted to my mentors, and I have nothing but respect for that legacy. Nevertheless, I now believe that neo-orthodoxy (and its Catholic counterparts) was the dying gasp of creedal Christianity—a last effort to salvage it for the modern world. In the half century that follows the end of the Second World War, it has become clear that neo-orthodoxy has failed, that we have moved beyond the reach of that noble effort. In plain language, neo-orthodoxy is dead. As that fact dawned on me, slowly and painfully, I found myself forced to re-evaluate all those doctrines that constitute the orthodox creed. I have done so at the behest of Jesus as the subverter of theological litmus tests. I began to wonder what, if anything, Jesus had contributed to the religion that regards him as its founder. Here are the preliminary results of my reflections, formulated as additional theses.

5. *We can no longer rest our faith on the faith of Peter or the faith of Paul.* I do not want my faith to be a secondhand faith. I am therefore fundamentally dissatisfied with versions of the faith that trace their origins only so far as the first believers; true faith, fundamental faith, must be related in some way directly to Jesus of Nazareth.

6. *Jesus himself is not the proper object of faith.* This proposition, I realize, is a radical departure from traditional views. Jesus called on his followers to trust the Father, to believe in God's domain or reign. The proper object of faith inspired by Jesus is to trust what Jesus trusted. For that reason, I am not primarily interested in affirmations about Jesus but

in the truths that inspired and informed Jesus. To call for faith in Jesus is to substitute the agent for the reality, the proclaimer for the proclaimed. (I hesitate to call Jesus' faith a faith in "God," since when we use the term "God" these days, we find it necessary to put quotation marks around it to indicate how problematic the term has become.)

Jesus pointed to something he called God's domain, something he did not create, something he did not control. I want to discover what Jesus saw, or heard, or sensed that was so enchanting, so mesmerizing, so challenging that it held Jesus in its spell. And I do not want to be misled by what his followers did: instead of looking to see what he saw, his devoted disciples tended to stare at the pointing finger.

Jesus himself should not be, must not be, the object of faith. That would be to repeat the idolatry of the first believers.

7. *In articulating the vision of Jesus, we should take care to express our interpretations in the same register as he employed in his parables and aphorisms.* Jesus quite deliberately articulated an open-ended, nonexplicit vision in his parables and aphorisms. He did not prescribe behavior or endorse specific religious practices. He was never programmatic in his pronouncements. His followers had and have the obligation to transmit his tradition in the same key. It is perfectly acceptable to specify what his pronouncements may mean for our time and place, but it is not commensurate with his vision to chisel them in stone. Our interpretation of parables should be more parables—polyvalent, enigmatic, humorous, and nonprescriptive. Yet we are invited by his example to be equally bold and innovative.

Once we pierce the veil of Easter, we are charged with an exciting new task. We are prompted to ask, What are the consequences of Jesus' vision for the religion we call Christianity? What does Jesus' gospel tell us about ourselves and about the precarious, fleeting world we inhabit? In answering these questions, we will only be describing the contours of God's domain as Jesus envisioned them.

Here I must add a caution. To accept Jesus' sense of the real naively is also a potential mistake. Just as Jesus challenged the immense solidity of his everyday world, we, too, must discover for ourselves in what respects our habituated sense of reality is illusory. In considering Jesus' glimpse of God's domain, we must test his perceptions of the real by our own extended and controlled observations on our world. We need not and should not place blind faith in what Jesus trusted. One tenet of the new creed for the post-Christian age is that nothing is protected, nothing is off limits.

RECOVERING THE ROOTS

Christianity as we have known it in the West is anemic and wasting away. Members are exiting the mainline churches but not moving to right-wing versions—or so I am told. The death of the churches is by no means imminent, yet their demise seems inevitable if their health does not improve. Nevertheless, Christianity has exhibited the power in the past to purge and reconstitute itself. It has been known to remember what it once was, to recover its roots and regain its strength. It is a resilient religion. The rediscovery and liberation of Jesus could conceivably result in a rebirth.

If Christianity recovers its roots, it will undergo a transformation. A new version of Christianity will involve a recision of many traditional elements and the creation of new symbols, stories, and a new cult. A reformation is imminent when a movement reviews and revises the records of how it got started. The renewed quest is the precursor of that revision.

A new reformation may not be of the magnitude of the reformation of the sixteenth century, but in some ways it may turn out to be as powerful. If it comes, it will modify the tradition that has gone before.

But there are difficulties. As Karen King remarked in assessing the significance of the Nag Hammadi Library for the history of early Christianity, it is unbelievably difficult to think our way back behind Nicea, the creeds, the formation of the New Testament, the emergence of orthodoxy.[1] We are relatively new at this game. Our first efforts will be stumbling and entirely provisional.

Some will not agree, but I think Christianity is a tradition worth reforming and saving. To be sure, it is not possible to foresee the complete shape of a reinvented Christianity. Yet some elements that will have to go into that process are clear enough. I have a few suggestions for launching a revision. I will again put them in the form of theses.

8. *Give Jesus a demotion.* We must begin by giving Jesus a demotion. He asked for it, he deserves it, we owe him no less.

As divine son of God, coeternal with the Father, pending cosmic judge seated at God's right hand, he is insulated and isolated from his persona as the humble Galilean sage. In the former there is not much left of the man who loved to laugh and talk at table, as Edward Beutner puts it, who never seemed to maintain a trace of social distance in the conversation.

A demoted Jesus then becomes available as the real founder of the Christian movement. With his new status, he will no longer be merely its mythical icon, embedded in the myth of the descending/ascending, dying/rising lord of the pagan mystery cults, but of one substance with us all. We might begin by turning the icon back into an iconoclast.

With Jesus as the actual leader, this movement will be subject to continuing reformations born of repeated quests for the historical Jesus.

9. *We need to cast Jesus in a new drama, assign him a role in a story with a different plot.* The creedal plot in which Jesus has been cast is the myth of

the *external* redeemer. In that story, the protagonist leaves a heavenly abode, enters human space, performs a redemptive function, and returns to the heavens. The movement is from and to an alien space. This plot is the essence of the Christ hymn in the second chapter of Philippians, the prologue to the Gospel of John, and the Hymn of the Pearl preserved in the Acts of Thomas, a third-century pseudepigraphical work.

It is also the plot of numerous stories well known to modern readers. Foremost among them is the film *Superman*. In this cinematic epic, we have a fairly complete redeemer myth: Superman descends to earth from another planet (heaven) by miraculous means (very advanced technology; arriving on the clouds, so to speak) as a precocious child. He is given the legacy of (divine) knowledge or wisdom in the form of a luminous crystal, which he is apparently not at liberty to utilize until he is mature—say, at about thirty years of age. To perform the rites of initiation he must withdraw to a desert region (the polar cap) and ponder his role. He subsequently launches his career as a savior in a large urban center (New York). He is sworn to fight for truth, justice, and the American way. His identity in the everyday world remains secret, however; he is disguised as a mild-mannered reporter. There is thus even a messianic secret. But in this secularized redeemer story, there is nothing corresponding to the Christian redeemer's death on a cross.

The same external redeemer story is at the base of the myth of the American West. In that myth, the cowboy hero rides into a town beleaguered by villains, has a shoot-out with the perpetrators of evil, rescues those who are unable to rescue themselves, and then rides off into the sunset. The Lone Ranger was the original radio version of this myth. His story, inaugurated in 1933, ran for 2,956 episodes, ending only in 1954. The movie *Shane* is another example of the external cowboy savior, played in this instance by Alan Ladd. This plot was used repeatedly in westerns for more than a half century. When the old West was no longer suitable as the setting for the drama, it was moved into space. *Star Trek* features the cowboy in a space suit.

The question regarding the historic creeds is not whether the plot of the external redeemer is believable—apparently it is for many moviegoers —but whether a hero from another world is salutary religiously, socially, and politically. We know that our perceptions of the world are decisively shaped by our mythic stories. How could such stories possibly be detrimental?

The redeemer hero in this plot comes from beyond and belongs to a reality not our own. The hero is not one of us; he or she (there are numerous woman versions, such as Wonder Woman) is qualitatively different from us. This feature of the redeemer suggests that the created world is basically flawed and must be redeemed from without.

In this flawed world, evil is stronger than human powers and cannot be overcome without superhuman aid. Mortal men and women are powerless within the framework of the myth because evil itself has cosmic dimensions. Spectator religion, morality, and politics are the inevitable result. Human beings are pawns in the cosmic drama being played out on a stage wider than their own. We are encouraged to rely on the powers above us, alien to us. Myths in this category tend to tranquilize, to function as escapist fare.

The action precipitated by the external redeemer is regularly violent and usually apocalyptic: since creation is defective and humans helpless, God must intervene as the only way to right wrongs and guarantee rewards for the faithful. Apocalypticists themselves are not infrequently tempted to assist God by supplying military muscle.

There is another type of hero who belongs to a different story. The hero with a thousand faces, according to Joseph Campbell, begins by leaving home. He or she undergoes trials and tribulations in an alien space but manages a victory over evil powers, usually assisted by helpers. The hero then returns home and is reintegrated into society, now able to bestow boons on others. We might dub this kind of story the myth of the *internal* redeemer.

The gospels and the creeds are structured around the myth of the external redeemer. But the temptation story reported by the synoptic gospels is a version of the internal redeemer tale. In that story, a troubled visionary goes on a vision quest into the desert where he fasts for a mythical forty days and forty nights. He reviews all the possibilities associated with the messianic and prophetic tradition and rejects all the standard features: turning stones into bread like Moses in the wilderness; assuming the role of divine magician by surviving a fall from the temple; offering allegiance to Satan as the means of coming to world power as a new caesar. After rejecting these options, the visionary returns to embrace the everyday world and endeavors to anoint every village and marketplace with touches of the divine, asking nothing for himself but daily bread.

A true savior incarnate—*incarnate* literally means embodied—a true savior embodied must submit to the same limitations imposed on the rest of us. If Jesus of Nazareth is a savior, it is only because he aspired to heaven as all mortals do but was sage enough to reject the temptation and accept the limitations of his finite existence. If he arrived via a miraculous birth, knew himself to be the messiah and son of God, and had foreknowledge that his death would be reversed in a few days, he is not qualified to function as my redeemer. I prefer a savior who understands my predicament—my double fettering that anchors mortals in both heaven and earth, as Franz Kafka put it—and is prepared to assist me in grappling with my insatiable longing for heaven while chained to earth and mortality.

But the temptation story is not the only available internal redeemer plot suitable for our purposes. We probably need a baker's dozen to give richness and variety to Jesus' story and the human story. We might try one suggested by Jesus himself.

There is the plot of the prodigal. In that story one can come home only by leaving home. The prodigal reflects Israel's foundational myth—the exodus and quest for the promised land. It also echoes Israel's exile and return. Departure and arrival, leave-taking and homecoming, are linked in inseparable tandem.

In exploring these and other possibilities, we will find it necessary to enlist the arts, performing and plastic, dramatic and musical, in the search for new and revised myths. We will find others have been there before us. In the ancient world, the myth of Prometheus and Homer's *Iliad* and *Odyssey* belong to the same genre as the tales of King Arthur and the knights of the Round Table. Among the fairy tales, "Hansel and Gretel" is a perfect example of the initiation myth. J. R. R. Tolkien has endeavored to create a circle of ordinary internal redeemers in his *Lord of the Rings*. In *The Return of the Jedi* George Lucas has elaborated yet another version of the myth of initiation utilizing this same plot. Lucas learned his craft at the feet of Joseph Campbell.

The principal deficiency in biblical scholarship currently is its lack of a myth criticism. We have developed historical criticism to a high art, but we have been unable to conceive a critical relation to the stories that undergird our tradition and limit our vision. In the next phase of our work, we must remedy this fundamental deficiency.

10. *We need to reconceive the vocation of Jesus as the Christ.* Jesus' functions as the Christ were assigned to him by his admirers in the first few centuries. But the real vocation of Jesus was assigned to him by his vision.

Jesus told his parables as though he were *hearing* them. He was not so much calling on God as God was calling on him. He was not making claims; he was being claimed. We know what it means to invoke something, or to revoke it, or to convoke a group. But we lack the simple form: voke. It is available in Latin: *vocare,* to call, which is related to *vox,* voice. Jesus was "voked," called. To be "voked" means to receive a vocation, a calling. Vocation is the noun that goes with the verb *voke.*

What interests me about Jesus is not so much what Peter and Paul thought of him, or even what Jesus thought about himself, but the call to which he was responding. To what divine manifesto did he succumb? By what vision was he both captivated and liberated? That is the interesting question. That is the determining issue.

As an external redeemer, in contrast to an internal savior, Jesus supplies our every need, fulfills all our fantasies. A steady diet of conception without sex, a salvific blood donor, and perpetual resuscitation goes together with fast food, soft ice cream, and the lottery. It is like a trip to McDonald's, where the menu is fixed, everything is cheap, and patience is not required. Such a diet has made the pious American fawning, flabby, and flatulent. Americans often don't want religion unless it is handed to them on a platter, effort free, sacrifice free, but not fat free. The sanctimonious need above all to go on a theological diet to shed the cumulative biliousness that accompanies self-satisfaction.

The historic Jesus is a reality anchor in a sea of unrealistic and potentially demonic dreams. The renewed quest is a reality check. It discourages self-indulgence and pandering. It represents the end of apologetic posturing and evasion. It demands honesty and candor. The real vocation of Jesus will displace the contrived vocations assigned him by later generations.

CHRISTIAN PRACTICE

The nodes of Jesus' epiphanic poetry—clusters of words that are revealing—sketched in Chapters Eight through Eleven suggest several areas in which his words and deeds are relevant to life and practice. It is appropriate to call it Christian life and practice, although the use of the term *Christian* may introduce confusion rather than clarity. I do not mean to limit my proposals to what goes on inside a church or among Christians, although I also include those activities. In any case, what follows are no more than initial proposals. They are suggested by obvious discrepancies between Jesus' words and deeds and current "Christian" practice.

Jesus was a social deviant. It is helpful to remember that. If Jesus was a social deviant, social deviancy may not be all bad. Recommending it is a kind of *imitatio christi* but with a different twist. In Jesus' company, rebels are welcome.

11. *Jesus kept an open table.* Jesus ate promiscuously with sinners, toll collectors, prostitutes, lepers, and other social misfits and quarantined people during his life. (He also hobnobbed with the affluent and powerful, but those associations seem to pose less of a problem for us.) Yet his followers, in ritualizing the meal Jesus ate periodically with his friends, began to limit participation to those who belonged to the Christian community. In the Didache, a first-century Christian manual, the rule is: "No one is to eat of the eucharist except those who have been baptized in the Lord's name. This is what the Lord said about this restriction: 'Don't give what is sacred to dogs.'"

We have to ask, would Jesus have condoned, to say nothing of authorized, a table open only to self-authenticating believers? Should we reconceive the scope of eating together in Christian communities, as well as the function of the eucharist?

12. *Jesus made forgiveness reciprocal.* Jesus tells the paralytic, the blind man, the adulteress that they are forgiven, without exacting penalties or promises from them. Jesus forgives because his Father forgives and on the same terms: without penalty or promise. The only requirement is reciprocity: one is forgiven to the extent that one forgives. Thus, one can

become the recipient of forgiveness only if one first becomes the agent of forgiveness. By acknowledging that forgiveness is in the hands of the human agents, Jesus precludes the possibility of vesting that matter in the hands of priests or clerics or even God. The power to forgive has already been conferred upon those who themselves need and want forgiveness. Human beings can have only what they freely give away.

13. *Jesus condemned the public practice of piety.* Jesus makes sport of displays of piety. He regards religious posturing as hypocritical. He advises his followers to conceal the acts of charity performed by the right hand from the intelligence of the left hand. He suggests that prayer is best conducted in the privacy of one's closet. The football players who kneel in the end zone and say a prayer for their success before millions of admirers have received the only reward they will ever get. Jesus robs me of any incentive to practice prayer in public. Piety should be practiced out of earshot of one's own voice.

14. *Jesus advocated an unbrokered relationship to God.* Jesus insisted that everyone has immediate and particular access to God. It is therefore not plausible that he would have commissioned certain disciples to broker that relationship in his vision of God's domain. The inauguration of a priesthood and clergy therefore appears to be inimical to Jesus' wishes.

The Jesus Seminar concluded, on the basis of the evidence, that, while Jesus enjoyed good companionship, he did not deliberately collect disciples, and he did not select "twelve" special followers or appoint leaders among them. Furthermore, he did not commission his followers to establish a church or inaugurate a world mission. The words and acts to this effect are found only in the framework stories of the narrative gospels, not in the authentic parables and aphorisms. (Awarding the keys to the kingdom to Peter in Matthew 16:16–19 and the great commission in Matthew 28:16–20 are stories without historical foundation, according to the seminar.)

To put the matter candidly, the canonical gospels endeavor to authenticate the leadership of the church then in power. The authentic words of Jesus reject the notion of privileged position among his followers: the first will be last and the last first; those who aspire to be leaders should become slaves of all.

15. *Jesus robs his followers of Christian "privilege."* As John Dominic Crossan so pointedly puts it, Jesus robs humankind of all protections and privileges, entitlements and ethnicities that segregate human beings into categories. His Father is no respecter of persons. Does that not include the label *Christian?* In that case, can it then be correct for Christian folk to distinguish themselves as "saved" or "redeemed" in relation to others? What is the basis for one denomination to claim superiority over

another? Is there any basis in Jesus' views for one individual to think that he or she has a favored position in God's eyes?

16. *Jesus makes it clear that all rewards and punishments are intrinsic.* According to Jesus, reward is integral to the activity for which it is a reward. The reward for loving one's neighbor is an unqualified relation to that neighbor. However, the church developed a doctrine of extrinsic rewards and sanctions to undergird its power and authority. If love is its own reward, why should human beings be rewarded for loving? Jesus asks rhetorically: Do not the pagans—those who have no such special incentive to love—do as much? In that case, pagan behavior is superior ethically: pagans love without a self-serving motive for doing so. But Christian behavior is not a prelude to some other kind of behavior; it is its own end. In simple terms: Are Christians being urged to be good here so they won't have to be good in the hereafter?

According to popular orthodoxy, we are promised eternal life following a bodily resurrection for believing the right things, for being theologically correct. How can that promise be anything other than self-serving? A version of Christianity that takes its cues from Jesus cannot be preoccupied with rewards and punishments.

NICEA REVISITED

In reviewing and revamping the decisions made along the way, it will be necessary to revisit Nicea. Nicea stands for all the sundry decisions that went to make up orthodoxy in the ancient church. We will want to look more closely at those leaders and movements that were branded as heretical to see what contribution they might have made to the richness and variety of the Christian movement. Specifically, we will want to examine very closely those items that combine to form the agenda of popular piety and orthodoxy today. For their part, the mainline churches have unwittingly endorsed a traditional theology that, in many cases, is not commensurate with their practice. It is probably time to substitute right behavior—orthopraxis—for right doctrine—orthodoxy. The mark of a Christian ought to be not what one believes but how one acts. We should either revise or eliminate the creeds.

Here is my short agenda.

17. *We will have to abandon the doctrine of the blood atonement.* The atonement in popular piety is based on a mythology that is no longer credible—that God is appeased by blood sacrifices. Jesus never expressed the view that God was holding humanity hostage until someone paid the bill. Nor did Amos, Hosea, or other prophets of Israel. In addition, it is the linchpin that holds the divinity of Jesus, his virgin birth, the bodily resurrection, and a sinless life together in a unified but naive package: God required a perfect sacrifice, so only a divine victim would do.

18. *We will need to interpret the reports of the resurrection for what they are: our glimpse of what Jesus glimpsed.* Reject the claims to apostolic privilege and authority based on personal appearances.

The reports of Jesus' appearances to certain followers function in the gospels and letters as commissioning stories. They endow certain leaders with authority and position—authority to proclaim the gospel as they understood it and the position of reliable and exclusive witnesses to the resurrection. These circular credentials exclude subsequent and independent claims to the same or similar vision and to authority. The appearance stories, consequently, are fundamentally self-serving. Furthermore, with the possible exception of Paul of Tarsus, the appearances of the risen Jesus supply the Christian faith with none of its essential theological and ethical content.

The reports of appearances of the risen Jesus to his followers, however, are a belated and oblique recognition of the vision Jesus had of God's dominion over creation. They are a diluted and not altogether satisfactory glimpse of what Jesus glimpsed. To claim that Jesus rose from the dead is a way of confessing that Jesus revealed what the world was really like, that he caught a glimpse of eternity. Affirmations of Jesus' resurrection should send his devotees searching through his parables and aphorisms for traces of that glimpse.

19. *Redeem sex and Mary, Jesus' mother, by restoring to Jesus a biological if not actual father.* Virginity is not necessarily godly, except in an ascetic, pleasure-denying, dualistic world. And Jesus is not necessarily a more effective savior for having been born without a father. Celebrate all aspects of life by giving Mary her rights as a woman, even if it means acknowledging that Jesus may have been a bastard. A bastard messiah is a more evocative redeemer figure than an unblemished lamb of God.

The virgin birth, in the light of other miraculous birth stories in the ancient world, is a mythical way to account for an unusual life. The gods frequently consorted with human beings in Greek and Roman mythology and gave birth to heroes and heroines. Within the limits of romantic folklore, the virgin birth of Jesus is an intriguing tale—not particularly well suited to adolescent Mary and baby Jesus, perhaps, but delightful; as a piece of literalized theology, it is contemptible. In any case, the virgin birth becomes an extraneous doctrine once the need for an unblemished sacrifice, for a blood atonement, is abandoned.

Augustine's notion that the consequences of Adam's sin is transmitted through male sperm is one of the great tragedies of theological history. He should be labeled as misguided and Manichean for his views. Furthermore, we should blow the whistle on the Roman curia for its ascetic proclivities—the self-justifying inclination to condemn sex for all purposes other than conception. Mary's plight is thereby linked to a celibate priesthood on the grounds that abstinence is godly and that sex is dirty, aside from necessary multiplication of the race, especially in

Catholic countries. In Genesis the Lord did not order human beings to multiply and *destroy* the earth.

The anti-abortion movement, sponsored by both Catholics and Protestants, pretends that it is solely concerned with the sacredness of life, a concern contradicted by its parallel endorsement of capital punishment. In fact, the so-called prolife people are driven by a fundamental disdain for the sex act if its intent is not to produce children. In the absence of such intent, sinners who indulge and conceive accidentally should be forced to pay the price of parenting unwanted progeny. Criminalizing abortion is a way of enforcing Puritanical sexual codes.

We must divorce the abortion issue from the concept of sex as sin. We should endorse responsible, protected recreational sex between consenting adults. That alternative premise is the foundation of universal birth control and family planning programs that will eventually reduce and then eliminate the abortions nobody really wants in the first place.

20. *Exorcise the apocalyptic elements from Christianity.* Apocalypticism at its base is world-denying and vindictive. The apocalypse is a protest against injustice in this life, which is what makes it appealing. But it is also ethically crippling because the apocalyptic mind looks for rectification in another world, rather than seeking justice in this one. In addition, the apocalyptic vision anticipates that those of us who have suffered in this life will be freed from pain in some future existence. That seems unobjectionable. But apocalypse adds that those who have prospered here, and especially those who have harmed us, will suffer in the hereafter. Those who advocate the apocalyptic solution are seeking vindication for their mistreatment in this life and punishment for someone else's corresponding unmerited favor. The desire to reward and punish in the next world is self-serving in its most crass, pathetic form. It is unworthy of the Galilean who asked nothing for himself, beyond his simplest needs.

21. *Declare the New Testament a highly uneven and biased record of various early attempts to invent Christianity.* Reopen the question of what documents belong among the founding witnesses. In a new New Testament, include dissenting points of view. Eliminate the less deserving parts.

In any case, the authority of an iconic Bible is gone forever. It cannot be restored. Recognize that fact and attempt to devise a new canon of scriptures that accurately reflects the diversity in Christian origins and that promotes literacy in religion.

These are my twenty-one theses. If I had a church, I would scotch tape them to the door.

Notes

CHAPTER 1
The Jesus Question

1. *The Quest of the Historical Jesus,* 403.
2. *The Quest of the Historical Jesus,* 401.
3. The author discusses these and related matters in her "Epilogue," pp. 151–54.
4. This is the judgment of Thomas Sheehan, *The First Coming,* 5.

CHAPTER 2
From Nazareth to Nicea

1. Matt 13:55.
2. Mark 6:3.
3. Mark 3:21, 31; John 7:5; Acts 1:14; 1 Cor 9:5.
4. Mark 6:3; Matt 13:56.
5. Matt 26:73.
6. Luke 4:16–30.
7. Mark 1:15.
8. Mark 8:31–33, 9:31, 10:33–34.
9. Mark 10:45.
10. Henry Bettenson, *Documents of the Christian Church* (New York: Oxford University Press, 1947), 72.

CHAPTER 4
The Renewed Quest

1. This point of view is current among many New Testament scholars who yearn for the old evangelical days. It was given expression recently in an article appearing in *The Christian Century* (February 1–8, 1995): 108–11.
2. "New Testament and Mythology," pp. 1–44 in *Kerygma and Myth* (New York: Harper & Row, 1961).
3. *Essays on New Testament Themes* (Philadelphia: Fortress Press, 1964 [1954]).
4. *Who Was Jesus?* (Grand Rapids, Mich.: Eerdmans Publishing, 1992), 17 f. Wright's list of third questers is to be found on pp. 12–17.
5. (Stanford, Calif.: Stanford University Press, 1988), 121.
6. DialSav 11:4.
7. *The Sayings of Jesus: The Second Source of St. Matthew and St. Luke,* trans. J. R. Wilkinson (London: Williams & Norgate; New York: G. P. Putnam's Sons, 1908 [1907]).
8. John S. Kloppenborg, *The Formation of Q* (Philadelphia: Fortress Press, 1987); *Q Parallels* (Sonoma, Calif.: Polebridge Press, 1988); Arland Jacobson, *The First Gospel: An Introduction to Q* (Sonoma, Calif.: Polebridge Press, 1992); and Leif Vaage, *Galilean Upstarts: Jesus' First Followers According to Q* (Valley Forge, Penn.: Trinity Press Int., 1994).

CHAPTER 5
Translation and Text

1. John 3:26.
2. Mark 14:36.
3. Rom 8:15; Gal 4:6.
4. Mark 5:41, *talitha koum,* "Little girl, get up!"; 7:34, *ephphatha,* "Be opened."
5. Mark 15:34; Matt 27:45.
6. Matt 1:19.
7. Matt 9:13.

8. Matt 20:4.
9. Matt 27:4.
10. Matt 27:19.
11. Luke 18:32.
12. Luke 12:30.
13. Luke 21:10.
14. Luke 2:32.
15. Luke 7:5.
16. Matt 3:7//Luke 3:7.
17. Matt 3:9.
18. Mark 2:17.
19. Matt 6:21.
20. Luke 14:11.
21. Luke 6:20.
22. Matt 8:20.
23. Matt 13:25.
24. Matt 25:14–30.
25. John 3:3.
26. Luke 9:58//Matt 8:20.
27. Ps 8:3–5 (New International Version).
28. *The Essential Jesus,* 54.
29. Mark 9:31.
30. Dan 7:13–14.
31. Mark 8:38.
32. Barnabas 12:10.
33. Ignatius to the Ephesians 20:2.
34. Mark 2:27–28.
35. Matt 8:2.
36. Matt 15:22, 25.
37. Matt 10:24–25.
38. John 4:11, 15, 19.
39. Isa 40:3, quoted in Mark 1:3.
40. Matt 11:25.
41. Mark 2:27–28.
42. Matt 12:8.
43. Luke 6:5.
44. Nestle, Eberhard, and Kurt Aland, eds., *Novum Testamentum Graece,* 26th ed. (Stuttgart: Deutsche Bibelstiftung, 1979).

CHAPTER 6
Testament

1. Aland, *The Text of the New Testament,* 77.
2. *The Canon of the New Testament,* 269; cf. a similar remark on p. 253.
3. *The Canon of the New Testament,* 253.
4. *The Canon of the New Testament,* 251.
5. Harry Gamble, "The Pauline Corpus and the Early Christian Book," pp. 265–80 in *Paul and the Legacies of*

Paul, ed. William S. Babcock (Dallas: Southern Methodist University Press, 1990), 276.
6. *The Canon of the New Testament,* 217.
7. *The Text of the New Testament,* 109.
8. *The Text of the New Testament,* 78.
9. Metzger, *The Canon of the New Testament,* has a full treatment of the influence of Montanism on the development of the canon, 99–106.
10. Metzger, *The Canon of the New Testament,* 226–27.
11. In addition to the works listed in "Suggested Readings" (pp. 322–25) under "Text and Canon," the reader may wish to consult the following: Philip W. Comfort, *Early Manuscripts and Modern Translations of the New Testament* (Wheaton, Ill.: Tyndale House Publishers, 1990); Lee Martin McDonald, *The Formation of the Christian Biblical Canon* (Nashville, Tenn.: Abingdon Press, 1988); Irven M. Resnick, "The Codex in Early Jewish and Christian Communities," *Journal of Religious History* 17 (1992): 1–17; C. H. Roberts and T. C. Skeat, *The Birth of the Codex* (Oxford: Oxford University Press, 1983); Robert W. Funk, "The New Testament as Tradition and Canon," in *Parables and Presence* (Philadelphia: Fortress Press, 1982), 151–86; Harry Y. Gamble, *Books and Readers in the Early Church* (New Haven: Yale University Press, 1955).
12. *Ancient Christian Gospels,* p. xxx.
13. Julian Hills is a Fellow of the Jesus Seminar and general editor of the Scholars Version.

CHAPTER 7
The Gospels

1. *The Infancy Gospels of James and Thomas* (Santa Rosa, Calif.: Polebridge Press, 1996).
2. Mark 1:1–15.
3. Luke 1:26–56.
4. Luke 2:41–52.
5. Mark 2:1–12.
6. John 5:1–18.
7. Mark 6:35–44//John 6:1–15.
8. Mark 6:45–52//John 6:16–21.

9. Mark 8:22–26//John 9:1–7.
10. Secret Mark 1:1–10//raising of Lazarus, John 11:1–44.
11. Mark 1:16–45.
12. *Ancient Quotes and Anecdotes* (Sonoma, Calif.: Polebridge Press, 1989).
13. "Beelzebul in Mark 3: Dialogue, Story, or Sayings Cluster?," *Forum* 4, 3 (1988): 93–108.
14. Mark 5:21–43.
15. Mark 6:35–44; 8:1–9.
16. Mark 8:22–26; 10:46–52.
17. Mark 11:1–11; 14:12–16.
18. Mark 3:21.
19. Matt 16:17–20.
20. Matt 17:24–27.
21. Matt 5:21–27.
22. Matt 6:1–18.
23. Matt 23:1–22.
24. Luke 14:16– 23//Thom 64:1–11.
25. Luke 19:12–27.
26. Mark 1:40–45; Luke 5:12–16.
27. *Die evangelische Geschichte kritisch und philosophisch bearbeitet* (Leipzig, 1838).
28. Luke 9:59–60.
29. Stephen J. Patterson, *The Gospel of Thomas and Jesus* (Sonoma, Calif.: Polebridge Press, 1993).
30. Luke 11:47–51, a passage taken from the Sayings Gospel Q.
31. A detailed discussion of the rules of evidence may be found in Robert W. Funk, *The Gospel of Mark: Red Letter Edition*, 29–52.
32. Mark 3:3.
33. Mark 4:35.

CHAPTER 8
The Search for the Rhetorical Jesus

1. *The Lost Gospel*, 192, 193.
2. Mark 2:18–20.
3. Matt 20:16; Luke 13:30.
4. Mark 10:31; Matt 19:30.
5. Thom 4:2–3.
6. Luke 11:9–13.
7. Thom 94.
8. Mark 11:24.
9. Thom 92.
10. John 15:7.
11. Luke 11:5, the friend at midnight.
12. Matt 18:12, the lost sheep.
13. Mark 2:17.

14. Mark 7:15.
15. Mark 2:27.
16. Luke 9:58.
17. Matt 16:25.
18. Luke 6:44.
19. Matt 10:24.
20. Mark 3:20–26.
21. Luke 10:30–35.
22. Thom 64:1–11; Luke 14:16–23.
23. Matt 20:1–15.
24. Luke 18:10–14a.
25. Luke 6:27b.
26. Matt 6:3, Thom 62:2.
27. Luke 17:33.
28. Matt 5:39–41; Luke 6:29.
29. Manual of Discipline 7:15.
30. In a contribution to a forthcoming volume on the wit and wisdom of Jesus.
31. Deuteronomy 24:10–13.
32. Manual of Discipline 7:12, 14.
33. Matt 13:33.
34. Exod 12:17–20.
35. Exod 23:18, 34:25; Lev 2:11, 6:17.
36. 1 Cor 5:6–8.
37. Ezek 17:22–24.
38. 1 Kgs 17.
39. Thom 97:1–4.
40. Matt 5:42.
41. Thom 95:1–2.
42. Luke 11:31//Matt 12:42.
43. Mark 3:21.
44. Luke 12:58–59//Matt 5:25–26.
45. Luke 10:30–35.
46. Matt 20:1–15.
47. Thom 64:1–11; Luke 14:16–23.
48. Luke 15:11–32.
49. Luke 15:8–9.
50. Luke 15:4–6; Matt 18:12–13.
51. Luke 15:11–32.
52. Luke 14:16–24.
53. Mark 2:15–17; Matt 9:10–13; Luke 5:29–32; GOxy 5:1–2; cf. Luke 19:1–10.
54. John 2:1–11.
55. Mark 14:22–25.
56. Mark 1:41.
57. Mark 2:5.
58. Luke 6:20.
59. John 8:12.
60. John 8:58.
61. John 14:6.
62. John 8:44.
63. Mark 10:33–34.

CHAPTER 9
In the Beginning Was the Parable

1. John 8:48.
2. Mark 3:20–21.
3. Thom 113:2–4.
4. Luke 17:20–21.
5. Mark 13:24–27, 30.
6. Luke 11:20.
7. Mark 3:22.
8. *The Parables of the Kingdom* (New York: Charles Scribner's Sons, 1961), 16.
9. Luke 17:18.
10. John 8:48.

CHAPTER 10
Profligate and Proper Sons

1. Rev. ed. Trans. by S. H. Hooke (New York: Charles Scribner's Sons, 1963).
2. *The Genesis of Secrecy: On the Interpretation of Narrative* (Cambridge: Harvard University Press, 1979).
3. Genesis 12:1–4.
4. Exodus 3:7–10.
5. Luke 16:31.
6. Luke 7:33–34.
7. Mark 2:15–17.
8. Mark 4:10–12.
9. Matt 21:31b.
10. Matt 18:17.
11. Matt 5:46.
12. Luke 6:32.
13. Luke 18:10–14.
14. Thom 64:1–11; Luke 14:16–23.
15. Matt 20:1–15.

CHAPTER 11
The Gospel of Jesus

1. Exod 20:12.
2. Luke 14:26.
3. Luke 9:59–60.
4. Mark 3:31–35.
5. Luke 3:8–9.
6. Mark 9:40.
7. *Pro Quinto Ligario* 33 (46 B.C.E.).
8. Joshua 10:40.
9. Matt 5:43.
10. Manual of Discipline 1:9–10. Similar remarks are found at 9:21–23 and 10:17–20.
11. Mark 13:2.
12. Mark 11:15–16.
13. Mark 1:40–45.
14. Mark 5:24–34.
15. Luke 7:11–17.
16. Luke 10:30–35.
17. Thom 14:4.
18. Thom 14:5.
19. Mark 7:15.
20. Mark 7:20–23.
21. Mark 6:11.
22. Thom 53:1–2.
23. Gal 2:3–5.
24. Acts 16:3.
25. Thom 89.
26. Oxyrhyncus 840 2:1–9.
27. Manual of Discipline 8:21–24.
28. Manual of Discipline 6:27–7:2.
29. Luke 11:2b//Matt 6:9b.
30. Luke 11:2//Matt 6:9.
31. Luke 6:21//Matt 5:6//Thom 69:2.
32. Matt 11:16–19//Luke 7:31–35.
33. Mark 2:19//Matt 9:15//Luke 5:34.
34. Luke 14:11//Matt 23:12; Luke 18:14, from Sayings Gospel Q.
35. Luke 18:12.
36. Mark 2:19.
37. Exod 20:8.
38. Mark 2:27.
39. John 5:18.
40. Acts 13:2–3.
41. Didache 8:1.
42. Luke 11:11–13//Matt 7:9–11, from Sayings Gospel Q.
43. Exod 16:1–36.
44. Luke 12:22–31//Matt 6:25–34//Thom 36.
45. Luke 12:7//Matt 10:30.
46. Luke 9:58//Matt 8:20//Thom 86:1–2.
47. Luke 9:1–6; 10:1–12//Mark 6:8–11//Matt 10:1–15//Thom 14:4.
48. Matt 6:11.
49. Luke 11:9–10//Matt 7:7–8//Thom 2:1–4, 92:1, 94:1–2.
50. John 9:1–41.
51. Matt 5:45; cf. Luke 6:35.
52. Matt 19:24.
53. Mark 10:23.
54. Thom 63:1–3//Luke 12:16–21.
55. Luke 16:13.
56. Thom 64:12.
57. Luke 6:37.
58. Matt 18:23–34.
59. Thom 26:1–2.
60. John 7:53–8:11.
61. Matt 5:42a.

62. Matt 6:3.
63. Luke 11:2–4//Matt 6:9–13.
64. Matt 6:5–8.
65. Luke 17:33.
66. Matt 20:1–15.
67. Mark 10:27.
68. Mark 10:29–30.
69. Mark 10:31.
70. *Parables and Paradoxes* (New York: Schocken Books, 1961), 81.

CHAPTER 12
The Death of Jesus

1. *Who Killed Jesus?*, 161.
2. *Jewish War* 5.11.1.
3. Raymond E. Brown, *The Death of the Messiah*, vol. 2, 1279–83.
4. Matt 27:22–25.
5. *The Historical Figure of Jesus*, 249.
6. Mark 15:1.
7. *Antiquities* 18.63–64.
8. *Annals* 15.44.
9. Crossan argues this point in detail in a chapter on the burial in *Who Killed Jesus?*, 160–88.
10. Luke 13:6–9.
11. Luke 7:37–50.
12. 1 Cor 11:23–25.
13. Mark 6:17.
14. Luke 22:35–38.
15. Luke 19:44.
16. John 2:19–22.
17. Zech 13:7 (LXX).
18. John 18:15–18; 25–27.
19. Mark 8:31.
20. 1 Cor 15:3–4.
21. Mark 14:49.
22. Matt 26:56.
23. Mark 1:3.
24. 2 Kings 1:8 (LXX).
25. *The Death of the Messiah*, vol. 2, 1445–67.
26. *Who Killed Jesus?*, 159, in conjunction with statements made throughout the book.
27. "Feminist Myth of Christian Origin" pp. 51–67 in *Reimagining Christian Origins*, ed. Elizabeth A. Castelli and Hal Taussig (Valley Forge, Penn.: Trinity Press International, 1996).
28. Matt 27:3–10.
29. Mark 15:42–47.
30. Mark 14:64.
31. Deut 21:22–23.
32. Matt 27:57–60.
33. John 7:50–52.
34. John 19:38–42.
35. Matt 27:3–10.
36. Acts 1:15–19.
37. Matt 27:62–66; Peter 8:1–6.
38. John 11:17, 39.
39. Matt 27:63.
40. Matt 27:19, 24–25.
41. Matt 27:51–53.
42. John 18:10.
43. Luke 22:51.
44. Matt 26:52; Rev 13:10; Jer 15:2, 43:11.
45. Luke 23:6–16.
46. Pet 1:1–2; 2:2–5.
47. 1 Cor 11:23–26.
48. Luke 14:27.
49. *The So-Called Historical Jesus and the Historic Biblical Christ* (Philadelphia: Fortress, 1964).
50. *History of the Synoptic Tradition*, 279.
51. *Ancient Christian Gospels*, 219–20; "Apocryphal and Canonical Gospels," 127.
52. *The Cross That Spoke* (San Francisco: Harper & Row, 1988).
53. *The Fourth Gospel and Its Predecessor* (Philadelphia: Fortress, 1988).
54. "Passion Narratives," in *The Anchor Bible Dictionary*, ed. David Noel Freedman, vol. 5, 172–77.

CHAPTER 13
Domesticating the Tradition and Marketing the Messiah

1. Luke 6:20.
2. Matt 5:3.
3. Matt 7:9–10.
4. Matt 6:11.
5. Luke 11:3.
6. Luke 11:9–10.
7. Luke 10:3–4.
8. Didache 11:3–9.
9. Luke 4:3–4.
10. Deut 8:3.
11. The Epistle of James issues a counter-warning regarding this trend (2:14–17): faith will not supply a needy brother or sister with food and clothing.
12. Luke 11:13.
13. John 6:35.
14. John 6:51.

15. Luke 6:30.
16. Didache 1:5–6.
17. Mark 10:23, 10:25.
18. Mark 10:27.
19. Mark 7:15.
20. Matt 15:11.
21. Matt 15:18–20, following Mark 7:20–23.
22. Matt 12:34.
23. Thom 14:5.
24. Luke 14:16–24.
25. Matt 22:10.
26. Matt 22:11–14.
27. Matt 5:5, derived from Psalm 37:11.
28. Matt 5:7.
29. Matt 5:8, derived from Psalm 24:3–4.
30. Matt 6:22.
31. Matt 6:34.
32. Luke 10:7.
33. Luke 6:44.
34. Matt 12:1–8//Mark 2:23–28//Luke 6:1–5.
35. Mark 2:27–28.
36. Mark 8:10–13. The oath is found in v. 12.
37. Luke 11:29–32.
38. Matt 12:38–42. Actually, Jesus was in the tomb, so to speak, for only a day and a half, but parts of three different days were usually reckoned as three days.
39. Matt 5:13–16.
40. Matt 13:10–17.
41. Mark 2:1–12//Matt 9:1–8//Luke 5:17–26; John 5:2–9.
42. The stories of the lame man in John 5 and of the blind man in John 9 make this point unequivocally.
43. Mark 2:10.
44. Matt 9:8. The term for "humans" is plural in Greek, although it is usually translated as a collective singular, "man."
45. This is the sort of question she raises in her book *The Gnostic Gospels*.
46. Luke 7:1–10//Matt 8:5–13; there is a parallel story in John 4:46–54.
47. Isaiah 26:19, 29:18–19, 35:5–6, 42:6–7, 61:1.
48. Luke 7:11–17; Elijah's miracle is reported in 1 Kings 17:17–24.
49. Mark 6:35–44, 8:1–9.
50. Mark 5:1–20.
51. Mark 1:15.
52. Mark 9:1.

53. Mark 13.
54. Luke 21:8–9.
55. Luke 19:11.
56. Luke 19:13.
57. Matt 19:28.

CHAPTER 14
Resurrection and Return

1. "The Primitive Christian Kerygma and the Historical Jesus" in Carl E. Braaten and Roy A. Harrisville (trans. and eds.), *The Historical Jesus and the Kerygmatic Christ: Essays on the New Quest of the Historical Jesus* (New York, Nashville: Abingdon Press, 1964), 42.
2. *Jesus: A Revolutionary Biography*, 95.
3. *First Coming*, 172–73.
4. 1 Cor 15:13–14.
5. 1 Cor 15:35.
6. 1 Cor 15:42, 44, 50.
7. Acts 9:3–19, 22:1–16, 26:9–19.
8. John 20:14–18.
9. Luke 24:13–33.
10. John 21:4.
11. Matt 28:17; Luke 24:11, 25–26, 41; Peter 14:2; Pseudo-Mark 16:11.
12. Mark 14:28.
13. Matt 27:51–54.
14. The entire story is found in Matt 28:1–20. The words of Jesus are reported in v. 10.
15. Luke 24:1–53.
16. Identified in Luke 8:3.
17. Luke 24:34.
18. Luke 24:33b–49.
19. Pet 9:1–4, 10:2–5.
20. Mary 7:1–3.
21. Appended in some manuscripts and translations to the Gospel of Mark and versified as 16:9–20.
22. 1 Cor 15:5–8.
23. Mark 9:2–8//Matt 17:1–8//Luke 9:28–36.
24. Luke 5:1–11; Mark 1:16–20.
25. Acts 9:3–19, 22:1–16, 26:9–19.
26. 1 Cor 15:8.
27. Acts 1:21–22, 13:31.
28. Rev 1:13–16.
29. Dan 7:9–10, translated from the Greek version.
30. "From Easter to Valentinus (or to the Apostles' Creed)." *Journal of Biblical Literature*, 101 (1982): 5–37.
31. Acts 9:3–9; Gal 1:17.

32. *Formation of the Resurrection Narratives*, 49.
33. Matt 28:16–20; Luke 24:47–49.
34. Matt 19:28.
35. John 20:23.
36. Pagels' sketch is found in "The Controversy over Christ's Resurrection: Historical Event or Symbol?" in *The Gnostic Gospels*, 3–27. The quotation is found on p. 6.
37. John 21; Matt 16:13–20.
38. Gal 1:11.
39. Gal 3:28.
40. Gal 2:11–14.
41. 1 Cor 10:27.
42. *Anchor Dictionary of the Bible*, vol. 5, 684–91.
43. Ezek 37.

CHAPTER 15
The Divine Child

1. Rom 1:3–4.
2. Acts 2:36.
3. Mark 14:62.
4. Luke 3:7–9, 22:28–30.
5. Mark 1:10–11.
6. "Infancy Narratives in the Ancient World," *The Fourth R* 5,5 (1992): 1–3.
7. The story of God's promise to Abraham and Sarah and of the conception of Isaac is recounted in Gen 17:15–27, 18:1–15, 21:1–7.
8. Luke's version is preserved in Luke 1:5–25, 57–80, to be analyzed later in this chapter.
9. Gen 17:18–22, 18:9–15.
10. The story of Samson's birth is found in Judg 13:2–25.
11. His story is recounted in the two books known as 1 and 2 Samuel. The tale of his birth is recorded in 1 Sam 1:1–2:10.
12. Jer 23:5–6. Similar prophecies are to be found in Isa 9:6–7, 11:1.
13. Tamar's story is recounted in Gen 38.
14. Ruth 4:18–22.
15. Ruth's story is told in the Book of Ruth, especially 3:6–9, 14, 4:15.
16. Matt 1:19–20.
17. *The Infancy Gospels of James and Thomas* (Santa Rosa, Calif.: Polebridge Press, 1996).
18. Phil 2:5–10.
19. John 1:1–5, 14.
20. Otto Rank, *The Birth of the Hero*, 13. The actual text is found in James B. Pritchard, ed., *The Ancient Near East* (Princeton University Press, 1958), 85–86.

EPILOGUE
Jesus for a New Age

1. In a lecture prepared for the Westar Institute in 1996.

Suggested Readings

Ancient Sources

Miller, Robert J., ed. *The Complete Gospels: Annotated Scholars Version*. Rev. and exp. ed. Sonoma, Calif.: Polebridge Press, 1994.

Robinson, James M., ed. *The Nag Hammadi Library*. 3rd, rev. ed. San Francisco: Harper & Row, 1988.

Vermes, Geza. *The Dead Sea Scrolls in English*. 3rd, rev. and aug. ed. London: Penguin Books, 1987.

Wise, Michael O., Martin G. Abegg, Jr., and Edward M. Cook. *The Dead Sea Scrolls: A New Translation*. San Francisco: HarperSanFrancisco, 1996.

The New Testament

Davies, Stevan L. *New Testament Fundamentals*. Santa Rosa, Calif.: Polebridge Press, 1994.

Harris, Stephen L. *The New Testament: A Student's Introduction*. 2nd ed. Mountain View, Calif.: Mayfield Publishing Co., 1995.

Mack, Burton L. *Who Wrote the New Testament? The Making of the Christian Myth*. San Francisco: HarperSanFrancisco, 1995.

Jesus

Borg, Marcus J. *Jesus: A New Vision*. San Francisco: Harper & Row Publishers, 1987.

Bornkamm, Günther. *Jesus of Nazareth*. San Francisco: Harper & Row, 1960.

Crossan, John Dominic. *Jesus: A Revolutionary Biography*. San Francisco: HarperSanFrancisco, 1994.

Sanders, E. P. *The Historical Figure of Jesus*. New York: Penguin Books, 1993.

Sheehan, Thomas. *The First Coming. How the Kingdom of God Became Christianity*. New York: Random House, 1988.

Vermes, Geza. *Jesus the Jew: A Historian's Reading of the Gospels*. Rev. ed. Philadelphia: Fortress Press, 1981.

The Quest of the Historical Jesus

Borg, Marcus J. *Jesus in Contemporary Scholarship*. Valley Forge, Penn.: Trinity Press International, 1994.

McAteer, Michael R., and Michael G. Steinhauser. *The Man in the Scarlet Robe: Two Thousand Years of Searching for Jesus*. Etobicoke, Ontario: The United Church Publishing House, 1996.

Robinson, James M. *A New Quest of the Historical Jesus*. Missoula, Mont.: Scholars Press, 1979 (1959).

Sanders, E. P. *Jesus and Judaism*. Philadelphia: Fortress Press, 1985.

Schweitzer, Albert. *The Quest of the Historical Jesus: A Critical Study of Its Progress from Reimarus to Wrede*. New York: Macmillan, 1961 (1906).

Tatum, Barnes. *In Quest of Jesus: A Guidebook*. Atlanta: John Knox Press, 1982.

Translation

Miller, Robert J., ed. *The Complete Gospels: Annotated Scholars Version*. Rev. and exp. ed. Sonoma, Calif.: Polebridge Press, 1994.

Text and Canon

Aland, Kurt and Barbara. *The Text of the New Testament*. 2nd ed., rev. and enl. Trans. Erroll F. Rhodes. Grand Rapids, Mich.: William B. Eerdmans, 1989.

Crossan, John Dominic. *Four Other Gospels. Shadows on the Contours of Canon*. New York: Winston Press, 1985.

Gamble, Harry Y. "Canon, New Testament." In *The Anchor Bible Dictionary*, edited by D. N. Freedman, et al. Vol. 1, 852–61. New York: Doubleday, 1992.

Hoover, Roy W. "How the Canon Was Determined." *The Fourth R* 5, 1 (January 1992): 1–7.

Koester, Helmut. "Apocryphal and Canonical Gospels." *Harvard Theological Review* 73 (1980): 105–30.

Metzger, Bruce M. *The Canon of the New Testament*. Oxford: Clarendon Press, 1987.

———. *Manuscripts of the Greek Bible. An Introduction to Palaeography*. Oxford: Oxford University Press, 1981.

———. *The Text of the New Testament. Its Transmission, Corruption, and Restoration*. 3rd ed., enl. Oxford: Oxford University Press, 1992.

The Gospels

Bultmann, Rudolf. *History of the Synoptic Tradition*. Rev. ed. Trans. John Marsh. San Francisco: Harper & Row, 1963.

Funk, Robert W. *New Gospel Parallels*. 3rd ed. Vol. I, 2, *Mark*. Santa Rosa, Calif.: Polebridge Press, 1995.

Kloppenborg, John S., Marvin W. Meyer, Stephen J. Patterson, and Michael G. Steinhauser. *Q Thomas Reader*. Sonoma, Calif.: Polebridge Press, 1990.

Koester, Helmut. *Ancient Christian Gospels: Their History and Development*. Philadelphia: Trinity Press International, 1990.

Mack, Burton L. *The Lost Gospel. The Book of Q & Christian Origins*. San Francisco: HarperSanFrancisco, 1993.

Patterson, Stephen J. *The Gospel of Thomas and Jesus*. Sonoma, Calif.: Polebridge Press, 1993.

Sanders, E. P., and Margaret Davies. *Studying the Synoptic Gospels*. Philadelphia: Trinity Press International, 1989.

Stanton, Graham. *Gospel Truth? New Light on Jesus and the Gospels*. Valley Forge, Penn.: Trinity Press International, 1995.

The Rhetorical Jesus: Parables and Aphorisms

Crossan, John Dominic. *In Fragments. The Aphorisms of Jesus*. San Francisco: Harper & Row Publishers, 1983.

———. *The Dark Interval. Towards a Theology of Story*. Sonoma, Calif.: Polebridge Press, 1988.

_____. _In Parables. The Challenge of the Historical Jesus._ Sonoma, Calif.: Polebridge Press, 1992.

Funk, Robert W. _Jesus as Precursor._ Rev. ed. Ed. Edward F. Beutner. Sonoma, Calif.: Polebridge Press, 1993.

Funk, Robert W., Brandon B. Scott, and James R. Butts. _The Parables of Jesus: Red Letter Edition._ Sonoma, Calif.: Polebridge Press, 1988.

The Gospel of Jesus

Bultmann, Rudolf. _Jesus and the Word._ Trans. Louise Pettibone Smith and Erminie Huntress Lantero. New York: Charles Scribner's Sons, 1958 (1934).

Crossan, John Dominic. _The Essential Jesus: Original Sayings and Earliest Images._ San Francisco: HarperSanFrancisco, 1994.

Funk, Robert W., and Roy W. Hoover. _The Five Gospels. The Search for the Authentic Words of Jesus._ A Polebridge Press Book. New York: Macmillan, 1993.

Funk, Robert W., and Mahlon H. Smith. _The Gospel of Mark: Red Letter Edition._ Sonoma, Calif.: Polebridge Press, 1991.

Mitchell, Stephen. _The Gospel According to Jesus: A New Translation and Guide to His Essential Teachings for Believers and Unbelievers._ New York: HarperCollins Publishers, 1990.

Tatum, W. Barnes. _John the Baptist and Jesus: A Report of the Jesus Seminar._ Sonoma, Calif.: Polebridge Press, 1993.

The Death of Jesus

Brown, Raymond E., S.S. _The Death of the Messiah. From Gethsemane to the Grave._ 2 vols. The Anchor Bible Reference Library. New York: Doubleday, 1994.

Crossan, John Dominic. _The Cross That Spoke. The Origins of the Passion Narrative._ San Francisco: Harper & Row Publishers, 1988.

_____. _Who Killed Jesus?_ San Francisco: HarperSanFrancisco, 1995.

Domesticating the Tradition and Marketing the Messiah

Fuller, Reginald H. _The Foundations of New Testament Christology._ London: Lutterworth, 1965.

Mack, Burton L. _A Myth of Innocence. Mark and Christian Origins._ Philadelphia: Fortress Press, 1988.

Resurrection and Return

Bowersock, G. W. _Fiction as History: Nero to Julian._ Berkeley: University of California Press, 1994.

Fuller, Reginald H. _The Formation of the Resurrection Narratives._ Philadelphia: Fortress Press, 1980 (1971).

Luedemann, Gerd. _The Resurrection of Jesus. History, Experience, Theology._ Minneapolis: Fortress Press, 1994.

Pagels, Elaine. "The Controversy over Christ's Resurrection: Historical Event or Symbol?" Pages 3–29 in: _The Gnostic Gospels._ New York: Random House, 1979.

Robinson, James M. "Jesus from Easter to Valentinus (or to the Apostles' Creed)." _Journal of Biblical Literature_ 101 (1982): 5–37.

Sheehan, Thomas. "The Resurrection. An Obstacle to Faith?" _The Fourth R_ 8 (March/April 1995): 3–9.

Spong, John S. _Resurrection: Myth or Reality? A Bishop's Search for the Origins of Christianity._ San Francisco: HarperSanFrancisco, 1994.

The Divine Child

Brown, Raymond E., S.S. *The Birth of the Messiah. A Commentary on the Infancy Narratives in the Gospels of Matthew and Luke.* New updated ed. The Anchor Bible Reference Library. New York: Doubleday, 1993.

McGaughy, Lane C. "Infancy Narratives in the Ancient World." *The Fourth R* 5, 5 (September 1992): 1–3.

Schaberg, Jane. *The Illegitimacy of Jesus. A Feminist Theological Interpretation of the Infancy Narratives.* New York: Crossroad, 1990.

Spong, John S. *Born of a Woman: A Bishop Rethinks the Birth of Jesus.* San Francisco: HarperSanFrancisco, 1992.

Jesus for a New Age

Berger, Peter L. and Luckmann, Thomas. *The Social Construction of Reality. A Treatise in the Sociology of Knowledge.* New York: Doubleday, 1966.

Boorstin, Daniel J. *The Image: A Guide to Pseudo-Events in America.* New York: Vintage Books, 1992 (1961).

Borg, Marcus J. *Meeting Jesus Again for the First Time.* San Francisco: HarperSanFrancisco, 1994.

Dundes, Alan. "The Hero Pattern and the Life of Jesus." In *In Quest of the Hero,* 179–223. Princeton: Princeton University Press, 1990.

Hawking, Stephen. *A Brief History of Time. From the Big Bang to Black Holes.* New York. Bantam Books, 1988.

Kuhn, Thomas S. *The Structure of Scientific Revolutions.* 2nd ed., enl. Chicago: University of Chicago Press, 1970 (1962).

Luck, Georg. *Arcana Mundi: Magic and the Occult in the Greek and Roman Worlds.* Baltimore: The Johns Hopkins University Press, 1985.

Pagels, Elaine. *Adam, Eve, and the Serpent.* New York: Random House, Inc., 1989 (1988).

――――. *The Gnostic Gospels.* New York: Random House, Inc., 1989 (1979).

Spong, John S. *Rescuing the Bible from Fundamentalism: A Bishop Rethinks the Meaning of Scripture.* San Francisco: HarperSanFrancisco, 1990.

Appendix

Catalogue of Authentic Words and Deeds

Sources are identified in parentheses:
Q = Sayings Gospel Q
L = Luke's special source
M = Matthew's special source
// links parallel versions
* preceding the page number indicates that the parable or aphorism is quoted in full

Parables

Parables parodying symbols

1. *Leaven* (Q, Thomas) 150, *156
   Luke 13:20–21//Matt 13:33//Thom 96:1–2
2. *Mustard seed* (Thomas, Mark, Q) 150, 157
   Thom 20:2–4//Mark 4:30–32//Luke 13:18–19//Matt 13:31–32
   He said to them, "It's like a mustard seed. ³It's the smallest of all seeds, ⁴but when it falls on prepared soil, it produces a large branch and becomes a shelter for birds of the sky."
3. *Empty jar* (Thomas) 157
   Thom 97:1–4
   The Father's imperial rule is like a woman who was carrying a jar full of meal. ²While she was walking along a distant road, the handle of the jar broke and the meal spilled behind her along the road. ³She didn't know it; she hadn't noticed a problem. ⁴When she reached her house, she put the jar down and discovered that it was empty.

Narrative parables (3 characters, 2 scenes)

4. *The Samaritan* (L) 154, 161, *170–71, 171–80, 196, 204
   Luke 10:30–35
5. *Vineyard laborers* (M) 153, 154, 161, 191, 195–96, 215
   Matt 20:1–15
   For Heaven's imperial rule is like a proprietor who went out the first thing in the morning to hire workers for his vineyard. ²After agreeing with the workers for a silver coin a day he sent them into his vineyard.
   ³And coming out around 9 AM he saw others loitering in the marketplace ⁴and he said to them, "You go into the vineyard too, and I'll pay you whatever is fair." ⁵So they went.
   Around noon he went out again, and at 3 PM he repeated the process. ⁶About 5 PM he went out and found others loitering about and says to them, "Why did you stand around here idle the whole day?"

⁷They reply, "Because no one hired us."

He tells them, "You go into the vineyard as well."

⁸When evening came the owner of the vineyard tells his foreman: "Call the workers and pay them their wages starting with those hired last and ending with those hired first."

⁹Those hired at 5 PM came up and received a silver coin each. ¹⁰Those hired first approached thinking they would receive more. But they also got a silver coin apiece. ¹¹They took it and began to grumble against the proprietor: ¹²"These guys hired last worked only an hour but you have made them equal to us who did most of the work during the heat of the day."

¹³In response he said to one of them, "Look, pal, did I wrong you? You did agree with me for a silver coin, didn't you? ¹⁴Take your wage and get out! I intend to treat the one hired last the same way I treat you. ¹⁵Is there some law forbidding me to do as I please with my money? Or is your eye filled with envy because I am generous?"

6. *Prodigal son* (L) 153, 161, 181–89, *182–83, 209

   Luke 15:11–32

7. *The dinner party* (Thomas, Q) 132, 150, 154, 161, 191, 195

   Thom 64:1–11//Luke 14:16–23; cf. Matt 22:2–13

   Someone was receiving guests. When he had prepared the dinner, he sent his slave to invite the guests. ²The slave went to the first and said, "My master invites you." ³The first replied, "Some merchants owe me money; they are coming to me tonight. I have to go and give them instructions. Please excuse me from dinner." ⁴The slave went to another and said, "My master has invited you." ⁵The second said to the slave, "I have bought a house, and I have been called away for a day. I shall have no time." ⁶The slave went to another and said, "My master invites you." ⁷The third said to the slave, "My friend is to be married, and I am to arrange the banquet. I shall not be able to come. Please excuse me from dinner." ⁸The slave went to another and said, "My master invites you." ⁹The fourth said to the slave, "I have bought an estate, and I am going to collect the rent. I shall not be able to come. Please excuse me." ¹⁰The slave returned and said to his master, "Those whom you invited to dinner have asked to be excused." ¹¹The master said to his slave, "Go out on the streets and bring back whomever you find to have dinner."

   ¹²Buyers and merchants will not enter the places of my Father.

8. *Shrewd manager* (L) 191

   Luke 16:1–8a

   There was this rich man whose manager had been accused of squandering his master's property. ²He called him in and said, "What's this I hear about you? Let's have an audit of your management, because your job is being terminated."

   ³Then the manager said to himself, "What am I going to do? My master is firing me. I'm not able to dig ditches and I'm ashamed to beg. ⁴I've got it! I know what I'll do so doors will open for me when I'm removed from management."

   ⁵So he called in each of his master's debtors. He said to the first, "How much do you owe my master?"

   ⁶He said, "Five hundred gallons of olive oil."

   And he said to him, "Here is your invoice; sit down right now and make it two hundred and fifty."

   ⁷Then he said to another, "And how much do you owe?"

   He said, "A thousand bushels of wheat."

   He says to him, "Here is your invoice; make it eight hundred."

   ⁸The master praised the dishonest manager because he had acted shrewdly.

9. *Unforgiving slave* (M) 191, 213–14

   Matt 18:23–34

   This is why Heaven's imperial rule should be compared to a secular ruler who decided to settle accounts with his slaves. ²⁴When the process began, this debtor was brought to him who owed ten million dollars. 25Since he couldn't pay it back, the ruler ordered him sold, along with his wife and children and everything he had, so he could recover his money.

26At this prospect, the slave fell down and groveled before him: 'Be patient with me, and I'll repay every cent.' 27Because he was compassionate, the master of that slave let him go and canceled the debt.

28As soon as he got out, that same fellow collared one of his fellow slaves who owed him a hundred dollars, and grabbed him by the neck and demanded: 'Pay back what you owe!'

29His fellow slave fell down and begged him: 'Be patient with me and I'll pay you back.'

30But he wasn't interested; instead, he went out and threw him in prison until he paid the debt.

31When his fellow slaves realized what had happened, they were terribly distressed and went and reported to their master everything that had taken place.

32At that point, his master summoned him: 'You wicked slave,' he says to him, 'I canceled your entire debt because you begged me. 33Wasn't it only fair for you to treat your fellow slave with the same consideration as I treated you?' 34And the master was so angry he handed him over to those in charge of punishment until he paid back everything he owed. 35That's what my heavenly Father will do to you, unless you find it in your heart to forgive each one of your brothers and sisters.

Finding parables

10. *Lost coin* (L) 161, 209
    Luke 15:8–9
    Or again, is there any woman with ten silver coins, who if she loses one, wouldn't light a lamp and sweep the house and search carefully until she finds it? 9When she finds it, she invites her friends and neighbors over and says, "Celebrate with me, because I have found the silver coin I had lost."

11. *Lost sheep* (Q, Thomas) 161, 209
    Luke 15:4–6//Matt 18:12–13; cf. Thom 107:1–3
    Is there any one of you who owns a hundred sheep and one of them gets lost, who wouldn't leave the ninety-nine in the wilderness, and go after the one that got lost until he finds it? 5And when he finds it, he lifts it up on his shoulders, happy. 6Once he gets home, he invites his friends and his neighbors over, and says to them, "Celebrate with me, because I have found my lost sheep."

12. *Treasure* (M, Thomas) 156, 209
    Matt 13:44//Thom 109:1–3
    Heaven's imperial rule is like treasure hidden in a field: when someone finds it, that person covers it up again, and out of sheer joy goes and sells every last possession and buys that field.

13. *Pearl* (Thomas, M) 209
    Thom 76:1–2//Matt 13:45–46
    The Father's imperial rule is like a merchant who had a supply of merchandise and then found a pearl. 2That merchant was prudent; he sold the merchandise and bought the single pearl for himself.

Other parables

14. *Pharisee & toll collector* (L) 154, 195
    Luke 18:10–14a
    Two men went up to the temple to pray, one a Pharisee and the other a toll collector.

¹¹The Pharisee stood up and prayed silently as follows: "I thank you, God, that I'm not like everybody else, thieving, unjust, adulterous, and especially not like that toll collector over there. ¹²I fast twice a week, I give tithes of everything that I acquire."

¹³But the toll collector stood off by himself and didn't even dare to look up, but struck his chest, and muttered, "God, have mercy on me, sinner that I am."

¹⁴Let me tell you, the second man went back home acquitted but the first one did not. For those who promote themselves will be demoted, but those who demote themselves will be promoted.

15. *Corrupt judge* (L) 153
    Luke 18:2–5
    Once there was a judge in this town who neither feared God nor cared about people. ³In that same town was a widow who kept coming to him and demanding: "Give me a ruling against the person I'm suing."
    ⁴For a while he refused; but eventually he said to himself, "I'm not afraid of God and I don't care about people, ⁵but this widow keeps pestering me. So I'm going to give her a favorable ruling, or else she'll keep coming back until she wears me down."

16. *The assassin* (Thomas)
    Thom 98:1–3
    The Father's imperial rule is like a person who wanted to kill someone powerful. ²While still at home he drew his sword and thrust it into the wall to find out whether his hand would go in. ³Then he killed the powerful one.

Aphorisms

Beatitudes

17. *Congratulations, poor!* (Q, Thomas) *85, *162, *242
    Luke 6:20//Thom 54//Matt 5:3
18. *Congratulations, hungry!* (Q, Thomas) 208
    Luke 6:21a//Matt 5:6//Thom 69:2
    Congratulations, you hungry! You will have a feast.
19. *Congratulations, sad!* (Q)
    Luke 6:21b//Matt 5:4
    Congratulations, you who weep now! You will laugh.

Case parodies

20. *Other cheek* (Q) *155
    Matt 5:39//Luke 6:29a
21. *Coat & shirt* (Q) *155
    Matt 5:40//Luke 6:29b
22. *Second mile* (Q) *155
    Matt 5:41

Global injunctions

23. *Give to beggars* (Q) *158, *214, *244–45
    Matt 5:42a//Luke 6:30a
24. *Lend without return* (Thomas, Q) 150, *158
    Thom 95:1–2//Matt 5:42b; cf. Luke 6:34//Luke 6:35c
25. *Before the judge* (Q) 160
    Luke 12:58–59//Matt 5:25–26
    When you are about to appear with your opponent before the magistrate, do your best to settle with him on the way, or else he might drag you up before the judge, and the judge turn you over to the jailer, and the jailer throw you in prison. ⁵⁹I tell you, you'll never get out of there until you've paid every last red cent.

Paradoxes

26. *Love of enemies* (Q) *154, *195
    Luke 6:27b//Matt 5:44b//Luke 6:32, 35a
27. *Leave the dead* (Q) 136, *198
    Matt 8:22//Luke 9:59–60
28. *Left & right hands* (M, Thomas) *154, *214
    Matt 6:3//Thom 62:2

Antithetical couplets

29. *Saving & losing life* (Q, Mark, John) *152, *155, *214
    Luke 17:33; cf. Matt 16:25, 10:39; Luke 9:24; John 12:25; Mark 8:35
30. *First & last* (Q, Thomas, Mark) *147, *215
    Matt 20:16; cf. Mark 10:31; Matt 19:30; Luke 13:30; Thom 4:2, 4:3
31. *What goes in* (Mark, Thomas) *204, *246, 246–47
    Mark 7:14–15//Thom 14:5//Matt 15:10–11
32. *Lord of the sabbath* (Mark) *92, *94, 248
    Mark 2:27–28; cf. Matt 12:8//Luke 6:5
33. *Foxes have dens* (Q, Thomas) 85, *90–91, *152, 212
    Luke 9:58//Matt 8:20//Thom 86:1–2

Caricatures & hyperboles

34. *Eye of a needle* (Mark) 213, *245
    Matt 19:24//Luke 18:25//Mark 10:25
35. *Sliver & timber* (Thomas, Q) 214
    Thom 26:1–2//Matt 7:3–5//Luke 6:41–42
    Jesus said, "You see the sliver in your friend's eye, but you don't see the timber in your own eye. ²When you take the timber out of your own eye, then you will see well enough to remove the sliver from your friend's eye."
36. *Pearls to pigs* (Matthew, Thomas)
    Matt 7:6//Thom 93:1–2
    Don't offer to dogs what is sacred, and don't throw your pearls to pigs, or they'll trample them underfoot and turn and tear you to shreds.
37. *Gnat & camel* (Matthew)
    Matt 23:24
    You strain out a gnat and gulp down a camel.
38. *Hating one's family* (Q, Thomas) *197, *238
    Luke 14:26; cf. Thom 55:1–2a; Matt 10:37; Thom 101:1–3
39. *God & sparrows; hairs of head* (Q) 212
    Luke 12:6–7//Matt 10:29–31; cf. Luke 21:18
    What do sparrows cost? A dime a dozen? Yet not one of them is overlooked by God. ⁷In fact, even the hairs of your head have all been counted. Don't be so timid: You're worth more than a flock of sparrows.

Prayer

40. *Abba, Father* (Q) *207–8
    Luke 11:2b//Matt 6:9b; cf. Matt 6:9c
41. *Lord's prayer: revere name* (Q) 208
    Luke 11:2d//Matt 6:9d
    Your name be revered.
42. *Lord's prayer: impose rule* (Q)
    Luke 11:2e//Matt 6:10a
    Impose your imperial rule.
43. *Lord's prayer: bread* (Q) 212, *243
    Matt 6:11; cf. Luke 11:3

44. *Lord's prayer: debts* (Q)
Matt 6:12; cf. Luke 11:4a–b
Forgive our debts to the extent that we have forgiven those in debt to us.

Admonitions

45. *On anxieties: don't fret* (Q, Thomas) 212
Luke 12:22–23//Matt 6:25//Thom 36:1
[22]He said to his disciples, "That's why I tell you: don't fret about life—what you're going to eat—or about your body—what you're going to wear. [23]Remember, there is more to living than food and clothing."
46. *On anxieties: lilies* (Q, Thomas) 212
Luke 12:27–28//Matt 6:28b–30//Thom 36:2
[27]Think about how the lilies grow: they don't slave and they never spin. Yet let me tell you, even Solomon at the height of his glory was never decked out like one of them. [28]If God dresses up the grass in the field, which is here today and tomorrow is tossed into an oven, it is surely more likely that God cares for you, you who don't take anything for granted!
47. *On anxieties: birds* (Q) 212
Luke 12:24//Matt 6:26
Think about the crows: they don't plant or harvest, they don't have storerooms or barns. Yet God feeds them. You're worth a lot more than the birds!
48. *On anxieties: clothing* (Q) 150, 212
Matt 6:28a
Why worry about clothes?
49. *On anxieties: one hour* (Q)
Luke 12:25//Matt 6:27
Can any of you add an hour to life by fretting about it?
50. *Emperor & God* (Thomas, Mark)
Thom 100:2b–3//Mark 12:17b//Luke 20:25b//Matt 22:21c
Give the emperor what belongs to the emperor, [3]give God what belongs to God.
51. *Become passersby* (Thomas) *87
Thom 42
52. *On divorce* (Mark, Q, Paul)
Mark 10:9; cf. 1 Cor 7:1–11; Matt 19:9, 5:32; Luke 16:18
Those God has coupled together, no one else should separate.
53. *Two good ears* (Common lore) *150
Mark 4:23, etc.
54. *Number one* (Mark) 132
Mark 9:35//Matt 23:11//Luke 9:48b
If any of you wants to be 'number one,' you have to be last of all and servant of all!
55. *Ask, seek, knock* (Q, Thomas) *212, 243
Matt 7:7–8//Luke 11:9–10//Thom 92:1//Thom 94:1–2; cf. Thom 2:1–4

Proverbs

56. *Sly as a snake* (M, Thomas)
Matt 10:16b//Thom 39:3
You must be sly as a snake and as simple as a dove.
57. *Placing the lamp, Lamp & bushel* (Q, Mark, Thomas)
Luke 8:16//Luke 11:33//Mark 4:21//Matt 5:15//Thom 33:2–3
No one lights a lamp and covers it with a pot or puts it under a bed; rather, one puts it on a lampstand, so that those who come in can see the light.
58. *Aged wine* (L, Thomas)
Luke 5:39a//Thom 47:3; cf. Luke 5:39b
Besides, nobody wants young wine after drinking aged wine. As they say, 'Aged wine is just fine!'

59. *Able-bodied & sick* (POxy 1224, Mark) 73, *85, 124, *151
POxy 1224 5:2//Matt 9:12//Mark 2:17a//Luke 5:31
60. *Mountain city* (M, Thomas)
Matt 5:14b//Thom 32
A city sitting on top of a mountain can't be concealed.
61. *No respect at home* (Thomas, John, Mark)
Thom 31:1//Luke 4:24//John 4:44//Matt 13:57//Mark 6:4
No prophet is welcome on his home turf.
62. *By their fruit* (Q, Thomas) *152, *246, *248
Matt 7:16b//Thom 45:1a//Luke 6:44b; cf. Matt 12:33a; Matt 7:17–18; Luke 6:43; Matt 7:20; Matt 12:33b; Matt 7:16a; Luke 6:44a; Luke 6:45a; Matt 12:35; Thom 45:2–3; Thom 45:1b; Thom 45:4; Matt 12:34; Luke 6:45b; Matt 7:19
63. *Two masters* (Q, Thomas) 213
Luke 16:13//Matt 6:24//Thom 47:2
No servant can be a slave to two masters. No doubt that slave will either hate one and love the other, or be devoted to one and disdain the other. You can't be enslaved to both God and a bank account.

"Better than" sayings

64. *Better than sinners: sunrise* (Q) *212
Matt 5:45b
65. *Better than sinners: love* (Q) *195
Luke 6:32//Matt 5:46

Instructions

66. *Instructions for the road: house* (Q) 212
Luke 10:7a
Stay at that one house, eating and drinking whatever they provide.
67. *Instructions for the road: eat* (Thomas, Q) 212
Thom 14:4a//Luke 10:8
When you go into any region and walk about in the countryside, when people take you in, eat what they serve you.

Difficult to classify

68. *Friend at midnight* (L) 150
Luke 11:5–8
Jesus said to them, "Suppose you have a friend who comes to you in the middle of the night and says to you, 'Friend, lend me three loaves, ⁶for a friend of mine on a trip has just shown up and I have nothing to offer him.' ⁷And suppose you reply, 'Stop bothering me. The door is already locked and my children and I are in bed. I can't get up to give you anything'—⁸I tell you, even though you won't get up and give the friend anything out of friendship, yet you will get up and give the other whatever is needed because you'd be ashamed not to."
69. *Castration for Heaven* (M)
Matt 19:12a
There are castrated men who were born that way, and there are castrated men who were castrated by others, and there are castrated men who castrated themselves because of Heaven's imperial rule.
70. *Satan's fall* (L)
Luke 10:18
I was watching Satan fall like lightning from heaven.
71. *Seed & harvest* (Mark, Thomas)
Mark 4:26–29; cf. Thom 21:9

And he would say:

God's imperial rule is like this: Suppose someone sows seed on the ground, [27]and sleeps and rises night and day, and the seed sprouts and matures, although the sower is unaware of it. [28]The earth produces fruit on its own, first a shoot, then a head, then mature grain on the head. [29]But when the grain ripens, all of a sudden that farmer sends for the sickle, because it's harvest time.

72. *Scholars' privileges* (Q, Mark) 208–9
Luke 20:46//Mark 12:38–39//Matt 23:5–7//Luke 11:43
Be on guard against the scholars who like to parade around in long robes, and who love to be addressed properly in the marketplaces, and who prefer important seats in the synagogues and the best couches at banquets.

73. *Coming of God's imperial rule* (Thomas, Q) *167
Thom 113:1–4//Luke 17:20–21; cf. Thom 51:2

74. *Good gifts* (Q) 211
Matt 7:9–11; cf. Luke 11:11–13
Who among you would hand a son a stone when it's bread he's asking for? [10]Again, who would hand him a snake when it's fish he's asking for? Of course no one would! [11]So if you, worthless as you are, know how to give your children good gifts, isn't it much more likely that your Father in the heavens will give good things to those who ask him?

75. *Powerful man* (Mark, Q, Thomas)
Mark 3:27//Matt 12:29//Thom 35:1–2//Luke 11:21–22
No one can enter a powerful man's house to steal his belongings unless he first ties him up. Only then does he loot his house.

76. *Salting the salt* (Mark, Q) 249
Mark 9:50a//Luke 14:34–35a//Matt 5:13b
Salt is good and salty—if salt becomes bland, with what will you renew it?

77. *Forgiveness for forgiveness* (Mark) *213
Luke 6:37c; cf. Mark 11:25; Matt 6:14–15
Forgive and you'll be forgiven.

78. *Satan divided* (Q, Mark) 152
Luke 11:17–18; cf. Matt 12:25–26; Mark 3:23–26
Every government divided against itself is devastated, and a house divided against a house falls. [18]If Satan is divided against himself—since you claim I drive out demons in Beelzebul's name—how will his domain endure?

79. *Hidden & revealed, Veiled & unveiled* (Thomas, Q, Mark)
Thom 5:2//Thom 6:5//Luke 12:2//Matt 10:26b//Luke 8:17; cf. Thom 6:6; Mark 4:22; Thom 5:3 (Greek); Thom 6:4; Matt 10:26a
For there is nothing hidden that won't be revealed.

80. *Inside & outside* (Thomas, Q) *206
Thom 89:1–2; cf. Matt 23:25–26; Luke 11:39–41

81. *Fasting & wedding* (Mark, Thomas) *146–47, 208, 209
Mark 2:19//Matt 9:15a//Luke 5:34; cf. Thom 104:2; Thom 104:3; Luke 5:35; Mark 2:20; Matt 9:15b

82. *Narrow door* (Q)
Luke 13:24; cf. Matt 7:13–14
Struggle to get in through the narrow door; I'm telling you, many will try to get in, but won't be able.

83. *Difficult with money* (Mark) 213, *245
Mark 10:23//Luke 18:24//Matt 19:23

84. *Barren tree* (L) 225
Luke 13:6–9
A man had a fig tree growing in his vineyard; he came looking for fruit on it but didn't find any.

⁷So he said to the vinekeeper, "See here, for three years in a row I have come looking for fruit on this tree, and haven't found any. Cut it down. Why should it suck the nutrients out of the soil?"

⁸In response he says to him, "Let it stand, sir, one more year, until I get a chance to dig around it and work in some manure. ⁹Maybe it will produce next year; but if it doesn't, we can go ahead and cut it down."

85. *Children in God's domain* (Mark, Thomas)
Mark 10:14b//Matt 19:14//Luke 18:16
Let the children come up to me, don't try to stop them. After all, God's domain belongs to people like that.

86. *Return of evil spirit* (Q)
Luke 11:24–26; cf. Matt 12:43–45
When an unclean spirit leaves a person, it wanders through waterless places in search of a resting place. When it doesn't find one, it says, 'I will go back to the home I left.' ²⁵It then returns, and finds it swept and refurbished. ²⁶Next, it goes out and brings back seven other spirits more vile than itself, who enter and settle in there. So that person ends up worse off than when he or she started.

87. *Fire on earth* (Thomas, Q)
Thom 10; cf. Luke 12:49
Jesus said, "I have cast fire upon the world, and look, I'm guarding it until it blazes."

88. *Have & have not* (Thomas, Mark, Q) 86
Thom 41:1–2//Mark 4:25//Luke 8:18b; cf. Matt 25:29; Matt 13:12; Luke 19:26
Jesus said, "Those who have something in hand will be given more, ²and those who have nothing will be deprived of even the little they have."

89. *For or against* (Mark, Q, POxy 1224) *199
Mark 9:40

90. *Glutton & drunk* (M) 208
Matt 11:18–19a//Luke 7:31–35
Just remember, John appeared on the scene neither eating nor drinking, and they say, 'He is demented.' ¹⁹The son of Adam appeared on the scene both eating and drinking, and they say, 'There's a glutton and a drunk, a crony of toll collectors and sinners!'

91. *Toll collectors & prostitutes in God's domain* (M) *194
Matt 21:31b

92. *No one knows the time* (Mark)
Mark 13:32//Matt 24:36
As for that exact day or minute: no one knows, not even heaven's messengers, nor even the son, no one except the Father.

93. *Into the wilderness* (Q, Thomas)
Matt 11:7–8//Thom 78:1–2//Luke 7:24–25; cf. Thom 78:3
What did you go out to the wilderness to gawk at? A reed shaking in the wind? ⁸What did you really go out to see? A man dressed in fancy clothes? But wait! Those who wear fancy clothes are found in regal quarters.

94. *Wineskins* (Thomas, Mark)
Thom 47:4//Luke 5:37–38//Mark 2:22; cf. Matt 9:17
Young wine is not poured into old wineskins, or they might break, and aged wine is not poured into a new wineskin, or it might spoil.

95. *False messiahs* (Mark)
Mark 13:21//Matt 24:23
And then if someone says to you, 'Look, here is the Anointed,' or 'Look, there he is,' don't count on it!

96. *Not one stone* (Mark) *202, 229–*230
Mark 13:2//Matt 24:2//Luke 21:6

Parabolic Acts

97. *Demons by the finger of God (by God's spirit)* (Q) 168
   Luke 11:19–20//Matt 12:27–28
   If I drive out demons in Beelzebul's name, in whose name do your own people drive them out? In that case, they will be your judges. [20]But if by God's finger I drive out demons, then for you God's imperial rule has arrived.

98. *Eating with sinners* (Mark, POxy 1224)
   Mark 2:16–17//Matt 9:11–13//Luke 5:30–32//Luke 15:1–2//POxy 1224 5:1–2
   And whenever the Pharisees' scholars saw him eating with sinners and toll collectors, they would question his disciples, "What's he doing eating with toll collectors and sinners?"
   When Jesus overhears, he says to them: "Since when do the able-bodied need a doctor? It's the sick who do. I did not come to enlist religious folks but sinners!"

99. *Paralytic* (Mark) 126, 129, 162, 250–51
   Mark 2:1–12//Matt 9:1–8//Luke 5:17–26; cf. John 5:1–9
   Some days later he went back to Capernaum and was rumored to be at home. [2]And many people crowded around so there was no longer any room, even outside the door. Then he started speaking to them. [3]Some people then show up with a paralytic being carried by four of them. [4]And when they were not able to get near him on account of the crowd, they removed the roof above him. After digging it out, they lowered the mat on which the paralytic was lying. [5]When Jesus noticed their trust, he says to the paralytic, "Child, your sins are forgiven."
   [6]Some of the scholars were sitting there and silently wondering: [7]"Why does that fellow say such things? He's blaspheming! Who can forgive sins except the one God?"
   [8]And right away, because Jesus sensed in his spirit that they were raising questions like this among themselves, he says to them: "Why do you entertain questions about these things? [9]Which is easier, to say to the paralytic, 'Your sins are forgiven,' or to say, 'Get up, pick up your mat and walk'? [10]But so that you may realize that on earth the son of Adam has authority to forgive sins, he says to the paralytic, [11]"You there, get up, pick up your mat and go home!"
   [12]And he got up, picked his mat right up, and walked out as everyone looked on. So they all became ecstatic, extolled God, and exclaimed, "We've never seen the likes of this!"

100. *True relatives* (Mark, Thomas) *198
   Matt 12:48–50//Thom 99:2; cf. Mark 3:33–35//Luke 8:21; Thom 99:3

101. *Leper* (Mark, GEger) 93, 133, 161, 204
   Mark 1:40–44//Matt 8:1–4//Luke 5:12–16//GEger 2:1–4
   Then a leper comes up to him, pleads with him, falls down on his knees, and says to him, "If you want to, you can make me clean."
   [41]Although Jesus was indignant, he stretched out his hand, touched him, and says to him, "Okay—you're clean!"
   [42]And right away the leprosy disappeared, and he was made clean. [43]And Jesus snapped at him, and dismissed him curtly [44]with this warning: "See that you don't tell anyone anything, but go, have a priest examine your skin. Then offer for your cleansing what Moses commanded, as evidence of your cure."

Index of Ancient Texts

Index of Selected Names and Subjects

THE JESUS SEMINAR

The Jesus Seminar is a project of the Westar Institute, a private, nonprofit research institute devoted to improving biblical and religious literacy by making the scholarship of religion available and accessible to the general public. As part of its literacy program, the Institute sponsors seminars, workshops, and publications in the field of religion.

Membership

Membership in the Westar Institute is open to professional scholars as Fellows and to others as Associates. Membership benefits include a subscription to the magazine of the Westar Institute—*The Fourth R*—and notices of national and regional meetings of the Jesus Seminar.

To learn more about the Westar Institute and its projects, please contact:

The Westar Institute
P.O. Box 6144
Santa Rosa, CA 95406
(707) 523-1323
(707) 523-1350 fax